# The Trees of
# Golden Gate Park
# and San Francisco

# The Trees of Golden Gate Park and San Francisco

*Elizabeth McClintock*

Edited and Arranged by
Richard G Turner Jr

HEYDAY BOOKS/CLAPPERSTICK INSTITUTE, BERKELEY, CALIFORNIA
IN COLLABORATION WITH PACIFIC HORTICULTURAL FOUNDATION,
STRYBING ARBORETUM SOCIETY, FRIENDS OF RECREATION AND PARKS,
FRIENDS OF THE URBAN FOREST, SAN FRANCISCO TREE ADVISORY BOARD

Library of Congress Cataloging-in-Publication Data

McClintock, Elizabeth May, 1912-
  The trees of Golden Gate Park and San Francisco / Elizabeth McClintock
; edited and arranged by Richard G. Turner, Jr.
      p. cm.
Includes bibliographical references (p.   ).
  ISBN 1-890771-28-7 (pbk.)
  1.  Trees--California--San Francisco--Identification. 2.
Trees--California--San Francisco--Pictorial works. 3.  Golden Gate Park
(San Francisco, Calif.)  I. Turner, Richard G., 1946- II. Title.
  QK149 .M3853 2001
  582.16'09794'61--dc21
                              2001000286

Front cover: Aging Monterey cypresses (*Cupressus macrocarpa*) tower over the
    evergreen foliage of kapuka (*Griselinia littoralis*) and the spring floral display of an
    Akebono cherry (*Prunus* x *yedoensis* 'Akebono') in Golden Gate Park. Photograph
    by RG Turner Jr
Back cover: Dominating the corner property at Willard Street North and McAllister
    Street, just one block north of Golden Gate Park, is the largest California buckeye
    (*Aesculus californica*) in the city, estimated to be over one hundred years old.
    Photograph by Jerry Robinson.
Cover and Interior Design: Rebecca LeGates
Printing and Binding: Publishers Press, Salt Lake City, UT

All photographs are courtesy of the Helen Crocker Russell Library of Horticulture
    unless otherwise noted.
All illustrations are credited on p. 242.
All maps created by Ben Pease.

Orders, inquiries, and correspondence should be addressed to:
      Heyday Books
      P. O. Box 9145, Berkeley, CA 94709
      510/549-3564, Fax 510/549-1889
      www.heydaybooks.com

Printed in the United States of America

10 9 8 7 6 5 4 3 2 1

# Table of Contents

# Preface

*Golden Gate Park in San Francisco is a most remarkable urban forest. San Francisco is not a city built in and around a forested or wooded area, but is—or was—situated in an area with few native trees. The early builders of the park, after its founding in 1870, realized that the site selected for the park—the western part of the San Francisco peninsula with its windswept grassland, interspersed with sand dunes and rocky outcrops—presented problems in creating a park. But they chose a variety of appropriate trees, brought from different areas of the world, and today we see the successful results of their early efforts: Golden Gate Park—a human-made, urban forest surrounded by a great city.*

*The remarkable feature of Golden Gate Park is that diversity of trees planted in the park's early days. Many of these are still to be seen as magnificent old specimens; to these others have been added. Unfortunately, no records exist today of when the oldest trees were planted, nor is there a complete list of the park's trees. I began this series of tree articles in 1976, and, to date, over one hundred trees have been described in sixty articles in* Pacific Horticulture. *The few remaining will conclude the series.*

Dr Elizabeth McClintock handed me those paragraphs shortly after I became editor of *Pacific Horticulture* in April 1997. Like other readers of the magazine since its founding in 1976, I had enjoyed her articles on the trees of Golden Gate Park. As a regular user of the park, I too was intrigued by the diversity of trees growing there. I encouraged Dr McClintock to continue writing the series, and she did so through the July 2000 issue of the magazine.

Dr McClintock and I frequently discussed the potential for a book of her collected articles about the park's trees. I soon learned of others in the community who shared our hope that such a book could be published. Late in 1997, a number of local non-profit organizations, each devoted to the study, appreciation, or care of trees, came together as a consortium to explore the notion of jointly publishing the book. We realized that this book could be a great service to a broad segment of San Francisco's residents, as well as to visitors to the city.

We recognized the constant challenges faced by city workers to properly maintain Golden Gate Park and the other parks in the city. A book about the diversity of trees in Golden Gate Park would not only acquaint

San Franciscans with the stories behind these trees, but also alert them to the tremendous responsibility that lies in the stewardship of a human-made forest such as that found in the park. The five groups (Pacific Horticultural Foundation, Strybing Arboretum Society, Friends of Recreation and Parks, Friends of the Urban Forest, and the Tree Advisory Board to the Department of Public Works) agreed to publish the book as a collaborative venture supporting the mission of each organization. *Trees of Golden Gate Park and San Francisco* is the result of countless volunteer hours spent editing and arranging text, gathering information and assembling data, drawing and photographing trees, creating maps and verifying locations of trees in the park (and in the city), and raising the funds necessary to publish the book.

We decided early on that *Trees of Golden Gate Park* should be more than a simple reprinting of Dr McClintock's articles from *Pacific Horticulture*. Working closely with the publisher, the team developed the concept of a field guide, with the stories of individual trees adapted from the original articles but reassembled in alphabetical order. From her seventy-one articles, written over twenty-five years, 170 trees were chosen to fill the book. (There are still many trees in the park that have not been written about and have not been included in the book—a task for future writers to complete the story of the park's trees.*)

New drawings were commissioned for each of the trees, color photographs gathered from a number of sources, and maps of the park drawn on which key tree locations could be noted. Pieces of the original articles were organized into a series of appendices that provide further background for the stories of the trees.

To properly frame the story of Golden Gate Park and its trees, landscape architect Russell Beatty provided an opening chapter. "The Planting of Golden Gate Park: Metamorphosis in Sand" (expanded from an article by Beatty originally published in the *California Horticultural Journal,* April 1970) tells the story of the tremendous effort involved in transforming shifting sand dunes into the forested park we know today. And it highlights the dedicated and creative individuals—most notably William Hammond Hall and John McLaren—who shaped the park that continues to give so much pleasure more than one hundred and thirty years after its beginning.

To bring the story of the park's trees up to date, park forester Peter Ehrlich provided the second chapter, on the reforestation program that began in the early 1980s. By that time, it had become clear that the park's trees were in a state of decline, in part due to natural causes inherent in a human-made forest, and in part due to the city's history of deferred maintenance for this priceless resource. The reforestation program is now an integral part of the park management program, and, more importantly, of the city's budget for the park.

Assisting the editor and publisher in the three-year development of *Trees of Golden Gate Park* has been a team of volunteers from the five

---

* Dozens more trees may be found in Golden Gate Park, and particularly in Strybing Arboretum and Botanical Gardens; check with the Helen Crocker Russell Library of Horticulture there for information on trees in Strybing. Other trees, common along the streets of San Francisco, may be found in Clifford Janoff's *Trees for San Francisco* (Friends of the Urban Forest, 1995).

sponsoring organizations. Heading that team has been Nancy Conner, who gathered information from many sources for the sidebar data accompanying each tree in the field guide and worked closely with the artist in the preparation of the park maps. Aiding her in assembling the sidebar material and in verifying tree locations were Julie Brook, David Brunner, Diana Cohen, Elliott Donnelley, John R Dunmire, Peter Ehrlich, Roy C Leggitt, Dan McKenna, Alicia Ramirez, Jake Sigg, Barbara Stevens, Bian Tan, Tony Walcott.

Artist Mimi Osborne, a frequent contributor to *Pacific Horticulture*, organized the team of artists (Kristin Jacob, Nancy Baron, Lee Boerger, and Martha Kemp) who provided line drawings for trees not previously illustrated in the magazine (by artists Lee Adair Hastings, Leslie Bohm, Virginia Gregory, and Carolyn Mullinex). George Waters, Saxon Holt, Jerry Robinson, and William McNamara offered images from their photographic libraries. Barbara Pitschel, head librarian for the Helen Crocker Russell Library of Horticulture at Strybing Arboretum, provided invaluable assistance at every stage of the project, and made available to us the library's extensive slide collection.

Aiding the editor in the preparation and review of the manuscript were George Waters, Pat Castor, Margot Sheffner, Donald Foley, Jack Spring, Walden Valen, and Scot Medbury. Guiding us in the early stages of conceptual development of the book was Shelly Moore.

An editor could not ask for a more accommodating and enthusiastic publishing team than that provided by Malcolm Margolin and Heyday books. From the beginning Malcolm's calm and nurturing presence helped us all through the challenges of assembling this book. Artist Rebecca LeGates transformed our ideas for the look of the book into a design that is both functional and attractive. Rina Margolin provided an extraordinary service as copy editor, in the process educating this still-fresh editor in the intricacies of this important aspect of publishing.

Our deep appreciation goes to all of these individuals for their help in the development of *Trees of Golden Gate Park and San Francisco*.

From the first meeting, Dr McClintock and the others on the team hoped that proceeds from the sale of the book could be put toward the management of the park's trees. Because of the success of a fund-raising campaign, spearheaded by Diana Cohen and marked by a generous initial grant from the Columbia Foundation, a significant portion of the sale of each book will be returned to Friends of Recreation and Parks. There it will be placed in the Elizabeth McClintock Fund for Park Trees—a fitting tribute to the book's author, without whom *Trees of Golden Gate Park and San Francisco* would never have happened.

Richard G Turner Jr, editor
April 2001

# Introduction

Trees are the cornerstone of Golden Gate Park, the crowning jewel among San Francisco's treasures. This magnificent park, serving more than fifteen million visitors each year—the largest human-made, urban park in the country—would not exist but for the presence of the forest and for the foresight of the park's early planners and planters. From its start near the end of the nineteenth century, this pioneer public garden was a grand horticultural experiment. With little native to preserve on the shifting sand dunes, early park superintendents were given free license to introduce plants from around the world that might prosper in our climate. A great many did survive, and the resulting forest stabilized the sand dunes, buffered the persistent west wind, and framed spaces for people and gardens throughout the 1,017 acres of the park.

The trees of Golden Gate Park—and San Francisco—are an extraordinary public resource, and they can be enjoyed freely by anyone, resident or visitor, rich or poor, young or old. They add immeasurable beauty, grace, dignity, and character to the city, yet they are widely undervalued and often taken entirely for granted, as if they were just part of the natural backdrop. They are not, of course. The original landscape of San Francisco was largely sand dunes, meadows, marshes, and rocky scrub, with few native trees. The forests and avenues of trees seen throughout the city are no less a human creation than the city's architecture. Almost all of San Francisco's trees were deliberately introduced, and if this wonderful and varied public horticultural legacy is to be preserved, the trees will need proper care and timely replacement.

The publication of this book is the center of a larger campaign to educate the public about the trees of San Francisco. The groups and individuals collaborating on this project all agree on the need to call attention to this exceptional civic resource, to cultivate an understanding and appreciation of it, and to rally support for its preservation.

# The Planting of Golden Gate Park:
# A Metamorphosis in Sand

Russell A Beatty

The greensward that slashes across the western half of San Francisco is an unparalleled nineteenth-century achievement. The confluence of political motives, powerful men, and bold, inventive, confident park builders transformed a Sahara-like landscape into one of the world's great urban oases: Golden Gate Park.

Such a miracle would be unlikely in today's climate of environmental consciousness and participatory politics. Yet, the trees and rich plantings, the glades and woodlands, and the unique facilities housing a great museum, science academy, conservatory, and world-class arboretum draw a multitude of visitors each year from around the world. Golden Gate Park is indeed one of San Francisco's crown jewels in its trove of riches.

First-time visitors, and no doubt many San Franciscans, are unaware of the park's remarkable transformation from windswept dunes to forest and glade—truly a metamorphosis in sand. The rich diversity of trees and woodlands we see today thrives despite natural conditions in which trees would not ordinarily grow. These trees exist by the grace of irrigation, protection from battering salt-laden winds, and the uncommon skill and bold experimentation of knowledgeable, persistent men—most notably William Hammond Hall and John McLaren.

One hundred and thirty years ago, skeptics, including Frederick Law Olmsted, designer of New York's

Sand dunes and dune vegetation on the site of the future Golden Gate Park.

Central Park and other large parks, warned San Franciscans that undertaking the building of a park in such an inhospitable place would be a monumental folly. As one San Francisco newspaper in 1868 put it: "Of all the white elephants the city of San Francisco ever owned, they now have the largest in Golden Gate Park, a dreary waste of shifting sand hills where a blade of grass cannot be raised without four posts to keep it from blowing away."

Were such a venture proposed today, there would be such an outcry that the park would die at inception. Imagine the environmental impact report! Instead of a romantic green park, these 1,000 acres would either be ripe for development or be protected as the last vestige of the greatest expanse of coastal dunes in Northern California.

But the social and political climate of the 1860s was different from that of today. The state of California was less than two decades old. San Francisco exploded onto the map as

Aerial view of Golden Gate Park from above the Pacific Ocean.

an instant city in the boom of the gold rush. Its population swelled from a mere 20,000 in 1849 to nearly 150,000 in 1870. The "big four"—Leland Stanford, Mark Hopkins, Collis P Huntington, and Charles Crocker—reaped immense rewards, not from mining directly, but from supplying the miners with dry goods, hardware, and even legal advice. In turn, these entrepreneurs bankrolled the completion of the first transcontinental railroad to San Francisco in 1869. These were heady times for a raw western town yearning to become a respectable city.

The era spawned bold, confident, adventurous men who faced insurmountable obstacles, yet saw them merely as challenges to overcome: chiseling a railroad across the Sierran granite, plowing up a million acres of the Central Valley while dredging for gold, or building a romantic park on windswept sand dunes at the edge of the continent. The challenge of the latter task fell to a gifted young man, William Hammond Hall, a surveyor and field engineer for the US Army Corps of Engineers. Though confident and skillful in his engineering work, he knew nothing about designing and building a park, let alone selecting and planting trees. Such "minor" obstacles posed no problem for him. No one else in the West knew any more. The yet-to-be-named profession of landscape architecture was dominated by Easterners. Such notable designers as Frederick Law Olmsted, Horace Cleveland, and Andrew Jackson Downing designed great parks and landscapes in the more refined cities of the East and Midwest. But this was San Francisco—raw, wild, and eager to mimic or even surpass those eastern relatives.

## Rationale for a Park

In the 1860s, San Francisco was struggling to become a real city, casting off its gold rush–era mantle of serving the nomadic culture of miners and speculators who erected seasonal tent neighborhoods or lived in boardinghouses. Across the bay, a great university was becoming the "Athens of the West," a significant step towards civilizing the region. In San Francisco, the city's leaders sought a stable, respectable culture to replace the live-for-today, money-seeking, hell-raising, hedonistic backwash of the gold rush—folks who had no vision for the city's future.

In midcentury America, one symbol thought to signify a stable, civilized city was the establishment of a large park or "pleasure ground." San Francisco had only a few dusty squares and several private parks, such as Woodward's Gardens, that served as sylvan retreats. But the city lacked the type of large, romantic, naturalistic park that had recently become a prominent addition to eastern cities. New York's Central Park and Brooklyn's Prospect Park were models for crowded industrial cities to create green oases for their citizens. Supporting the movement for such great urban parks was the popular belief that these pleasure grounds would improve the health and morality of urban dwellers. Park advocates asserted that contemporary urban society was unacceptable but could be improved when a city was connected to a rural, "country-like" nature in parks. Urban reformers, including Olmsted, posited that the ills of the urban environment—its crowded, ugly, disorderly, and artificial features—predisposed citizens to such moral disorders as poverty, tyranny, crime, and disease. To counter such evils, the argument went, people should be exposed to an open, beautiful landscape that recalled an eastern North American woodland.

In 1865, Olmsted responded to a query from San Franciscan park advocates by observing that the city should distance itself from the discovery of gold to forge a civilizing influence and to seek something deeper, richer, and more lasting than the restless "city of strangers and sojourners" he saw there. He argued that the lack of such congenial influences as parks would result in capital flight back to real cities such as New York. Olmsted saw in parks a strong democratizing influence which forged unique bonds among disparate races and classes. He also believed that pleasure grounds functioned as pressure release valves for all laborers toiling under considerable hardship and stress.

San Francisco was ripe for such arguments. Not only had the city expanded in a haphazard, uncontrolled, and crowded manner, but the surrounding countryside was bleak and forlorn—the antithesis of the lovely green woodlands found around eastern cities. One park advocate complained: "Looking at our city from the bay, or the Golden Gate, in summer and fall, we see a mass of yellow houses on yellow hills of yellow sand or yellow rock....We want a place where, under the protection of our hills, we can have fifty, a hundred, or two hundred acres, sown with grass, planted with trees and laid off with roads pleasant for walking and driving. We need the reviving influences of beautiful nature." The simplicity of this argument was obvious: by creating a beautiful park, the city could promote moral order and a healthy, wealthy, crime-free democracy.

The surrounding landscape certainly must have seemed inhospitable, especially seen through the eyes of emigrants from the eastern states. People welcomed, even demanded a lush green park as respite from the sere, dry California landscape. Any trees that could be called woodlands probably had been stripped for firewood during the frenetic gold rush days. The decade of the 1860s was a period of wild climatic swings—the wettest and driest years on record—leaving the natural landscape variously inundated or parched, but ultimately bone-dry and inhospitable for much of the year.

Making matters worse for San Franciscans were the lands to the west of the settlement—a vast 3,000-acre coastal landscape of barren, shifting sand. Little wonder upper-class San Franciscans petitioned to establish a public park, as in this appeal to the board of supervisors in August 1865: "The great cities of our own country, as well as of Europe, have found it necessary at some time period of their growth, to provide large parks, or pleasure grounds, for the amusement and recreation of the people....No city in the world needs such recreation grounds more than San Francisco. A great park...is the great want of the city."

Park advocates identified a number of places suitable for a large urban pleasure ground. As so often happens, politics drove the selection process rather than the logic espoused by Olmsted—to locate the park in a comfortable environment sheltered from the westerly winds, one that would be conducive to growing trees and other plants. The acquisition of the "outside lands" (west of Divisadero Street) had puzzled city authorities for some time. They believed the establishment of a large park in these lands could stake the city's claim. Nevertheless, three sites were considered for the park: the Presidio, Mission Valley, and the sand wastes west of the hills to the ocean.

Despite being the least suitable environment for a park, the tract of sand from Stanyan Street to Ocean Beach was selected for a variety of political reasons. Squatters had laid claim to much of this area. As a candidate for mayor, Supervisor Frank McCoppin cut a brilliant deal that satisfied both the squatters and the city. He offered legal title to their claims if they agreed to grant ten percent of their holdings to the city for a park and to pay the city five years of back taxes. In one brilliant stroke, McCoppin expanded the city's depleted tax base, resolved the knotty problem of the western land titles, and designated a large tract for a park that would arrest the shifting sands invading the city. No doubt the move also helped solidify his election as the next mayor.

In short order, the man selected to accomplish this Herculean task was appointed: William Hammond Hall. It was no coincidence that he came highly recommended by Colonel Barton S Alexander, the ranking officer of the Army Corps of Engineers, under whom Hall had worked as a surveyor. Alexander clearly believed that by supporting Hall to survey the park, the city's interest in the Presidio as a park site would be diverted.

## Visionary Park Engineer— William Hammond Hall

Imagine a twenty-four-year-old man with no formal education, trained as an apprentice land surveyor by military engineers, working as a draftsman and surveyor, and with absolutely no training or experience in horticulture or landscape design. Would this man be the best qualified to assume the task of designing a one-thousand-acre park on land comprising two-thirds shifting sand dunes with the other third barely supporting scrub oak and grasses? Illogical as it would seem today,

William Hammond Hall, engineer and designer of Golden Gate Park.

this is the person who was selected to oversee the initial development of what has become one of the country's great urban parks.

Consider also that no parks and very few gardens had been designed in California by 1870, and that horticulture, as we know it today, was in an embryonic stage of development. A number of nurseries had become established in San Francisco and elsewhere in the Bay Area and were importing seeds and plants from the East Coast and Australia. The decades between 1850 and 1870 saw rampant, almost frantic experimentation with whatever plants would grow in California, especially in the northern part of the state.

In retrospect, however, Hall was the most qualified man to assume the challenge of designing Golden Gate Park, arresting the dunes, and firmly establishing the groundwork for the park we see today. Between 1866 and 1870, he had served as field engineer for the Corps of Engineers on the Pacific Coast. He had surveyed and conducted detailed topographical mapping of a wide array of places from San Diego to the state of Washington for fortifications, navigation, and hydrography. He had also surveyed the three thousand acres of sand dunes west of the city and, at the recommendation of Colonel Alexander, had studied European sand-dune reclamation. This combination of experience and expertise made Hall the logical choice to survey the park. Hall also subscribed to the prevailing theory that environments influenced people and that parks served as physical and moral antidotes for the evils of urban society.

On April 4, 1870, the "Act to Provide for the Improvement of Public Parks in the City of San Francisco" was approved by the state legislature. In May, the first Board of Park Commissioners was named with SF Butterworth, president; Andrew J Moulder, secretary; and Abraham Seligman, treasurer. The commissioners advertised for bids to survey the outside lands and, in a fortuitous move, selected William Hammond Hall.

Hall's approach to the survey and design of the park, as well as the taming of the dunes, employed his discipline as an engineer: he saw it as a problem to be solved systematically and methodically. During his survey of the land, he began research on park design. A voracious reader and accustomed to educating

himself, he studied the work and writings of Olmsted, Downing, Charles Sprague Sargeant, and other prominent designers and landscape theorists. In correspondence with Olmsted, he discovered, to his great surprise, that Olmsted had submitted a proposed park design to San Francisco five years earlier.

Olmsted and his partner, Calvert Vaux, had proposed a modest 120-acre park located in Hayes Valley, an area sheltered from the west winds. The park would extend into the city by a narrow promenade, sunk below grade for protection from the wind and running from Hayes Valley to the bay along what is now Van Ness Avenue to Aquatic Park, with another narrow arm to the southwest. Thus the park would reach deep into the heart of the expanding city in accessible locations that would be conducive to the planting of trees as well as to the comfort of people. Equally significant to the sound logic of the park's location was Olmsted's belief that the traditional romantic, green, pastoral English landscape was inappropriate for California's Mediterranean-type climate. He proposed employing landscape models derived from the Mediterranean region: minimal areas of lawn, selection of Mediterranean plants, and compositions of plants to create the illusion of lushness without extensive summer irrigation—all concepts employed in his design of Mountain View Cemetery in Oakland. Though Olmsted was absolutely correct in both his plan and logic (as we have come to appreciate only recently), he was rebuffed by San Franciscans whose motives for the

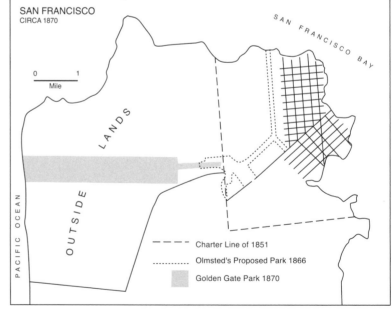

San Francisco circa 1870

park were political and whose landscape tastes were forged by the English landscape traditions of parks they had known in East Coast cities.

Innocently and unknowingly, Hall had hoped to consult with Olmsted on his park design. Understandably disappointed by his rejected ideas, Olmsted was deeply skeptical about the possibility of successfully developing a park in the outside lands. A few years earlier he had written:

> Determining that a pleasure ground is needed which shall compare favorably with any in existence, it must...be acknowledged that, neither in beauty of greensward, nor in great umbrageous trees, do the special conditions of the topography, soil, and climate of San Francisco allow us to hope that any pleasure ground it can acquire will ever compare in the most distant degree with those of New York or London.
>
> There is not a full grown tree of beautiful proportions near San Francisco, nor have I seen any young trees that promised fairly, except, perhaps, of certain compact clump forms of evergreens, wholly wanting in grace and cheerfulness. It would not be wise nor safe to undertake to form a park upon any plan which assumed as a certainty that trees which would delight the eye can be made to grow near San Francisco....It is perhaps true that the certainty of failure remains to be proved...and it may be urged that experiments on a small scale should be set on foot at once to determine the question for the benefit of future generations...

Realizing the need for an experienced park designer, Hall suggested that the park commissioners secure the services of Olmsted either to develop the plan or to serve as an advisor. The expense of Olmsted's travel and insufficient funds thwarted the idea. Olmsted probably would not have accepted such an offer, considering his earlier rejection and his doubts of the likelihood of success in developing a park on the chosen site. Nevertheless, Olmsted was cordial in offering whatever help and encouragement he could to Hall, though he could not mask his skepticism. In correspondence with Hall, Olmsted wrote:

> I have given the matter of pleasure grounds for San Francisco some consideration and fully realize the difficulties of your undertaking. Indeed, I may say that I do not believe it practicable to meet the natural but senseless demand of unreflecting people bred in the Atlantic States and the North of Europe for what is technically termed a park under the climatic conditions of San Francisco. Experience in Persia, Turkey, Smyrna, Spain & Portugal would afford more suggestions for what is practicable and desirable than any that could be derived from English authorities.

Clearly now facing the challenge alone, Hall began his self-imposed crash course in park and landscape design by ordering the plans and writings of the eastern designers from publishers in New York and Philadelphia. The prevailing text on naturalistic landscape design of the day was Downing's Treatise on the Theory and Practice of Landscape Gardening Adapted to North America (1850). In it, Hall discovered not only the design principles for romantic and picturesque landscapes but also lists of trees used to create such landscapes. According to Downing, trees were selected by form and character to reflect and create two landscape ideals: the "beautiful" and the "picturesque." The former was represented by the soft, rounded, luxuriant growth typified by many deciduous trees. The picturesque was more dramatic, wild, and bold and could be achieved through the use of more irregular or emphatic trees such as conifers and rugged oaks.

Downing's book, with its clear prescriptions for the design of romantic landscapes, confirmed what Hall had observed and gleaned from the plans and writings of Olmsted and other park designers. Certainly, Hall's original plan for the park demonstrates that this inexperienced young engineer sought to emulate Downing's vision of the romantic landscape in the layout of paths and roads as well as the massing and grouping of trees. He may also have adopted, initially, the types of trees suggested by Downing.

The design principles Hall employed, if not copied, resulted in the type of park San Franciscans expected. The pressure to quickly create a park in the fashion of Central Park was enormous. And Hall's determination to disprove his detractors and the park's critics allowed him no time for a lengthy education in either landscape design or horticulture, nor to explore the less familiar Mediterranean design concepts as suggested by Olmsted. Within six months, Hall completed not only a detailed topographic survey but also a preliminary design plan for the park. In his report at the completion of his commission for the survey, he wrote with supreme confidence:

*The Golden Gate Park contains about 1,000 acres, of which 270 acres at the eastern end is good arable land covered in many places with trees and shrubbery; this portion may at once be converted into an attractive resort. The remaining 730 acres, stretching down to the ocean beach, is a waste of drifting sand. Forbidding as it appears at present, it is confidently believed that it can be reclaimed by proper appliances. Should the necessary means be placed at the disposal of the Commissioners, they will undertake the experiment of reclamation, and if successful, will continue the work until the barren sand-hills are converted into verdant fields.*

No doubt relieved and satisfied, the park commissioners appointed Hall as Engineer of the Park in August 1871 at a salary of $250 per month. Now the work began in earnest for the indefatigable 25-year-old superintendent. The execution of his plan fulfilled two facets of his personality: the aesthetic or spiritual visionary, and the pragmatic, problem-solving engineer. The first is expressed in this reflection on his work:

*When man undertakes to make a woodland park, his object and sustained endeavor must be to cause the result to seem to be the work of nature of this kind....[Park goers must] instinctually take it for granted that nature made it. One of the most difficult tasks in mind-control is to make oneself fully realize and accept as art that, man-made, which closely simulates pleasing and restful nature....[A]n English park presents open landscapes of meadow, lawn and slope, interspersed with irregular plantations, and meandered by winding walks and drives of diversified character—in seeming imitation of the ever variable climate. These pleasure grounds present, in their broad, free, and simple features, a constant invitation to the health-giving exercises and amusements of the English people, to which they are prompted by the bracing atmosphere of their country.*

The engineer in him considered the transformation of the windblown landscape into the envisioned English woodland as a challenge, not unlike a military battle. He devised a three-pronged attack to accomplish this task.

*First, the improvement of the Avenue [Panhandle] of approach and about 300 acres of the main reservation as a finished modern pleasure ground,*

*whose works of utility are fashioned after those of Eastern Parks, and whose aesthetic design is governed by due consideration of local circumstances; Second, the reclamation of the dune sands, the cultivation of forest trees thereon, and the construction of two drives—one near the northern boundary of the reservation, and one near its southern limit—westward from the finished park, through this young forest, to the Ocean Beach; and Third, the improvement of this beach by the erection of an artificial sand dune upon its outer half, to be in time surmounted by a road, the building of a broad sheltered drive upon its inner side...and the construction of a large tidal lake of salt water inside of this drive...*

## The First Plantings

With this strategy, Hall began an exhaustive analysis of the site, its soil, plants, the water table, and methods of reclaiming the sand dunes. Somehow, without formal training, he learned about the existing native plants and observed their growth characteristics. Only a few plants grew on the sandy western two-thirds: willows around ponds plus shrubs such as bush lupine (*Lupinus albifrons, L. arboreus*) and goldenbush (*Ericameria ericoides*). Wild strawberry (*Fragaria* sp.) colonized Strawberry Hill, along with scrubby coast live oaks (*Quercus agrifolia*), California cherry (*Prunus ilicifolia*), elderberry (*Sambucus* sp.), and sage (*Artemisia pyncnocephala*). On eastern and northern slopes of ridges farther inland, the dominant cover was coast live oak and California lilac (*Ceanothus thrysiflorus*), with scattered cherry and elderberry.

A nursery and a greenhouse were established to grow trees needed both for planting the Avenue and for establishing cover on the dunes. By propagating and growing his own trees, Hall not only saved great sums of money but also had firm control over the operation and was able to experiment with new and exotic plants. This raised the hackles of disgruntled local nurserymen who thought he should purchase from them. As with this and virtually everything Hall did, there were detractors and critics quick to pounce on him and his methods. Fortunately, he was hard shelled and, as Kevin Starr described him, "a little stiff-necked and defensively arrogant....Smallish in stature, a self-centered, defensive, but superior man in a trim beard and well-tailored tweeds." A weaker man would have succumbed to all the petty accusations.

His experimentation with plants in the nursery began one of the hallmarks of planting that continues today—the search for new trees and other plants suitable for San Francisco and the region. By December 1871, after only four months as superintendent, Hall had three thousand trees ready to plant and planned to set out seventeen thousand more in 1872. Among the first trees were blue gum *(Eucalyptus globulus)*, Monterey cypress *(Cupressus macrocarpa)*, Monterey pine *(Pinus radiata)*, maritime pine *(P. pinaster)*, plume albizia *(Acacia lophantha,* now *Albizia lophantha)*, and Sydney golden wattle *(Acacia latifolia,* now *A. longifolia)*.

Discrepancies on what trees were initially planted appear in several historical publications about the park. The essence of these differences is the assertion that Hall planted many trees that were not well suited to San Francisco, particularly in the wind- and sand-battered environment he was trying to tame. Helen and Guy Giffen (1949) state: "The first trees to be planted were Norway Maple, Sycamore, Maritime Pine, English Yew, Austrian Pine, Elder, Monterey Cypress, Alders, and Cottonwood, several varieties of Oak, Acacia and Blue Gum Eucalyptus. With the exception of the Monterey Pine [not listed above] and Cypress the trees did not survive, except in the more sheltered areas…" Terrence Young (1994) cites another source that noted the planting of black walnut, elms, and ash in addition to these trees.

However, Hall identified a different group of trees, with only some overlap, in his first two biennial reports. For the eastern part of the park, he listed the following being grown for planting in his first report:

| | |
|---|---|
| *Eucalyptus* (15 species) | 1,500 plants |
| *Acacia* sp. | 1,200 plants |
| *Pinus* sp. | 6,500 plants |
| Cypress (presumably *Cupressus macrocarpa*) | |
| | 3,500 plants |
| *Schinus molle* | 350 plants |
| *Sequoia giganteum (Sequoiadendron giganteum)* | |
| | 400 plants |
| *Sequoia sempervirens* | 500 plants |
| *Chamaecyparis lawsoniana* | 500 plants |
| *Pittosporum* sp. | 500 plants |

In his Second Biennial Report, he listed many more trees and shrubs, only one of which, black alder *(Alnus glutinosa)*, was mentioned by the Giffens.

Although Hall was not a horticulturist, and the field of horticulture in California was almost unexplored then, he was not likely to have planted Norway maples and others on the Giffens' list in such an environment. These are primarily deciduous trees listed in publications by such writers as Downing and Olmsted for eastern parks. Hall was astute enough to realize that the unique conditions of Golden Gate Park demanded planting and experimentation with mostly evergreen species from coastal California and from similar climates such as Australia.

In November 1871, he hired Patrick Owens as an assistant to oversee the greenhouse and plant propagation and reported, "…many thousands of young trees of the best varieties have been raised from seed, and are now growing finely, and it is expected that this nursery will supply all the ornamental and shade trees necessary to stock the Park, at a trifling cost."

Hall discovered to his delight that his nursery-reared trees grew at an astonishing rate. In only two years, eucalyptus seedlings shot up to eighteen feet with a caliper of four inches. Monterey pines and Monterey cypress reached fourteen feet with a spread of ten to twelve feet during the same period. He adopted an intelligent planting scheme, planting the trees closely so that they would support each other against the buffeting winds; the trees would later be thinned as they matured.

The work of grading the roads and planting the Avenue and main, eastern part of the park began and was accomplished with little difficulty. Seedling trees quickly became established in the sandy loam soil. The development of this part of the park proceeded so well that in three years over sixty-six thousand trees had been planted, fences built, twenty-two entry gates erected, and most of the roads and paths completed. Samuel Williams recorded in a book describing San Francisco in 1875: "Three years ago it [Golden Gate Park] was a howling waste of sand; today it has several miles of drives, lovely plateaus covered with grass, flowers and young trees…"

Though much of Hall's effort was to quickly establish a forest, he was selecting and placing trees following a well thought-out design strategy. He adapted the principles used by Olmsted and other Easterners to the unique conditions of Golden Gate Park. Through

Leveling the sand dunes in the process of building Golden Gate Park

observation, he developed an understanding of how plants could influence microclimate. He realized that the park would be visited year-round, and he studied how people might use the park. Evergreen conifers were selected to moderate the foggy winds by removing moisture from the lower stratum of air. He knew the sandy soil would freely absorb solar heat, conduct it slowly, and radiate it gradually. If the winds could be tempered and the moisture removed, comfortable glades could be developed.

> The character of [the park's] improvement should...embody alternate heavy plantations and open spaces; the former so disposed as to best shield the latter from the winds, with glades situated and of such size that they may be thus protected, without being under the influence of the woods...which would render them damp....The great breadth of landscape effect will thus be to the comfort and health of those who will find other elements of attraction, made possible by its absence.

Rather than declaring all existing vegetation as unfitting for the park, Hall preserved even the scrubbiest of shrubs and trees. These became nurse thickets to protect his young seedlings that were interplanted, with the intent of removing the native material when the new trees became established. He felt that the oaks were "not sufficiently in keeping with the class of vegetation desirable in the more finished portions of the Park...." Nevertheless, they were to be "retained in certain suitable localities...and accompanied by such other trees as will harmonize with them to produce a

class of scenery desirable at these points." For these uses of the native plants he apologizes. "The above fact[s] will explain certain seeming transgressions of the rules of taste in groupings which are now apparent in the Park." This negative attitude toward native vegetation was common then and probably understandable given the deeply ingrained preferences for lush, green woodland parks. This may explain why relatively few native oaks are found in the park today.

Initially, Hall's main concern for completing the eastern part of the park was the establishment of major groupings of trees. Fine lawns, shrub masses, and flowers were unimportant. "The more delicate elements of beauty and grace have been overlooked for the time being." A few roses, shrubs, and other flowering plants were received as gifts from public-spirited citizens, but Hall kept them in the greenhouse, planting only a few at the main entrance. He did establish about two acres of lawn and promised more, once money was relieved from the pressure of the initial reclamation efforts. Thus, through skillful horticultural techniques, detailed understanding of the site and microclimates, and a well-developed, though rapidly learned sense of landscape design, Hall set the character of Golden Gate Park in only five years. The finished "pleasure ground" was indeed largely established by 1876, to a point west of where the conservatory now stands.

## Water

With its Mediterranean-type climate, where over eighty percent of annual rainfall occurs in the winter portion of the year, irrigation is essential to sustain a garden or park in San Francisco. The question of how much supplemental water is needed is driven by the character and nature of the designed landscape. In the last quarter of the twentieth century, Californians began to reflect upon the reality of this semiarid climate in the design and management of landscapes. Still, today, as in the 1870s, the preference for lush, green landscapes is derived from the English rather than Mediterranean models. Despite Olmsted's sound advice for modeling Golden Gate Park on landscapes of the semiarid Mediterranean region, the park was designed and planted to satisfy the understandable tastes for a well-watered landscape. It is easy to criticize this approach in retrospect today, as have some authors (Black, 1994; Young, 1994).

On the other hand, it is apparent from examining Hall's work that he was conscious of the need to adapt both landscape design and plant selection to the environmental constraints of the park's landscape—incessant summer wind and salt air, aridity, and sandy soil. Where lawns were to be located, they were relatively small and compact. Tons of loam were imported to afford good growth and reduce water loss through the porous sand. (Robbing other parts of the city of good soil is another contentious topic!) Covering the entire thousand acres with loam was impractical, so deposits were made only on the refined eastern end. For the forested areas, tons of street sweepings (horse manure) were spread to build humus, increasing both the water- and nutrient-holding ability of the sand.

The majority of trees selected (and those that survived through self-selection) were relatively drought tolerant—eucalypts, acacias, pines, and cypress. Most of the trees and shrubs listed in the first biennial reports are from similar, semiarid climates or are native to coastal California and, therefore, well-suited and logical choices for experimentation in the park's tree plantations.

Space here does not afford a detailed discussion of the irrigation of the park trees and other plantings. The topic is well covered by Black (1995) and Clary (1980). Suffice it to say that, as an engineer, Hall was resourceful in tapping the existing lakes, ponds, and aquifers with wells and piping, in constructing a large reservoir on Strawberry Hill, and in connecting water mains to the city's eventual supplier, Spring Valley Water Company. The amount of water required to irrigate the high maintenance areas of the park remains a controversial subject today, just as the park itself, as a microcosm of California's water use and supply, remains a topic of endless debate. There are probably ways to reduce water consumption in the park. But it is difficult to imagine how the "howling waste of sand" could have been transformed into the lovely oasis of today in a more water-efficient manner during those early years of tree planting.

## Taming the Dunes

As though the achievement of completing the eastern part of the park was not enough, Hall had simultaneously been forging ahead with the other two prongs of his plan of attack. He was equally successful with the taming of the more difficult western two-thirds of the park.

As Colonel Alexander had anticipated, Hall needed to learn sand-dune reclamation techniques by studying reclamation work done in France, Great Britain, Denmark, Holland, and North Africa. By analyzing the characteristics of the sand dunes in each country, he concluded that those most closely resembling the dunes in San Francisco were along the Gulf of Gascony in France, an area one hundred times larger than the San Francisco dunes. Nevertheless, he studied the reclamation techniques and adapted them to the park.

Two types of plants were required. Where the drifting sand could be checked away from the front line of the beach, tap-rooted plants such as the native lupine could be used. Nearer the beach, where the greatest drift occurred, mat-forming plants with fibrous spreading roots could be employed, thriving on the constant build-up of sand, ultimately controlling the dunes. For this he found that a beach grass (*Ammophila arenaria*) imported from Europe worked best. Hall was assisted in this research by a Frenchman, Paul Rousset, who owned a large tract near the park. A native of the southwestern coast of France, where dune reclamation had been accomplished, Rousset offered Hall his knowledge of dune reclamation. Local seedsman Frank Pixley imported seeds of the beach grass from France.

With this research and the proper seeds in hand, Hall devised his reclamation program:

1. Erect a bulkhead, an artificial dune of wooden walls piled high with brush, along the Great Highway, and cover the sand with beach grass plants grown from seed in the nursery.
2. Stop the shifting sand dunes by establishing such native vegetation as lupine and suitable imported

trees and shrubs such as *Pinus pinaster, Albizia lophantha,* and *Acacia longifolia.*

3. Plant stabilized dunes with seeds and the various plants previously listed.

One problem puzzled Hall—how to keep sand drift from burying the slow-germinating lupine. Always the keen observer, Hall noticed that moist barley, spilled from feeding draft horses, germinated in five days. So he soaked the barley seed, as well as the lupine seed, to hasten the process. This enabled him to arrest sand drift in twelve days so that the lupine could germinate, binding the sand with its roots as deep as twenty-five feet in search of water. In turn, other woody plants could be planted in the stabilized sand. Basically, he was stabilizing the dunes by initiating a form of artificial ecological succession.

Hall's expectations for this monumental task demonstrated the confidence he had when he became

Golden Gate Park and Sunset District sand dunes

superintendent. After two years, he anticipated converting the dunes into "heaths" covered with native vegetation. And after only six years, he expected to have young forests of evergreen trees established so as to give a decidedly parklike appearance in twelve years. The records and descriptions of the park clearly show that all this was easily accomplished with a combination of systematic engineering, self-education, insightful research, and keen observation. With a large dose of self-confidence, Hall wrote: "Man, as the director, with the forces of nature as laborers in the field, now

readily converts these wandering hillocks into fixed and productive features of topography."

As with any planting of this scale, there were some setbacks. The winters of 1872 and 1873 were unusually severe with several violent storms and heavy frosts. Some ten-foot-tall trees were buried with sand and an initial planting of tender *Albizia lophantha* succumbed to frost. His first seed of maritime pine proved to be poor and only a few plants survived. Those that did live were either scorched by the sun or choked by the competing lupine. The winters of 1874 and 1875 brought uneven distribution of rains preceded by high winds and long, intervening spells of drying north winds. The lupine plantings suffered during this period, but the situation gradually improved.

In the long run, the plants did survive and the "howling waste of sand" was largely tamed in only three years. The costs proved nominal even for that day. About eight hundred acres were reclaimed at a total cost of $30,750, or $43.93 per acre of seeding with barley and lupine and nearly $100 per acre for forested areas.

Hall was a master at saving money and improvisation, perhaps due in part to his Scottish heritage and to his sense of self-discipline. This led to his later undoing. He understood large-scale tree planting and how to accomplish his goal in the challenging circumstances of the park. Recognizing that the strong northwest winds would bend and contort the young trees, he planted trees close together in large masses, the trees as close as four or five feet apart. Gradually as they grew, he thinned the saplings out and regulated the outline of the groups. "The planting at Golden Gate Park has nearly all been done with this view. The trees selected were chosen for their...rapid growth and hardy disposition under existing circumstances and it is expected that many of them will be supplanted by specimens of other varieties as the primary end is attained." In another statement he said that by planting the trees close together, staking became unnecessary after the first year, thereby saving substantial time and money and producing a better effect than by using any other method. (We have something to learn from this even today!) Undoubtedly, Hall knew that trees transplanted in the thinning process would not survive.

Never losing sight of the finished design of the park, Hall apologizes: "The real works of Landscape Gardening...have been very limited at the Park and it cannot be expected...that any marked effects produced by the exercise of this art will be apparent until the primary object, before alluded to, shall have been accomplished."

## Hall's Legacy

So, in only five years (1871–1876), William Hammond Hall succeeded in fulfilling his early goals and was well on the way to refining the reclaimed sand dunes to the standard of the eastern part of the park.

Behind the scenes, however, all was not well. Political opponents in City Hall began to cut off the flow of money. Stirred by a bitter park employee, DC Sullivan, previously fired for dishonesty, the "City Hall Gang" arranged for an investigation of the park's operation by an Assembly Special Committee from Sacramento. Sullivan had been elected to the state legislature and was named chairman of the investigating committee! The investigation took the form of petty faultfinding and complaints by other "ill-treated" park employees. Among other things, Hall was accused of

- wanton and useless destruction of one-third of all trees planted. "These trees might have been transplanted at a small expense, and large sums of money thus saved..." went the testimony;
- neglect of duty by making private surveys in San Mateo and Marin counties while being paid $400 per month at the park;
- waste of money: wells dug and not being used continuously.

The park commissioners, caught in a squeeze play, attempted to appeal the investigating committee's report in a well-documented letter to Governor William Irwin in 1876. Each accusation was categorically refuted and documented by the testimony of horticulturists and other witnesses. The sound technique of planting thickly and later thinning trees was endorsed by horticulturists. All of Hall's private surveys had been completed prior to his salaried appointment and were known to the park commissioners. Some wells were test wells; others were used intermittently as the water table fluctuated.

But the damage had been done. Harassed and defeated, this travail heaped upon years of criticism despite his great successes, Hall submitted his resignation as Landscape Engineer and Superintendent. Thus ended an astonishing period in the development of the park. A great park had been created where once only sand dunes shifted under the relentless wind. Hall had battled the elements in one of the great stories of landscape transformation. But he could not win against the pettiness, jealousies, and mean-spirited temperament of his fellow men.

Over the years, the legacy of Hall's achievements in the establishment of the foundation for Golden Gate Park as we know it has been overshadowed by the long tenure and achievements of John McLaren. Yet, his efforts and accomplishments against all odds—environmental, personal, and political—are astonishing. In only five years, Hall achieved what is, perhaps, the most remarkable landscape transformation anyone has ever seen. He essentially disproved all skeptics in creating one of the world's most renowned urban parks. Even the great Olmsted paid him high compliments in correspondence in 1874:

*I have been inclined to regard the attempt to prepare a large city park on this site given you for that purpose an ill considered one. I must now say, however, that I feel much more confidence than I have hitherto been able to do, that if you are allowed to continue your work, and are adequately sustained, the thorough study, good taste, and sound judgment which appear to me manifest in your papers and plans, will certainly produce results of striking interest and value....I heartily congratulate you on the success which has thus far attended your studies, and on your good prospect of accomplishing more than, with my limited knowledge of the local conditions, I have hitherto thought practicable.*

And, in 1876, Olmsted wrote:

*I cannot too strongly express my admiration of the spirit and method which characterizes your undertaking, and I do not doubt that it will be rewarded with results such as I have not hitherto thought it reasonable to expect under the circumstances. There is no like enterprise anywhere else, which, so far as I can judge, has been conducted with equal foresight, ingenuity, and economy.*

## The Dark Years

Following Hall's resignation, the park entered a dark decade in which funds were cut, superintendence was tossed from one unwitting hand to another (three in all), and the visionary work of William Hammond Hall fell into disrepair from neglect and ignorance. Trees that were now beginning to buffer the wind in the western end received no irrigation. The thickly planted trees were left unthinned. Throughout the park, maintenance was reduced to the barest minimum. One of the superintendents was told he had to assume the duties of the head gardener who had resigned.

In 1886 Hall was called back again, but it was too late. He was about to be appointed state engineer for California. Even so, Hall agreed to advise on park improvements, including the construction of the Sharon Building and its Children's Playground. He agreed to accomplish one final task, one that opened a new and lasting era in the development and nurturing of the park—that of the selection and training of a new superintendent. His choice was another Scotsman, a gardener named John McLaren.

## The McLaren Era— White Elephant to Green Oasis

According to *Chronicle* columnist Herb Caen, John McLaren

> was a dour, dedicated Scotsman...who, in 1887, took over the job of transforming a desolate area of windswept sand into a public park second to none in the world...and the lush evidence of his spectacular success grows on every inch and in every corner. "Uncle John," a benevolent despot who brooked no interference from anyone, ran the park with a green-thumbed iron fist until his death...in 1943. During his...reign he planted well over a million trees and acres of tough beach grass to hold the shifting sands, created lakes and wild canyons, brooks and waterfalls, and did his job so fast and so well that by 1894 the Park was ready for the world to marvel at as the scene of the California Midwinter Exposition.

This statement, along with many others referring to the long tenure of John McLaren, implies that he was solely responsible for the transformation of the barren

sand wastes into the park as we know it. In 1926, an editorial in the *San Francisco Chronicle* that Park Commission President Herbert Fleishacker approved gave full credit for the development of the park to McLaren. William Hammond Hall vigorously protested this assumption in an open letter to the park commission and the newspaper. Such lack of recognition of Hall's role in the park's early development has persisted and causes an unfortunate and unnecessary competition for credit between Hall and McLaren, detracting from the significance of both men's contributions.

Indeed, Hall laid the groundwork and accomplished a remarkable achievement under the most difficult circumstances. When Hall was recalled in 1886 to help rectify years of damage to the park from neglect and mismanagement, he hand-picked John McLaren as his assistant. After three years of training McLaren and working with him to resume his strategies for creating the park, Hall turned over to him a park, a forest, and relatively stabilized dunes for continuation and refinement. Hall, on leave from his position as state engineer, left as park consultant in 1889 when William Stow was appointed to the park commission. Stow had been responsible for crippling the park during its dark years by cutting the state appropriation for the park in half. Ironically, when Stow

John McLaren, superintendent of Golden Gate Park from 1887 to 1943.

Conservatory of Flowers in Golden Gate Park, 1879, shortly after completion of construction. A native woodland of coast live oak *(Quercus agrifolia)* can be seen beyond and dune vegetation in front of the new conservatory; young Monterey pines *(Pinus radiata)* are in the foreground.

work force of over one thousand men was employed to repair the damaged park.

A massive tree planting and reclamation effort was launched in addition to repairing roads, structures, and utilities. Over twenty thousand trees and shrubs were planted. The commissioners, in a moment of enlightenment, developed a plan to build fences piled with brush along the ocean end of the park to stop invading sand and to permit construction of a highway. Due to memory loss from the board's lack of continuity, they had forgotten that Hall had outlined exactly this procedure twenty years earlier!

Not intimidated by politicians, McLaren resumed the tasks of stabilizing the dunes, planting and thinning out the forest plantations, and refining the eastern end of the park. He subscribed to Hall's method of planting trees closely, followed by thinning in a few years to promote fuller growth: "plant thick, thin quick," as he called it. By 1887 more than seven hundred thousand trees and shrubs were growing in the park. McLaren continued this massive planting effort but with more diversity, now that the planting environments had been improved by arresting the sand and were protected by the maturing forest.

As a knowledgeable plantsman, McLaren increased experimentation with a variety of tree species. Seeds and plants were imported for propagation in the park nursery from a wide array of firms and botanic gardens all over the world: India, China, Japan, Australia, New Zealand, Tasmania, England, France, and Switzerland, as well as throughout the United States. In 1895, the park commissioners' *Catalogue of Trees and Shrubs in Golden Gate Park* listed 825 kinds of trees along with 225 species of vines and herbaceous plants. The 1910 report included 2,730 kinds of plants. And by 1924, the list had grown to 3,600.

The park nursery served not only as incubator for park plantings, but was also McLaren's "boot camp" for gardeners. He insisted that new gardeners work in the nursery at least one year to learn the cycle of plant

became commission president, he complained about insufficient funding!

Fortunately, McLaren was not only a tough, no-nonsense Scot cut from the same mold as Hall, but he also was a knowledgeable plantsman and horticulturist. Originally educated and trained as a landscape gardener in Scotland, McLaren came to California in 1872 to work on several large estates in San Mateo County. With so few expert gardeners available, McLaren apparently caught Hall's attention and made the fortuitous move to San Francisco.

Had the new superintendent been development- or recreation-oriented, as in many park departments today, the tree planting and the character of the park would have taken on a different appearance. There would have been less experimentation in tree selection, less skilled management, and, perhaps, fewer trees in deference to an emphasis on recreational facilities. Quite possibly, Hall's work would have been eroded or undone and, conceivably, the park might have failed, succumbing to the harsh coastal environment.

None of this happened. The canvas begun by Hall was placed in the best possible hands and in July 1890, John McLaren was appointed superintendent, a title he held for fifty-three years until his death at age ninety-six in 1943. He inherited a park quite well developed but suffering from neglect, poor management, inadequate funding, and a damaging storm of 1889. But he assumed the onerous task with confidence, skill, and boundless energy. The '89 storm had caused widespread unemployment in addition to severe damage to the park. Money was raised to hire the needy, and a propagation and growth before being assigned to beats in the park.

Under McLaren's ironfisted management and horticultural skill, Golden Gate Park became an enormous garden with a wide array of growing conditions and microclimates. Many trees no doubt failed, succumbing either to the harsh elements or to their unsuitability for the conditions. Many trees would thrive in one environment but fail in others. In this way, the trees we see today have survived a filtering process—the survival of the fittest.

The character of the park is likewise determined by this process evolving as environmental conditions have improved over time. Success, too, was predetermined by McLaren's skill in plant selection. He avoided deciduous shrubs and many deciduous trees, declaring that these types of plants were all the unfortunate gardeners back East could grow, so we should plant broad-leafed evergreens and leave the deciduous plants to them.

McLaren insisted on proper planting techniques to ensure survival of the trees. As standard practice, tree holes were to be large and square, as large as six feet square and six feet deep. Backfill consisted of a mix of as much straw, manure, leaves, and loam as possible to provide for good moisture retention. To ensure high survival rates, he frequently planted a broad-leafed tree in the same hole as a conifer. At least one of the two would live; if both lived, there was a choice of which to leave and which to remove, no doubt a dilemma for his gardeners.

## Defending the Park

After repairing damage from the 1889 storm, McLaren's first big challenge was to prepare the park for the 1893–1894 Midwinter International Exposition. MH de Young had arranged for many of the exhibits from the Columbian Exposition in Chicago to be moved to San Francisco for a similar fair, to jump-start the lagging economy here. Nearly two hundred acres of the park east of Strawberry Hill were selected for the fair site. A large piece of the park had to be cleared and graded to accommodate the exposition. Such destruction of the park engendered considerable opposition.

McLaren was appointed landscape designer for the fair, but he resigned immediately upon learning he would have to take orders from de Young, the fair director. According to Clary (1980), "McLaren took orders from no one, except perhaps his gracious wife."

One of the lasting contributions of the fair to the park was the Japanese Tea Garden. The garden was built by a local merchant, George Turner Marsh, who had a large Japanese garden and four Japanese families living on his Mill Valley estate. The site for the Japanese Village, which remains today as the Japanese Tea Garden, was selected because of its large number of tall pine trees, reminiscent of Japan. Bonsai trees, shrubs, vines, and flowers were imported from Japan to create an authentic exhibit. The entry gate was brought by ferry from Marsh's garden and reassembled as the entrance to the village, where it remains today as the main entrance to the garden. The Japanese Village quickly became one of the favorite attractions of the fair. However, the exhibit and its operation stirred considerable criticism within the local Japanese community. Later on, the Japanese family who created, maintained, and lived in the Japanese Tea Garden were forced out—the ugly consequence of anti-Asian sentiment during World War II.

Repairing the damage from the fair must have irked McLaren and occupied his effort and budget for years afterward. Yet another challenge occurred a few years later when the park became a refugee camp for thousands of victims made homeless by the 1906 earthquake. An "instant city" of tents and barracks

A scene in the Japanese Village at the Midwinter International Exposition of 1893–1894. The village was such a popular feature of the fair that it was retained after the fair closed and became the Japanese Tea Garden.

hastily arose. One company of soldiers was ordered to find a level spot in which to pitch its tents. Before anyone noticed, least of all McLaren, it had selected the perfect site—McLaren's prized bowling green! As an avid lawn bowler, McLaren erupted at this discovery and probably singed the ears of the unwitting soldiers. Repairing the greens and the rest of the park took over a year of hard work.

True today as then, parks are viewed as opportunities not only to hold large events, but also to erect monuments and buildings by self-serving politicos. McLaren steadfastly defended the park as well as he could against such incursions. The promoters of the 1915 Panama–Pacific International Exposition eyed Golden Gate Park as the logical site for their event. After all, boosters argued, the land west of Strawberry Hill was little more than a wilderness that could only be improved by the exposition. An enormous wave of opposition arose after President Taft broke ground in the park. Even William Hammond Hall joined the fray, writing an impassioned, eloquent, sixteen-page argument against the proposal.

*A great city park is necessarily the country place of the poor...used by tens of thousands of positively poor and often sick and decrepit people. The rich...can go to the real country for the weekend or summer vacation. The poor have only the great city park for their country...*

*The day will come when San Francisco will have probably quite as large a proportion of park dependers as have other great cities. This climate braces people for a bold, short strenuous dash of life and then breaks them down. Wait a generation...and her park area will not be nearly enough for the safety valve which she will need.*

*This is no so-called "nature lovers" argument. It is the accepted argument of social humanity, of modern sanitary science, of civic economics.*

*Keep buildings out of the park. Make parks of our "parks," and keep them as such to contribute, as such open, restful spaces in cities alone can, towards the health of mind and body of the people...*

This time wiser men prevailed and the Panama–Pacific International Exhibition was located in Cow Hollow, now the Marina District. Following the fair, a great variety of trees was planted in Golden Gate Park. During the fair, numerous dignitaries visited San Francisco. As a publicity stunt, a troop of cavalry would escort each person to the exposition, where a tree was planted honoring the visitor's city, state, or country. Since none of the trees could remain on what was to become part of the Presidio, they were transplanted to Golden Gate Park. Examples included a white oak for Maryland, a cedar for New Jersey, an Oriental plane tree with soil from Central Park for New York, a maple for Indiana, a pine for China, and so on. Many of the trees representing the states were clustered together just east of the Pioneer Log Cabin, where some of them can still be seen. Trees were also planted in the park by former presidents Roosevelt and Taft, as well as other dignitaries from Washington. A grove of redwoods honoring the dead of World War I was planted near Fulton Street on the north side of the park.

Over the years, McLaren's reputation as "the man who planted a million trees" grew along with his trees. His reputation as a passionate and steadfast defender of the park was legendary. He won many battles and endured the jabs, false accusations, and wrath of impetuous politicians and other detractors. His accomplishments, too numerous to elaborate here, are legion and in a large measure have incrementally built upon Hall's foundation to leave a lasting legacy for all future generations of San Franciscans.

Many others followed in McLaren's footsteps and made significant contributions to the refinement of the park—Roy Hudson, Eric Walther, and John Spring, to name a few. Each planted trees, weathered both natural storms and the vagaries of political climate, defended the park against exploiters, and continued to shape an urban oasis second to none.

As San Francisco rose from the ashes of the earthquake and fire to become one of the world's most beautiful cities, Golden Gate Park rose from the desolate, shifting sand wastes to emerge miraculously as one of the world's most beautiful parks. Its trees are living testaments to the undaunted spirit, skill, and bold confidence of men like Hall and McLaren. They tell a great story of world geography, of human collaboration with nature, and of the contentious effort to provide a unique place of comfort, respite, and health-giving calm for all—a democratic, uplifting Eden, a soft counterpart to an increasingly hard world.

# The Reforestation of Golden Gate Park

Peter Ehrlich

*It should be recognized that because the Park's unique landscape character is a wholly artificial creation its care and maintenance is highly labor-intensive. Significant numbers of qualified personnel must be retained to ensure the park's continued preservation and maintenance.*

*1979 Plan for Golden Gate Park*

By the 1970s, the forest that is Golden Gate Park had long since begun to decline. Two reasons for its decline can be identified: certain trees had reached a natural stage of senescence or old age, while other trees had succumbed to the challenging and artificial conditions of the park. In the first category were Monterey cypress and, particularly, Monterey pines, whose natural life spans are not much more than one hundred years. In the second category were many different trees aging more rapidly than normal due to the combination of persistent wind, salty air, sandy soil, severe storms, occasional freezes, and prolonged droughts. In addition, the park's trees have had to deal with the pressures brought about by the number of visitors to the park each year, resulting in trampling and compacting of soils in the root zone, or in erosion of the soil away from the roots. Years of steadily declining city budgets for park maintenance had resulted in deferred maintenance that, sadly, further impacted the health and vigor of this human-made forest.

The *1979 Plan for Golden Gate Park* set forth the broad principles for a renovation of the forest. An inventory conducted in that same year showed a large part of the park's forest to be in poor or only fair condition. Seventeen percent of the park's thirty-three thousand trees were dead, dying, or in need of immediate replacement; eighty-seven percent of those were in the western end of the park. The results of this inventory were published in the *Golden Gate Park Forest Management Plan* (1980), which further established guidelines for the reforestation of the park.

Several salient points were expressed in Objective I of the *1979 Plan for Golden Gate Park*. Policy A states: "Ensure that the essential design elements that give the Park its unique landscape character are retained and protected." This would be accomplished in the following ways: (1)"The existing form of wooded areas and their relationship to the meadow areas should be maintained. The size, the basic texture, and color of the Park woods should not be significantly altered..." and (2) "It should be recognized that the Park, by design intent, is basically evergreen. Large scale introduction of flowering trees in areas other than horticultural gardens should be discouraged."

## A Fifty-Year Plan

With the inventory complete and guidelines established, the imposing task of replacing the park's forest canopy and the windbreak it provides was begun during the 1979–1980 winter planting season. The initial goal was to replace the aging forest with a new forest in twenty-five years. This twenty-five year rotation was deemed adequate to create an uneven-aged, "second growth" forest, which would not age and decline as precipitously and uniformly as the original forest.

Two-year saplings of Monterey cypress *(Cupressus macrocarpa)* in a cleared reforestation block. Photograph by RG Turner Jr

17

The park's forest was divided into a series of plots of trees to be replaced. Within a selected plot, those trees were removed that were dead, in decline, or structurally unsound to the point of creating a public hazard or causing damage to the park's infrastructure. The size of each plot, or plantation, was a compromise between the need to admit sufficient sunlight to grow replacement trees and the need to minimize public displeasure with large openings in the historic forest. Monterey cypress, Monterey pine, maritime pine, and Torrey pine (initially the primary forest replacement trees) are intolerant of shade, needing full sunlight for best growth.

Silviculture (the cultivation of trees for wood production), though different from the purpose of Golden Gate Park's forest, nevertheless provides a procedure called "group selection" that was borrowed for the park's reforestation program to balance adequate sunlight and visual impact. In an area that has a group of declining or structurally weak trees, openings are created that are approximately one and a half times the height of the surrounding, untouched trees. In the park's forest, this produces openings of approximately 0.3 acres. Each area is selected both for the decadence of its overstory and for its reforestation potential

Three-year saplings of Monterey pine *(Pinus radiata)*. Photograph by RG Turner Jr

(aspect, slope, and proximity to water). These decisions are made by a council composed of the urban forester, arborist supervisor, and reforestation supervisor.

The original desire to replace the 628 forested acres of parkland over twenty-five years has now been changed to a fifty-year rotation for a number of reasons. A twenty-five-year rotation would have meant that extensive areas of the park would be occupied by sapling trees. This, it was felt, was aesthetically unacceptable to park users. The rate of overstory removal that would have been necessary to attain a twenty-five-year replacement would have significantly diminished the protection that the old overstory provides to the new plantings. Wind velocities would increase, to the detriment of the new plantings. The twenty-five-year rotation would not have provided a true, uneven-aged forest in the park. The fifty-year rotation means that the aging of the second growth forest will occur over a more extensive period of time. Also, more varied-age classes of overstory trees would be present in the park, increasing the quality of bird habitat through varying canopy heights; this would enhance an important recreational activity within the park—birdwatching.

The decline of Monterey pine has been the most precipitous in the past twenty years, dropping from twenty-two percent of the park overstory in 1980 to seventeen percent of the canopy in 1993. A stump found in the Cambria stand, a natural population of Monterey pine on California's central coast, was 125 years old. This age should be considered as the upper end of the potential life span of Monterey pine in a wild population. Considering the more extreme environment of Golden Gate Park, one hundred years could be considered the upper limit of this pine's expected life span in the park. Eighty- to hundred-year-old trees often have a poor structure (co-dominant stems and heavy lateral limbs) or are in decline due to a number of pests and diseases (western gall rust, red turpentine beetle, Monterey pine engraver beetle, and pitch canker). Dramatic declines such as that of Monterey pine will be avoided with a fifty-year rotation.

## Reforestation Procedures

Seeds of replacement trees are started in long white tubes (leach cells) in the Golden Gate Park Nursery. When the seedlings reach sufficient size, they are transplanted to bottomless, one-gallon tree pots and grown in these containers until they are planted in the park.

Tree pots are tall, slender containers that allow the plants to develop deeper root systems than in conventional one-gallon containers. Experience has shown that root development and establishment is better on trees planted from such containers; as a result, most trees in the reforestation program are handled this way.

The park environment, especially its soils with their low organic composition, has made the reforestation process a labor-intensive one. All new tree plantings are hand watered for three to four years. Hand watering entails the building of a small berm, or mound, around the tree at the drip line and filling the resulting basin at least twice at each watering to wet the soil thoroughly and deeply. The deep watering of the trees is one means of overcoming the hydrophobicity and poor water-holding capacity of the park's soils. Most reforestation plantings are done in the rainy season (late fall and winter). By taking advantage of the natural, deep rains, labor-intensive watering schedules can be reduced. Watering is more frequent during the first summer after planting, then is reduced in subsequent years.

The sand dunes on which Golden Gate Park was built are Holocene dune sands, which have a poor water-holding capacity due to the lack of organic matter incorporated at any level in the soil profile. This results in a lack of the organisms necessary to break down the organic layer that has been deposited on the sand's surface since the forest became established. Although the mature canopy drops as much as forty-five thousand pounds of organic matter on the park's sands, little of this breaks down, especially under pines, cypress, and eucalypts. The chemical composition of this leaf litter—high in natural oils—is also responsible for its resistance to decay organisms. (Amundsen and Tremback, *Pacific Horticulture,* Winter 1989). This lack of decomposition results in a poor development of the "A" horizon (upper level) in the soil profile. Most tree root development normally occurs in that layer, but only when there is adequate moisture held in the soil. The systematic and intensive watering regimes in the park are necessary to maintain sufficient water in this primary root zone.

Attempts to amend reforestation sites with well-rotted manure from the Golden Gate Park Stables have produced only a moderate increase in the water-holding capacity of the soils. Deep watering for at least three to four years has consistently proven to be the most effective way to produce healthy, vigorous trees.

An eight-year-old Monterey pine *(Pinus radiata).* Photograph by RG Turner Jr

Future plans call for top-dressing plantations with compost made from the chipped and shredded branches and leaves of prunings and tree removals in the park.

Trees are overplanted in reforestation plantations, though not as thickly as in William Hammond Hall's time, when there was no established forest to provide protection from the wind. Trees today are planted ten to fifteen feet apart with the expectation that some of the trees will succumb to vandalism and disease. When plantations are five years of age, they are assessed for potential thinning. Defective, diseased, and dead trees are removed, along with those of low vigor, to reduce competition with the more vigorous trees displaying a good structure.

Trees compete with each other for light and moisture. When the crowns of plantation trees touch, the thinning process begins again. Growth potential is then transferred to the remaining trees. Ultimately, after numerous thinning operations, the plantation is left with healthy, well-spaced trees with good structure. Sometimes the trees that are left are pruned during a thinning to remove co-dominant stems from otherwise healthy trees. The necessity of thinning as a management strategy was well understood by William

A small grove of ten-year-old Monterey pine *(Pinus radiata)* and Monterey cypress *(Cupressus macrocarpa)*. Photograph by RG Turner Jr

Hammond Hall and John McLaren in their early plantings in Golden Gate Park.

## Species Selection

The selection of tree species for the replacement of the park's evergreen forest canopy and windbreak has changed over the years. The spread of the fungal disease pine pitch canker *(Fusarium subglutinans)* into the Bay Area and the southern part of San Francisco has resulted in a suspension of the planting of Monterey pine in Golden Gate Park. This pine is the most susceptible of the conifers to the pitch canker disease. Maritime pine *(Pinus pinaster)* and Torrey pine *(P. torreyana)* are still used even though they are relatively susceptible to this pest. Several other pines have been tested in the park to increase the species diversity in the canopy: Eldar pine *(P. eldarica,* syn. *P. brutia* ssp. *eldarica),* Austrian black pine *(P. nigra),* Mexican weeping, or Jelecote, pine *(P. patula),* and Canary Island pine *(P. canariensis).* The last has proven to be one of the most resistant pines to pitch canker. It easily reaches seventy-five to eighty feet in height and can serve as an adequate overstory tree. The most resistant trees are Japanese black pine *(P. thunbergii)* and Italian stone pine *(P. pinea),* but they do not reach overstory stature.

Monterey cypress is still the most commonly planted reforestation tree and the best for overstory replacement due to its wind tolerance, height, and characteristic branching pattern. It requires adequate deep watering for four summers after planting. If stressed due to unavailability of water, it can become prey to a variety of pests such as cypress tip moth, cypress canker, and oak root fungus *(Armillaria mellea).* Some of our oldest and best specimens from reforestation plantings are ten to twenty years old and already fifty feet tall.

A modest, but controversial, effort to replant eucalypts in Golden Gate Park has been attempted. Eucalypts represent twenty percent of the park's current overstory. Since the reforestation program is mandated to preserve the character of this overstory, it is felt that eucalypt replacement should occur. It is also felt that blue gum *(Eucalyptus globulus)* should not be used because of its invasive nature. Other species that have been used are swamp gum *(E. ovata),* bangalay *(E. botryoides),* forest red gum *(E. tereticornis),* and river red gum *(E. camaldulensis);* spotted gum *(E. maculata)* will be tried in the future. New eucalypts are planted only in areas where older ones have been removed or where they have occupied a significant part of the landscape.

In the twenty years of the reforestation program, fourteen thousand trees have been planted. They have been planted on 328 plantations, resulting in 110 acres of reforested parkland. Of the several trees used, Monterey cypress has been planted the most—3,059 trees in all.

## Special Park Areas

In the 1999–2000 planting season (November to April), replanting of the forest canopy began in the park's Rhododendron Dell. The devastation wrought on the dell by winter storms in 1995 and by the area's severe problem with oak root fungus has led to a great loss of trees there. The first plantings were of coast redwood *(Sequoia sempervirens)* and dawn redwood *(Metasequoia glyptostroboides)* on the western edge of the dell. Both species are resistant to the fungus, can take the frequent irrigation that rhododendrons require during the dry season, and will provide some high shade for the understory planting, as well as some protection from the wind.

Reforestation of the Panhandle has also begun. This area, the first planted in Golden Gate Park in 1871, is in need of overstory replacement. However, this replacement will be done on a tree-by-tree basis, not by clearing plots of forest as in the western end of the park. The large trees along Fell and Oak streets will be replaced with smaller, specimen trees. Large trees were planted in the Panhandle in the 1870s when the area was known as The Avenue, and the only vehicles passing beneath were infrequent horse carriages. Today a huge volume of traffic passes under these monarchs and the risk of damage and injury from an aged tree falling is of serious concern. All large tree replacements will be planted in the interior of the Panhandle. Planted along the edge of the Panhandle have been specimen trees such as red maple *(Acer rubrum* 'Red Sunset'), Mexican swamp cypress *(Taxodium mucronatum),* and a pendulous selection of Nootka cypress *(Chamaecyparis nootkatensis* 'Pendula'). These plantings help fulfill the Panhandle's original role as a "tree walk."

The eastern end of Golden Gate Park has been extensively reforested with coast live oak *(Quercus agrifolia).* The native stands in the park are being augmented with seedlings grown from acorns collected from trees in the native oak grove at Stanyan and Fulton streets.

The intent is to preserve the genetic integrity of the park's oak population. (Likewise, tree plantings in the reforestation effort at Buena Vista Park are made with trees grown from seed collected at Buena Vista Park.)

Planning for windbreak and overstory replacement in Strybing Arboretum is more complex than in the rest of the park. The challenge here is to remove the old canopy trees without damaging the valuable plant collections below them. Options are labor intensive and will require setting aside space for the stacking of logs and brush. The use of a crane may be considered where access is available for large equipment. Otherwise, all trees have to be lowered and removed slowly, section by section, to avoid damage to the understory plantings. The Golden Gate Park tree crew will perform all the work. Replacement trees for the overstory in the arboretum will be determined in consultation with the arboretum staff.

Recognizing the continuing need to evaluate, maintain, and replace our urban trees, the Recreation and Park Department has shown its long-term commitment by incorporating into its regular budget permanent funding for an urban forester to administer the program and an urban forestry division to carry out field operations. This long-range, carefully planned program is ensuring a future for this great park.

# The Trees of
# Golden Gate Park
# and San Francisco

# Reading the Field Guide

## Tree Names

Three names are provided for most trees (in this order):

**Common names** are usually in English; some trees have not been grown long enough to have gained a common name. Check the list of common names on page 221 to learn the corresponding botanical name of a tree.

**Botanical names** are in Latin and *italicized*. The first word is the genus; the second word is the species (or specific epithet). Some plants have a third name, either a variety or subspecies (in Latin and *italicized),* or a cultivar (in English, surrounded by single quotes). The field guide is organized alphabetically by the botanical names of the trees. Synonyms (syn.) are given when older names are still in occasional use. **Family name**s usually end in –aceae; check the list of tree families on page 220 for related trees.

## Tree Number

Use this number to locate a tree on the maps on pages 212–219

## Illustration

A simple line drawing showing details of leaves, flowers, or fruit to help in identifying a tree, generally shown at less than actual size. Artists are listed on page 242

## Sidebar Data

(in order of presentation)

**Tree locations in GGP** (always with map number and coordinates for the maps found on pages 212–219)

**Tree locations beyond GGP** (in San Francisco)

**Evergreen or deciduous** leaves / growth rate / mature size in cultivation

**Brief description** of flowers / fruit or cones

**Cultural preferences:** sun or shade / watering frequency for established trees*

**Climate zone adaptability** *Sunset Western Garden Book* zones

**Street tree suitablity** (if noted)

**Color plate(s)** (if noted)

*Watering frequency in San Francisco's cool, summer-dry, mediterranean climate: regular = weekly in dry months; occasional = once every two weeks in dry months; infrequently = once a month in dry months. (These are average recommendations.)

## Main Text

Adapted from articles originally appearing in *Pacific Horticulture* magazine (1976–2000), the main text gives full descriptions of the trees, their natural distribution, their history of discovery, and their introduction to horticulture (when known). An introduction to a genus precedes a group of species that belong to a single genus.

Key features of the trees are highlighted in **bold** for quick access to descriptions. In some cases, the descriptions of flowers or fruit are given only once in the introduction to the genus and not for each species.

Check the glossary on page 233 for definitions of botanical terms.

Check "People and Places" on page 224 for additional information about some of the people and nurseries mentioned in the text.

Check the maps on pages 212–219 for key locations of trees in Golden Gate Park. Additional locations may be noted in the main text for trees within the park and elsewhere in San Francisco. Locations beyond San Francisco are provided to demonstrate the range of adaptability of the trees.

# The Wattles
# *Acacia*
## Leguminosae

*Acacia,* a member of the legume family or Leguminosae (also known as Fabaceae), is a large genus of about 1,200 species of trees and shrubs that occur in warm temperate and tropical regions of the world. More than half are found in Australia, where acacias and eucalypts are the dominant woody plants. The **leaves** of acacias are generally bipinnately compound and somewhat featherlike in appearance; in many Australian acacias, however, the feathery or fernlike leaves are replaced by modified leaflike structures called phyllodes, which are actually the leaf stalks or petioles enlarged and expanded. Phyllodes carry on photosynthesis as do leaves, but are thought to be an adaptation for survival under drought conditions. They vary in shape and size, from those that are definitely leaflike, as in blackwood acacia *(Acacia melanoxylon)* to those that are more or less spiny, as in star acacia *(A. verticillata).*

Acacias and other leguminous plants with similar flowers are sometimes put into a family of their own, the Mimosaceae. The individual, small, yellow **flowers** of acacias are grouped into two kinds of clusters: globose heads and short spikes. The numerous stamens make up the showy part of the flower, while the petals are small and inconspicuous. **Fruits** of acacias, like other legumes, are beanlike pods of varying sizes and colors, although mostly brown; each pod contains several flat seeds. In Australian acacias, the **seeds** generally have threadlike appendages of varying lengths and shapes in different species. These aid in dispersal of the seeds by birds or ants and are useful in distinguishing related species.

The name *Acacia,* derived from the Greek word for sharp point, was used by the Greeks for the spiny tree of northern Africa that we now know as *Acacia nilotica* (syn. *A. arabica).* The hard wood of this tree was used in ancient Egypt for building purposes. Wattle, meaning a flexible rod, was applied as a common name early in the settlement of Australia, where the slender branches of some acacias were used for construction of windbreaks, hedges, and "wattle and daub" shelters. Another common name for acacias is mimosa, but this name is less accepted since *Mimosa* is also the botanical name of another genus related to *Acacia.*

Acacias, along with eucalypts, were among the earliest trees introduced into California. Both are natives of Australia and were brought into the state by early nurserymen. Among these was Colonel James Warren, proprietor of a nursery in Sacramento. The 1855 catalog of his Warren and Son's Garden and Nurseries listed four species: *Acacia armata, A. dealbata, A. longifolia,* and *A. floribunda.* Of these, the first three are commonly grown in California today.

Another early nurseryman, William Walker of San Francisco, in his 1885 Golden Gate Nursery catalog, listed the above acacias and several others, including *Acacia melanoxylon;* later he listed some thirty or forty species. Today a few of the names he listed cannot be identified, but Walker was introducing acacias directly from Australia early in the history of California as a state and, according to HM Butterfield (1938), probably "no nurseryman since [Walker's] time has listed so many Australian acacias."

William Hammond Hall used acacias in the earliest plantings in Golden Gate Park. In later years, under John McLaren, thousands of acacias were planted in the park, both to stabilize the sand and as ornamentals. According to Butterfield (1964), "50,000 acacia trees were set out in Golden Gate Park in a single year." One of the early sand stabilizers was *Acacia longifolia,* well known for this use in Australia, especially in New South Wales. Acacias are fast-growing plants, but tend to be weak wooded and short-lived. Some have been reported to grow about twelve feet in four months, twenty-five feet in six years, and to reach maturity in about thirty years; within a few years after that, many begin to decline. During the early years of the park's development, as many as thirty different species were used. Only a few species can be found in the park today.

The acacias that have been planted in Golden Gate Park are also seen in many California cities. In and around a few urban areas some have reseeded and become naturalized along roadsides and other disturbed sites. Although occasionally locally abundant, they have not become widespread in the state and apparently have not spread into areas of undisturbed native vegetation, as has happened in South Africa, where several species are now considered noxious weeds.

# 1

## Cootamundra wattle
# *Acacia baileyana*

Leguminosae

Cootamundra wattle, also called Bailey acacia in the United States, is usually a shapely, small- to medium-sized tree with a round head. It has blue green, feathery, bipinnately compound **leaves** less than 3 inches long and lacking a terminal leaflet; its bright yellow **flowers** are in globose heads in midwinter (late January and February in San Francisco). The new foliage is often purplish or reddish in color. Typically short-lived, mature plantings of Cootamundra wattle have disappeared from the park. Today, one large and several small trees of this acacia can be seen at the top of Hippie Hill, near a single tree of *Lagunaria patersonii*. One old, leaning specimen can be seen on the south edge of the meadow west of the conservatory. A fine, vigorous tree of the purple-leafed cultivar, 'Purpurea', is on the north slope of the AIDS Memorial Grove, near the western end of de Laveaga Dell. Excellent examples of all foliage variations are grown at the UCSC Arboretum. They are commonly planted as street trees throughout California.

Hippie Hill (IV-R2); N slope
of AIDS Memorial Grove (IV-P2)
1342-1348 Cabrillo Ave; 423 Laguna St; 3652
20th St; 25 Cerritos; 2401 15th St; 485 29th St
Evergreen/Fast growth/20' - 40'
Fragrant, yellow globose flower heads (Jan-Feb)/
Brown seed pods
Full sun/Water infrequently
Sunset Zone 7-9, 13-24
Suitable as a street tree

# 2

## Silver wattle
# *Acacia dealbata*

Leguminosae

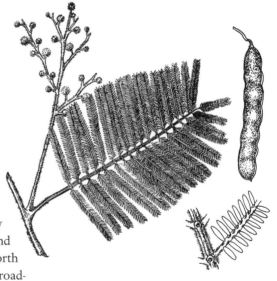

Silver wattle has whitish or gray, somewhat hairy stems and leaves. Trees are medium-sized, often irregular in shape, with feathery compound **leaves** 3 to 5 inches long. **Flowers** are bright yellow, in globose heads arranged in branched clusters generally longer than the leaves, and showy in late winter and early spring (February and March in San Francisco). One large tree and two adjacent smaller ones are on Conservatory Drive East, just north of the Fuchsia Garden. This species has naturalized in parks and roadside areas in many parts of California though it is not widespread. Silver wattle is sometimes mistakenly called *Acacia decurrens*, the name of a related species not commonly planted in California.

Conservatory Dr East, N of
Fuchsia Garden (IV-R1)
Opposite 378-80 Funston Ave; 875 Church St
Evergreen/Fast growth/50'
Fragrant, bright yellow globose flower heads in
branched clusters (Feb-Mar) /Brown seed pods
Full sun/Water infrequently
Sunset Zone 8, 9, 14-24

# 3

## Sydney golden wattle
### *Acacia longifolia*

Leguminosae

Sydney golden wattle is a small tree or large shrub often branching from the base of the trunk. It has modified **leaves** (phyllodes) similar to those of blackwood acacia but generally lighter green and 3 to 6 inches long. In **flower,** it may easily be distinguished from blackwood acacia by its bright yellow, spikelike flower clusters. Sydney golden wattle has been widely planted in the park, especially in the western end where it continues to be important in stabilizing the sand dunes; it is also in the background planting along Kennedy Drive east of Conservatory Drive East, and is scattered along Lincoln Way. It is commonly used as a small street tree throughout coastal California.

Kennedy Dr, E of Conservatory Dr East (IV-R2)
1108-1110 Balboa Ave
Evergreen/Fast growth/15'; shrublike
Bright yellow, spikelike flower clusters (Mar)/
   Brown seed pods
Full sun/Water infrequently
Sunset Zone 8, 9, 14-24
Suitable as a street tree

# 4

## Blackwood acacia
### *Acacia melanoxylon*

Leguminosae

Blackwood or black acacia, is a large tree, to 90 feet tall at maturity, though usually under 40 feet in cultivation; it has a well-shaped, oval crown. The broad, lanceolate, modified **leaves** (phyllodes), 2 to 5 inches long, generally have three parallel, longitudinal veins. On seedlings and young branches, however, both kinds of acacia leaves are seen—feathery, bipinnately compound leaves, and modified leaf-like phyllodes—with intermediate stages between the two. The cream to pale yellow, rather dull **flowers** are in globose heads on stalks generally shorter than the modified leaves and do not stand out from the foliage. Blackwood acacia is widely planted throughout coastal California as an ornamental tree, often clipped into a rounded, compact crown. Its use as a street tree is being phased out because of its propensity for lifting pavements and damaging underground plumbing. In Golden Gate Park, blackwood acacia may be seen on Conservatory Drive East opposite the Fuchsia Garden; a mature specimen is on the bank southwest of McLaren Lodge.

Blackwood acacia occurs in southeastern coastal Australia. It was first identified in Tasmania by Scottish botanist Robert Brown. The wood has been used in Australia for cabinetry, decorative work, veneer, and furniture.

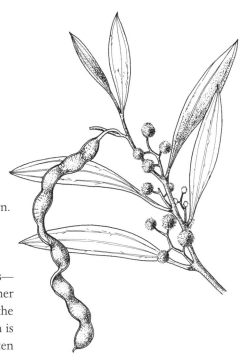

SW of McLaren Lodge (IV-S2); Conservatory Dr
   East opposite entrance to Fuchsia Garden
   (IV-R1)
37 + 50 Fifth Ave; 76 Laurel St; 400 block of
   Belvedere St; 1060 Dolores St
Evergreen/Fast growth/40'
Cream-colored, spherical flowers in short clusters
   (March - April) /Black seed pods
Full sun/Water infrequently
Sunset Zone 8, 9, 13-24

## 5

### Everblooming acacia
# *Acacia retinodes*
Leguminosae

Formerly much planted in Golden Gate Park and seen elsewhere in California, *Acacia retinodes* is, however, not always recognized, and the name *A. floribunda* is sometimes mistakenly applied to it. *Acacia retinodes* is a small tree about 15 to 20 feet tall, with an oval but not always well-formed crown. Its modified **leaves** (phyllodes) generally are narrowly lanceolate, 2 to 6 inches or more long. **Flowers** are in globose heads arranged on a stalk shorter than the leaves. The tree tends to flower sporadically during the year, and so is often called everblooming acacia. It may be distinguished from blackwood acacia by its longer, narrower phyllodes, each with only a single longitudinal vein, the midvein. Like most acacias, *A. retinodes* is short-lived, and few specimens have been found recently; one large one can be seen on the south side of Mallard Lake, next to a giant California buckeye (*Aesculus californica*).

S side of Mallard Lake (II-I4)
Evergreen/Fast growth/15'-20'
Yellow globose flower heads (sporadic through-
    out the year) /Brown seed pods
Full sun/Water infrequently
Sunset Zone 8, 9, 13-24

## 6

### Star acacia
# *Acacia verticillata*
Leguminosae

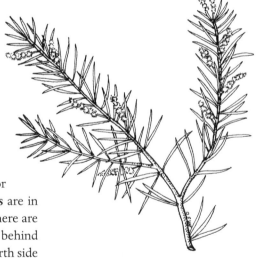

Star acacia, or prickly Moses, is a small tree or large shrub with spiny modified **leaves** (phyllodes) about ½ inch long, generally two or three together, and grouped in whorls around the stem. Its **flowers** are in spikelike clusters. It has been planted in various places in the park; there are several old trees with crooked trunks on Conservatory Drive West behind the conservatory; other star acacias are along the footpath on the north side of the meadow west of the conservatory, and scattered along Lincoln Way.

Conservatory Dr West
    behind conservatory (IV-
    Q1); on path N of meadow W of conservatory
    (IV-Q1)
Evergreen/Fast growth/15'; shrublike
Short spikes of pale yellow flowers (Apr-May)/
    Light brown seed pods
Full sun/Water infrequently
Sunset Zone 14-24

# 7

## Pineapple guava
# *Acca sellowiana* (syn. *Feijoa sellowiana*)

### Myrtaceae

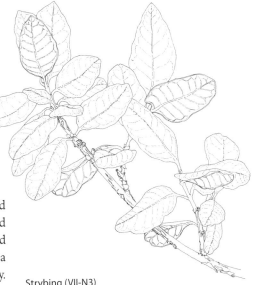

Pineapple guava is a large shrub or small tree to 18 feet tall. The young **bark** is smooth, light reddish brown to brown, and flaky. The opposite, oblong **leaves** are gray and hairy on the lower surface, somewhat hairy to nearly hairless above, with short leaf stalks. **Flowers** have four sepals and four petals. The nearly round petals are ½ inch long, reddish to pink, and edible with a sweet taste; the numerous stamens are nearly 1 inch long and similar in color. **Fruits** are fleshy ovoid berries, 1 to 3 inches long, with a spicy fragrance when mature. They are tasty raw and make excellent jelly. The fruits show a close relationship to common guava *(Psidium guajava)* and strawberry guava *(P. cattleianum)*, both of which are tropical in origin. Native to southern Brazil and Argentina, pineapple guava is often cultivated in areas with moderately cool climates for its attractive flowers that appear in spring. Its fruits need summer heat to ripen well and are commercially important in Israel, New Zealand, and California.

Strybing (VII-N3)
Evergreen/Slow growth/18'; shrublike
Reddish to pink, 1 1/2" flowers with many
    showy stamens (May) /Greenish, fleshy,
    1"-3" long berries with spicy fragrance
Full sun/Water infrequently, though
    tolerates more
Sunset Zone 7-9, 12-24

Recently it has been pointed out that pineapple guava should be placed in the genus *Acca*, a generic name that has priority over the better-known *Feijoa*. The name *Acca* is taken from the Peruvian name for the tree. The species name *sellowiana* honors Friedrich Sellow, a German naturalist who collected plants in Brazil and found the pineapple guava in 1819 in the southern state of Rio Grande do Sul. The earliest listing for pineapple guava in California was by Francesco Franceschi in Santa Barbara in 1906. In Golden Gate Park, it was first listed in the *Annual Report of the Park Commissioners* for 1924. There are two pineapple guavas in Strybing's Garden of Fragrance.

## The maples
# *Acer*

### Aceraceae

Most maples are deciduous, erect trees with five- to seven-lobed, opposite **leaves;** a few are shrubby, particularly those native to montane regions. Maple **flowers** are small and generally not showy, lacking for the most part visible petals; because they are wind-pollinated, the stamens are the most prominent feature of the flowers, which usually hang in clusters from the branches as the leaves are unfolding in spring. Individual fruits of maples, called samaras or keys, consist of two halves, each with a thin, winglike extension above the seed. These winged **seeds** are distributed by wind.

The botanical name *Acer* was used by the Romans for maples; the word meant sharp, and refers to the hardness of maple wood, which the Romans used for making spear handles. The maple family consists of only two genera, *Dipteronia* and *Acer,* both represented in Golden Gate Park. Although unrelated botanically, maples *(Acer)* and sweet gums *(Liquidambar)* have similar features, and trees of the two genera are sometimes confused. The leaves of sweet gums are arranged alternately, and their fruits are grouped together into prickly, spherical clusters.

*Acer,* with about 150 species, is distributed in the Northern Hemisphere in North America, Central America, Europe, northern Africa, and Asia. Many species are grown as ornamentals in gardens, streets, and parks, and several are excellent for use in bonsai. The hard wood of maples has had many uses in construction and furniture making. The chief source of commercial maple wood has been sugar maple *(Acer saccharum)*. Bird's-eye maple, much used for veneers in furniture making a couple of generations ago, was obtained from the burls or knots of sugar maple. Maple syrup and sugar are also obtained from this tree. Early colonists in New England learned of this use from the native Americans, whose sugar making was recorded by Captain John Smith. Maples, including sugar maple, are among the trees that contribute to the spectacular autumn color in the eastern deciduous forests. The national emblem of Canada is a stylized maple leaf.

Five maples occur naturally on the Pacific Coast. Of these, three are cultivated as landscape trees: big-leaf maple *(Acer macrophyllum),* vine maple *(A. circinatum),* and box elder *(A. negundo).*

# 8

## Hedge maple

# *Acer campestre*

### Aceraceae

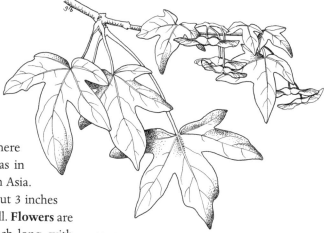

Hedge maple is the only maple native to the British Isles, where it is often seen in hedgerows and along roadsides, as well as in open fields. It is also found through Europe and into western Asia. **Leaves** of this deciduous maple are three- to five-lobed, about 3 inches long, somewhat downy on the underside, and yellow in the fall. **Flowers** are small, green, and insignificant. The **fruits** are samaras, 1 inch long, with wide-spreading wings. Hedge maple has hard, smooth-textured wood that in the past has been carved into bowls, spoons, and other utensils.

Music Concourse (II-O2); Strybing (VII-O4)
SE corner of California and Steiner Sts
Deciduous/Slow growth/30'
Inconspicuous green flowers (Apr) /Paired winged seeds
Full sun to part shade/Water occasionally and deeply
Sunset Zone 1-9, 14
Suitable as a street tree

Early plantings of pollarded trees in the Music Concourse included a number of hedge maples; they have been replaced by the more common London plane tree. A single tree can be seen among other maples just west of the small parking lot in Strybing. Hedge maple is occasionally seen in parks and gardens and as a street tree in cities along the West Coast.

## 9

### Vine maple
### *Acer circinatum*

Aceraceae

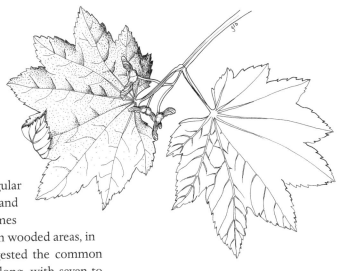

Vine maple is a small to medium tree with an irregular rounded crown or else a shrub with a crooked trunk and branches, often with a widely spreading habit. Sometimes the lower branches trail along the ground, particularly in wooded areas, in search of light, and this trailing habit may have suggested the common name. **Leaves** are simple, nearly round, 1 to 4 inches long, with seven to nine irregular lobes that are sharply toothed along their margins. **Flowers** are small, few, and in hanging clusters. The paired samaras making up the **fruits** are 1 to 1½ inches long and spread almost horizontally.

Vine maple occurs from southern British Columbia to Northern California. It was discovered on the Lewis and Clark Expedition of 1804–1806, and named and described by Friedrich Pursh. It was later found by David Douglas, who introduced it to England. A desirable tree, vine maple is cultivated on the Pacific Coast from San Francisco north to British Columbia. There are several specimens in Strybing's Redwood Grove and the Arthur Menzies Garden of California Native Plants. A number of fine specimens can be seen in the Regional Parks Botanic Garden in Tilden Regional Park, Berkeley. It is also cultivated in Victoria and Vancouver, British Columbia, and more widely in Seattle.

Strybing (VI-M4)
Deciduous/Slow growth/35'
Small red flowers in hanging clusters (Apr)/
    Paired winged seeds
Full sun to part shade/Water occasionally and
    deeply
Sunset Zone 1-6, 14-17

## 10

### Big-leaf maple
### *Acer macrophyllum*

Aceraceae

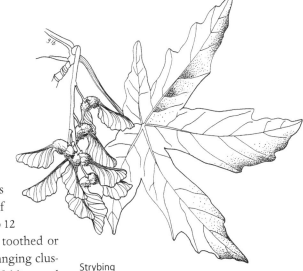

Big-leaf maple, an attractive, erect tree with a broad crown, is found from Alaska south to California and east to Idaho. Big-leaf maple has simple, palmate **leaves,** heart shaped at the base, up to 12 inches wide, and generally five-lobed with each lobe coarsely toothed or lobed. The many small, yellow white **flowers** are in slender, hanging clusters, 2 to 4 inches long; the flowers appear as the leaves are unfolding and can be quite showy. **Fruits** are 1 to 2 inches long, the two samaras attached at right angles to each other; the **seeds** are densely hairy.

Strybing
    (VI-N4)
Deciduous/Fast growth/30'-95'
Small yellow white flowers in drooping clusters
    (Apr-May) /Clusters of 3" winged seeds
Full sun to part shade/Water occasionally and
    deeply

Big-leaf maple is often cultivated in the Pacific Coast states. In Seattle it is said to be the city's most abundant tree and, at 120 to 130 feet, among the tallest. One tree in Washington has been measured at over 155 feet. At the turn of the century in Seattle, big-leaf maple was the most widely planted street tree, and some neighborhoods still have large landmark trees, but it is no longer used in street-side plantings because of the damaging effects of its roots on sidewalks.

In the Northwest, big-leaf maple is an important source of hardwood for furniture, paneling, cabinets, and musical instruments. Older trees sometimes produce knots or burls with patterns that make the wood useful for veneer. In California, native big-leaf maples grow along stream banks and in other areas where moisture is likely to be available during the long, dry summers. The tree is occasionally cultivated in urban areas such as the San Francisco Bay Area, Santa Barbara, Santa Monica, and Los Angeles. A fine specimen can be seen on the edge of Strybing's Redwood Trail.

According to Butterfield (1964), big-leaf maple was first offered in California as an ornamental in 1854 by Commercial Nurseries of San Francisco. It was grown in Golden Gate Park in the 1890s, but no trees known to have been planted at that time exist today.

Big-leaf maple was first seen on the Northwest coast by Archibald Menzies of the Vancouver Expedition in 1794; it was later collected at the rapids of the Columbia River during Lewis and Clark's first American transcontinental expedition from 1804 to 1806. In 1814 it was named and described by Friedrich Pursh in his early work on North American plants.

# 11

## Japanese maple
# *Acer palmatum*
## Aceraceae

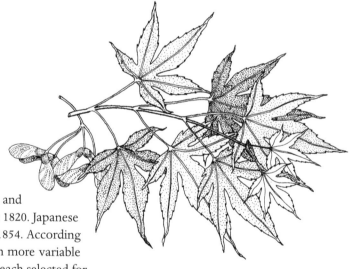

Japanese maple is native to southwestern China, Korea, and Japan. It was introduced to cultivation in England about 1820. Japanese maples were offered by a California nursery as early as 1854. According to Jacobson (1996), no ornamental tree species has been more variable in cultivation. Hundreds of cultivars have been named, each selected for a distinct variation in some character such as: size and habit of growth; color, shape, and size of leaf; or bark color. **Leaves** are 2 to 3½ inches long, sharply toothed, and palmately five- to seven-lobed. The small **flowers** are arranged in loose clusters in spring. In the **fruits,** the wings of each samara are 1 to 2 inches long and ¼ inch wide, spreading nearly horizontally.

Japanese maples are common and popular small garden trees throughout most of North America and all of the West Coast. They are particularly familiar from their use in Japanese gardens, as for instance the

Japanese Tea Garden (V-N2); Strybing (VI-N3 & VII-O3)
Deciduous/Slow growth/20'
Inconspicuous flowers (Apr-May) /Paired winged seeds
Part shade/Water regularly
Sunset Zone 1-10, 12, 14-24

many trees in Golden Gate Park's Japanese Tea Garden and in Strybing's Moon-viewing Garden in the Asian section. A notable cultivar is the coral bark maple ('Sango Kaku'), whose bright red winter bark stands out in a mixed planting near the Thomas Church-designed pavilion in Strybing's Demonstration Gardens.

# 12

## Five-leaf maple
# *Acer pentaphyllum*
### Aceraceae

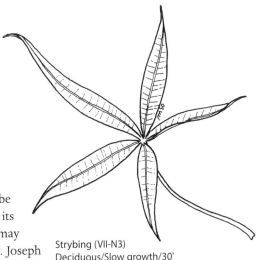

Strybing (VII-N3)
Deciduous/Slow growth/30'
Upright clusters of yellow green flowers (Apr-May) /Paired winged seeds
Full sun to part shade/Water occasionally and deeply
Sunset Zone 5-9, 14-17

*Acer pentaphyllum* has no accepted common name, but it might be called five-leaf maple. It is rare in cultivation, and information on its distribution in the mountains of western China suggests that it may either be rare in its native area or have been infrequently collected. Joseph Rock first found it in 1929 in the valley of the Yalong River near Muli, south-western Sichuan, at about 10,000 feet. At that time, Rock was on an expedition to western China sponsored by the National Geographic Society. Rock introduced the tree into Europe in the same year, and plants were raised and distributed by Hillier and Sons' Nursery, Winchester, England.

Joseph Rock recorded this species in his field notes as being about 30 feet tall, with opposite **leaves** palmately divided generally into five separate leaflets, an unusual trait among the maples. Leaflets are about 2 to 3 inches long, glossy, dark green above and gray green below. Leaves are on petioles about the same length as the leaflets. Clusters of pale yellow **flowers** appear in late spring, but are not showy and are seldom seen in cultivation. The **fruits** (samaras) are ¾ inch long and are likely to form without the flowers being fertilized.

At one time, Strybing had three trees of this maple, the only ones in Golden Gate Park. The acquisition date of the oldest of the three was not recorded, but the tree was already in the arboretum when records were begun in the late 1950s; it was, therefore, among the early trees planted in the arboretum. Its source is not known, but it may have come from the UC Botanical Garden (Berkeley). Toichi Domoto of Domoto Nursery in Hayward obtained scions of the Strybing tree from Eric Walther in the early 1950s. The scions were grafted first on Japanese maple and later, more successfully, on sugar maple (*Acer saccharum*). Domoto also grew plants from seed, finding that seeds germinated well and seedlings grew more successfully than grafted plants. Marshall Olbrich of Western Hills Nursery in Occidental obtained a plant grafted on sugar maple from Mr Domoto and from it distributed seeds and seedlings. Virtually all specimens of *A. pentaphyllum* in gardens in America today are thought to have been derived from these three Strybing trees, which unfortunately succumbed to storm damage in the 1990s. A younger tree remains near the fence north of Heidelberg Hill.

# 13

## Lilly pilly
# *Acmena smithii*
### Myrtaceae

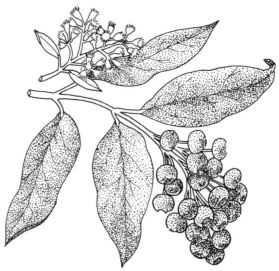

Lilly pilly is a small to medium tree with densely spreading branches and scaly, brown **bark.** The simple, evergreen **leaves** are opposite, ¾ to 4 inches long by ½ to 1 ¼ inches wide, dark green and shiny above, pale below, and usually with a pointed tip. Its spring **flowers** are small, white, and numerous, clustered on branched stems or panicles. The most colorful aspect of the tree is the **fruit:** round, fleshy berries, about ½ inch in diameter produced in abundance and varying in color from purple to almost white.

N of Kennedy Dr, W of Conservatory Dr West (IV-P1); Strybing (VI-N3)
Evergreen/Moderate growth/25'
Small, white flowers in branched clusters (Mar)/ Showy, fleshy, purple, pink or white berries
Full sun/Water regularly
Sunset Zone 15-17, 19-24
Color plate

Our knowledge of *Acmena*, a small genus in the myrtle family, dates from 1828 when it was first described. The genus occurs in most of Australia as well as southeastern Asia, and is closely related to two larger genera with which it has often been included: *Eugenia* and *Syzygium*. Recently, however, *Acmena* has been recognized as a valid genus separate from *Eugenia*, mostly of the New World, and from *Syzygium* of the Old World. The common name, lilly pilly, presumed to be of Australian Aboriginal origin, has followed *Acmena smithii* through its several name changes, showing unusual stability and widespread acceptance of a common name. The Latin Acmena is said to be one of the names of the goddess Venus. The specific name honors James Smith, an important English botanist at the turn of the eighteenth century.

Lilly pilly occurs in eastern Australia from Victoria in the south to Queensland in the north. It is widely cultivated there as an ornamental tree and as a hedge since it responds well to clipping and shaping. It is also cultivated in Europe. Not commonly planted here on the West Coast, only a few trees can be found in Golden Gate Park: one large, spreading tree stands on the north side of Kennedy Drive, west of Conservatory Drive West, while another fine specimen can be seen just west of Strybing's Friend Gate in the Eastern Australian Collection. Both of these trees display fruit of a particularly bright purplish pink color. Landscape architect Thomas Church used lilly pilly in a number of his gardens in the Bay Area during the 1950s; they were often shaped or sheared in formal settings. Muller et al lists it in Franceschi Park and as a street tree along at least one thoroughfare in Santa Barbara.

Buckeyes and horse chestnuts
# *Aesculus*
## Hippocastanaceae

Horse chestnuts and buckeyes are a distinctive and easily recognized group of deciduous trees or large shrubs. Of special appeal are their large palmately divided **leaves,** attractive flower clusters, and fruits with handsome seeds. The opposite leaves are generally made up of five to seven separate leaflets. The **flowers,** individually small, with a cup-shaped to more or less tubular calyx and four separate petals, are numerous, colorful, and arranged in large, showy, upright clusters. The globose or pear-shaped **fruit,** a smooth or somewhat prickly capsule, splits to release a single large, shiny brown inedible **seed,** superficially resembling the edible chestnut. All parts of the horse chestnut or buckeye contain aesculin, a glycoside poisonous to cattle and humans, but it is the seeds that are generally involved in human poisonings, which occur mostly in children. Fatalities have been reported in Europe, but none are known in the United States.

The genus, a member of the horse chestnut family, consists of about thirteen species. Those in North America are called buckeyes, because of the resemblance of the partially opened fruit to the eye of a deer. Those from southeastern Europe and Asia are known as horse chestnuts. Horse chestnuts, however, are sometimes called chestnuts. Perhaps the best known example of the shortened common name is in the opening lines of Longfellow's poem, *The Village Blacksmith:* "Under a spreading chestnut tree the village smithy stands." The smithy's chestnut tree was a European horse chestnut.

# 14

California buckeye
# *Aesculus californica*
## Hippocastanaceae

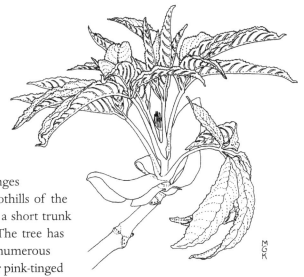

California buckeye occurs only in California, in the Coast Ranges from Mendocino to San Luis Obispo and in the western foothills of the Sierra Nevada from Shasta to Kern counties. It is a tree with a short trunk and a spreading crown, generally 25 to 30 feet in breadth. The tree has sticky buds, **leaves** with five leaflets 4 to 6 inches long, and numerous **flowers** in more or less cylindrical clusters with white, pink, or pink-tinged petals. The pear-shaped **fruits,** 2 to 3 inches long, have a rough but not prickly surface. In California the trees leaf out as early as March, but often by July the leaves turn brown and begin to drop, in response to the drying soils of summer.

Thomas Nuttall collected California buckeye in 1836 and gave it its name, which was published two years later by Asa Gray and John Torrey in the first volume of their *Flora of North America.* In 1850, William Lobb introduced it to England by way of seed sent to the Veitch Nursery, where a tree flowered in 1858. In Golden Gate Park, fine specimens can be seen on the south side of Mallard Lake and in Strybing's Arthur Menzies Garden of California Native Plants.

Mallard Lake (II-I4); Strybing (VII-N4)
McAllister at Willard North; 22nd St and
 Pennsylvania; Levant St at Lower
 Terrace
Deciduous/Slow growth/20' or more
Fragrant, white to pink flowers in upright
 cylindrical, 8"-10" long clusters (spring)/
 Large, dark, shiny, 1 1/2" diameter seeds
 in a leathery fruit
Full sun/No water once established
Sunset Zone 4-10, 12, 14-24
Color plate

Aside from the occasional present-day use of California buckeye as a landscape tree, it was used by Native Californians for catching fish and for food. Seeds were commonly ground to a meal that was floated in streams, where fish were incapacitated by the toxins released and so easily caught. Less commonly, leaves and young shoots were used for this purpose. For food, the toxic substance was leached from the seeds, but this was a longer process than with acorns and done only in years when the acorn crop was poor.

# 15

### Red horse chestnut
# *Aesculus* × *carnea*

## Hippocastanaceae

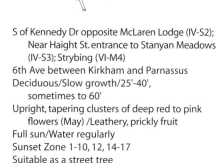

Red horse chestnut is a smaller tree than horse chestnut (*Aesculus hippocastanum*). It is a hybrid between the latter and red buckeye (*A. pavia*). The origin of the tree is not known, but it probably was a chance garden hybrid, and it apparently appeared in Germany before 1820. It is intermediate between the parents, particularly in the habit, with the leaves of horse chestnut and the flower color and glandular-edged petals of red buckeye. Red horse chestnut has a rounded crown, generally 25 to 40 or sometimes 60 feet tall, with slightly sticky winter buds and **leaves** with five to seven leaflets, 3 to 6 inches long. The **flowers,** with a red cup-shaped calyx and four red petals, are in a more or less open cluster, and the **fruits,** less than 2 inches across, have relatively few prickles.

Red horse chestnut, with colorful flowers varying from deep red to pink, is an attractive landscape tree, long cultivated in Europe and the United States. It was offered first in California in 1884 by RD Fox at his Santa Clara Valley Nursery, San Jose, and has been in Golden Gate Park since the early 1900s. At present, the park has two trees near its eastern entrance on the south side of Kennedy Drive opposite McLaren Lodge. These trees, about 20 feet tall, are probably less than forty years old. A third tree is near the Haight Street entrance to the park. In Strybing, in a mounded bed northeast of the Succulent Garden, is a tree of the cultivar 'Briotii' with brighter red flowers. Trees of red horse chestnut are reported elsewhere in California from Berkeley and Sacramento to Santa Barbara and Santa Monica. In the Pacific Northwest, it is common in the Seattle and Portland areas.

S of Kennedy Dr opposite McLaren Lodge (IV-S2);
    Near Haight St. entrance to Stanyan Meadows
    (IV-S3); Strybing (VI-M4)
6th Ave between Kirkham and Parnassus
Deciduous/Slow growth/25'-40',
    sometimes to 60'
Upright, tapering clusters of deep red to pink
    flowers (May) /Leathery, prickly fruit
Full sun/Water regularly
Sunset Zone 1-10, 12, 14-17
Suitable as a street tree

## 16

### Horse chestnut
# *Aesculus hippocastanum*

Hippocastanaceae

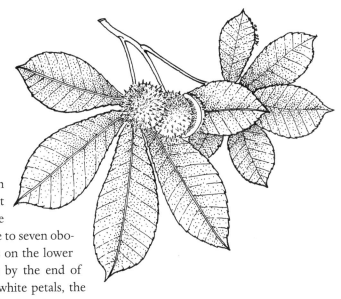

Horse chestnut is native to southeastern Europe (northern Greece, Albania, and Bulgaria) and is one of the best known, largest, and handsomest of shade trees. Horse chestnut has sticky winter buds, opening to **leaves** with five to seven obovate leaflets, each 5 to 12 inches long with scattered hairs on the lower surface; leaves often appear scorched along the margins by the end of California's dry summers. The **flowers** have four to five white petals, the lower one splotched with yellow turning reddish after pollination; the pyramidal flower clusters are up to 12 inches tall. **Fruits** are 2 to 3 inches in diameter, with a prickly husk.

N of McLaren Lodge (IV-S1); E of Pioneer Log
    Cabin (III-M2); Strybing (VII-O3)
945 Dolores St
Deciduous/Moderate growth/60'-100'
White flowers in upright, pyramidal clusters, up
    to 12" tall (May) /Leathery, spiny fruits
Full sun/Water occasionally
Sunset Zone 1-10, 12, 14-17
Color plate

Horse chestnut has been used to great effect in European cities such as Paris and Madrid, where it lines major streets and boulevards. The tree has little other economic value. Its soft timber lacks strength and is not long lasting; it has been used mostly in the manufacture of kitchen utensils and toys. Its greatest claim to fame may be the use of its seeds by small boys (more in Europe than in the United States) for the game of conkers.

Horse chestnut was an early introduction into California. According to Butterfield (1964), it was offered first in 1854 by Commercial Nurseries, San Francisco, and probably was planted in the early 1900s in Golden Gate Park. Of several horse chestnuts in the park, the largest and most impressive is at the edge of the lawn north of McLaren Lodge. Of an unknown age, it is about 50 feet tall, with a trunk diameter of more than 3 feet and a broadly spreading crown of about 70 feet. This magnificent old specimen is surely one of the park's landmark trees. Other horse chestnuts in the park are in the meadow east of the Pioneer Log Cabin, near Alvord Lake, and near the Garden of Fragrance in Strybing. California cities having horse chestnut trees include Davis, Sacramento (capitol grounds—an old one about 60 feet tall), Santa Barbara, and Santa Monica. Horse chestnuts are also found in the Pacific Northwest; the trees are common in Seattle and Portland, where numerous streets are lined with magnificent specimens.

# Horse Chestnut History

The earliest record of the cultivation of horse chestnut comes from Constantinople by way of the Flemish diplomat and writer, Ogier de Busbecq, who was the ambassador of Ferdinand I of Austria to the court of Suleiman the Magnificent, sultan of the Ottoman Empire in the mid-1500s. In 1556 de Busbecq sent fruits and seeds from Constantinople to the botanist Pierandrea Mattioli in Venice. The Turks were reported to have ground the seeds and mixed them with the meal of one of their grains as a medication for "horses suffering from broken winds or coughs." The seeds were called *at kastanesi* (horse chestnut) in Turkish. Mattioli, alluding to the Turkish name, used the Latin phrase, *castaneae equinae,* for the seeds.

In 1576, an ambassador to the court of Suleiman II, Baron David von Ungnand, sent seeds of horse chestnut to Vienna, where they were received by the botanist Clusius (Jules Charles de l'Ecluse), who described and named the seed *Castanea equina* in 1583. This Latin version of horse chestnut, which can likewise be traced back to the Turkish name, has been suggested as the origin of the common name used today. Another suggestion, however, is that the common name may have come from the resemblance of the tree's prominent leaf scar to a horseshoe. When Linnaeus named the genus in 1753, he chose to call it *Aesculus,* the Latin name for an oak with edible acorns, but to designate the species he used *hippocastanum*

(derived from the Greek for horse and chestnut), giving us *Aesculus hippocastanum.*

Seeds of horse chestnut were taken, again from Constantinople, to France in 1615 and probably about the same time to England. In Thomas Johnson's revised edition of Gerarde's *Herbal* (1633), the tree was reported as growing in John Tradescant's garden near London. Wilson (1930) described the impressive avenue of horse chestnuts in Bushy Park near Hampton Court on the banks of the Thames River. The avenue, 170 feet wide and about a mile long with 137 trees in a line on each side, was planted in 1699 by Sir Christopher Wren. At one time, the trees were so impressive at the height of their spring flowering that a special day, Chestnut Sunday, was set aside to honor them. According to Wilson, the largest trees were about 100 feet tall with trunks from 2 to 20 feet across and with broad, handsome crowns.

Horse chestnut was introduced to colonial Philadelphia in 1741, when seeds were received by John Bartram from his correspondent, Peter Collinson of London. In 1763, Collinson wrote to Bartram of being pleased to learn "that our horse chestnut has flowered." In the intervening years, horse chestnut has become a popular landscape shade tree in the eastern United States, but an overplanted one according to Donald Wyman, who obviously did not share Wilson's enthusiasm for the tree.

# 17

### Red buckeye
## *Aesculus pavia*
Hippocastanaceae

Red buckeye, a parent of red horse chestnut, occurs in the southeastern states from Virginia to northern Florida and west to Louisiana. It is a small tree, generally under 20 feet, or sometimes a large shrub, with sticky winter buds. The **leaves** have five to seven leaflets, 2 to 6 inches long. The **flowers** are generally red to scarlet but sometimes yellow. The calyx is more or less tubular, the four petals remaining somewhat erect (more so than in other buckeyes), making colorful, more or less open flower clusters 4 to 8 inches long. The **fruits,** about 2 inches across, lack prickles.

Strybing (VI-N3)
Deciduous/Slow growth/20'
Upright, tapering, 4"-8" long clusters of red to scarlet flowers (May-June) /Smooth roundish fruit
Full sun/Water regularly
Sunset Zone 3-9, 14-24

Red buckeye was introduced to England in 1711, but is infrequently grown there today. It is sometimes cultivated elsewhere in Europe and in the United States. San Francisco's Commercial Nurseries offered it in 1854, but it is rarely grown in California. The only tree in Golden Gate Park is in Strybing, in a bed between the New Zealand and Asian collections. It can be seen in the Washington Park Arboretum in Seattle, but is not commonly planted in the Northwest.

# 18

## African fern pine

# *Afrocarpus gracilior*

(syn. *Podocarpus gracilior*)

## Podocarpaceae

Japanese Tea Garden (V-N2); knoll
   E of Academy of Sciences (III-P2);
   Strybing (VII-N3)
10th Avenue between Moraga and Noriega
Evergreen/Slow growth/60'
(Conifer) Round, fleshy berrylike fruit
Full sun to part shade/Water occasionally
Sunset Zone 8, 9, 13-24
Suitable as a street tree

African fern pine is a slow-growing tree reaching 60 to 70 feet in height, with a smooth brown **bark.** Its branches are more or less upright to spreading, with linear **leaves,** 2 to 4 inches long and about ¼ inch wide, arranged irregularly on the stems; leaves remain on the branches for an extremely long time, resulting in relatively little leaf litter. The rounded **fruits,** generally containing a single seed, are fleshy, berrylike, and about ½ inch in diameter; usually one or two occur at the end of short, leafy branchlets. As suggested by the common and generic names, Afrocarpus is native to Africa; this species is found in the mountains of Uganda, Ethiopia, and Kenya in eastern subtropical Africa.

Recent studies of the genus *Podocarpus* have resulted in the separation of many of its species into other genera. Among those is African fern pine, formerly *Podocarpus gracilior* but now *Afrocarpus gracilior.* This new generic name is taken from the prefix *afro* and the Greek word for fruit, *karpos.* *Afrocarpus* is distinguished from *Podocarpus* by its fruit, which lacks the basal fleshy receptacle seen in *Podocarpus. Afrocarpus, Podocarpus,* and the several other genera in the podocarpus family are seed-bearing plants called gymnosperms, their seeds lacking the protection of an ovary as in the flowering plants (angiosperms). Other gymnosperms are the cone bearers (pines, cedars, cypresses, and redwoods), yews, cycads, and ginkgo.

African fern pine is the most widely cultivated ornamental species of *Afrocarpus.* Popular as a patio or plaza tree because of its tidiness, it is also used as a street tree in coastal communities and in the interior regions of California's Central Valley. Outstanding mature specimens can be seen on the campuses of UCLA and UC Santa Barbara. A mature, low-branched tree, fruiting reliably, can be seen on the knoll east of the Academy of Sciences in Golden Gate Park. Another tree is next to the Tea House in the Japanese Tea Garden. In Strybing, a small cluster of trees, planted in 1953, is southwest of the fountain.

## The Kauris
# *Agathis*
### Araucariaceae

Trees belonging to the genus *Agathis* have straight trunks with a thick **bark** that emits a milky sap when punctured. **Leaves,** even less coniferlike than those of the related genus *Araucaria,* are lanceolate to oval, flat and leathery, with short petioles and many parallel veins. Juvenile leaves often differ from adult leaves. Mature leaves may remain on the tree for several years and on falling, leave a cushionlike scar. The name "Agathis," taken from a Greek word meaning ball of thread, comes from the appearance of the young cones, which have a blue gray coating partially covering the cone scales. The **cones** are ovoid to globose, and take two years to mature. The genus has about twenty species in Australia, New Zealand, the Philippines, Malaysia, New Caledonia, and New Guinea. Most are tall, massive trees, and some are valuable for timber and resins.

# 19

### New Zealand kauri
# *Agathis australis*
### Araucariaceae

New Zealand kauri is one of the world's largest and oldest trees. It occurs naturally only in a limited area near Auckland on New Zealand's North Island, where magnificent trees, some over 150 feet in height, may still be seen. It was once much more abundant, but unfortunately has been exploited for commercial uses. New Zealand kauri has pale, smooth **bark** and **leaves** that are ¾ to 2¼ inches long and about ⅓ to ⅔ inch wide. Its globose **cones** are from 3 to 4 inches long. It has been in Golden Gate Park since the late 1890s, but no specimen remains from those early years. Today the park has several young trees in the New Zealand Collection at Strybing. This kauri is rarely cultivated in the United States; trees grown under the name are usually *Agathis robusta*. In addition to being cut for lumber, New Zealand kauri provides a hard resin used in the manufacture of linoleum and other products.

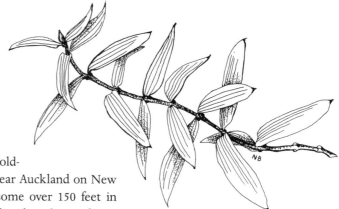

Strybing (VI-N3)
Evergreen/Slow growth/Over 150'
(Conifer) Globular, woody cones, 3"-4" across
Full sun/Water occasionally
Sunset Zone 16-24

# 20

Queensland kauri
## *Agathis robusta*
Araucariaceae

Queensland kauri may grow from 120 to 140 feet tall and 3 to 4 feet in trunk diameter in its native habitat. The **bark** is gray brown and exfoliating. Adult **leaves** are narrow and oblong, 2 to 4 inches long, and about 1 inch wide. The globose **cones** are 4 to 5 inches long. The tree occurs only in dense rainforest areas of northeastern and southeastern Queensland, Australia, from sea level to 3,000 feet; it has been an important timber tree in these areas. Although recorded in California as early as 1865, today it is rarely cultivated in the state. Trees have been grown in Berkeley, Santa Barbara, San Diego, and San Francisco. The species has been in Golden Gate Park since the late 1890s. Today several trees are known in the park. One is on the east side of Strawberry Hill near the Chinese Pavilion, and another is near the walk connecting the Music Concourse with the Rhododendron Dell. A third tree is in Strybing, south of the Eric Walther Succulent Garden.

E side of Strawberry Hill near Chinese Pavilion (III-M3); Strybing (VI-M4)
Evergreen/Slow growth/120'-140'
(Conifer) Globular, woody cones, 4"-5" across
Full sun/Water occasionally
Sunset Zone 15-24

# 21

Willow myrtle
## *Agonis flexuosa*
Myrtaceae

Willow myrtle is a member of the genus *Agonis,* which includes about ten species, all occurring only in southwestern coastal areas of Western Australia. The name of the genus comes from the Greek word for a gathering or assembly and alludes to the grouping of seeds in the fruit. Willow myrtle, named for its willowlike habit, is the best known of the species in cultivation.

Willow myrtle is a medium-sized tree to 30 or 40 feet, with a pendulous habit and widely spreading branches that have a somewhat zigzag growth pattern at their tips. The tree has a broad crown and dark brown, fibrous, furrowed **bark. Leaves** are alternate and when young are lanceolate, often broadly so, in contrast to the narrower, almost linear older leaves, which are 3 to 5 inches long. The leaves, which hang more or less vertically, have a peppermint smell when crushed, and give rise to a second common name, peppermint tree. The nearly sessile **flowers,** grouped into loose

W side of Conservatory Dr West (IV-Q1); SE corner of King Dr and Chain of Lakes Dr (I-D4); S of King Dr, E of Crossover Dr (III-M4)
Richmond Mini-Park, on 7th Ave between Geary and Anza; 3456 22nd St
Evergreen/Moderate growth/30'-40'
Small white flowers along the branches (June)/ Small woody capsules
Full sun/Water infrequently
Sunset Zone 15-17, 20-24
Suitable as a street tree

clusters, are scattered along the hanging branches. The white, spreading petals are the showy part of the flower and surround fifteen to twenty stamens. The flowers are followed by rounded, loosely clustered **fruits,** about ½ inch in diameter. Willow myrtle is attractive as a specimen tree, and it is often used in place of the more common weeping willow (*Salix* spp.), which, like all willows, has invasive roots and demands plenty of water.

Willow myrtle is widely distributed in the southwestern part of Western Australia, mostly in forests and woodlands dominated by several species of eucalypts. The tuart forests *(Eucalyptus gomphocephala),* heavily logged for their valuable timber, have been transformed into forests of understory trees, including willow myrtle, with only a few remaining tall tuarts. Because of the willow myrtle's medium size and wide-branching habit, its wood is of little commercial value.

Willow myrtle was introduced to California before 1871, when it was listed for the first time by Stephen Nolan at his Belle View Nursery in Oakland. The first mention of the tree in Golden Gate Park was in 1924.

A large old specimen of willow myrtle, about 25 to 30 feet tall, is in Strybing Arboretum along one of the main paths of the Demonstration Gardens. It has two basal trunks, a broadly spreading crown, and characteristically drooping branches. According to records, it is one of the oldest trees in the arboretum; recent storms have badly disfigured it. Other large specimens can be seen along the west side of Conservatory Drive West and at the southeast corner of King Drive and Chain of Lakes Drive East. Younger trees can be seen along the Strybing fence east of Crossover Drive on the south side of King Drive. Willow myrtle is commonly used as a street tree in the Bay Area and is also seen in Santa Barbara, Santa Monica, and Pacific Palisades.

# 22

## Tree of heaven

# *Ailanthus altissima*
Simaroubaceae

Tree of heaven belongs to the quassia family, the Simaroubaceae, a mostly tropical family known in California only from the introduced tree of heaven and the native crucifixion thorn *(Castela emoryi)* from the Colorado and Mojave deserts. This is a tall deciduous tree to 60 feet or more with bronze green new growth in spring. The alternate **leaves** are pinnately compound, 1 to 2 feet or even 3 feet long with eleven to twenty-five leaflets, each leaflet 3 to 6 inches long. The **flower**s are small and greenish in large terminal clusters. Male and female flowers are on separate trees. Male flowers are strongly, and unpleasantly, scented; **fruits** produced by the female

Deciduous/Fast growth/60' or more
Greenish flowers at ends of branches (May-June)/
    Clusters of reddish brown, winged seed pods
Full sun/Needs no watering
Sunset Zone 1-24

flowers are attractive, papery winged **seeds** or samaras, about 1 to 2 inches long, reddish brown at first, later light brown. The tree may be distinguished from other trees with pinnately compound leaves by the two to four glandular teeth at the base of each leaflet of both male and female trees, and by the characteristic odor of the crushed leaves. So unpleasant is this odor that in some areas the tree has the common names of stink tree or stink wood. The clusters of reddish brown samaras are decorative and are often used in dried arrangements. The samaras with their papery wings are carried by the wind, sometimes for long distances.

Wood of tree of heaven was prized at one time for fuel and cabinet making. As fuel, it ranked with such trees of the eastern United States as white oak, black walnut, and birch. Its heavy, strong, light yellow wood was valuable in cabinet making because it did not warp on drying, and, although coarse grained, it took a fine polish. Another use, at one time with industrial possibilities, was in the production of silk. Leaves are eaten by the larvae of an insect that produces a particular kind of silk; experiments for its production were carried out in the southern United States, France, and Algeria.

Tree of heaven was being offered in 1853 by Colonel James Warren at his nursery in Sacramento, but the source of his material is not known. Chinese immigrants working in California mines during the gold rush were presumed to have brought seeds of the tree from its native China. These seeds were planted in the Sierra Nevada foothills around the placer mining camps, producing trees that eventually spread spontaneously from established colonies still to be seen in and around some of the old mining camps. From the Sierra foothills, tree of heaven was taken or spread to other parts of California. Colonel Warren's material may have come from there. In any event, the tree became so widespread throughout most of California that Jepson (1936) referred to it as the only introduced tree in California which is "aggressively spontaneous."

According to reports of the park commissioners, tree of heaven was being grown in Golden Gate Park's nursery in the 1890s. By 1899, these trees (or at least some) had been planted in the park, and subsequent reports list this tree. However, today it is not found in the park. It is also an uncommon tree in San Francisco. Probably the cool, foggy summers and mild winters of the central California coast are not conducive to its growth.

# The Tree That Grew in Brooklyn

From northern China where it is native, seeds of tree of heaven were sent to England in 1751 by Pierre d'Incarville, a French Jesuit missionary. He sent, to the Royal Society in London, seeds of a tree that he considered to be lacquer or varnish tree *(Rhus verniciflua)*, a tree well known even at that time from the Himalayas and China. The seeds were turned over to Philip Miller of the Chelsea Physic Garden, and to Philip Carteret Webb of Busbridge near London, both of whom grew plants from the seeds. Miller recognized his tree as being different from varnish tree and in 1768 described it as a new species, *Toxicodendron altissimum*. John Ellis, another contemporary botanist, gave the plant at Busbridge another name, *Rhus sinense*. Réné Desfontaines, in 1786, recognized that this tree was not related to varnish tree, but belonged to a new genus and species which he named *Ailanthus glandulosa*. For years, tree of heaven was known by that name, but in 1916 it was realized that the specific epithet first given to it in 1768 by Miller had priority over later names; hence, it is now called *Ailanthus altissima*.

The name *Ailanthus* was given by Desfontaines to the new genus because he considered that it was related to a tall tree growing in Amboina, now called Ambon, an island in the Moluccas, and now part of Indonesia. The tree in Amboina was known by the local name of *aylanto,* a word meaning tree of the sky, or heaven tree, because of its height. From this relationship we have both the botanical name, *Ailanthus,* and the common name, tree of heaven.

Tree of heaven was introduced into the United States from England in 1784 to The Woodlands, the estate of William Hamilton near Philadelphia. Hamilton introduced many hardy fruit and ornamental trees including ginkgo, Norway maple, and Lombardy poplar. A second introduction was recorded by Andrew Jackson Downing in 1841, when trees came directly from China to Rhode Island. Following this introduction, root sprouts from the original trees were distributed to nurseries in the eastern United States.

Today, tree of heaven is one of the commonest trees in urban areas of the United States. Since colonial times, it has been planted extensively in the eastern United States, where today it is one of the few trees which flourishes in the polluted atmosphere of industrial cities—"the tree that grew in Brooklyn." Apparently it has no particular soil requirements and will grow in the poor soil of disturbed areas. It is fast growing and when pruned properly makes an attractive specimen; in some areas it has been a useful street tree. Unfortunately, from cultivated and landscaped areas, it has spread into cities and between cities until it has become a widely naturalized weed tree.

# 23

## Titoki
# *Alectryon excelsus*
### Sapindaceae

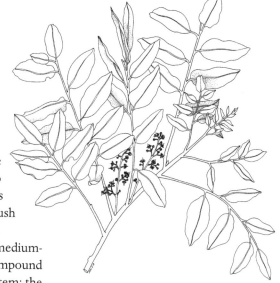

*Alectryon* is a small genus with about fifteen species occurring in the western Pacific, including New Zealand and Australia. It belongs to the soapberry family, one not represented on North America's Pacific Coast except by introduced trees such as the hopseed bush (*Dodonaea viscosa*) and the golden rain tree (*Koelreuteria paniculata*).

*Alectryon excelsus,* known by its Maori name of titoki, is a medium-sized tree with fairly smooth, dark gray **bark.** The pinnately compound **leaves,** 4 to 12 inches long, have an alternate arrangement on the stem; the four to six pairs of leaflets usually have an entire margin but sometimes display a few coarse teeth. The new growth is clothed in rusty hairs, but mature leaves are a glossy deep green on the upper surface. The **flowers,** small and inconspicuous, occur in spring on branched clusters forming panicles. **Fruits,** which take about a year to develop, are somewhat woody, rounded capsules, ¼ to ½ inch long and fairly smooth. At maturity, each capsule splits to reveal a shiny black **seed** partially embedded in a showy, bright red, somewhat fleshy aril, an appendage of the seed. The partially open fruits with seed and aril visible are the main attraction of the tree, far more than the insignificant flowers.

The earliest mention of titoki in Golden Gate Park was in the 1924 *Annual Report of the Park Commissioners.* A superb specimen of titoki, nearly 20 feet tall and of greater width, can be seen on the west side of Conservatory Drive East, south of the entrance to the Fuchsia Garden. A

N of Hippie Hill (IV-R2); W side of Conservatory Dr East (IV-R1); Strybing (VI-N3)
NE corner Dolores Park
Evergreen/Slow growth/20'-30'
Inconspicuous flowers on branch tips (spring)/ Red, fleshy fruit with partially exposed, shiny black seed
Full sun/Water regularly
Sunset Zone 16-24

cluster of three small trees is on the north side of Hippie Hill; other specimens are in Strybing's New Zealand Garden, though some were damaged in the ferocious storm of December 1995. A number of titokis can be seen as street trees in the Santa Barbara area.

In its native New Zealand, the tough, elastic wood of titoki was used for small tools, for such items as harness yokes for oxen and horses, and in coach building. In addition, the Maori extracted oil from the seeds that they used for skin ailments and sore eyes, as a hair cream, and in ritual ceremonies.

## Araucarias
# *Araucaria*
### Araucariaceae

The genus *Araucaria,* with about twenty species, occurs in eastern Australia, New Caledonia, New Guinea, Norfolk Island, and southern South America. Mature **leaves** are of two kinds. In some species, they are linear or awl-shaped to scalelike and more or less overlapping on the branchlets, while in others, they are lanceolate to ovate and scattered along the branches. Male and female **cones** are usually borne on separate trees; the female cones ripen in two to three years and break apart when mature. Trees are often large with tall, straight trunks and branches radiating in whorls from the trunk. The genus takes its name from the Arauco Province of Chile, which was inhabited by the Araucanian people and is home to monkey puzzle *(Araucaria araucana).* Seven species of Araucaria were introduced into cultivation in California between 1859 and 1884, according Butterfield (1964). Of the six known today in California cities, five are in Golden Gate Park; the sixth, *Araucaria columnaris,* is found only in Southern California.

## 24

### Paraná pine
# *Araucaria angustifolia*
### Araucariaceae

Trees of *Araucaria angustifolia* have more or less horizontal branches, lanceolate **leaves,** 1 to 2¼ inches long and about ¼ to ½ inch wide, sharply acute with a noticeable midrib. Mature **cones** are 5 inches high and 6½ inches in diameter. A tree in Santa Barbara is 70 feet tall, but mature trees may reach 90 feet or more. The species is native to southern Brazil and northern Argentina, where it was important for lumber and provided edible seeds; it is sometimes called the Brazilian pine. Although grown in California as early as 1884, this species is rarely cultivated today. In addition to the large tree in Santa Barbara, it is grown in The Arboretum of Los Angeles County and in Golden Gate Park, where the only specimen is about 35 feet tall in Strybing's South American Collection. Unfortunately, its age and date of accession are not known.

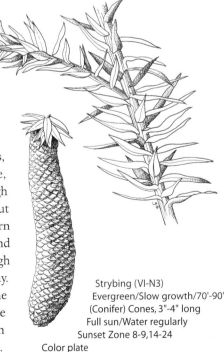

Strybing (VI-N3)
Evergreen/Slow growth/70'-90'
(Conifer) Cones, 3"-4" long
Full sun/Water regularly
Sunset Zone 8-9,14-24
Color plate

# 25

Monkey puzzle tree
## *Araucaria araucana*
Araucariaceaea

The common name of monkey puzzle is said to have originated in Cornwall in southern England. The owner of a young tree, proudly showing it to friends and apparently wishing to emphasize the tree's unusual shape and sharply pointed leaves, reputedly remarked that "it would puzzle a monkey to climb it." It is also sometimes known as the Chile pine. Monkey puzzles are stiffly branched, sometimes irregularly so, giving the tree an unusual shape, particularly when young. The upper branches tend to spread upward, while the lower are pendulous. **Leaves** are broadly ovate, rigid and leathery, sessile, abruptly and sharply pointed, 1 to 2 inches long, ¾ to 1 inch wide, densely arranged, and overlapping; they persist for many years. Mature trees in their natural habitat may reach 90 to 100 feet; in cultivation they are much shorter. The mature globose **cones**, 5 to 7 inches thick, take one to two years to mature. The large, oval **seeds,** about 1½ inches long, were eaten in the past in Chile.

A native of the cool, moist western slopes of the Andes in Chile and southwestern Argentina, monkey puzzle was first discovered in 1780 in Chile. Later, Archibald Menzies, with the Vancouver Expedition, picked up some seeds that were served for dessert when he and other ship's officers were dining with the governor of Chile. From these seeds, germinated onboard ship, Menzies took five young plants to England in 1795, one of which survived until 1892.

Monkey puzzle is the most hardy of all araucarias. It has been so successfully grown in England that, according to Bean (1970), it "is the most remarkably hardy tree ever introduced into Britain." In the United States it is hardy from southern Maryland south and west to Texas. It is occasionally planted in California; trees are known in Sacramento, Santa Barbara, Santa Monica, and San Diego. It has been in Golden Gate Park since the 1890s. Today, a small grove of these trees is at the northwest corner of Kennedy and Transverse drives; young ones can be seen in Strybing's Primitive Plants Garden southeast of the Friend Gate. Large and magnificent trees exist in the Portland and Seattle areas.

Kennedy Dr at Transverse Dr (II-K2)
Evergreen/Slow growth/70'-90'
(Conifer) Globose cones, 5"-7" thick, in tree tops
Full sun/Water regularly
Sunset Zone 4-9, 14-24

*Except during the nine months before he draws his first breath, no man manages his affairs as well as a tree does.*

GEORGE BERNARD SHAW, 1903

# 26

Bunya-bunya
## *Araucaria bidwillii*

Araucariaceae

The common names for this tree, bunya-bunya and bunya pine, were taken from the Bunya Mountains of northeastern Queensland, one of the regions in which the tree is native. Mature trees are large, fairly symmetrical in shape, and densely branched, particularly above the middle. The secondary branches or branchlets are long and pendant and tend to be clumped toward the ends of branches. **Leaves** are lanceolate, spirally arranged, almost overlapping, stiff, and leathery; they narrow gradually to a sharp point and vary in length from ½ to 1½ inches, varying from shorter to longer leaves on a single branchlet. **Cones** are large and heavy, nearly globose, 10 to 12 inches long, sometimes weighing as much as ten pounds, and are borne out of sight on the uppermost branches. They contain up to 150 pear-shaped edible **seeds,** 2 to 2½ inches long. The cones of araucarias usually break up when mature, but some cones of the bunya-bunya fall while still intact, perhaps from their weight. A large cone could cause injury to anyone struck by one.

The large edible seeds, the bunya nuts, were a staple food of Australian Aborigines. They are starchy, with something of the texture of a boiled potato, and were eaten raw, roasted, ground into flour, or boiled. Because of this use, at one time the Australian government placed restrictions on cutting bunya-bunya for timber.

Bunya-bunya has been planted in California cities from north to south, including Sacramento, Palo Alto, Menlo Park, Oakland, Santa Barbara, Santa Monica, Arcadia, and San Diego. It has been in Golden Gate Park since the late 1890s, and today two specimens can be seen. A large specimen is on Strawberry Hill near the Chinese Pavilion, and another is east of the Stow Lake Boathouse parking area; a young specimen, approaching 20 feet tall, is in the lawn inside Strybing's Friend Gate.

In Australia, bunya-bunya occurs in two areas in the coastal mountains of southeastern Queensland, one to the east of Brisbane and the other near Port Douglas. The species was named for JC Bidwill, a government botanist in New South Wales and later commissioner of crown lands in Queensland.

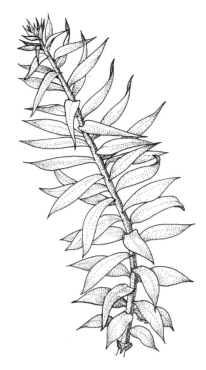

E side of Strawberry Hill near Chinese Pavilion
(III-M3); Strybing (VII-N3)
Evergreen/Slow growth/80'
(Conifer) Heavy cones, up to 12" long, in treetops
Full sun/Water regularly
Sunset Zone 7-9, 12-24

# 27

## Hoop pine
### *Araucaria cunninghamii*
Araucariaceaea

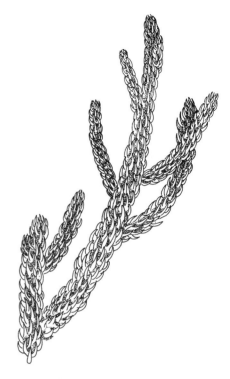

Commonly called hoop pine, mature trees of this araucaria are smaller and less densely branched than those of bunya-bunya, and the branchlets are more crowded toward the ends of the branches. **Leaves** are linear to narrowly triangular or awl-shaped, sharply pointed, nearly straight, ⅓ to ⅔ inch long, crowded, and more or less overlapping. **Cones** are ovoid to almost globose, 2 to 4 inches long, each scale terminating in a lanceolate reflexed tip; the **seeds** are ¼ to ½ inch long. Hoop pine is somewhat more widely distributed than bunya-bunya, occurring in coastal southeastern Queensland south to northern New South Wales and also in New Caledonia.

The wood of hoop pine, just as that of bunya-bunya, has several economic uses in Australia, and in addition the tree is cultivated as an ornamental. It was named in honor of Alan Cunningham, a pioneer botanist and explorer of eastern Australia.

In California, hoop pine is cultivated less frequently than bunya-bunya and Norfolk Island pine. It is known from Santa Barbara and The Arboretum of Los Angeles County, in addition to Golden Gate Park. The park's single specimen, an old tree over 35 feet tall, is along a path between Kennedy Drive and Hippie Hill.

On path between Kennedy Dr and Hippie Hill
  (IV-R2)
Evergreen/Moderate growth/25'-30' or more
(Conifer) Ovoid cones, 2"-4" long
Full sun/Water regularly
Sunset Zone 7-9, 12-24

# 28

## Norfolk Island pine
### *Araucaria heterophylla*
Araucariaceaea

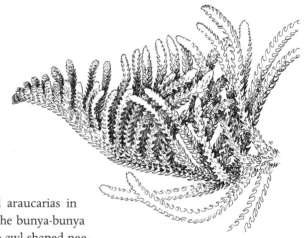

Norfolk Island pine is the most frequently seen of all araucarias in California, but it is found mostly in coastal areas while the bunya-bunya can be grown away from the coast. Its mature **leaves** are awl-shaped needles similar to those of the hoop pine, but they are shorter (about ¼ inch long), incurved, and more strongly overlapping; juvenile leaves are softer, more slender, and about ½ inch long. The squat, ovoid **cones** are 3 to 5 inches long. Norfolk Island pine is a tall tree, often exceeding 100 feet in California. It has branches spreading horizontally from the main trunk, with branchlets arranged more or less uniformly along the length of the branches, giving the tree a decidedly symmetrical shape.

On the lawns W and S of McLaren Lodge (IV-S2);
  King Dr and Middle Dr East (III-O3); Strybing
  (VII-N3)
3625 20th St
Evergreen/Moderate growth/100'
(Conifer) Roundish, squat cones, 3"-5" long
Full sun/Water occasionally
Sunset Zone 17, 21-24

This araucaria is found only on Norfolk Island in the South Pacific, about 900 miles off the eastern coast of Australia. Both the island and the tree were discovered in October 1774 by Captain James Cook on his second voyage. Captain Cook and his crew called this tree a spruce-pine. Before coming to Norfolk Island, Captain Cook had discovered New Caledonia and its several spruce-pines, including the one we know today as the New Caledonian pine *(Araucaria columnaris),* a close relative of the Norfolk Island pine. Today Norfolk Island pine still flourishes on its island home but not in the abundance of Captain Cook's day.

The Norfolk Island pine was introduced into England through Joseph Banks in 1793 and grown at Kew. It is not hardy in most of England but is occasionally grown in Cornwall in southern England. It was an early introduction into California by William Walker in 1859, and today it is grown in coastal California from the San Francisco Bay Area to San Diego. It is particularly tolerant of the sandy soils and windy conditions of coastal areas such as Golden Gate Park. At a distance, its symmetrically arranged branches give it a characteristic silhouette. This effect can be appreciated by viewing the two trees in the lawn to the south and to the west of McLaren Lodge. There is also a group of three trees near the intersection of King Drive and Middle Drive East. Trees of this species are included in Strybing's Primitive Plants Garden. Young Norfolk Island pines are often grown indoors in containers.

# Pines and Araucarias

European explorers who first discovered the trees now placed in the genera *Araucaria* and *Agathis* called them pines because they were evergreen and superficially resembled familiar European cone-bearing trees. They are the only genera in the araucaria family. Trees of this family, related to the much larger pine family of the Northern Hemisphere, differ from the pines and their relatives in having cones that shatter at maturity and a single seed on each cone scale. In the pine family, the cones usually remain intact at maturity (firs are an exception), and each cone scale has two seeds. Leaves also differ in the two families. In the araucaria family, mature leaves vary from awl-shaped to ovate, sometimes broadly ovate, while members of the pine family mostly have needle-like leaves.

*Conifers stand in the sacred temple yards of Japan, where, with venerating care, their old limbs are supported by pillars. They line the solemn approaches to the tombs of the Chinese emperors at Jehol. Solomon sought them in the peaks of Lebanon for his temple. But in all the world there are none like those in our western states.*

DONALD CULROSS PEATTIE, *The Flowering Earth*

# 29

## Coast banksia
## *Banksia integrifolia*
### Proteaceae

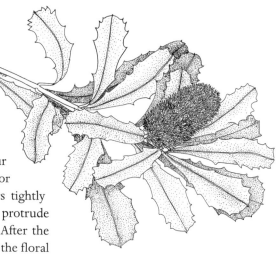

Banksias are distinctive members of the protea family that occur entirely in Australia and on neighboring islands. Their cylindrical or rounded flower clusters may contain as many as 3,000 flowers tightly arranged along a central woody stalk. The slender styles, which protrude from the flowers, give the cluster its characteristic appearance. After the flowers mature and fall, a limited number of fruits protrude from the floral stalk. These eventually split open to release the seeds; each seed has a wing that aids in distribution.

Banksias were named after Joseph Banks who, with Daniel Solander, collected the first banksias and other plants on Australia's eastern coast while accompanying Captain James Cook's voyage around the world on the ship *Endeavor* (1768–1771). The majority of banksias occur in Western Australia.

Coast banksia, or tree banksia, occurs over a broad area of eastern Australia, from coastal regions to harsher interior and mountainous settings. Always a robust, evergreen tree, it may vary in height from low and shrubby to as much as 70 feet tall, making it the tallest of the banksias. Its **bark** is rough with small, irregularly spaced depressions. The 2- to 4-inch long **leaves** are alternate or whorled, obovate to narrowly elliptic, generally with entire margins. They are green above and white below with a tightly compressed covering of fine hairs. The cylindrical flower clusters, appearing in fall and winter, vary from 2 to 6 inches long and consist of densely packed, pale yellow **flowers;** the winged **seeds** are about ⅜ to 1 inch long, held in persistent woody capsules on conelike **fruits.**

Coast banksia is among the most easily and widely cultivated species of banksia in Australia; a number of the more temperamental species, particularly those from Western Australia, are grafted onto the roots of coast banksia to make them more tolerant of garden conditions. On North America's Pacific Coast, it is grown only in California, so far as is known. Its earliest listing for Golden Gate Park is in the 1924 *Annual Report of the Park Commissioners.* A large tree on Hippie Hill is about 40 feet tall, estimated to be seventy to eighty years old. The bark is thick, sparsely rough, and the tree has four large trunks from its base. Another tree can be found in Strybing Arboretum, thought to have been planted by Eric Walther in the early 1940s in what is now the South African Garden; young specimens are north of the Duck Pond on the edge of the arboretum's Primitive Plants Garden. The species is also listed for Orpet Park in Santa Barbara, and in the Australian Garden at the UCSC Arboretum.

Hippie Hill (IV-R2); Strybing (VII-N3)
Evergreen/Moderate growth/40'-70'
Cylindrical, 2"-6" clusters of pale yellow flowers
    (fall and winter) /Winged seeds in woody
    capsules
Full sun/Water infrequently
Sunset Zone 15-24

# 30

### English boxwood
## *Buxus sempervirens*

Buxaceae

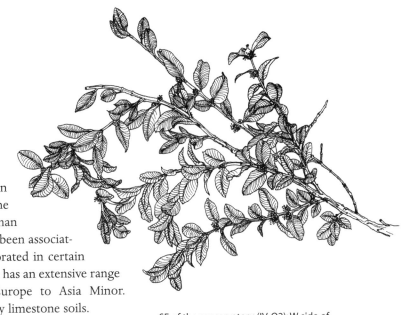

Of all of the broad-leafed evergreens in Golden Gate Park, English boxwood, or box, is one of the best known for its long association with human activities. Box, together with holly and yew, has been associated in Europe with ancient legends and incorporated in certain religious festivals. It is native to Europe, where it has an extensive range from southeastern England across central Europe to Asia Minor. Throughout its range, it is typically found on dry limestone soils.

Boxwood is variable in habit, growing either as a low shrub or as a small, shrubby tree with arching branches. Its simple, dark green, glossy **leaves** are about 1 inch long and narrow ovate in shape with a rounded tip. The yellowish **flowers** are small, clustered within the foliage, and insignificant.

The wood of box is hard, heavy, densely and uniformly grained, and bright orange brown in color. It can be polished to give a smooth and attractive surface and has been used in Europe from ancient times to the present. Virgil, Pliny, and Ovid mention its use for musical instruments and small objects. In modern times it has been used for rulers and drawing instruments that must be exact in size and have neat and accurate scales, for flutes and other musical instruments, and for turnings, inlays, and small carvings. One of its most important uses has been for wood engravings. For these, an artist uses very fine and sharp tools to cut the design on the end grain of a piece of boxwood, which is considered "the only completely satisfactory surface for wood engraving."

In gardens and parks, boxwood is used as both a shrub and a small tree. Shrubs are often clipped to form hedges and have been trained into various shapes in the art of topiary. There are numerous named cultivars, some particularly low growing, available in nurseries. In its tree form, box becomes 15 to 20 feet tall and may eventually reach 30 feet with a trunk 2 feet across.

Box has been in the park since about 1900, and in California since 1884. It was introduced to the eastern coast of North America in 1652 when a plantation of box was set out on eastern Long Island. In Golden Gate Park, there are several box trees in a planting southeast of the conservatory; another large, multi-trunked specimen is along the west side of the Sixth Avenue entrance from Fulton Street. Sheared hedges of boxwood are in Strybing Arboretum, near the Stow Lake Boathouse, at the Kennedy Drive entrance to the Rhododendron Dell, and in public and private gardens throughout the West Coast.

SE of the conservatory (IV-Q2); W side of
  6th Ave S of Fulton St (III-P1)
Evergreen/Slow growth/15'-20'; shrublike
Clusters of small, greenish yellow flowers in
  spring
Sun on coast, part shade inland/Water
  occasionally
Sunset Zone 5-6, 15-17

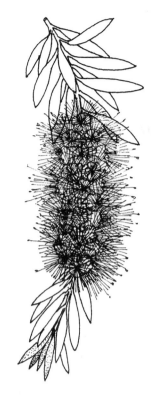

# 31

Weeping bottlebrush

# *Callistemon viminalis*

Myrtaceae

Bottlebrush is the common name for three genera of cultivated trees and shrubs in the myrtle family: *Callistemon, Melaleuca,* and *Metrosideros.* All are native to Australia; some species have a long history in cultivation in that country and abroad, particularly in California. They have numerous flowers characteristically arranged in a showy, leafless, spikelike inflorescence.

The botanical name *Callistemon* comes from two Greek words meaning beautiful and stamen, alluding to the colorful stamens of many species including weeping bottlebrush. The species name, *viminalis,* refers to the long, slender stems, often weeping in this species. Weeping bottlebrush is a small to medium tree, 30 to 40 feet tall, with somewhat flaky **bark. Leaves** are arranged alternately and are lanceolate, to 4 inches long, with pinnate venation; numerous oil dots can be seen when leaves are held against the light, and they may be fragrant when crushed. Its numerous **flowers,** produced sporadically year-round but most heavily in spring and summer, are in the typical bottlebrush-like spikes, 3 to 7 inches long. The five sepals and petals are inconspicuous, much shorter than the long, showy, red stamens, which are united at their bases and are the conspicuous part of the flowers. **Fruits** are small, roundish, woody capsules that persist on the stem after the flowers have fallen.

Native to stream sides in northeastern Australia, weeping bottlebrush was introduced to California by Evans and Reeves Nurseries in Los Angeles in 1942 and was found to be adaptable to a range of conditions from damp to dry. The species is variable, and many cultivars are offered by Australian nurseries. On the West Coast, the species is the most commonly grown, along with one cultivar ('McGaskillii'), selected for its more prolific flowering on a smaller weeping tree. Weeping bottlebrush appears commonly as a street tree and in public and private gardens throughout California and the Southwest. In Golden Gate Park, a fine specimen can be seen just inside and to the west of Strybing's Friend Gate. Several mature trees can be seen on the campuses of UC Berkeley and UCLA, and at the Huntington Botanical Gardens.

Strybing (VI-N3)
End of 100 block of Bocana St; 1370 Sanchez St
Evergreen/Fast growth/30'-40'
Pendant spikes of bright red bottlebrush flowers
  (spring-summer and sporadically year round)/
  Woody seed capsules
Full sun/Water occasionally
Sunset Zone 8, 9, 12-24
Suitable as a street tree

## 32

Incense cedar

# *Calocedrus decurrens*

(syn. *Libocedrus decurrens*)

Cupressaceae

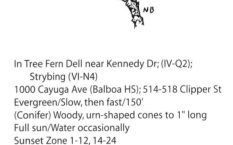

Incense cedar occurs in the Cascade Mountains of Oregon, southward into California, throughout the Sierra Nevada, the Coast Ranges, the mountains of Southern California, and northern Baja California. Trees are more or less conical, up to 150 feet tall, with trunks 3 to 6 feet in diameter. The **bark** is thin on young trees, thicker on old trees, reddish brown, somewhat fibrous, and furrowed. The flat branchlets are fully green on both surfaces and lack any white blotches on the underside. The scalelike **leaves** are in pairs that are closely appressed, ⅛ to ¼ inch long, with minute spreading tips; the crushed leaves release a pleasantly pungent odor. The somewhat urn-shaped **cones,** up to 1 inch long, have two to three opposite pairs of scales that spread apart as cones mature. It is still occasionally known by its old name, *Libocedrus decurrens.*

Wood of incense cedar, which is durable, light in weight, and reddish brown, has had limited commercial value, although it was important in the manufacture of pencils after the supply of eastern red cedar (*Juniperus virginiana*) became scarce. According to Butterfield (1964), incense cedar was introduced into cultivation in California in 1859 by William Walker through his Golden Gate Nursery in San Francisco. Today, it is occasionally cultivated in parks throughout California; a few cultivars have been selected in Europe. Two tall incense cedars are just east of the entrance to the Tree Fern Dell on the south side of Kennedy Drive; others are in Strybing's Arthur Menzies Garden of California Native Plants.

In Tree Fern Dell near Kennedy Dr; (IV-Q2); Strybing (VI-N4)
1000 Cayuga Ave (Balboa HS); 514-518 Clipper St
Evergreen/Slow, then fast/150′
(Conifer) Woody, urn-shaped cones to 1" long
Full sun/Water occasionally
Sunset Zone 1-12, 14-24

## 33

Cape chestnut

# *Calodendrum capense*

Rutaceae

Strybing (VII-N3)
Evergreen/Slow growth/25′-70′
Terminal pyramidal flower clusters, 5"-10" long, pink or lavender to white with conspicuous stamens (June-July) /Large, woody, five-angled fruit
Full sun/Water regularly
Sunset Zone 17, 19, 21-24, worth a try in 15, 16
Color plate

Cape chestnut belongs to the rue, or citrus, family. The generic name (sometimes misspelled as *Calodendron*) is taken from two Greek words meaning beautiful and tree. The common name refers to its native land and the similarity of the fruits to those of the edible chestnut *(Castanea sativa)*. Trees are evergreen, about 25 to 70 feet tall, with a broadly spreading crown. **Leaves** are opposite, somewhat ovate, to 5 inches long, with many parallel veins, and on short petioles. In early summer, the numerous showy **flowers** form a pyramidal cluster 5 to 10 inches long; the five narrow, 1-inch-long, spreading petals are pink or lavender to almost white. Adjacent to the petals are five stamens and five petal-like staminodes, conspicuously dotted with purple glands. The large, woody, five-angled **fruit** has knobby projections and is split into five parts, each with two large shiny black seeds.

Cape chestnut is a tree of southeastern Africa, with a geographical distribution extending from eastern Cape Province northward to Kenya, generally throughout mountain and coastal forests from sea level to about 6,000 feet elevation. In Africa, the wood of the Cape chestnut has been used for planking and furniture; the seeds, for obtaining small amounts of oil; and the roots, for a hot water infusion used by native people there to treat wounds.

It was introduced into cultivation from the Cape region to England in 1789 by Francis Masson of Kew Gardens. The plant was lost to cultivation for a number of years, but in 1883 it appeared again and was reported in England and Germany as a handsome tree that required the protection of a greenhouse. From Europe it was taken to Australia, where it grew outdoors in Sydney; in 1905, JH Maiden, government botanist and director of the Botanic Gardens there, described it as a fine, large tree completely covered with flowers.

Cape chestnut has been in California since at least 1897, when Dr Francesco Franceschi had it in Santa Barbara, according to Butterfield (1964). It has become a popular tree in California, where it is grown in Santa Barbara, Riverside, Claremont, San Diego, and probably elsewhere. An unusually large tree in Chavez Ravine, Elysian Park, Los Angeles, has a spread of nearly 80 feet; it flowers profusely in early summer and is one of the most striking flowering trees in the Los Angeles area. Other fine trees can be seen at The Arboretum of LA County. Strybing Arboretum has several trees, planted in the mid-1980s, in the South African Garden.

## She-oaks
# *Casuarina*
## Casuarinaceae

Casuarinas are a distinctive group of trees and shrubs found mostly in Australia, though there are about thirty species of *Casuarina* occurring on several Pacific islands in addition to Australia. They make up the only genus in the casuarina family. Characteristic of the genus are the minute scalelike **leaves** arranged in whorls on slender, green, grooved, and jointed branchlets. She-oaks have many common names based on their leaves and wood. The branchlets, which may be pulled apart at each joint, superficially resemble the much thicker, jointed stems of horsetails *(Equisetum),* which has given them a common name of horsetail trees. Branchlets are often clustered and drooping, giving them a superficial resemblance to pines, hence the common name of Australian pines. Europeans who came to Australia in early colonial times discovered that the hard wood of casuarinas had certain oaklike properties and called them oaks. Another common name, beefwood, was given because of the redness of the wood. The botanical name, *Casuarina*, is said to have been derived from the resemblance of the clustered branchlets to the feathers of the cassowary *(Casuarius)*, a large flightless Australian bird.

The small, inconspicuous **flowers** of casuarinas lack petals and are unisexual; in some species, both male and female flowers are on the same tree while in others, they are on separate trees. Male flowers are arranged in slender, cylindrical, terminal spikes, while females are grouped into small clusters on the old wood among the branchlets. At maturity, the clusters of female flowers develop into woody conelike **fruits** containing small winged **seeds.**

Casuarinas are sometimes confused with tamarisks *(Tamarix* spp.), particularly with athel tamarisk *(T. aphylla)* which also has fine, slender branchlets. However, in tamarisk the somewhat larger scalelike leaves are alternate and not whorled as are the tiny ones of the casuarinas.

Casuarinas have been used in various ways in Australia: the foliage as browse and fodder for cattle, and the wood for furniture, small articles such as tool handles, and fuel. Some are attractive and have been planted in cities as ornamental trees.

# 34

## River she-oak
# *Casuarina cunninghamiana*
## Casuarinaceae

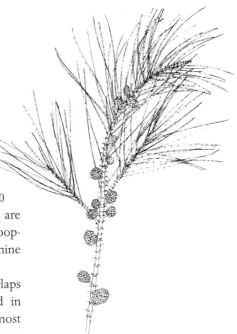

River she-oak is the tallest casuarina in Australia, often attaining 70 to 90 feet, but in some areas trees are only 40 feet tall. Its rounded **cones** are about ⅓ to ½ inch long. Branchlets do not droop as distinctly as in drooping she-oak, and are much finer. The scalelike **leaves** number seven to nine (usually eight) at each node. Insignificant **flowers** appear in summer.

River she-oak, in part of its distribution in New South Wales, overlaps that of the river red gum *(Eucalyptus camaldulensis)*—also planted in California—and extends northward into Queensland and northernmost Northern Territory. Found along the banks of streams and watercourses, as its name would suggest, it effectively prevents erosion of the banks, and, as early as the end of the 1800s, was being planted in the US to protect disturbed watercourses.

River she-oak has been in Golden Gate Park since the early 1900s; it was listed in the 1910 *Annual Report of the Park Commissioners*. A single tree is at the eastern end of McLaren Lodge, beside the driveway.

Although easily recognized, in the past there has been confusion regarding the identity of *Casuarina cunninghamiana*. It was probably first introduced under the name of *C. equisetifolia*, another species not easily distinguished from *C. cunninghamiana*. We now know that trees in California called *C. equisetifolia* are actually *C. cunninghamiana*.

Behind McLaren Lodge (IV-S2)
Jefferson Square, Laguna at Turk; Ninth St
    between Harrison and Bryant
Evergreen/Fast growth/40'-90'
Inconspicuous flowers (summer) /Small, round,
    conelike fruits to 1/2" across
Full sun/Needs no watering once established
Sunset Zone 8, 9, 12-24
Suitable as a street tree

# 35

Drooping she-oak

## *Casuarina verticillata*

**(syn.** *C. stricta***)**

Casuarinaceae

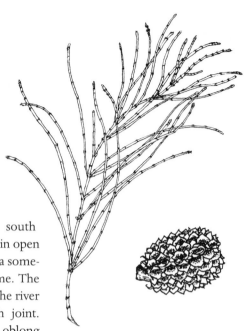

Drooping she-oak occurs in Australia from New South Wales south through Victoria to South Australia and Tasmania. It is often found in open country, on dry ridges, and other rocky sites. Up to 40 feet tall with a somewhat rounded crown, its branchlets droop, hence the common name. The branchlets are noticeably thicker and appear coarser than those of the river she-oak. There are ten to twelve tiny scalelike **leaves** at each joint. Insignificant flowers appear in winter and spring. The woody **cones,** oblong in shape and 1 to 3 inches long, are among the largest in the genus.

    Drooping she-oak was introduced into California before 1858, when William C Walker offered it at his San Francisco nursery. It is planted in California cities from the San Francisco Bay Area south to San Diego. It has been in Golden Gate Park since the early 1900s when it was listed in the 1910 *Annual Report of the Park Commissioners.* Several trees of drooping she-oak can be seen near Fulton Street opposite 17th Avenue.

Fulton St opposite 17th Ave (III-L1)
Evergreen/Fast growth/40'
Inconspicuous flowers (winter-spring) /Oblong
   conelike fruits, 1"-3" long
Full sun/Needs no watering once established
Sunset Zone 8, 9, 12-24
Suitable as a street tree

---

The Cedars

## *Cedrus*

Pinaceae

The true cedars comprise the small genus *Cedrus*, consisting of several trees that occur in widely separated geographic areas. The trees are so similar that botanical authorities have not always agreed on the number of species they represent. In the 1800s, Sir Joseph Hooker, the well-known English botanist, as well as others, regarded them all as geographical variants of a single species. Later, botanists thought of them as four separate species. A recent study recognized only two species, *Cedrus deodara* and *C. libani,* the latter with four subspecies—*atlantica, brevifolia, stenocoma,* and *libani*—and that is how they are known today.

    The cedars are generally tall conifers with irregular crowns and dark gray **bark,** smooth on young trees but becoming scaly and fissured on older trees. There

are two kinds of branchlets: terminal shoots with single, spirally arranged **leaves;** and short, spurlike shoots with dense clusters or whorls of needlelike leaves that are three-angled in cross section and last for three to five years on the trees. The clustered leaves are similar to those of the larches *(Larix),* although larch leaves are deciduous while those of cedars are evergreen. Male and female **cones** of cedars occur on the same tree. The male cones are erect, finger-shaped, 2 to 3 inches long, ½ to ⅝ inch wide, and shed vast quantities of pollen. The female cones are stout, more or less barrel-shaped, erect, blunt or notched at the apex, with thin, broad, densely overlapping scales, hairy on the outside. They mature in two to three years, when they disintegrate while still on the tree, leaving a slender, erect stalk and a woody, platelike base. The **seeds,** two to each scale and winged, are released when the cones disintegrate. Sometimes, though, the cones fall intact, probably from disturbance or injury.

In their native mountain regions, the four cedars discussed here can be easily recognized, but in cultivation it is not always possible to place a single specimen in the species in which it probably belongs. Each species is more or less variable, and variants have been selected and named as cultivars for such characters as leaf color (golden yellow and various shades of green) and habit (dwarf, prostrate, and pendant). These trees are all cultivated, often in parks and large gardens, but because of their potential size, they are not suitable for small gardens.

# 36

## Deodar
# *Cedrus deodara*

Pinaceae

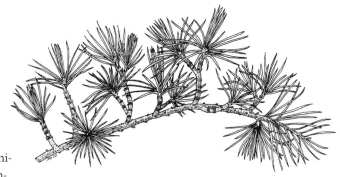

Deodar, or Himalayan cedar, is a large, broadly pyramidal tree, generally to 150 feet tall at maturity, occasionally reported at 250 feet. The leading stem is erect but drooping at its tip, and along it are drooping branchlets, generally with densely hairy tips. The large lower branches are horizontal with gracefully pendulous side branches. The short lateral shoots have clusters of fifteen to thirty leaves, 1½ to 2 inches long. **Leaves** are gray green, becoming darker on older trees. The barrel-shaped **cones** are 2½ to 5 inches long and 2 to 3 inches wide.

Deodars can be distinguished from other cedars by their pendulous branches, generally longer leaves, and slightly larger cones. They are most attractive as young trees; few conifers are as graceful. They are considered less hardy than other species of cedar, but are commonly grown throughout the West Coast, from Vancouver and Seattle to San Diego. Deodars can be seen in Golden Gate Park at the entrance to the Rhododendron Dell, at Stanyan and Waller streets, and, interspersed with Atlas cedars, along Transverse Drive; a single tree is on Strybing's Main Lawn.

Deodar was introduced into England when seed was obtained from its native range in the western Himalayas in 1831, then again in 1856. It has been in Golden Gate Park since 1893.

Stanyan at Waller St (IV-S3); entry to
    Rhododendron Dell (III-P2); along Transverse
    Dr (II-K2); Strybing (VII-O4)
1300 Balboa Ave; 1000 Cayuga Avenue
    (Balboa HS)
Evergreen/Fast growth/150'
(Conifer) Dark bluish green, barrel-shaped cones,
    3" wide x 5" long, that disintegrate on the tree
Full sun/Needs no watering
Sunset Zone 2-12, 14-24
Color plate

*There is nothing like the true cedars in the whole coniferous kingdom. Not even the pines produce a tree of such majestic architecture. Partly no doubt because of their biblical background—they are the trees most mentioned in the Bible and always as an image for fruitfulness and strength—[we] regard them with something approaching awe. Countless cedars in English churchyards and on the lawns of country houses are celebrated in village lore as having come back with the crusaders.*

HUGH JOHNSON, *The International Book of Trees*

# Not All Cedars Are *Cedrus*

Cedar is a common name for several kinds of conifer other than the true cedars, which are only those that belong to the genus *Cedrus;* true cedars have needlelike leaves, typical of trees in the pine family.

The word cedar derives from the ancient Greek word for resinous tree and may originally have been applied to species of *Juniperus,* the junipers. Today, certain junipers are also called cedars; for instance, *Juniperus virginiana,* a native of the eastern United States, is known as Virginia, pencil, or red cedar. Other coniferous trees called cedars include incense cedar *(Calocedrus decurrens),* Port Orford cedar *(Chamae-*

*cyparis lawsoniana),* yellow cedar *(C. nootkatensis),* western red cedar *(Thuja plicata),* and Hiba cedar *(Thujopsis dolabrata).* These trees are all members of the cypress family (Cupressaceae). The sharing of the common name cedar calls attention to the similarity of their scalelike leaves, flattened branchlets, and more or less resinous character.

Interestingly, the cedar wood used for making furniture comes from *Cedrela odorata,* a West Indian tree of the mahogany family (Meliaceae) of flowering plants, not from any of the conifers.

## 37

Atlas cedar

# *Cedrus libani* ssp. *atlantica*

(syn. *C. atlantica*)

Pinaceae

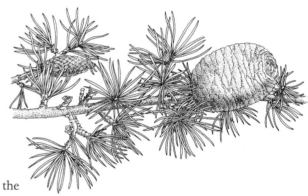

Atlas cedar, sometimes called North African cedar, originates in the Atlas Mountains of Algeria and Morocco, and is well known in cultivation. It is a tall tree to about 120 feet, but heights of as much as 160 feet have been recorded. Its pyramidal habit is somewhat reminiscent of the cedar of Lebanon and the deodar. However, Atlas cedar may be recognized by its uppermost branches, which are fewer and more open. Its leader remains dominant, not forming the dense crown of the cedar of Lebanon. Its branches are obliquely erect, differing from the pendulous branches of the deodar. Young branchlets of Atlas cedar can have minute hairs or be hairless. The **leaves,** about twenty to twenty-five in each whorl, are ½ to 1 inch long and vary in color from a muted greenish blue to blue gray, to silvery, and to yellowish in some of its cultivars. The blue gray leaves are best seen in the cultivar 'Glauca', easily recognizable and the most popular of the cedars. **Cones** are 2 to 3 inches long and about 1½ inches wide.

Atlas cedar is widely planted in cities along the West Coast; its size makes it suitable only for parks and public gardens, however. It has been in Golden Gate Park since 1893; fine specimens displaying a variety of foliage colors can be seen along Transverse Drive. A younger tree is on Strybing's Main Lawn.

Along Transverse Dr near Kennedy Dr (III-K2); Strybing (VII-O4)
431 Yerba Buena Ave; 1000 Cayuga Ave (Balboa HS); 89 Amber Way; 1040 Dolores
Evergreen/Slow growth/120'
(Conifer) Bluish green, 2"-3" long, barrel-shaped cones, that disintegrate on the tree
Full sun/Needs no watering once established
Sunset Zone 2-23

# 38

### Cyprus cedar

## *Cedrus libani* ssp. *brevifolia*

**(syn. *C. brevifolia*)**

### Pinaceae

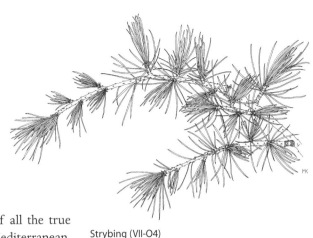

Cyprus cedar has the most restricted natural distribution of all the true cedars; it occurs only on the island of Cyprus in the eastern Mediterranean, in a national park where it is now protected. It is a medium-sized tree to about 40 feet, usually much branched, sometimes sparsely branched. **Leaves** are bluish green, about ¼ to ½ inch long, with twenty to thirty on the short shoots. These short leaves distinguish the species from other cedars. Its **cones** are 3 to 4¼ inches long with a depression at the tip.

Cyprus cedar is the least commonly planted of the true cedars. Only one tree of this species exists in Golden Gate Park, planted in 1960 on Strybing's Main Lawn.

Strybing (VII-O4)
Evergreen/Slow growth/40'
(Conifer) Green cones to 3" long, that disintegrate on the tree
Full sun/Needs no watering once established
Sunset Zone 5-24

# 39

### Cedar of Lebanon

## *Cedrus libani* ssp. *libani*
### Pinaceae

Cedar of Lebanon is a large tree to 120 feet tall with a trunk diameter of 4 to 8 feet. The numerous uppermost branches, densely arranged and spreading more or less horizontally, eventually give it the characteristic broad, somewhat flattened crown. The young branchlets generally have minute hairs but sometimes are without hairs. The **leaves** on the short shoots are one to twenty in a whorl and ½ to 1½ inches long. The **cones** are 3 to 5 inches long and 1½ inches wide.

Cedar of Lebanon was known in biblical times and even earlier, when Lebanon and the surrounding region had extensive cedar forests. These forests in Lebanon and the Taurus Mountains of western Turkey are now much reduced in size, but are protected.

Michael Zohary (1982), of Jerusalem, mentions negotiations between King Solomon and Hiram, King of Tyre, a seaport in the ancient Mediterranean, about obtaining the wood of cedar of Lebanon for building King Solomon's temples. Both the First and Second Temples of Jerusalem were built of cedar. According to Zohary (1982), the word *erez*, mentioned seventy times in the Bible, has been translated as cedar. Most of these translations

Japanese Tea Garden (V-N2); Strybing (VII-O4)
Evergreen/Slow growth/120'
(Conifer) Green cones, 2"-3" wide x 2 1/2"-5" long, that disintegrate on the tree
Full sun/Needs no watering once established
Sunset Zone 2-24

refer to trees of the genus *Cedrus*. The Phoenicians also used wood of this cedar to build ships that sailed the Mediterranean.

Elwes and Henry (1908) mention that John Evelyn, prominent in many fields of natural history in seventeenth-century England, probably introduced the tree to England. Evelyn (1769), in a book on practical arboriculture, says that he received seed from Lebanon, but he gave no date. Since its introduction, this cedar has been much cultivated in England, where it has added greatly to the charm of the English landscape.

Cedar of Lebanon has been in Golden Gate Park since 1893. It can now be seen in the Japanese Tea Garden, as a small carefully shaped dwarf tree in the Sunken Garden near the small bridge. A young tree has recently been added to the collection of *Cedrus* on Strybing's Main Lawn. It is occasionally planted elsewhere on the West Coast; a number of trees can be seen in Portland, Oregon, especially at Hoyt Arboretum.

## Coachwood and Christmas bush
# *Ceratopetalum*
## Cunoniaceae

*Ceratopetalum* is a genus of five species of handsome trees and shrubs endemic to moist forests in Australia and New Guinea. It belongs to the cunonia family, which is little known in California. The generic name comes from the Greek words for horned and petal, and alludes to the flowers of an Australian species with petals resembling a stag's horns. The tiny **flowers** are arranged in much-branched clusters, lack petals, and are not showy. The calyx, however, swells as the **fruit** develops and becomes colorful when ripe—much showier than the flowers. Both species discussed have suffered a decline in popularity as landscape subjects in California; they were mentioned in Bailey's *Hortus Third* (1976) and in his much earlier *Standard Cyclopedia of Horticulture* (1914), but are not listed in present-day sources of landscape trees in California.

# 40

## Coachwood
# *Ceratopetalum apetalum*
## Cunoniaceae

Coachwood is found in the rain forests of New South Wales, the Blue Mountains north and south of Sydney, and north into southern Queensland; it is primarily a tree of moist gullies. The species name, *apetalum,* refers to its lack of petals. The one specimen of coachwood in Strybing Arboretum is among the oldest trees in the Eastern Australia Collection; it is more than 40 feet tall with a branched trunk and smooth

Strybing (VI-N3)
Evergreen/Slow growth/40'
Small white flowers (early summer) /Reddish sepals hold maturing fruit
Full sun to part shade/Water regularly
Sunset Zone 16-24
Color plate

gray brown **bark.** Its **leaves** are 3 to 6 inches long, evergreen, opposite, leathery, and broadly lanceolate, with scattered teeth along the margins. The early summer **flowers** are small and not showy but numerous, arranged in branched clusters in the leaf axils. The persistent sepals, however, enlarge, turn red or rose, and become conspicuous and petal-like as the fruit matures. The ripe **fruit** is a hard nut and does not open to release its single seed.

The fragrant, pinkish wood of coachwood was used in Australia for building horse-drawn carriages, from which came the common name. During World War II it was used for rifle fittings and in the construction of the Mosquito fighter-bomber airplane.

# 41

### New South Wales Christmas bush
# *Ceratopetalum gummiferum*
## Cunoniaceae

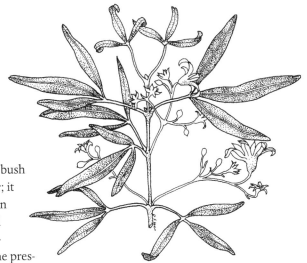

In Australia, this species of *Ceratopetalum* is called Christmas bush because its fruits mature and are particularly colorful in December; it occurs only in New South Wales, where it is widespread in open forests, in gullies, and sometimes on old sand dunes. It is a small tree or large shrub, generally about 15 to 30 feet tall. The arboretum's original Christmas bush died in 1964, and was replaced by the present plant, now a large shrub over 8 feet tall near the main walk west of the Friend Gate. The second part of its scientific name, *gummiferum*, alludes to the gummy, ruby red substance exuded when a branch is cut or wounded. The **leaves** of Christmas bush are divided into three leaflets, each 1 to 3 inches long. The spring **flowers** have white petals about as long as the sepals. The sepals enlarge and become showy and reddish as the **fruit** matures.

Strybing (VI-N3)
Evergreen/Slow growth/15'-30'
Small white flowers (spring) /Reddish sepals
    hold maturing fruit
Full sun to part shade/Water regularly
Sunset Zone 16-24

*The wonder is that we can see these trees and not wonder more.*

RALPH WALDO EMERSON

False cypress
# *Chamaecyparis*
Cupressaceae

*Chamaecyparis* is a small genus of conifers with about six species. It occurs on the Atlantic and Pacific coasts of North America, as well as in Japan and Taiwan. Like *Cupressus* and *Thuja,* other members of the cypress family, leaves of seedlings and young plants of false cypress are different from those of adult plants. Juvenile **leaves** are needle- or awl-shaped, while adult leaves are scalelike, generally about ⅓ inch long and spreading, forming flattened, fan-shaped sprays of branchlets. **Cones** usually occur at the ends of the upper branchlets; they are small, round, and composed of six to twelve peltate scales. Each cone scale usually has two (rarely five) winged **seeds.**

# 42

Lawson cypress, Port Orford cedar
# *Chamaecyparis lawsoniana*
Cupressaceae

Lawson cypress, or Port Orford cedar, is native to the West Coast of North America, its range extending from Coos Bay, Oregon, south along the coast into northwestern California. It is also found on the slopes of the Siskiyou Mountains on the California-Oregon border and on the southern slopes of Mt Shasta in Northern California.

Lawson cypress is a forest tree 50 to 75 feet tall (often much taller in the wild) with horizontal or pendulous branches forming a narrow pyramidal crown. The acute scalelike adult **leaves** are usually from ⅛ to nearly ¼ inch long, with glands and indistinct whitish markings on the underside. The round **cones** are about ⅓ inch in diameter.

This species was introduced into cultivation in the British Isles in 1854 when seeds were sent from California by William Murray to Scotland's Charles Lawson, for whom the tree was named; its other common name alludes to a town on the coast of Oregon where the tree is particularly common. It was offered for sale in 1854–1859 in San Francisco by Golden Gate Nursery. It is commonly grown today, particularly in Europe where numerous cultivars have been named and described, including many that are dwarf in stature and others with distinctly colored foliage. In cultivation, some cultivars lose their distinctive characters with age and cannot always by identified and named. Several mature specimens can be seen in Golden Gate Park near the southwest corner of the Conservatory; in Strybing Arboretum, specimen trees are immediately west of the parking lot behind the County Fair Building, and near the Dwarf Conifer pond. It is frequently grown in parks and public gardens from San Francisco north to Vancouver.

Near SW corner of conservatory (IV-Q2);
    Strybing (VII-O4)
Evergreen/Fast growth/50'-75'
(Conifer) Roundish, reddish brown cones, 1/3"
    across, with shieldlike scales
Full sun/Water occasionally
Sunset Zone 4-6, 15-17

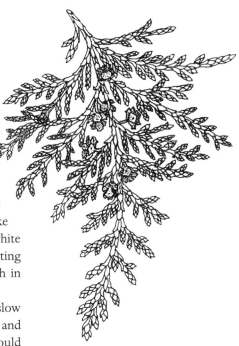

## 43

Hinoki cypress
### *Chamaecyparis obtusa*
Cupressaceae

Hinoki, or hinoki cypress, is native to Japan where it occurs on all the main islands and on Taiwan. As a cultivated tree, it is generally 10 to 30 feet tall, but in Japan, it may reach 100 feet or more. The scalelike **leaves** are not glandular like the previous species but have distinct white lines on the lower surface; the obtuse leaves are arranged in alternating pairs of differing lengths. The round solitary **cones** are about ⅓ inch in diameter with eight to twelve peltate scales.

Hinoki has numerous named cultivars, most of them dwarf or slow growing. In Japan it has a long history of cultivation, both for its beauty and its useful timber. In 1861, it was introduced into England by John Gould Veitch. Today, it is one of the most valuable ornamental trees of Japanese origin. Hinoki can be seen in several locations in Strybing Arboretum, including the beds around the Dwarf Conifer pond and in the Moon-viewing Garden; a number of specimens are prominent in the Japanese Tea Garden as well. It is a common tree of public gardens throughout California and the Northwest.

Japanese Tea Garden (V-N2); Strybing (VII-N4)
Evergreen/Slow growth/10'-30'
(Conifer) Roundish, brown cones to 1/3" across
Full sun/Water regularly
Sunset Zone 4-6, 15-17
Color plate

## 44

Hand-flower tree
### *Chiranthodendron pentadactylon*
Sterculiaceae

A tree of Mexico and Guatemala, *Chiranthodendron pentadactylon* is best known for its unusual flowers. Their shape suggests diminutive hands with long, outstretched, clawlike fingers. Various common names allude to the flower: in Spanish, *arbol de las manitas, flor de manita,* or *mano de mico;* in Nahuatl, *macapal-xochital* and *mapasúchil;* and in English, hand-flower tree, tree of the little hands, monkey's hand, and devil's hand. The scientific name of the tree, taken from the Greek, also alludes to the shape of the flowers. The genus has only a single species and is sometimes placed in the bombax family (Bombacaeae).

The **flower** lacks separate petals; instead it has a floral cup combining sepals and petals. The cup, about 1½ to 2 inches long, dull red and covered with brown hairs on the outside, is distinctly five-lobed and has

Strybing (VI-M4 & VII-N4)
11th Ave near Irving
Evergreen/Moderate growth/20'-100'
Dull red, 1"-2" long flower, with protruding bright
    red stamens, like a five-fingered hand (May-
    Oct) /Oblong woody capsule, 3"-4" long
Full sun/Water occasionally
Sunset Zone 17-24
Color plate

a nectar-containing pouch at the base of each lobe. Five stamens are united at their base to form a tube, and from it extend five finger-like anthers. Each anther opens along its lower side to release the pollen; the narrow anther tips eventually curl like claws. The style, which projects from the staminal tube, is shorter than the anthers and appears as a thumblike sixth finger. The "hand," with its slender wrist and clawlike fingers, is bright red and stands out against the dull red of the floral cup. The flowers, generally appearing throughout the summer, are thought to be pollinated by nectar-feeding bats. The **fruit** is an oblong, woody, deeply five-lobed capsule, 3 to 4 inches long, and covered with soft, brown hairs. It eventually opens to release numerous black **seeds.** Evergreen **leaves** are ovate to round in outline, 6 to 10 inches long, and generally five-lobed, with five prominent veins from the base, brown and hairy beneath, pale green and almost glabrous above; their petioles are generally shorter than the leaf blades.

The hand-flower tree occurs in the Mexican states of Oaxaca, Morelos, and Chiapas and in adjacent Guatemala; it grows on wet slopes and ridges in forest belts extending up to 9,000 feet. In these areas, trees may be 35 to 90 feet tall, with trunks 3 to 6 feet in diameter. Trees in cultivation in California are not so tall, generally only 20 to 30 feet.

Dr Francesco Franceschi is credited with introducing the hand-flower tree to California in 1908 in Santa Barbara, where several trees are still growing. Other hand-flower trees are at the UC Davis Arboretum, the UC Botanical Garden (Berkeley), and in Santa Monica, San Diego, and the Los Angeles area. Strybing Arboretum has several trees of these trees. The oldest, located at the edge of the Eric Walther Succulent Garden, was grown from seed brought from Mexico by Mr Walther about 1935. This broad-spreading tree, now about 30 feet tall, first flowered in 1953. It has continued to flower every year throughout the summer. Another tree, planted in the mid-1980s in the New World Cloud Forest collection, has developed a strongly upright habit, typical of forest-growing specimens in the Mexican highlands and, though younger, exceeds the older tree in height.

# A cherished tree

The hand-flower tree was known to the Aztecs, who venerated it for its flowers, which they made into amulets, and for its medicinal uses. According to the Badianus Manuscript, an Aztec herbal of 1552, "juice of the bark and of the leaves [was] pressed out and used with other ingredients in a lotion to relieve pain." The Aztec rulers created extensive gardens, which so impressed the Spanish conquerors that their chroniclers included accounts of them. Montezuma II (1466–1520) had several gardens and of these, the one considered to be the finest had been inherited from his predecessor, Montezuma the Elder. This garden, located at Oaxtepec (near Cuernavaca in Morelos), contained many plants brought from other parts of Mexico. Among those mentioned for their medicinal uses in the writings of Dr Francisco Hernandez was the hand-flower tree. Hernandez was a Spanish physician commissioned by Philip II, King of Spain, to survey and report on the natural resources and political history of Mexico. He arrived in Mexico in 1570 and spent several years there. During this time, he traveled to various parts of the country and visited the important gardens. From the garden at Oaxtepec, he learned much about Mexican plants and their uses.

In 1786, more than two centuries after the extended visit of Hernandez to Mexico, Spain's King Charles

III issued a royal order to establish in Mexico a "botanical garden and a scientific expedition to make drawings, collect the natural products, and illustrate and complete the work of Dr Don Francisco Hernandez." The scientific expedition, directed by Martin de Sessé y Lacasta, was underway in August 1787. In May of the following year, the study of botany was inaugurated as part of the Royal and Pontifical University of Mexico. Among the students of botany at the university was Joseph Dionisio Larreategui, who graduated in 1794 and later gave *Chiranthodendron pentadactylon* its first scientific name in a paper published in 1805 in Paris.

In December 1787, Sessé and his expedition went to Toluca to see the renowned hand-flower tree that was reputed to have been planted 500 years before by a king of Toluca. The inhabitants of Toluca believed the tree to be the only one of its kind and regarded it with superstitious awe. They would not, however, propagate it for fear of offending the gods. Sessé and his party made cuttings from it and from these, a tree was grown in Mexico City. This tree lived until 1848, and from it, another tree was propagated that lived until 1935. It was reported in the 1980s that a third-generation tree, which owed its origin to the Toluca tree, was still growing in Mexico City. A later Sessé exploration found hand-flower trees in Guatemala. The legend that the tree in Toluca was the only one of its kind was proved wrong.

After Sessé and his expedition, the tree at Toluca was observed by two other Europeans, Alexander von Humboldt and Aimé Bonpland. They came to Mexico early in 1803 and remained for nearly a year during the five years of their expedition to the New World. They collected specimens and seeds from the hand-flower tree and, after their return to Europe, published an early account of the tree under the name *Cheirostemon platanoides*.

# 45

## Naranjillo
# *Citronella mucronata*

### Icacinaceae

Trees of *Citronella mucronata* are evergreen, to about 25 feet tall. The **leaves** are stiff, thick and leathery, ovate, and 1½ to 3 inches long, with entire margins on mature branches while being coarsely spiny (like those of English holly) on young branches. Small circular openings, or pore cavities, can be found on the undersides of the leaves; these are often inhabited by tiny insects or mites. The small greenish white fragrant **flowers** occur in densely crowded, spikelike clusters, 1 to 2 inches long, at the tips of the branches.

*Citronella mucronata* occurs only in Chile. It is found along the central coast from Coquimbo south to Osorno and in the Andes at elevations to about 3,600 feet in shaded places, mostly along the slopes of ravines and gorges where it mingles with other forest trees. It was first collected near Concepción in 1782 or 1783 by the Spanish pharmacist-botanists Hipolito Ruiz and José Pavon, who had been sent by the scientifically minded King Charles III of Spain to study the vegetation of the vice-kingdom of Peru (now Peru and Chile). The tree is not well enough known to have an English name, but one of its Spanish names in Chile is *naranjillo*. The **fruit,** which is oval, semi-fleshy, and nearly ½ inch long, certainly does not resemble an orange. However, Ruiz and Pavon said that the tree looked like a *citronnier*. Probably the Spanish name *naranjilla* and the reported similarity to a citrus tree suggested the botanical name of *Citronella*.

Strybing (VI-N3)
Evergreen/Slow growth/25'
Inconspicuous, fragrant, greenish white
    flowers in spiky clusters, 1"-2" long, at
    tips of branches /Semi-fleshy, oval fruit,
    1/2" long
Part shade/Water regularly
Sunset Zone 17-24

*Citronella mucronata* is not new to cultivation. It was introduced into England about 1840 in a garden in Abbotsbury, Dorset, where the species is still found. Another *naranjilla* in the British Isles is in the National Botanic Garden, Glasnevin, Ireland. The specimen in Strybing's South American Section was probably planted by Eric Walther in the late 1930s after the arboretum was established.

This plant was listed in the 1924 report of the park commissioners as *Villaresia mucronata,* a name now considered a synonym of *Citronella mucronata.* The icacina family does not occur in North America, being native mostly to the Southern Hemisphere. Its members, with their inconspicuous flowers and fruits, are not ornamental, and their economic uses are few, even in South America. So far as is known, the plant in Strybing represents the only species introduced into the United States, and it may well be the only plant of this species in the country.

In Chile, *Citronella mucronata* has been cultivated as a park or shade tree, and the wood has been used for fuel and paper pulp. A closely related South American species, *C. gongonha,* has been used as a substitute for *Ilex paraguariensis* in making maté. The leaves of *C. gongonha,* however, contain only small amounts of the essential oil that gives maté its distinctive flavor, and it is considered an inferior substitute.

# 46

Cabbage tree

# *Cordyline australis*
Agavaceae

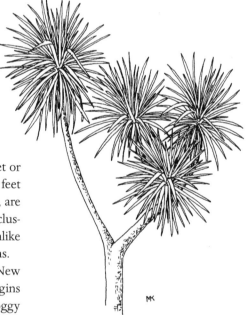

The trunk of cabbage tree can be branched or unbranched and is 25 feet or taller, with terminal clusters of strap-shaped **leaves,** each as much as 3 feet long. The numerous small, fragrant, white **flowers,** produced in spring, are borne in large showy panicles emerging from the centers of the leaf clusters; the **fruits** are small berries ripening later in the year. Although palmlike in appearance, this plant is not a palm but is related to agaves and yuccas.

Cabbage tree is native on both North and South islands of New Zealand. It grows from coastal lowlands to the mountains, on the margins of forests, in open places, along riverbanks, and near swampy or boggy areas. Its palmlike appearance gives a distinctive character to the landscape.

The common name of cabbage tree was given by early European settlers who used the youngest inner leaves and the adjacent stem as a raw or cooked vegetable. The earlier Maori name was *ti-kouka,* ti being an overall name used by the native peoples of the Pacific islands for the several species of *Cordyline* that they knew and utilized. The botanical name *Cordyline* is from the Greek for club and alludes to the shape of the roots; *australis* is from the Latin word for southern.

Along Stow Lake Dr (III-M2 & M3); Strybing
(VII-N3)
Valencia at Mission; 3428 22nd St
Evergreen/Slow growth/25' or more
Small, fragrant, white flowers in showy 3'
panicles (May) /White, red or purple
berries
Full sun/Water occasionally
Sunset Zone 5, 8-11, 14-24

On his first voyage (1768–1771), Captain James Cook circumnavigated New Zealand. Accompanying Cook on this voyage were the young Joseph Banks and Daniel Solander. Among their important collections of New Zealand plants was the cabbage tree. Captain Cook also visited New Zealand on his second voyage (1772–1775), accompanied by three naturalist-botanists: Johann Reinhold Forster, his son Georg, and Anders Sparmann. The younger Forster gave cabbage tree its botanical name in 1786.

The Maoris used *Cordyline australis,* as well as the other species in the genus, as a source of fiber for thatching, cordage, baskets, bird snares, rain capes, and sandals. The medicinal uses of the plant include the application of leaf scrapings as an ointment to treat skin lesions, and infusions of the leaves as a treatment for dysentery, diarrhea, and cuts. Early European settlers found the leaf fibers useful for twine and cordage. They also found that the leaves could be used for making paper, and material was sent to England as early as the 1860s to explore the possibility of its commercial use. An unusual Maori use of a single exceptionally large specimen of a cabbage tree was reported by William Colenso, an early New Zealand botanist. Within the trunk of this living tree, which had a circumference of twenty feet at the base, a room was constructed for the storage of baskets and tools.

The major present-day use of cabbage tree is as an ornamental for its palmlike habit. It was introduced into England in the 1820s and, by the late 1800s, was grown in such mild climate areas as Cornwall in the south and the west coast of Scotland. It was probably introduced into California in the early 1900s although no dates are available. It is first recorded in Golden Gate Park in the 1924 *Annual Report of the Park Commissioners.* A number of cabbage trees may be seen in the park around Stow Lake and in Strybing's New Zealand collection. This tree can also be seen in many neighborhoods in San Francisco, the Bay Area, and throughout milder regions of California.

# 47

New Zealand laurel
## *Corynocarpus laevigatus*
Corynocarpaceae

New Zealand laurel occurs on both North and South islands of New Zealand, mostly along the coast. The two naturalist-botanists, Joseph Banks and Daniel Solander, accompanying Captain James Cook on his first voyage, were, in 1769, the first Europeans to see this tree. New Zealand laurel is a handsome evergreen tree about 20 to 30 feet tall as seen in California. In New Zealand, however, trees are reported to reach 50 feet or more, with trunks from 1½ to 2½ feet in diameter. The glossy **leaves,** dark green above and paler beneath, are usually 3 to 6 inches long and somewhat laurel-like in shape, hence the common name. The small, greenish, inconspicuous

W side of Kezar Dr, near Kennedy Dr (IV-S2);
    Strybing (VI-N3)
9th Ave between Lincoln and Irving
Evergreen/Slow growth/20'-30'
Inconspicuous greenish flowers (spring) /Showy,
    poisonous fruits resembling orange olives or
    small plums
Full sun to part shade/Water regularly
Sunset Zone 16, 17, 23, 24
Suitable as a street tree

**flowers** occur in narrowly erect clusters, 2 to 4 inches long. The **fruits,** in contrast to the flowers, are showy. They somewhat resemble olives or small plums, and are 1 to 1½ inches long. The name of the genus, derived from two Greek words meaning club and fruit, alludes vaguely to the shape of the fruit. The large **seed** is surrounded by a thin, orange-colored fleshy layer and enclosed by a tough, netlike fibrous cover.

Long before the Europeans arrived in New Zealand, the Maoris used the starchy seeds as an important food staple. The raw seeds, however, are bitter, unpalatable, and contain a toxic compound, karakin, that causes convulsions, permanent rigidity of the muscles, and often death. The Maoris removed the toxin and made the seeds palatable by baking or boiling. When properly prepared, seeds could be stored for future use. The Maoris called the tree *karaka,* and cultivated it in small groves in coastal areas. They used the trunks of large trees for canoes.

New Zealand laurel has been in Golden Gate Park since at least 1889 when it was listed in the *Annual Report of the Park Commissioners.* Trees may be seen in Strybing's New Zealand collection. At the eastern end of the park on Kezar Drive, near Kennedy Drive, is a small group of trees with a few young ones that may be seedlings. Elsewhere in California, New Zealand laurels are found in Santa Barbara, Santa Monica, and The Arboretum of LA County.

# 48

Mexican Hawthorn

## *Crataegus pubescens*
Rosaceae

Mexican hawthorn is a deciduous tree to 30 feet or, rarely, a shrub, generally with a broad crown and branches with or without thorns. **Leaves** are ovate, rounded to wedge-shaped at the base, pointed at the tip, irregularly toothed, and 2 to 4 inches long, with a short leaf stalk. **Flowers** with four white petals, about ½ inch across, occur in terminal clusters 2 to 3 inches across; stamens number fifteen to twenty. Small, applelike **fruits** are ½ to ¾ inch in diameter, yellow, yellow orange, or red, and release the fragrance of grapes when fully ripe.

Mexican hawthorn is widespread in Mexico from the central tableland south to Chiapas, but it has been so long cultivated for its edible fruits that it is not always possible to determine whether a particular tree is wild or domesticated. This hawthorn has been reported in Guatemala too, but the plants may have been introduced from Mexico and the existence there of native trees is questionable. Fruits of Mexican hawthorn, hard before maturity, become soft when ripe. They may be eaten raw but generally are cooked with sugar or honey and used for preserves or jelly.

Strybing (VI-M4)
Deciduous/Slow growth/30'
Masses of white flowers in terminal clusters, 2"-3"
    across (spring) /Fragrant yellow to red edible
    fruits, to 3/4" diameter
Full sun/Water infrequently
Sunset Zone 1-12, 14-17

Several Europeans who came to Mexico during the sixteenth, seventeenth, and early eighteenth centuries wrote of the Mexican hawthorn in accounts of their explorations. In the 1570s, Dr Francisco Hernandez, recorded the Mexican hawthorn under the names *texocotl* and *pomum saxeum* (rock apple). He observed that the fruits were widely used as a conserve. In 1788, Vicente Cervantes arrived in Mexico from Spain to teach at the ill-fated Royal Botanical Garden in Mexico City. He referred to the hawthorn as *tejocotl* and reported that the fruits and seeds were astringent and a tonic. Sessé and Mociño, who explored large areas of Mexico between 1795 and 1804, wrote of *texocotl* in the vicinity of Mexico City and of the use of the fruits. Their beautiful and accurate drawings were later turned over to the Swiss botanist De Candolle, who used them in 1825 as the basis for his species *Crataegus mexicana,* a name by which the plant has also been known.

Throughout its wide range in Mexico, plants of Mexican hawthorn show much variation. Early European botanists, recognizing minor variants, named new species from them. These names are now listed as synonyms of *Crataegus pubescens.* The best known are *C. mexicana* and *C. stipulacea.*

Mexican hawthorn was introduced into England in the 1820s. The first mention of its cultivation may have been in 1826, when it was listed by nurseryman Conrad Loddiges in his *Catalogue of Plants;* he called it *Crataegus stipulacea.* A second introduction was listed and illustrated in Sweet's *British Flower Garden* in 1835. Seed from this collection was received by Aylmer Lambert in 1829; the plant flowered in 1834.

Mexican hawthorn has been in California at least since 1869, according to Riedel (1957). It was offered by Franceschi in 1900; he introduced it again later as *Crataegus guatemalensis* and *C. stipulacea.* Popenoe (1920) wrote that "the tree has done well in southern California."

San Francisco's old Laurel Hill Cemetery, which no longer exists, had a Mexican hawthorn reported to have been planted by Mexicans who had brought it from their native land. A fine old tree in Strybing Arboretum predates the arboretum. It is in the Eric Walther Succulent Garden, perhaps acquired by Walther from Laurel Hill Cemetery. This hawthorn, among the oldest trees in the arboretum, should be considered one of the park's heritage trees and every effort should be made to preserve it.

# The Hawthorns

Hawthorns belong to *Crataegus,* a large genus of the Northern Hemisphere, and are found in the eastern United States, Mexico, Europe, and Asia. In the eastern United States as many as 1,500 species were described during the early years of the twentieth century. More recently, that number has been greatly reduced as the reproductive biology of the genus has become better understood. Only three species are found naturally in the western United States: Columbia hawthorn (*C. columbiana*), black hawthorn (*C. douglasii*), and *C. suksdorfii.*

Hawthorns are cultivated for their shapely habit, their attractive masses of white flowers in spring or early summer, and their red fruits in fall. Many species and cultivars are grown in gardens in the eastern United States and Europe, but, according to Sunset Western Garden Book, only about a dozen are grown in the West. Golden Gate Park has several species in addition to Mexican hawthorn (*Crataegus pubescens*): cockspur hawthorn (*C. crus-galli*), Washington thorn (*C. phaenopyrum*), black hawthorn (*C. douglasii*), and Lavalle hawthorn (*C. x lavallei*).

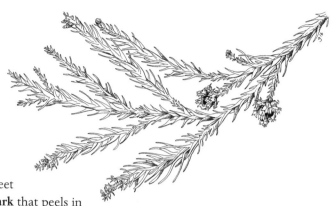

## 49

Japanese redwood
# *Cryptomeria japonica*
Taxodiaceae

Japanese redwood, generally a pyramidal tree 50 to 80 feet tall (to 180 feet in the wild), has thin, reddish brown **bark** that peels in narrow strips. **Leaves,** spirally arranged, are needlelike, curved more or less inward toward the tip, decurrent at the base, keeled on both upper and lower surfaces, and ¼ to ½ inch long. They remain on the tree for several years, often turning reddish brown in late fall. **Cones** are brown, rounded, solitary, ½ to ¾ inch long, composed of twenty to thirty loosely arranged bracts that remain on the tree for months after shedding their seeds.

On lawn S of conservatory (IV-Q2);Japanese
   Tea Garden(V-N2); Strybing (VII-O4)
8th Ave at Moraga
Evergreen/Moderate growth/50'-80'
(Conifer) Brown, rounded cones of loosely
   arranged bracts, 1/2"-3/4" long
Full sun/Water occasionally
Sunset Zone 4-9, 14-24

The Japanese redwood is widely cultivated in Japan, Europe, and the United States. In cultivation it has produced many variants, and over 300 cultivars have been described, mostly in Japan and Europe. These are based on habit and height of the tree, and on size, shape, and color of the leaves, including a number that are variegated. The best known and most easily recognized cultivar is 'Elegans', in which the juvenile leaves are retained permanently. Its narrowly linear, flexible, irregularly spreading leaves are ½ to 1 inch long, soft to the touch, and change from green in spring and summer to reddish brown in autumn and winter.

*Cryptomeria japonica* was introduced to California by William C Walker in 1859. It has been in Golden Gate Park at least since the 1890s. RD Fox of San Jose introduced 'Elegans' in 1884. Today, several fine old trees of this cultivar are in the Japanese Tea Garden adjacent to the pagoda. Other trees are near the tunnel entrance south of the conservatory. The species is in Strybing Arboretum's Asian sections, one opposite the Moon-viewing Garden and the other east of the Dwarf Conifer Garden. Elsewhere in California, cryptomerias are found on the grounds of the state capitol, the UC Berkeley campus, and in Santa Monica and Santa Barbara. Trees are also found in Portland and Seattle and in Vancouver, British Columbia.

# From Japan to the World

The first European to observe the Japanese redwood was the German-born physician and naturalist Engelbert Kaempfer, who spent two years (1690–1692) in Japan as a medical officer in the employ of the Dutch East India Company. At that time, Japan was closed to the outside world, with the exception of a trading post operated by the Dutch on the artificial island of Deshima in Nagasaki Bay. After returning to Europe, Kaempfer published his observations on Japanese customs and plants, providing Linnaeus with the only contemporary source of information about Japanese plants. Kaempfer briefly described the Japanese redwood under its Japanese name of *sugi*, a name referring to the timber cut from the trees and used for the construction of boats and temples.

Kaempfer was followed by two other physician-naturalists. Carl Thunberg, Swedish-born and a student of Linnaeus, visited Deshima from 1775 to 1776.

German-born Philipp Franz von Siebold lived on Deshima from 1823 to 1829. Although virtual prisoners on the island, both made substantial contributions to Japanese botany. Thunberg collected many plants on Deshima, as well as on the Nagasaki mainland and on a journey to Tokyo, then called Edo, to pay homage to the shogun. Thunberg made some of his collections by sorting through the hay for livestock kept on the island. After returning to Europe, he published the first flora of Japan by a European. Included was a description of the Japanese redwood under the name of *Cupressus japonica*. In 1841, this tree was determined to represent a distinct genus with a single species, *Cryptomeria japonica*. The generic name comes from two Greek words meaning to hide and a separate part; its meaning is obscure.

It was von Siebold who recognized the horticultural potential of cryptomeria. During his stay on Deshima, he introduced it to the botanical garden in Buitenzorg (now Bogor) on the island of Java, where the Dutch had a settlement. In 1853, William Lobb obtained seeds from von Siebold's introduction and sent them to the Veitch Nursery in England.

Cryptomeria had been introduced to England from collections make in its native range in China. In 1842, seeds were sent to Kew from the Zhoushan Islands off the east coast of Chekiang (now Zhejiang), and in 1844, Robert Fortune sent seeds from Shanghai to the Horticultural Society of London. In 1855, then in the employ of the United States government, Fortune introduced cryptomeria to this country through the US Patent Office, and plants were grown in the Government Experimental and Propagating Garden in Washington, DC.

EH Wilson saw cryptomeria in 1914 on Yakushima, a small island in southern Japan, south of Kyushu. In dense forests between 750 and 3,800 feet elevation, it was often the dominant tree. Wilson also saw cryptomeria at other locations, on the islands of Shikoku and Honshu, but because of its long history in cultivation, it was difficult to determine whether the trees had been planted or grew naturally. Wilson described cryptomeria as the "noblest of Japanese conifers" and the "most useful and popular tree in Japan…planted there from time immemorial." Many famous places in Japan, he observed, "owe their charm to the stately avenues and groves of this impressive tree." In 1906, Augustine Henry described the well-known avenue at Nikko, where the largest and most impressive cryptomeria was 145 feet tall; others were 110 to 120 feet tall with trunk diameters of 12 to 20 feet.

# 50

## Leyland cypress
# x *Cupressocyparis leylandii*
## Cupressaceae

Leyland cypress is a hybrid species generally intermediate between its parents, Nootka cypress *(Chamaecyparis nootkatensis)* and Monterey cypress *(Cupressus macrocarpa)*. Trees are often pyramidal, reaching heights in excess of 100 feet, with scalelike **leaves** resembling those of Nootka cypress. Gray green leafy branches, sometimes variegated, are generally dense except toward the top of the tree. Some trees have the somewhat flat-pinnate branches of Nootka cypress, while others tend to be angular-pinnate as are those of Monterey cypress. **Cones** are about ½ to ¾ inch in diameter, and cone scales are generally about eight in number with about five seeds on each scale. **Seeds** are about ⅓ inch wide with small projections.

Strybing (VII-O3)
Evergreen/Fast growth/60'-70'
(Conifer) Small, spherical, female cones, 1/2"-3/4" in diameter
Full sun/Water occasionally
Sunset Zone 3-24

Leyland cypress is an important and popular conifer in England, often planted for reforestation. It is one of the fastest growing conifers and is vigorous and hardy. More than twenty cultivars are listed, mostly in the British Isles. Unfortunately, the rapid growth of these trees usually results in weak wood; as trees mature, they often lose the attractive habit exhibited in their youth.

Golden Gate Park has a small group of Leyland cypresses on Strybing's Main Lawn. One received in 1965 from Pacific Nurseries in Colma, California, was planted that year by the Assistant Secretary of the Interior under Secretary Udall. Elsewhere on the Pacific Coast, Leyland cypresses are found in Santa Barbara and Los Angeles, in Portland and Seattle, and in Vancouver, British Columbia. They are commonly planted by developers of new subdivisions, particularly in coastal regions, because of their rapid growth; unfortunately, the trees often age poorly and require removal after a decade or two. They do tolerate shearing and are often used as tall, formal hedges.

# Naming a Hybrid

This bigeneric hybrid, *Leyland cypress*, originated from a cross between Nootka cypress (*Chamaecyparis nootkatensis*) and Monterey cypress (*Cupressus macrocarpa*). These two trees from western North America had long been cultivated in Britain, where the hybrid first occurred at Leighton Hall, near Welshpool, in the 1880s. Seedlings from it were grown at Haggerston Castle, Northumberland, the estate of CJ Leyland, for whom the tree is named. About 1911, the same cross occurred again, and from it, several trees were produced. In 1925, these puzzling hybrid trees came to the attention of two well-known English botanists, William Dallimore and BD Jackson, who published a description of the hybrid under the name *Cupressus* x *leylandii* and established its origin and parentage. Although *Chamaecyparis* was recognized as a genus separate from *Cupressus*, it was not until 1938 that the bigeneric

hybrid genus x *Cupressocyparis* was proposed. This name was established to include any hybrid between the genera *Chamaecyparis* and *Cupressus*. The earlier name *Cupressus* x *leylandii* was then transferred, and the hybrid became known as x *Cupressocyparis leylandii*. The common name of Leyland cypress was also established.

More recently, some botanists have recognized the close relationship between *Chamaecyparis nootkatensis* and the genus *Cupressus*. In *The Jepson Manual: Higher Plants of California* (1993), this species was transferred to *Cupressus* as *Cupressus nootkatensis*. If that change is accepted, x *Cupressocyparis leylandii* no longer represents a bigeneric hybrid but a hybrid between two species of *Cupressus*, and the original name, *Cupressus* x *leylandii*, given in 1926, could again be used for Leyland cypress. We have chosen, however, to retain the bigeneric hybrid status of this tree.

*"I rank arboriculture as one of the fine arts. I have studied it in all its various schools—the palms of Africa, the cypresses of Mexico, the banyans and peepals of India, the birches of Sweden, the elms of New England. In my mind there is a gallery of masterpieces, which I should not be afraid to place beside those of the Vatican or the Louvre."*

BAYARD TAYLOR, *At Home and Abroad*

## Cupressus
# *The Cypresses*
### Cupressaceae

The genus *Cupressus* occurs in North and Central America, the Mediterranean region of Europe, and from the Himalayas east to Japan. It includes approximately twenty species, all evergreen, cone-bearing trees with tiny scalelike **leaves** in pairs, so closely held to the twigs that the wood is not visible; the effect of such tightly held leaves is of a braided cord. The upper side of the leaves usually display a glandular pit that sometimes exudes a white resinous dot. Twigs will branch in more than one plane, unlike members of the genera *Chamaecyparis* and *Thuja,* also in the cypress family. **Cones** of cypresses are woody, globose or ovoid, with peltate scales. The **bark** on the trunks is often flaky or exfoliating in slender strips.

The cypresses are, on the whole, handsome trees, densely foliaged, and popular for their relatively fast growth under good conditions. A few have been important for their lumber. The greatest number of species is found from California through Mexico to Guatemala.

# 51

## Guadalupe cypress
# *Cupressus guadalupensis*
### Cupressaceae

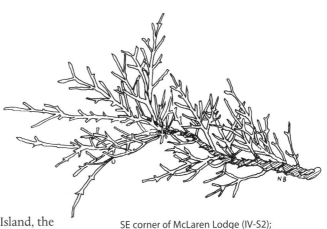

SE corner of McLaren Lodge (IV-S2);
    Strybing (VII-N4)
Evergreen/Slow growth/50'
(Conifer) Nearly round, brown cone, 1" in
    diameter
Full sun/Water infrequently
Sunset Zone 17-24
Color plate

Guadalupe cypress is a rare tree, endemic to Guadalupe Island, the westernmost of several islands belonging to Mexico, located about 150 miles from the coast of Baja California and 250 miles south of San Diego. This cypress occurs at this volcanic island's northern end on Mt Augusta, its highest point with an elevation of about 4,500 feet.

The several characters that generally distinguish Guadalupe cypress include its cherry red to gray brown, smooth, peeling **bark** and narrow, leafy branchlets about ¹⁄₁₆ inch wide, soft to the touch and blue green to gray blue. The scalelike **leaves** are initially about ¹⁄₁₆ inch long but later are longer, and the glandular pit in each is obscure. The nearly round **cones** are usually 1 inch long or slightly more, with eight to ten scales, each generally with conspicuous hornlike projections. **Seeds** may number as many as one hundred. A specimen in cultivation with this combination of characters, originating on Guadalupe Island would undoubtedly be Guadalupe cypress. But this species is closely related to the Tecate cypress *(Cupressus forbesii),* from southern California and northern Baja California. Some botanists have combined the two into a single species, for which the older name *C. guadalupensis* should be used.

Guadalupe Island has only a few inhabitants, all on the staff of a Mexican naval station. Since 1875, however, several naturalists have visited the island. Plant explorer Edward Palmer spent several months on the island in 1875 and made the first collection of plants there, including the cypress.

Palmer's collection was named and described by Harvard University botanists Asa Gray and Sereno Watson. Additional collections, including the cypress, were made in April 1885 by California botanist EL Greene and in January 1893 by Santa Barbara horticulturist Francesco Franceschi. In July 1923, an expedition sponsored by the National Geographic Society made a collection of seeds of the cypress, some of which were turned over to John McLaren of Golden Gate Park. John Thomas Howell of the California Academy of Sciences, visited the island in 1931 and 1932. He made a collection of specimens and seeds of this cypress as well as a number of other plants. Howell gave most of his cypress seeds to Carl Wolf of Rancho Santa Ana Botanic Garden, who wrote of Guadalupe cypress in his monograph, *The New World Cypresses,* published in 1948.

Visitors to Guadalupe Island since Palmer have reported on the widespread destruction of the island's plants by goats introduced even before Palmer's day. Most have said that seedlings were eaten as soon as they appeared. Through the years, many plants there have suffered the same fate as the Guadalupe fur seal, which in the 1800s was exterminated by hunters.

Guadalupe cypress, according to Wolf, was an early introduction into cultivation. Seeds apparently were sent to Europe about 1880 and were available in California about the same time. In California, Wolf knew of cultivated trees 50 feet or more in height in coastal areas, including the San Francisco Bay region, and Southern California, as far inland as Riverside. According to Butterfield (1964), the cypress was on the capitol grounds in Sacramento in 1871 and in Napa County about 1884.

Guadalupe cypress has been in Golden Gate Park at least since 1902. Though no information is available on the age or origin of the cypresses in the park, we may assume that seed for them came from one or more of the early naturalists who visited Guadalupe Island. Cypresses in the park are found at the southeast corner of McLaren Lodge near the corner of Fell and Stanyan streets, on Tenth Avenue near the intersection with Kennedy Drive, and in Strybing's Arthur Menzies Garden of California Native Plants. Other trees of this species can be seen in the UC Davis Arboretum, Santa Barbara Botanic Garden, and Huntington Botanical Garden.

The production of cones and seeds by Guadalupe cypress in cultivation is rare. Seed cones on a tree in the UC Davis Arboretum are the only known occurrence in California. According to Warren Roberts, arboretum superintendent, the only other known tree to have cones is at Villa Thuret, Antibes, France.

*A man does not plant a tree for himself; he plants it for posterity.*
ALEXANDER SMITH, 1863

# 52

## Monterey cypress
## *Cupressus macrocarpa*
### Cupressaceae

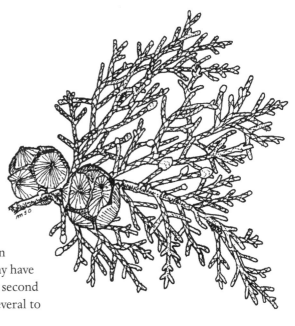

Monterey cypresses vary in height from 15 to 75 feet, depending on their habitat. Trunks 2 to 6 feet in diameter are covered with thick, fibrous **bark**. Small scalelike **leaves** about ¹⁄₁₆ inch long overlap on stout, cylindrical branchlets. **Cones** are brown, globose or oblong, 1 to 1 ½ inches long, on short stalks. The eight to ten cone scales are almost flat with a central raised point. Each cone may have as many as 140 brown, angled **seeds.** Cones mature during the second summer, shed their seeds in autumn, but remain on the tree for several to many additional seasons.

In front of McLaren Lodge (IV-S2); W edge of
    GG Park (I-B3); Strybing (VII-O4)
Sutro Heights; Great Highway at Lawton St
Evergreen/Fast growth/75'
(Conifer) Roundish, brown cones to 1-1/2" long,
    with scales like a soccer ball
Full sun/Needs no watering once established
Sunset Zone 17
Color plates

Monterey cypress occurs naturally only on the Monterey Peninsula in two localized groves. Its distribution is the most restricted of any California tree and perhaps of any conifer in the world. The Cypress Point grove extends along the shore from Pebble Beach near Pescadero Point northward for about two miles to Cypress Point. The grove at Point Lobos to the south is much smaller. Because of its narrowly circumscribed distribution, Monterey cypress is listed in the California Native Plant Society's *Inventory* as endangered in part of its range.

Monterey cypresses growing on the Monterey headlands in exposed situations are much affected by the wind. Old, asymmetrical trees with buttressed trunks have long been picturesque subjects for both artist and photographer. Trees a short distance away from the cliffs protect each other and have more symmetrical shapes similar to those seen in cultivated trees growing under favorable conditions. Such trees resemble old deodar cedars *(Cedrus deodara)* with broadly spreading, somewhat horizontal branches. Two particularly attractive trees are to be seen in Golden Gate Park. One, at the entrance to the park in front of McLaren Lodge, is decorated with lights every year as a Christmas tree; another is on a low mound at the eastern edge of Strybing's Main Lawn. Trees planted at the western edge of the park, immediately back from the ocean, show the effects of their windswept environment.

The first introduction of Monterey cypress into England was in 1831 by Aylmer B Lambert. Lambert's seeds, given to the Horticultural Society of London, were from an unnamed cypress of unknown origin. The plants raised appeared new and distinct and were informally called *Cupressus lambertiana*. Two or three years after their introduction, these plants were judged to be the same as cypresses raised at Hugh Low's nursery in Clapham; those trees had been grown from seeds of a new cypress from California received from the Russian botanist, Friederich EL Fischer, director of the Imperial Botanic Garden, St Petersburg. The second introduction of Monterey cypress into England was made about 1848 by Karl

Theodor Hartweg, who, like David Douglas earlier, had been sent to North America by the Horticultural Society of London. He spent nearly two years in California, arriving in Monterey in 1846. This cypress was among his collections.

Monterey cypresses have been planted extensively as park and boulevard trees and in windbreaks in the coastal zone of California. They thrive in areas where they are drenched in moisture from the annual summer fogs along the coast. In recent years, a canker fungus has begun to attack Monterey cypresses, affecting most seriously those trees planted away from the cool coast; the fungus can kill trees and there is no known cure.

Along with Monterey pines, Monterey cypresses have been the dominant trees in the forest planted in the late 1800s to create Golden Gate Park. They have grown well in the park and some seedlings have been produced, but they have not established themselves in great numbers. Now, over a century since the first plantings in the park, old pines and cypresses have reached the end of their natural life span and are being replaced by young trees in an extensive reforestation program begun in the 1980s.

# 53

## Rimu
# *Dacrydium cupressinum*
## Podocarpaceae

One of the most historically important trees in Strybing Arboretum is rimu, originally brought to California for the New Zealand pavilion at the Panama–Pacific International Exposition held in San Francisco in 1915. The New Zealand plants used to landscape the grounds around this pavilion were furnished by Duncan and Davies Nursery of New Plymouth, New Zealand, with assistance from Leonard Cockayne. After the close of the exposition, at the suggestion of John McLaren, many of these plants were taken to Golden Gate Park, and among those eventually planted in the arboretum was rimu.

Strybing (VI-N3)
Evergreen/Slow growth/25'-80'
(Conifer) Red or orange fruit with a single dark
    seed
Full sun to part shade/Water regularly
Sunset Zone 16, 17
Color plate

**Leaves** of young rimu trees are linear, up to ¼ inch long, spreading, and soft, while those of older trees are narrowly lanceolate, about ⅛ inch long, stiff, and curved inward toward the stem. Male and female **cones** are on separate trees. **Fruit** (not seen on cultivated trees) is similar to that of *Podocarpus* trees, and shows the relation of the two genera as both are in the same family. The fleshy cones of rimu consist of two parts, one above the other; the lower part is red, succulent, cup-shaped, and generally referred to as an aril, while the upper part, containing the seed, is smaller, dark blue, and pulpy. Superficially, the fruit resembles that of a yew *(Taxus),* except that, in yew, the seed is surrounded by the red fleshy aril.

Next to kauri *(Agathis australis),* rimu is the best known of New Zealand's forest and timber trees and was once common on both North and

South islands from near sea level to about 2,500 feet. It occurs generally in podocarp-mixed broadleaf evergreen forests, where it is one of the principal trees, along with several species of *Podocarpus*. Rimu trees at maturity are 80 to 150 feet tall, with straight trunks 2 to 4 feet in diameter and branches mostly in the upper half of the tree. This habit has made them one of New Zealand's most important timber trees; the excellent wood has been used extensively for houses, furniture, and many other purposes.

Rimu is slow growing; the tree in Strybing's New Zealand collection is 35 feet tall after about eighty-five years in the garden. In cultivation, young rimu trees are attractive with their dense, pendant branches and numerous close-set, slender leaves. Other trees in California are at the UC Botanical Garden in Berkeley and the Huntington Botanical Gardens.

Rimu was discovered during Captain James Cook's first expedition, about 1770, by Joseph Banks and Daniel Solander. The plant was later named by Solander. *Dacrydium* is from the Greek for tear; the rimu exudes tearlike drops of resin.

# 54

Tree dahlia
# *Dahlia imperialis*

Asteraceae

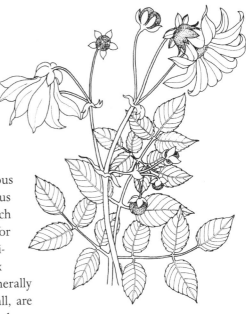

Tree dahlias constitute three of the twenty-seven species in the genus and are less known and less frequently grown than herbaceous garden dahlias. *Dahlia imperialis* is like other dahlias in having tuberous **roots.** Its stems are woody at the base and 6 to 12, sometimes as much as 20, feet tall. Current-year stems are usually unbranched except for the uppermost flowering branches. The **leaves** are large, opposite, bi- or tripinnately compound, and 2 to 3 feet long. There are four to six paired leaf branches from the midrib, and each has three to six generally paired leaflets. The daisylike **flower** heads, which appear in late fall, are often nodding and sometimes numerous (as many as 150 to 300 have been observed on a single plant). The heads may vary in width from 3 to 6 inches; the ray flowers vary in color from white or whitish lavender to rose purple; the central disk flowers are yellow.

Arizona Garden, E of conservatory (IV-R1);
    Strybing (VII-N4)
Deciduous/Fast growth/6'-20'
Nodding flower heads, 3"-6" across, in white,
    whitish lavender, or rose purple with yellow
    centers (Nov-Dec) /Flat, papery seeds
Full sun to part shade/Water regularly
Sunset Zone 4-6, 8, 9, 14-24

The stems, hollow except at nodes, are often filled with a watery sap that can quench thirst. The sap, apparently, was known to at least one group of native people of Mexico, whose name for tree dahlia was *acocotli*, or water cane. The stems, reminiscent of bamboo fishing poles, can be used in propagation; cut into lengths of several inches and inserted into the ground, they root and produce new shoots. Planted in rows these can become dahlia fences.

The geographical distribution of *Dahlia imperialis* extends from Chiapas in southern Mexico to Guatemala, El Salvador, Costa Rica, and northern Colombia, at elevations from 2,500 to 9,000 feet. Its habitat is rocky slopes and fields.

Best known of the tree dahlias, *Dahlia imperialis* has several synonyms: *D. arborea, D. lehmannii, D. maximilliana,* and *D. maxonii;* in addition, it is sometimes incorrectly called *D. excelsa,* the name of a closely related tree dahlia that is rarely cultivated. The original description of 1838 says that it came from the Valley of Mexico, where Mexico City is located, and that it appears to have been long cultivated in the botanical garden of that city. No tree dahlias, however, are native to the area around Mexico City.

*Dahlia imperialis* was described in 1863 from a plant collected at an unknown location in Mexico by Benedict Roezl, a Czechoslovakian gardener and botanist who traveled extensively in Mexico and introduced many tropical plants into Europe. Tubers of his tree dahlia were taken to Zurich, where it was cultivated. Later, plants were taken to the Royal Botanic Gardens, Berlin, where it was cultivated, named, and described.

*Dahlia imperialis* has been in Strybing Arboretum since at least the 1950s; fine specimens displaying an array of flower colors can be seen there in the New World Cloud Forest collection. It has been in Golden Gate Park since the 1920s and 1930s and can be seen today in the Arizona Garden east of the conservatory. Attractive as the tree dahlia is, it is not a common garden plant. Perhaps because plants are unwieldy and difficult to handle in ordinary nursery practice, it is uncommon in nurseries. Where it is grown, the stems are usually cut to the ground in winter after flowering is complete, to encourage tall, unbranched stems in the following growing season.

# 55

## Dove tree

# *Davidia involucrata*
## Cornaceae

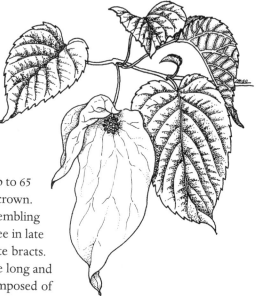

Dove tree, or handkerchief tree, is deciduous, 25 to 40 feet tall (up to 65 feet in its native China), with a broad, somewhat irregular crown. **Leaves** are heart-shaped, prominently veined, superficially resembling those of linden and basswood trees. The special feature of the tree in late spring is the pendant **flower** clusters, each with two showy white bracts. The bracts, unequal in length, are generally 3 to 6 inches or more long and surround the flower cluster. Clusters are nearly 1 inch wide, composed of small flowers that are inconspicuous except for the reddish to purplish anthers of the numerous male flowers. Each flower cluster also has a single female flower that eventually forms a hard, nutlike brown **fruit,** generally with reddish dots when ripe. It contains three to five seeds.

Seeds may take up to two years to germinate. Trees flower within ten years under favorable conditions. Propagation is generally by seed, often abundantly produced, or by cuttings.

Strybing (VI-M3 & VII-N4)
Deciduous/Slow growth/25'-40'
Hanging globose clusters of reddish flowers with 2 showy, white, 3"-6" long bracts (May)/ Round, greenish brown fruit, about 1" in diameter
Full sun to part shade/Water regularly
Sunset Zone 4-9, 14-21
Color plate

The dove trees in Strybing Arboretum (one above the Moon-viewing Garden and another near the south edge of the gardens) are the only ones in Golden Gate Park and were planted by Eric Walther in the early 1950s. Other trees are in the UC Botanical Garden in Berkeley and at Sonoma Horticultural Nursery in Sebastopol. Dove trees are occasionally cultivated in Southern California and the Pacific Northwest.

# A Treasure from China

Dove tree is one of the most unusual trees discovered in China in the late nineteenth century. It was found in 1869 by the French missionary and naturalist, Abbé Armand David, at Moupin in western Sichuan. A specimen of the dove tree, sent to the Natural History Museum in Paris, was named *Davidia* in honor of its discoverer. Another French missionary, Père Paul Farges, sent seeds of davidia from northeastern Sichuan in 1897 to the nursery firm of Vilmorin at Les Barres in France. But after two years only a single seed had germinated. Cuttings from the young plant were rooted and sent to the Jardin des Plantes in Paris, the Royal Botanic Gardens at Kew, and the Arnold Arboretum in Boston.

Meanwhile, Irish-born Augustine Henry was sent from England to China in 1881 to join the Chinese Imperial Customs Service. He arrived in Ichang (now Yichang), in eastern Sichuan, where his duties as customs officer allowed him periods of time to explore the area; with encouragement from William Thiselton-Dyer, director of the Royal Botanic Gardens at Kew, he began to collect botanical specimens. In 1889, near Ichang, he discovered a single dove tree, and a specimen of it was sent to Kew. Henry wrote of his dismay at observing the rapid deforestation of the countryside, so rich in unusual and unknown plants. He suggested that it would be worthwhile to send a full-time collector to the area, but Kew was unable to underwrite such a venture at that time. Harry Veitch, however, was interested in the idea. Thiselton-Dyer, who knew Ernest H Wilson, then a young gardener at Kew, suggested that Wilson be asked to go to China as Veitch's collector. Wilson turned out to be the last and greatest of the Veitch collectors.

The object of Wilson's first expedition to China was to obtain seed of the dove tree. According to Coats (1969), his instructions from Veitch were to "stick to the one thing you are after and do not spend time and money wandering about" since "probably almost every worthwhile plant in China has now been introduced to Europe." History tells us that Wilson did not follow these instructions; the plants collected on this and later expeditions made him the most outstanding collector in eastern Asia.

Wilson left for China in April 1899 and was to go directly to meet Henry in western China. Henry gave him good directions for locating the one dove tree he had found near Ichang, but when local villagers led him to the spot where the tree was supposed to be, Wilson found only a stump. The tree had been cut down to build a house.

Undismayed, Wilson made plans to go to the area where Abbé Armand David had discovered the tree in 1869, a thousand miles to the west. But while still at Ichang the following May, quite by chance he found a 50-foot dove tree in full flower. The tree was more beautiful than he had imagined. He later wrote, in *Aristocrats of the Garden,* "The flowers and their attendant bracts are pendulous on fairly long stalks, and when stirred by the slightest breeze they resemble huge butterflies or small doves hovering amongst [the branches of] the tree." Later that year, he collected large quantities of seed from the tree. In the following year, in northwestern Hupeh, he found more than a hundred dove trees and obtained more seeds. On later expeditions, he found many trees, but never again with the amount of seed as on the tree at Ichang.

Having collected an abundance of davidia seeds, as well as many other fine horticultural specimens, Wilson returned to England in April 1902 and went directly to Veitch's nursery. There he hoped to see young plants from the davidia seeds that had been sent earlier, but not a single one had germinated. A month later, however, hundreds of seedlings suddenly appeared.

At about the same time, Père Farges had sent another lot of seeds to Vilmorin in France, and these also successfully germinated. With young plants in the two nurseries in England and France, the introduction of davidia to European gardens was assured. Wilson's plants in Veitch's nursery first flowered in 1911.

# 56

Tasmanian tree fern
## *Dicksonia antarctica*
Dicksoniaceae

Most of the tree ferns in the Tree Fern Dell belong to *Dicksonia antarctica,* sometimes called Tasmanian tree fern from its native range in Tasmania; it is also native to mainland eastern Australia from Queensland south to Victoria. Plants in the Tree Fern Dell range up to 15 feet tall; in Australia they may reach well over 20 feet. This tree fern is easily recognized by the appearance of the **trunk,** which is covered with the upturned bases, 3 to 4 inches long, of the dark petioles that persist after the fronds fall. The **leaf** crown may have up to twenty-five fronds, each up to 10 feet long; the fronds are bi- and tripinnately divided, with toothed margins on sterile fronds and lobed margins on fertile fronds that carry the spore-bearing sori on their undersides. The petioles are covered with gray or brown hairs and scales. It is also seen in Strybing's New Zealand collection. This species is among the hardiest of tree ferns, popular in mild-winter gardens from Southern California to Seattle.

Two other dicksonias occur in the park, particularly in Strybing Arboretum, but are less numerous than *Dicksonia antarctica;* their trunks are also covered with the persistent petiole bases. A native of New Zealand, *D. fibrosa* has generally shorter trunks, to about 7 feet, and fronds somewhat stiffer and more erect. A third species, *D. squarrosa,* is also a native of New Zealand. It can be distinguished from *D. antarctica* and *D. fibrosa* by persistent petiole bases that are noticeably longer and more or less appressed to the trunk, creating a somewhat fluted appearance.

Tree Fern Dell (IV-Q2); Strybing (VI-N3)
Evergreen/Slow growth/12'-15'
(Fern) Spores under fertile fronds
Part shade to full sun on coast/Water regularly
Sunset Zone 8, 9, 14-17, 19-24

# Ferns as Trees

The stems of some ferns rise a few inches above ground, but most are either underground or spread more or less horizontally on the ground. The fronds or leaves, sometimes numerous and clustered, are the conspicuous part of the plant. A few ferns, however, produce tall stems that are slender and treelike; these are called tree ferns. Of various heights, these stems are crowned with an attractive and graceful cluster of large, spreading fronds, giving the plants a palmlike appearance. Two families of tree ferns are represented in California, Dicksoniaceae and Cyatheaceae; few of their 700 or so species are cultivated in Europe or elsewhere in the United States.

In their native habitats, tree ferns grow in tropical rain forests and cool, moist forests of temperate regions, where the temperature does not fluctuate greatly during the year. Some tree ferns succeed best where temperatures are lower at night than during the day, and several that come to us from Australia and New Zealand do very well in coastal California, where temperature differences between day and night are sufficient for successful growth. Those from tropical regions, where there is little difference between day and night temperatures, are best grown in southern Florida. In coastal California, where winters are mild and nights are cooler than days throughout the year, about fifteen species of tree ferns have been successfully grown.

San Francisco provides an ideal climate for growing tree ferns, and those in Golden Gate Park are among the park's outstanding plant collections. The success of tree ferns in the park may be attributed not only to climatic conditions but to the protection and shelter afforded them by surrounding trees. The park's tree ferns belong to three genera that come from New Zealand and Australia. The largest, oldest, and best-known planting is in the Tree Fern Dell on Kennedy Drive across from the conservatory. This planting extends to Quarry Lake to the south.

Tree ferns have been in the park since the early years of this century. According to the 1924 *Annual Report of the Park Commissioners,* the following three were in the park at that time: *Alsophila australis* (this name probably refers to *Sphaeropteris cooperi,* which has also been called *Alsophila cooperi* and *Cyathea cooperi), Dicksonia antarctica,* and *D. squarrosa.* A photograph in this report showing a scene with two young tree ferns is captioned "Tangles of Giant Ferns." Another photograph of a park scene appeared in the 1912 annual report accompanied by the caption "Tree Ferns in de Laveaga Dell," suggesting that tree ferns were in this area of the park before 1912, though no specific tree ferns were listed. A third planting of tree ferns in the park, dating from sometime in the 1950s, is along King Drive west of Nineteenth Avenue. Several species of tree ferns may also be seen in Strybing Arboretum, and in many other parks and gardens along the West Coast.

# 57

## Dipteronia
# *Dipteronia sinensis*
### Aceraceae

Dipteronia belongs to the maple family, which has only two genera, *Dipteronia* and *Acer. Dipteronia* has two species, of which one, *D. sinensis,* is occasionally cultivated. Strybing Arboretum has one specimen in its Asian section, just north of the Moon-viewing Garden, and it has been grown in the Washington Park Arboretum in Seattle.

Dipteronia differs from the maples in its pinnately compound leaves, with more leaflets than those of the few species of pinnate-leafed maples (most maples have palmately lobed leaves). Dipteronia also differs in its fruits: each of the pair of **seeds** is surrounded by a wing. *Dipteronia sinensis* is a small tree with **leaves** to 12 inches long, each with seven to eleven leaflets. **Flowers** are small, numerous, and in showy clusters in summer. The tree occurs in central China, where it is a rare and threatened species. EH Wilson collected it for the Veitch Nursery about 1900 and introduced it to England. No information is available on the source of Strybing's tree.

Strybing (VI-M3)
Deciduous/Slow growth/30'
Small greenish white flowers in showy, upright
    clusters (summer) /Winged, reddish brown
    seeds
Full sun to part shade/Water regularly
Sunset Zone 4-9, 14-21

# 58

Hopseed bush
## *Dodonaea viscosa*
Sapindaceae

Hopseed bush is an evergreen shrub or small tree to 30 feet tall, with a spreading habit; its leaves and stems are usually somewhat viscid, and its reddish brown **bark** peels in narrow strips. The simple alternate **leaves** may reach 5 inches in length and 1 inch or more in width; narrowly elliptical or obovate, the leaves have revolute margins and are held on short petioles. The small, inconspicuous male and female **flowers,** appearing in spring, are separate, lack petals, and occur on short racemes along the stems; the two to five sepals are more or less ovate and pubescent below. The **fruit** is a capsule, somewhat flattened, about ½ inch wide, with three conspicuous wings.

Hopseed bush is one of the most widely distributed of all woody flowering plants, occurring in the warmer parts of all continents, except Europe and Antarctica, as well as some of the Pacific islands, including Hawaii and New Zealand, where it was known as *akeake*. Maoris used its hard black wood, variegated with white streaks, in the manufacture of clubs and weapons of war. European settlers in New Zealand used the leaves for medicinal purposes, while the early settlers in Australia used the fruits as a substitute for hops (hence, its common name). The genus was named for the Belgian-born Rembert Dodoens, a publisher of early botanical books.

Hopseed bush has been widely planted for screening and in hedgerows throughout California, originally in its green-leaf form. In the early 1950s, a purple-leafed selection was introduced by Eric Walther of Strybing Arboretum; now this selection, 'Purpurea', notable for both its foliage and its showier pink fruits, is much more widely grown than the green form. Good specimens can be seen just west of the Tree Fern Dell entrance, where it forms a high screen along with *Luma apiculata*. It is also in the shrub planting north of the bowling greens on the west side of Bowling Green Drive, along Chain of Lakes Drive, and in other parks within San Francisco and most other cities in California. Trained on a standard, hopseed bush is sometimes used as a street tree in San Francisco and elsewhere.

Kennedy Dr W of Tree Fern Dell (IV-P2); N of
    bowling greens (1V-Q3); Chain of Lakes Dr N
    of King Dr (I-D4)
Buena Vista Park
Evergreen/Fast growth/15'
Insignificant flowers with no petals (spring)/
    Winged capsules, pink, reddish brown, light
    brown, or purple
Full sun/Water infrequently
Sunset Zone 7-9, 12-24
Suitable as a street tree
Color plate

## 59

### Winter's bark
# *Drimys winteri*
### Winteraceae

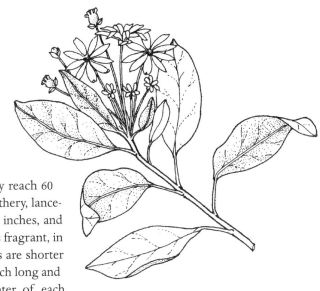

Winter's bark is an evergreen tree or large shrub that may reach 60 feet in height in the wild, with gray, aromatic **bark** and leathery, lanceolate **leaves,** variable in size from 1 to 7 inches by ½ to 3 inches, and whitish beneath. **Flowers** are white to cream, more or less fragrant, in few-flowered umbels on long flower stalks; the two sepals are shorter than the eight to twelve lanceolate petals, each about ½ inch long and spreading. Numerous stamens are clustered in the center of each flower along with four to ten separate ovaries. The **fruit** is a glossy black berry.

Strybing (VI-N3)
Evergreen/Slow growth/25'
Clusters of jasmine-scented, creamy white flowers, 1" wide, on the branch tips (winter and spring) /Glossy black berries
Full sun to part shade/Water regularly
Sunset Zone 8, 9, 14-24

*Drimys* is a genus in the Winteraceae, a family closely allied to the magnolias, with twenty to thirty species of evergreen trees and shrubs occurring in the southern hemispheres of both Old and New worlds. The genus name comes from the Greek, meaning acrid, a reference to the bitter taste of the bark. *Drimys winteri* was the first species in the genus to be described, in 1776. It was named for Captain William Winter, who accompanied Sir Francis Drake on his voyage around the world.

On his return in 1578, Captain Winter brought the bark of *Drimys winteri* from the Strait of Magellan, where he had found it to be useful as a treatment for scurvy for the ship's crew and as a seasoning for their meat. It was not named and described in botanical literature for another two centuries, and then only from a specimen collected on Captain Cook's second voyage.

Winter's bark has a wide geographical distribution from Mexico through South America to its southern tip, Tierra del Fuego. The species varies throughout this area, with several named variants. Occasionally available from nurseries, it is uncommon in cultivation except at botanical gardens such as Strybing. There, a fine old specimen is in the raised planting bed at the north end of the County Fair Building, just inside the main gate. Younger specimens can be seen elsewhere in Strybing, including several in the South American section. Other trees are found in Santa Barbara and Santa Cruz.

*You must take your tree as you find it. To the keen observer in the active seasons, it will seldom be the same two weeks, or even two days, together.*

HERBERT L. EDLIN, *The Observer's Book of Trees,* 1975

# 60

## Tree heath
# *Erica arborea*

Ericaceae

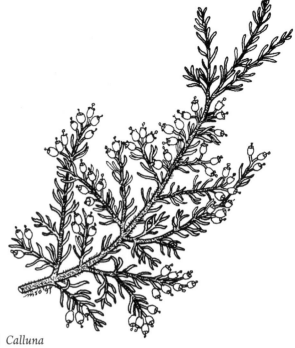

Heaths belong to the genus *Erica,* which encompasses over 600 species, nearly all of them in South Africa, but with a small number found in Europe and northern Africa. The common name heath is generally used for the ericas while heather is applied to *Calluna,* a related genus with only one species *(C. vulgaris),* the white or Scottish heather. The many heaths are recognizable by their usually shrubby habit, short evergreen, needlelike leaves, and small, rounded or bell-shaped, white or sometimes colorful flowers, which may be produced in great numbers. *Erica and Calluna* belong to the heather family, which also includes rhododendrons, mountain laurels, blueberries, cranberries, manzanitas, and madrones.

Tree heath is a tall shrub or small tree sometimes reaching 20 feet in height. It has slender, linear **leaves** about ¼ inch long; its numerous, white, bell-shaped **flowers,** about ⅛ inch long, are showy in mass, especially when plants are in full flower in spring. **Fruits** are tiny capsules produced in such quantity as to color the branches light brown.

A native of southern Europe, northern Africa, the Canary Islands, and Asia minor (including the foothills of the western Caucasus Mountains), tree heath's range extends south to the mountains of eastern and central Africa. In the early 1900s, the knobby, ground-level roots of the tree heath were used for making briar-root pipes for smoking tobacco, particularly in southern France, where the wood was once abundant along the coast from Marseilles to Genoa. Briar is a corruption of *bruyere,* the French word for heath.

Tree heath is at the eastern edge of the park along Stanyan Street, opposite St Mary's Hospital, where several can be found above the retaining wall on a steeply eroding bank. The species is also found in Strybing Arboretum northwest of the reservoir, and has been grown at the Washington Park Arboretum in Seattle.

Stanyan St S of Fulton St entrance (IV-S1);
  Strybing (VI-N4)
Evergreen/Slow growth/20'
Fragrant, bell-shaped, white flowers among
  leaves (spring) /Papery capsules
Full sun to part shade/Water occasionally
Sunset Zone 15-17, 21-24

# 61

## Escallonia
## *Escallonia revoluta*

### Grossulariaceae

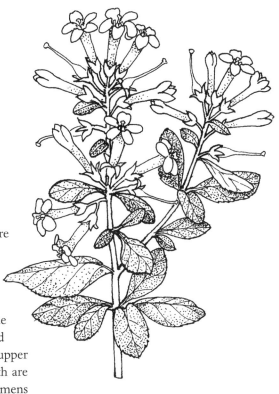

Most escallonias grown in California are shrubs, although a few are large enough to be called small trees. *Escallonia revoluta*, which reaches 20 to 25 feet, is one that attains enough height to be considered a tree. Like all escallonias, *E. revoluta* is evergreen. Its angled stems are softly hairy, as are the opposite **leaves,** which are obovate, to 2¼ inches long, about ¾ of an inch wide, narrowed at the base to a somewhat broadened petiole, and have irregularly toothed margins. The white **flowers** are dense to scattered at the ends of the upper stems. The petals are about ½ inch long and for most of their length are erect and form a tube. The rounded petal tips are spreading, the stamens and styles barely extending beyond the petal tube.

Evergreen/Slow growth/25'
White, tubular flowers, 1/2" long, along ends of
    upper stems (spring and summer) /Small,
    globular capsules
Full sun to part shade/Water occasionally
Sunset Zone 4-9, 14-17, 20-24

*Escallonia revoluta* occurs in central Chile from Coquimbo south to Osorno, usually in ravines and along watercourses. In some places, it is associated with other trees and shrubs that are also in Golden Gate Park or elsewhere in California: *Peumus boldus, Maytenus boaria, Gunnera tinctoria (G. chilensis), Azara integrifolia, Coriaria ruscifolia, Nothofagus dombeyi, Escallonia rubra, E. illinita,* and *E. pulverulenta.* The tree was introduced into England in 1887 and is listed in the fifth edition of *Hillier's Manual of Trees and Shrubs.*

As a landscape tree, *Escallonia revoluta* is not among the most striking, but as a broad-leafed evergreen it can be used in background plantings and as a specimen tree. The flowers of escallonia form rather showy clusters. It was in Golden Gate Park in 1924, when it was listed in the *Annual Report of the Park Commissioners.* It flourished in the park without special care—even with neglect—and would seem well adapted to local conditions of climate and soil. However, the specimen in the park apparently no longer exists; it may have been the only one in California. A young plant has been acquired for Strybing's South American collection and will be planted in that section of the arboretum in 2001.

# Gums and other eucalypts
# *Eucalyptus*
## Myrtaceae

The genus *Eucalyptus* is large, with over 500 species; with two or three exceptions, it is confined to Australia. Excluding vegetation of the deserts and semi-deserts, most of Australia's natural vegetation consists of communities of woody plants in which eucalypts are predominant. In fact, no other genus of trees and shrubs dominates so large and climatically diverse an area as does *Eucalyptus* in Australia. Eucalypts produce a variety of hardwood timber with a wide range of uses in Australia. Their leaves produce valuable essential oils that are used in pharmaceutical and perfume industries. Tannins, obtained from the bark and wood of some species, are also used commercially. With so large a genus, the identification of individual species presents difficulties in Australia and in cultivation. However, among broad-leafed evergreen trees in cultivation, a eucalypt can always be recognized by its characteristic leaves and buds, its numerous, generally showy stamens (the conspicuous part of the flower), and its woody, flat-topped fruit.

Because many species grow rapidly and have economic value, a large number have been introduced into cultivation in warm to moderately warm climates around the world. Here in California, at least 125 species, perhaps more, have been introduced and grown since the late 1850s, when the San Francisco nurseryman, William Walker, listed several in his catalog for 1858–1859. Among those in Walker's catalog were *Eucalyptus globulus* and *E. robusta,* grown from seeds received from Sydney, Australia. Walker was probably the first to import eucalypt seeds into California directly from Australia. He was followed by Stephen Nolan, who established Belle View nursery in Oakland in 1860 and listed about a dozen species in his 1871 catalog.

During the 1860s and continuing through the next two to three decades, the Australian botanist Baron Ferdinand von Mueller, began to promote the exportation and use of eucalypts outside Australia. Born in Germany, Von Mueller went to Australia as a young man in 1847 and spent the rest of his life exploring the country, collecting plants, and eventually becoming the greatest of Australia's nineteenth-century botanists. He was aided in his promotion of eucalypts by equally enthusiastic visitors to Australia, who returned to their home countries carrying the news of the many uses and advantages of this group of trees. In some cases, the tree's virtues were greatly exaggerated, but nevertheless, eucalypts continued to be taken around the world, until today they are established in some forty countries on all of the continents except Antarctica.

Eucalypts range from tall, stately trees to small, multi-trunked trees or shrubs called mallees. Mountain ash *(Eucalyptus regnans),* from Victoria and Tasmania, is often 200 to 300 feet tall, but measurements of over 350 feet have been recorded. It is said to be the tallest broad-leafed evergreen tree in the world, rivaling in height the redwoods of California. At the other extreme in size are some of the mallees, such as *E. macrocarpa,* a somewhat straggly shrub usually 6 to 10 feet tall. Its 2-inch-diameter red flowers are striking against the silvery leaves, the largest flower of all the eucalypts. This species has been grown in California and in Strybing Arboretum. Generally the tallest species are found in areas of summer or year-round rainfall, while the lower, shrubby mallees originate in arid regions or those with a summer-dry mediterranean climate.

The showy part of the flowers of a eucalypt is the cluster of numerous, variously colored stamens. **Flowers** are variable in size, often only ¼ inch across, and are noticeable only because several to many are grouped in a cluster. In the bud stage, the stamens are enclosed in a cap, known in eucalyptus terminology as the operculum, which consists of the united petals and sepals. The name *Eucalyptus* means "well-covered" and refers to this operculum. The cap falls away as the stamens develop and the flower opens. After the flowers have matured and the stamens have fallen, the **fruit,** a capsule, develops. It often becomes hard and woody and, at its apex, are several openings through which the small seeds are released. The shapes of the bud caps and the capsules are significant, and should be carefully examined when identifying species.

Another useful character to note in the identification of eucalypts is the **bark.** Species are sometimes arranged into several bark groups. Gums are trees with peeling bark and smooth trunks. Generally speaking, trees with hard, furrowed barks are called ironwoods: those with soft, furrowed barks, bloodwoods; those with shallowly furrowed, fibrous bark, easily pulled away in "strings," stringybarks. The boxes are another group with persistent bark that is thin, finely furrowed, and so firmly attached that only small pieces can be pulled away. The peppermints, distinguished more by their fragrant leaf oils, usually have furrowed, short-fibered bark or sometimes peeling bark.

Perhaps because the blue gum was so successful among Golden Gate Park's earliest plantings, it was followed by other eucalypts during the years when new plants were being added to the park. The 1924 *Annual Report of the Park Commissioners* lists over fifty species, including most of those discussed here.

# 62

River red gum
# *Eucalyptus camaldulensis*
## Myrtaceae

River red gum is a moderately tall tree from 80 to 100 feet, with a trunk several feet in diameter in Australia; the trunk branches to form a spreading crown. In Australia, it is a frequently photographed tree, but in California, most trees are less picturesque. Here, although branched above, most have dense, pendant masses of foliage and bear little resemblance to the attractively spreading, open, broad-crowned trees seen in Australia. The **bark** usually persists at the base of the trunk but, higher on the trunk, peels in long strips or irregular flakes. **Leaves** have a slender lanceolate shape like those of blue and manna gums. The small **flowers** are borne in summer in clusters of five to ten; the bud cap is cone-shaped with a long, pointed or beaked apex, and the stamens are creamy white. The **fruit** is less than ¼ inch long with four tiny protrusions above the apex where the seeds are released.

S of Music Concourse near King Dr (III-N3)
146 Cortland Ave; Mt. Lake Park; E side of Park
    Presidio S of Clement
Evergreen/Fast growth/80'-100'
Clusters of 5-10 flowers of creamy white stamens
    (summer) /Woody seed capsules
Full sun/Needs no watering once established
Sunset Zone 5, 6, 8-24

River red gum is the most widely distributed eucalypt in Australia, found almost throughout the continent, in all of the states except Tasmania. It is known in Australia by several other common names, including red gum, Murray red gum, and river gum. It and blue gum are the two most widely planted eucalypts around the world. In California, it is frequently seen in warmer areas such as the San Joaquin Valley, where it has seeded spontaneously in a few localities. It was introduced into Golden Gate Park prior to 1893 but today is rare there. A single tree may be seen close to King Drive, to the rear of the Verdi statue, south of the Music Concourse. Immediately outside the park, many red gums are to be seen along Park Presidio Boulevard and on the western edge of Mountain Lake Park.

The species name, *camaldulensis,* is taken from a garden near Naples, Italy, that belonged to the Duke of Camaldoli in the early 1800s. Frederick Dehnhardt, the German botanist in charge of the garden, published a catalog of the garden's plants in 1829 and 1830, in which he named and described three eucalypts grown from seeds received earlier from France. *Eucalyptus camaldulensis* was among them. These early nineteenth century introductions of eucalypts into Europe show that even before von Mueller was promoting the genus, several species had already made their way to Europe.

## 63

### Red-flowering gum
# *Eucalyptus ficifolia*
## Myrtaceae

Red-flowering gum is the only one of the eucalypts discussed here which has large clusters of colorful, showy, red **flowers.** It is a much-branched small tree 20 to 30 feet tall with a broadly spreading crown. The rough **bark,** persistent on the small branches, thick and somewhat flaky but not stringy on the trunk, puts it in the bloodwood bark group. In spite of its common name, it is not one of the gums. Broad, somewhat leathery **leaves,** resembling those of some of the tropical figs (*Ficus* species), have noticeable lateral veins, almost at right angles to the midvein. The woody **fruits** are 1 inch wide and resemble small dice cups.

Red-flowering gum has a restricted distribution in Australia. It is limited to a small area on the southwestern corner of Western Australia from near sea level to about 500 feet, and is so rare that it is included in a list of endangered Australian eucalypts. Fortunately, most of the trees are within a national park and therefore protected.

Because of its attractive red flowers, appearing throughout the summer, red-flowering gum is a widely planted ornamental within Australia and elsewhere. It does best in areas of mild climate and winter rainfall. It is well suited to coastal California, where it was introduced in the latter part of the nineteenth century. It was listed as growing in Golden Gate Park in 1902. Two trees may be seen on Kennedy Drive at the junction of Conservatory Drive East, and a third tree is on the north edge of the meadow west of the conservatory; another is on Strybing's Great Lawn. It is commonly used as a street tree in San Francisco and other coastal communities; a fine row of them can be seen along Bay Street on the southern edge of Fort Mason.

NW corner of Kennedy Dr and Conservatory Dr
   East (IV-R2); W of conservatory (IV-Q1);
   Strybing (VII-O4)
Bay St at Fort Mason
Evergreen/Moderate growth/20'-30'
Showy clusters, to 1' across, of scarlet, cream,
   pink, or orange stamens (summer) /Woody
   seed capsules
Full sun/Needs no watering once established
Sunset Zone 5, 6, 8-24
Suitable as a street tree

*A stricken tree, a living thing, so beautiful, so dignified, so admirable in its potential longevity, is, next to man, perhaps the most touching of wounded objects.*

EDNA FERBER

# 64

## Blue gum
# *Eucalyptus globulus*
### Myrtaceae

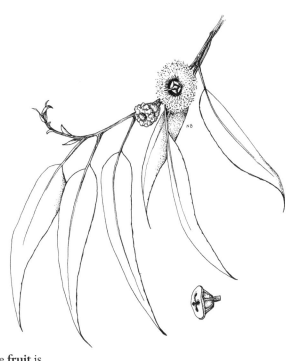

A tall tree, blue gum is often 50 to 100 feet in height or more, with rough, persistent **bark** at the base, peeling in long ribbonlike strips on the trunk and branches. The 5- to 10-inch long, alternate, mature **leaves,** lanceolate with a noticeable leaf stalk, contrast with the seedling, or juvenile, **leaves** which are opposite, ovate, covered with a waxy bloom, and clasp the square stem. The flowers, appearing from December through March and almost always borne singly, have a warty cap about ½ inch across. The stamens are pale yellow and large enough to be noticed, even if not particularly showy on the trees. The **fruit** is a top-shaped or buttonlike capsule, nearly 1 inch across, usually with four ribs.

*Eucalyptus globulus* was one of the earliest eucalypts to be discovered by European explorers. It was found by the French botanist Jacques-Julien Houtou de Labillardiere, a member of an expedition under Joseph-Antoine Bruni d'Entrecasteaux. The expedition stopped in Tasmania at Storm Bay in 1792, where, in the coastal forest, they saw tall trees with fruits like coat buttons. The biggest trees were about 150 feet tall, and one had to be cut down in order to see its flowers. Later, upon returning to Paris, de Labillardière described and named this tree.

Blue gum is the most commonly planted eucalypt, not only in California but around the world. It was one of the eucalypts promoted by von Mueller, who said that of all of the species of *Eucalyptus* in Australia, *E. globulus* "takes the first position of importance, and among its own kind it is the prince of eucalypts." Today, his statement might be challenged by many people. However, we must remember that, in von Mueller's, time much less was known about *Eucalyptus*. Of the species introduced into California, among the earliest was *E. globulus* in 1859. So frequent is the blue gum seen in California today that many Californians look upon it as a native tree. Indeed, it is so much at home in California that it has seeded itself and spread from its planted areas in many parts of the state, from north to south. Its distribution in Australia is limited to two small areas in southernmost Victoria and a fairly large area in southeastern Tasmania.

Blue gum is one of the three most important trees in the forest canopy of Golden Gate Park, planted along with Monterey pine and Monterey cypress in the earliest years of the park. Unlike the two conifers, this eucalypt has expanded its place in the park by spawning copious seedlings, many of which are now large trees. The seedlings have the ability to establish even in the shade of other trees, such as the conifers, and could threaten to overwhelm this human-made forest community if not carefully managed. Magnificent mature blue gums can be seen throughout the park and the Panhandle. A fine specimen is in the planting above the lawn west of McClaren Lodge; another is west of Strybing's Succulent Garden.

In planting above lawn W of McLaren Lodge (IV-R2); Strybing (VI-M4)
Center of Parade Grounds in the Presidio; Mt. Sutro.
Evergreen/Fast growth/100'
Showy, pale yellow stamens (Dec-Mar) /1" wide, blue grey, woody buttonlike seed capsules
Full sun/Needs no watering once established
Sunset Zone 5, 6, 8-24

# 65

Messmate stringybark
## *Eucalyptus obliqua*
Myrtaceae

Messmate stringybark, sometimes simply called messmate, differs from the gum trees in having a persistent stringy bark, though the interlacing fibers of the brown, furrowed **bark** are not as coarse as those of some stringybarks. Messmate is a tall tree with a straight trunk for more than half its height. In Australia, trees may be 150 to 225 feet tall with trunks 5 to 10 feet in diameter; they are generally shorter in cultivation in California. The bases of the broadly lanceolate **leaves** are unequal or oblique; the species name refers to this distinguishing character. Summer **flowers** usually occur in clusters of seven to twelve. The bud caps are short and cone-shaped, the stamens creamy white, and the **fruits** usually almost rounded below but flat and sunken at the apex.

*Eucalyptus obliqua* is of historical interest because it was the first eucalypt to be discovered by European explorers, and it was the first species of the genus to be named and described. David Nelson and William Anderson collected it on an island in Adventure Bay in southern Tasmania on Captain James Cook's third voyage in 1777. The specimen, along with others from the expedition, was taken to England and added to the collections accumulated by Sir Joseph Banks in London. The French botanist, Charles Louis L'Héritier de Brutelle, while in London in 1786 and 1787, using the specimen from Adventure Bay, named and described *Eucalyptus* as a new genus and at the same time named the new species *E. obliqua*. Accompanying L'Héritier's description was a drawing of *E. obliqua* by Pierre Joseph Redouté, the great French botanical artist, well known for his paintings of roses. Redouté's drawing is the first known illustration of a eucalypt.

In Australia, the messmate occurs mostly in Victoria and Tasmania, and to a limited extent in South Australia and New South Wales. In its homeland, it is sometimes grouped with eucalypts called ashes, a name applied in the early days of Australian settlement because of a superficial resemblance of the timber to that of the European ashes (*Fraxinus* species). The messmate is an important hardwood where it is native.

The messmate was introduced into Golden Gate Park before 1893, but today it is rare in the park. A single messmate near the eastern end of the Panhandle is located in the block between Central and Lyon streets, near Oak Street. Though rarely planted in California, one example can be seen on the UC Berkeley campus.

Panhandle near Oak & Lyon streets
Evergreen/Fast growth/150'
Clusters of flowers with creamy white stamens
    (summer) /Woody capsules rounded at base
Full sun/Needs no watering once established
Sunset Zone 5, 6, 8-24

# The Panhandle of Golden Gate Park

The Panhandle of Golden Gate Park was the first area to be planted by William Hammond Hall in the 1870s. This eight-block long, one-block wide eastern extension of the park was the most protected from the persistent ocean winds, making tree planting easier than elsewhere in the park. The Panhandle was to serve as a gracious carriage entrance to the park, and incorporated a winding road landscaped on both sides with trees and shrubs of all kinds.

Other than some nearby coast live oaks that predated Hall's early park plantings, the Panhandle contains the park's oldest trees. In 1965, it was estimated that there were fifty different kinds of trees in the Panhandle. Some had been planted in great numbers: Monterey cypress *(Cupressus macrocarpa),* Monterey pine *(Pinus radiata),* blue and manna gums *(Eucalyptus globulus* and *E. viminalis),* various pittosporums and acacias. Other trees were used as single specimens. Many evergreen shrubs edged the walkways and served as backdrops for colorful flowerbeds.

Today, the Panhandle serves as a neighborhood park, with a children's playground, basketball courts, and pathways for strolling and bicycling. The carriageway was removed many years ago and replaced with broad lawns, now used for sunning and picnicking. Much of the shrubbery has been eliminated in the interest of public safety. Some of the oldest trees in the Panhandle have succumbed to age and weather, but many large eucalypts, pines, and cypresses remain to give a sense of the grandeur planned for more than one hundred years ago by William Hammond Hall.

# 66

## Snow gum
## *Eucalyptus pauciflora*
Myrtaceae

Snow gum was introduced in 1874, but has never become common in spite of a beautiful form and bark. It may reach 40 feet in height, with a crown spread about equal to its height. The trunk's white **bark** peels in irregular strips, revealing patches of cream and gray. The lanceolate **leaves** are about 6 inches long and thickish, with veins more or less parallel to the midvein, a pattern different from most other eucalypts. About seven to twelve small white **flowers** occur in summer in umbels—more than the few suggested by the name *pauciflora,* which means few-flowered. The buds are pointed and the small white-stamened flowers are not showy, nor are the small woody **fruits** that follow.

Snow gum occurs in southeastern Australia on the coast from New South Wales to Tasmania and on inland mountains up to nearly 5,000 feet elevation, where snow is common in winter. The tree's mountain habitat, together with its white trunk, suggests the common names of snow gum and ghost gum. Variable throughout its natural range from upright trees to stunted and contorted shrubs, some are undoubtedly among the most cold hardy of all eucalypts; specimens are known in public and private gardens in Portland and Seattle, and in Victoria, British Columbia, as well as in

Strybing (VI-N3 & VII-N3)
Evergreen/Moderate growth/40'
Clusters of 7-12 small, white or creamy flowers
    (late spring-summer) /Cup-shaped capsules,
    1/2" diameter
Full sun/Needs no watering once established
Sunset Zone 5, 6, 8-24

northern Scotland. In Golden Gate Park, two fine specimens are within and on either side of the Friend Gate to Strybing Arboretum, in the Eastern Australian collection. Several beautiful multi-trunked snow gums, planted in the 1970s, can be seen at the UCSC Arboretum. A single specimen, demonstrating the species' tolerance of heat as well as cold, is at home in The Ruth Bancroft Garden in Walnut Creek, thirty miles east of San Francisco. The Huntington Botanical Gardens in San Marino has a fifty-year-old tree from a USDA seed collection.

## 67

Swamp mahogany
# *Eucalyptus robusta*
Myrtaceae

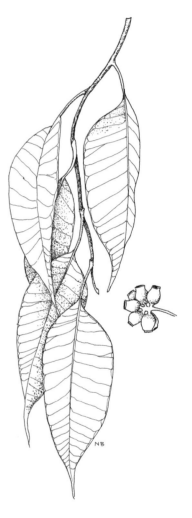

Swamp mahogany, sometimes called swamp messmate, has red brown, rough, thick, spongy, and somewhat fibrous **bark**, persistent on the smaller branches. The dark green **leaves** are thick and leathery; their fine venation is more or less parallel and almost at right angles with the midvein. **Flowers** are fairly large, five to ten occurring in somewhat showy clusters in spring and summer. Bud caps are conical with a conspicuous but bluntly pointed apex. The stamens are white, and the **fruit** capsules deeply cup shaped with three or four openings for seed dispersal. It is a tall, densely foliaged tree, reaching 80 to 90 feet in height.

Swamp mahogany occurs in Australia in a narrow strip along the middle part of the eastern coast, mostly in New South Wales but extending into southern Queensland. It is restricted, as the common name suggests, to swampy and other wet areas. Its timber, being in limited supply and light for a eucalypt, has had only minor utilization in Australia. The tree has had occasional use as an ornamental and has been planted in many countries around the world, doing best where there is enough water.

The swamp mahogany was introduced into California in the late 1800s as an ornamental. It was found to be fairly fast growing in plantings made at Hanford, Fresno, and Santa Barbara, where trees twelve years old had an average height of 45 feet and a trunk diameter of 7½ feet.

The earliest mention of swamp mahogany in Golden Gate Park was in 1902. It is rare in the park today. A fine specimen of the tree is on the northeast corner of Kennedy Drive and Tenth Avenue.

NE corner of 10th Ave and Kennedy Dr (III-O1)
905-907 Diamond St
Evergreen/Fast growth/80'-90'
Masses of pink-tinted, creamy white flowers (late
    winter to early summer) /Cylindrical seed
    capsules
Full sun/Water infrequently
Sunset Zone 5, 6, 8-24

## 68

## Manna gum
# *Eucalyptus viminalis*
### Myrtaceae

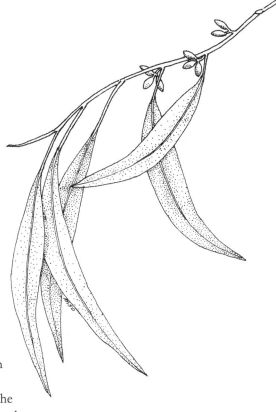

Manna gum has a tall, straight trunk with peeling **bark** and graceful branching. From a distance, it strongly resembles blue gum. Close examination, however, shows that its **leaves,** although the same general shape as those of blue gum and many other eucalypts, are usually neither as long nor as broad as those of blue gum. However, the flowers and fruits of the two differ and readily distinguish them. The **flowers** of manna gum are usually in groups of three, buds are about ¼ inch long, the bud caps are smooth and cone-shaped, the stamens creamy white and not showy, and the **fruit** is a top-shaped capsule, about ¼ to ⅓ inch long.

Manna gum has been given this common name because the bark exudes a pleasantly sweet tasting, manna-like substance that Australian Aborigines used for food. Widely distributed in southeastern Australia, including Tasmania, it is the chief food tree of koalas and, because it is widely cultivated in California, it is also used to feed koalas exhibited in California zoos. It was discovered in southern Tasmania in 1792 by the d'Entrecasteaux expedition and later named and described by de Labillardière.

Manna gum was introduced into California in 1861. Just when it was introduced into Golden Gate Park is not known; however, it was previous to 1893, when it was already listed in the *Annual Report of the Park Commissioners.* Today, manna gum is scattered throughout the park and seen along with the blue gum, although not as abundantly. Magnificent specimens, noticeable for their nearly white trunks, can be seen at Stanyan and Fulton streets, at Kezar Drive and Waller Street, just west of the Sixth Avenue entrance from Fulton Street, and in Strybing's Demonstration Gardens.

On Stanyan near Fulton St (IV-S1); NE corner of
    Waller and Kezar Dr (IV-S3); 6th Ave S of
    Fulton St ((III-P1); Strybing (VII-O3)
Evergreen/Fast growth/150'
Clusters of 3-7 creamy white flowers (throughout
    the year) /Top-shaped, woody, seed capsules
Full sun/Needs no watering once established
Sunset Zone 5, 6, 8-24

*In all countries where trees grow, the noblest specimens ought to be preserved as national monuments since...no nation can boast anything more magnificent than the forest giants Nature gave it.*

ERNEST H. WILSON, *Aristocrats of the Trees*

93

# 69

## European beech
# *Fagus sylvatica*
### Fagaceae

*Fagus* is a small genus of deciduous trees; the name is derived from the ancient Latin for European, or common, beech, whose specific name comes from the Latin for forest, which is its natural home.

This large, densely foliaged tree has a smooth, silvery gray **bark,** and produces simple, alternate **leaves,** elliptical in outline and obscurely toothed; the leaves are 2 to 4 inches long and generally have five to nine pairs of prominent, parallel veins. The small **flowers** are not showy, appearing in headlike clusters with separate male and female flowers on the same tree. **Fruits** are pear-shaped cups, about 1 inch long, covered with soft bristles and enclosing two oily seeds that are triangular in cross section.

European beech is a well-known tree, widely cultivated as an orna-mental. It is native over central and southeastern Europe, where it often occurs in pure stands in the mountains. In 1752, it was introduced into North America, where it has become an important cultivated tree. Few trees are more pleasing in the landscape, either as specimen trees or with others of its kind.

European beech is variable throughout its wide range. Of the many variants produced, some have originated in the wild, others in cultivation. As many as thirty cultivars have been named. These can be grouped into selections with leaves variously cut (the cut-leaf or fern-leaf beeches), with leaves variously colored (including the purple and copper beeches), and with growth habits varying from strictly erect to pendant (the fastigiate and weeping beeches, respectively).

European beech has had several uses in the past. The seeds are edible when roasted, and the oil produced by the seeds was used in the manufac-ture of soap and for illumination. The hard, heavy, easily split wood was used for kitchen utensils, wagons, agricultural implements, and furniture, especially chairs. At one time in England, Windsor chairs, made of beech wood, were particularly popular, and a small furniture industry remains near High Wycombe, where beeches are common. Preparations made from beeches have been used medicinally for the treatment of worms, con-sumption, and heart trouble; to purify the blood; as a poultice for burns; and as a wash for poison ivy.

The largest specimens in Golden Gate Park today are two 30-foot trees in the Rhododendron Dell. A number of young trees, planted in the 1960s, can be found in Strybing Arboretum: one is just outside the main gate on South Drive, while others are along the lawn panel near the Zellerbach Garden in the northwest corner of the arboretum. A good-sized tree with deep, coppery foliage can be seen on the north side of Alvord

Rhododendron Dell (III-P2); N edge Alvord Lake
    (IV-S3); Strybing (VI-N3)
Deciduous/Slow growth/80'
Inconspicuous flowers (May) /Bristly, pear-
    shaped capsules
Full sun/Water regularly
Sunset Zone 1-9, 14-24
Color plate

Lake. Magnificent specimens, some quite large, are on the UC Berkeley campus near the Life Sciences Building. A selection of cultivars can be seen at the Washington Park Arboretum in Seattle. Other specimens can be found in parks and estate gardens from central California north to British Columbia, but are only occasionally seen in Southern California.

# The beech family

The beech family, *Fagaceae,* contains some of the most popular park and garden trees in the world. In addition to the true beeches *(Fagus),* it includes the chestnuts *(Castanea),* the oaks *(Quercus),* and the tanbarks *(Lithocarpus),* all found throughout the Northern Hemisphere; and the southern beeches *(Nothofagus),* found in South America, New Zealand, and Australia. Strybing Arboretum has a several species of *Nothofagus* in its collections, along with trees of tanbark *(Lithocarpus densiflorus).*

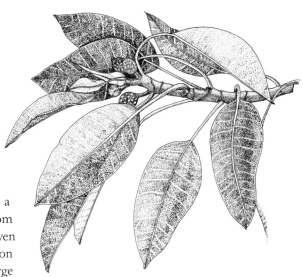

## 70

Moreton Bay fig
### *Ficus macrophylla*
Moraceae

Along the eastern coast of Australia, the Moreton Bay fig is a familiar native. Never more than 100 miles inland, it occurs from Moreton Bay (near Brisbane) on the north to the Shoalhaven River (south of Sydney) in rain forests, along coastal streams, on hillsides, in mountainous areas, and in eucalypt forests. Large trees in the wild are reported to be over 200 feet tall, with widely spreading canopies and bulky, buttressed trunks over 50 feet in girth. When trees are crowded, however, the crowns may be narrower. Trees in cultivation are generally not over 100 feet tall.

**Leaves** are leathery, 4 to 8 or 10 inches long, 3 to 6 inches wide, smooth, dark green above, more or less rusty felted below. The bud at the tip of each twig is surrounded and protected by a thin, showy sheath, the stipule, often 3 or 4 inches long, which falls as new leaves unfurl, leaving a conspicuous circular scar around the twig at the base of the petiole. This stipular scar is a distinguishing character on the twigs of all figs. **Flowers** are small and insignificant. The **fruits,** one or two at the base of the upper leaves, are purplish or reddish brown with light spots, round or ovoid, slightly less than 1 inch in diameter. In Australia, mature fruits are said to be edible, but in cultivation elsewhere, they do not fully mature and are inedible.

Because of its handsome appearance and its broadly spreading branches, the Moreton Bay fig has long been cultivated in Australia for ornament, shelter and shade in parks and gardens and sometimes as a street tree. Its

N of Alvord Lake (IV-S3); Strybing (VI-N3)
Valencia St at St Luke's Hospital
Evergreen/Moderate growth/100'
Inconspicuous flowers /Round or oval, 1", pur-
    plish or reddish brown fruits
Full sun/Water occasionally
Sunset Zone 17, 19-24

large size makes it unsuitable for small gardens or even as a street tree, although Ferdinand von Mueller, the eminent Australian botanist of the nineteenth century, described it as the "grandest of Australian avenue trees."

Sometime before the end of the eighteenth century, the Moreton Bay fig was taken to Europe. A tree grown in Paris was the basis for the name and description of *Ficus macrophylla,* published in 1804. Later, it was introduced into Italy. Today, Moreton Bay figs are grown in many warm temperate and semitropical regions, including the Canary Islands, southern Florida, and Hawaii. In southern California, where Moreton Bay fig trees are often planted, two exceptionally large trees can be seen. Outstanding for its size and age is one in Santa Barbara at the corner of Chapala and Montecito streets, adjacent to the old Southern Pacific (now Amtrak) Railroad Station. Planted in 1877 as a small tree, it is Santa Barbara's best known tree. Today it has a trunk circumference of over 30 feet and a crown spread of more than 170 feet. Its tremendous branch structure is braced with hundreds of feet of steel cable. A second magnificent tree, in Balboa Park in San Diego, stands alone in a lawn to the north of the Natural History Museum. Planted in 1915 from a five-gallon can, it is over 60 feet tall and has a crown diameter of more than 100 feet. Both the Santa Barbara and the San Diego trees have massive trunks with extensive buttresses.

The Moreton Bay fig was an early introduction into California. According to Butterfield (1940), William Walker imported seeds of this ornamental tree from Australia in 1859 along with seeds of other Australian plants. The Moreton Bay fig has been in Golden Gate Park since at least 1893, when it was listed in the *Annual Report of the Park Commissioners.* Today, a large tree of unknown age may be seen at the eastern end of the park near the restrooms north of the Haight Street entrance to the park. It is closely surrounded by neighboring trees and does not have the broadly spreading crown and buttressed trunk seen in other trees of this species. A younger tree with buttresses beginning to develop can be seen in Strybing Arboretum, west of the Friend Gate; unfortunately, it was badly damaged in the violent windstorm of December 1995. An outstanding specimen can be seen on the east side of St Luke's Hospital on Valencia Street in San Francisco.

# A Large, Worldwide Family

The genus *Ficus* is large, with approximately 700 to 800 species of trees, shrubs, and vines widely distributed around the world, mostly in tropical regions. Most are evergreen and with a milky sap. In tropical forests, many fig trees begin life as seedlings in the moist crotch, or niche, of a branch of another type of tree. From the seedling, many roots grow downward, forming a netlike mesh around the trunk of the host tree, which eventually is strangled and dies. The fig, growing in place of the host tree, puts out basal buttresses that add to its support. In its homeland the Moreton Bay fig may be, but is not always, a strangler. Certainly, trees in cultivation are not.

The strangling habit of many figs is remarkable but not unique; other tropical trees develop in the same manner. A unique feature of most figs is the method of pollination and the development of their fruits and seeds. Fig flowers, small and not visible to us, are borne inside a hollow receptacle, called a syconium, that develops into the fig fruit. The best-known fig fruit is the edible common fig. Within the syconium may be three kinds of flowers—male, female, and gall flowers. Pollination is carried out by gall wasps, each species of fig having its own special wasp.

# 71

Shamel ash
## *Fraxinus uhdei*
Oleaceae

*Fraxinus* is a genus of about sixty species in the Northern Hemisphere. Most of these ashes are deciduous, the evergreen *F. uhdei* being an exception. Shamel ashes are fast growing, quickly becoming large trees. They may reach 25 to 30 feet in ten years, 40 feet in twenty, and eventually 70 feet in height. All ashes have opposite **leaves** that are divided into several leaflets. Shamel ash **leaves** vary in length from 4 to 8 inches. The five to seven leaflets are 2 to 3 inches long and ¾ to 1 ¼ inches wide with small teeth along the margins.

**Flowers** in the ashes are small, inconspicuous, and generally either male or female; many occur in clusters of different sizes and shapes. Flowers may appear for only a short time in spring and may be overlooked. Often the flowers do not have corollas or petals; exceptions are the flowering ashes, *F. dipetala* of California and the European *F. ornus*. Shamel ash flowers lack a corolla, but they do form elongated clusters (panicles) several inches long. **Fruits,** also in clusters, consist of a single seed (a samara) with a conspicuous wing that aids in dispersal on the wind. Generally, seeds are abundantly produced.

*Fraxinus uhdei* is widely distributed in Mexico from Sinaloa and San Luis Potosi south to Oaxaca and Chiapas and into Guatemala. In Chiapas, it has been observed in the pine-oak-liquidambar forest, where it generally occurs along drier streams with other deciduous and semideciduous trees. It is frequently planted as a street tree in Mexican cities, including Mexico City and Guadalajara. In Chiapas, it is occasionally planted in hedgerows around homes and is used for tool handles and for fuel.

The date of introduction of Shamel ash into California is not known. Riedel (1957) reports that several trees were planted in Fairmont Park, Riverside, by Dr Archie Shamel. Dr Shamel lived in Riverside during the 1920s and for many years was a member of the parks commission there. Because his name is associated with the ash, it may be presumed that he introduced it to Riverside and from there it was taken to other parts of California.

In Golden Gate Park, a single tree of Shamel ash is in Strybing Arboretum at the edge of the Succulent Garden, next to a tree of Mexican hawthorn *(Crataegus pubescens)*. Both are among the trees that were in the park when the arboretum was laid out in 1937.

As an ornamental in California, Shamel ash has been used most frequently as a street tree. In San Francisco, it was set out after street tree plantings were begun in the 1950s. Unfortunately, its shallow roots, like those of other species of *Fraxinus,* eventually cause problems with curbs and pavement. This ash has been frequently planted in both Northern and Southern California, including low-elevation deserts.

Strybing (VI-M4)
200 block of Noe St
Evergreen/Fast growth/70'
Pendant elongated flower clusters, not showy
    (spring) /Winged seeds
Full sun/Water occasionally and deeply
Sunset Zone 9, 12-24

# 72

## Ginkgo
# *Ginkgo biloba*
### Ginkgoaceae

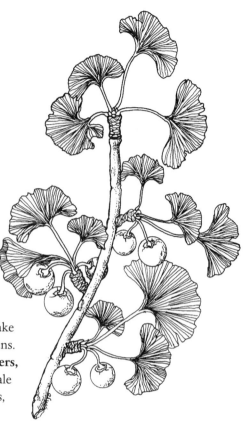

Ginkgo, or maidenhair tree, is one of the most distinctive, attractive, and easily recognized of temperate deciduous trees. Its fan-shaped, parallel-veined **leaves** are unmistakable. When leafless, it is easily distinguished from other deciduous trees by the short, stout, spur shoots scattered on the long branches. Leaves, seeds, and pollen sacs are borne on these spur shoots. These characters, together with the plant's adaptability to a wide range of climatic and soil conditions, its disease resistance, and its golden yellow autumn foliage, combine to make it one of our best-known urban trees on streets and in parks and gardens.

Ginkgo trees are either male or female. There are no true **flowers,** only unprotected ovules on female trees and catkinlike pollen sacs on male trees, both produced at the tips of spur shoots. Being gymnosperms, ginkgoes have "naked" **seeds,** that is, seeds not enclosed in a fruit, as are the seeds of flowering plants (angiosperms). The fleshy ginkgo seed is produced singly on a long stalk; though plumlike in appearance, it is not a fruit in the botanical use of the term. Male and female trees can be recognized only when these reproductive structures are present on the trees.

The success and popularity of ginkgo as a landscape tree are due to its generally attractive habit, golden yellow fall color, long life, fairly low maintenance, minimal litter, and a lack of pests and diseases. A feature that detracts from the landscape use of the tree is the fleshy seed produced on female trees in autumn. These have a disagreeable odor and are often in large enough quantity to be smelly and messy after falling to the ground. This undesirable character, however, can be avoided by planting only male trees.

In recent years, especially in the United States, male trees have been identified, given cultivar names, propagated, and made available for planting. In California, the Saratoga Horticultural Research Foundation began a program in 1951 of selecting and propagating male trees. The most promising ones from that program are still available: 'Autumn Gold', having an upright habit; 'Fairmont', a narrow habit; and 'Saratoga', a compact habit.

For centuries, ginkgoes have been trained in Japan as bonsai, and many American enthusiasts show bonsai ginkgoes, sometimes as miniature groves, in their collections. Young ginkgo trees are occasionally seen informally espaliered against walls. In China and Japan, ginkgo seed is a highly prized food. After removal of the fleshy covering, the seed is considered a delicacy when boiled or roasted.

Ginkgo also has medicinal uses known to the Chinese for centuries. Chemical compounds called ginkgolides, obtained from ginkgo leaves, have been identified; in Europe and Asia these are prescribed for a number of diseases, including asthma and Alzheimer's.

Fuchsia Garden near Conservatory Drive East (IV-S1); N of Kennedy Dr W of Conservatory Dr West (IV-R1); Japanese Tea Garden (V-N2); Strybing (VII-O4)
21-27 Fifth Ave; 1046 Diamond St; 3322 22nd St
Deciduous/Slow growth/80'
Pollen catkins on male trees; inconspicuous flowers on female trees (spring) /Smelly, yellow green, plumlike fruits.
Full sun/Water infrequently
Sunset Zone 1-10, 12, 14-24
Suitable as a street tree
Color plates

Just when ginkgo was introduced from China to Japan is not known, but it may have been during the Sung Dynasty. In Japan, there are trees said to be nearly a thousand years old. Engelbert Kaempfer was the first European to observe and publish his writings about ginkgo. The Dutch East India Company had a trading post in Nagasaki Bay, Japan, where Kaempfer lived for two years (1690–1692). In 1712, following his return to Europe, Kaempfer published a description and illustration of the plant and gave it the name "ginkgo."

Ginkgo was introduced into Europe from Japan in 1727 and first planted in the Dutch city of Utrecht. It was introduced into the United States from England in 1784 when two trees—today the oldest in the country—were planted by William Hamilton on his estate near Philadelphia. Ginkgoes were introduced into California in 1854, and trees today are scattered in and around most West Coast cities.

Ginkgo was not an early introduction into Golden Gate Park; only the 1924 *Annual Report of the Park Commissioners* lists it. The Japanese Tea Garden, with seven ginkgoes, has the largest number of any section in the park. Of these, the most easily located are east of Trestle Bridge near the great bronze Buddha, on the east side of the Pagoda, and on the edge of Main Pond inside the South Gate. Of those in Strybing Arboretum, one is across the path from the Dwarf Conifer Garden. Others in the park are on the north side of Kennedy Drive, west of Conservatory Drive West, and at the entrance to the Fuchsia Garden from Conservatory Drive East.

# An Ancient Tree

Ginkgo, as the only living representative of an ancient group of gymnosperms, has probably existed on earth longer than any other plant known today. It has been called a living fossil, a term used for plants surviving today from very long evolutionary lines. The geological record of ginkgo goes back in time about 200 million years or more to the Mesozoic Era. Fossil leaves similar to those of living trees have been found in Triassic and Jurassic rocks on the Pacific Coast.

Ginkgo is believed to be native to the mountains of southeastern China. Although the existence of natural stands within the past century is questionable, the history of ginkgo points to its occurrence in that part of China. In early Chinese civilizations along the Yellow River in northern China, many plants were domesticated, but among those mentioned in their literature, ginkgo is conspicuous by its absence, leading to the inference that it was not native in that area. Much later, in the Sung Dynasty (AD 960–1279), records of ginkgo appear. Literature from the period refers to ginkgo as being in present-day Anhui Province, south of the Chang Jiang (Yangtze) River. Additional references are made to it in poetry and paintings.

Modern botanists have tried to establish the natural occurrence of ginkgo in China. Professor Hui-Lin Li, an eminent Chinese botanist at the University of Pennsylvania, has reviewed the observations of Chinese botanists as well as those of Robert Fortune, EH Wilson, and Frank Meyer, all of whom explored several areas in China during the past century and a half. All agreed that the natural area of ginkgo is centered in and around the mountains known as Tien Mu Shan in eastern Anhui and adjacent Zhejiang provinces, east of Shanghai. Ginkgo is said to grow in this area with conifers and broad-leafed trees. These observations agree with those of Professor Li, who lived for many years in this part of China and traveled in the region. It appears, therefore, from early historical records and observations of modern botanical explorers, that the mountains of southeastern China are the last refuge of ginkgo, and also that this is the area from which originated all cultivated ginkgo trees taken from China to Japan and the rest of the world.

Sung Dynasty literature reports that ginkgo was cultivated during the Sung and later dynasties, but according to Professor Li, its cultivation was not associated with Buddhism, contrary to statements made by Wilson and others. Professor Li believes that cultivation of the ginkgo tree had no religious origin or significance and its preservation was not attributable to planting by Buddhist or Taoist priests. The tree, however, has been preserved through its extensive cultivation in China, later in Japan, and still later in Europe and North America. Fine old ginkgoes are found today on Chinese temple grounds and elsewhere. In the ancient and attractive city of Yangzhou in the Chang Jiang River valley, a venerable and aged ginkgo, said to be 1200 years old, still stands. Scattered in this city are eighteen ginkgoes over 500 years old and 290 that are more than 300 years old.

# 73

## Silk oak
# *Grevillea robusta*
## Proteaceae

Silk oak is a fast growing tree, symmetrical and pyramidal when young, but developing a spreading crown when older. In Australia, mature trees reach 50 to 60 feet or more in height. The fernlike, pinnately compound **leaves** are alternate on the stems and may be up to 10 inches in length and 6 inches wide. Trees in full flower are strikingly attractive; the numerous bright orange, showy **flowers** are held in pairs on racemes 3 to 4 inches long. Individual flowers are slender, about 1 inch long, and arranged along one side of their stems. The **fruits** are small, leathery follicles.

N of Bowling Greens (IV-Q3); Strybing (VII-N3)
601 Diamond St
Evergreen/Fast growth/60'
Bright orange flowers in showy clusters, 3-4"
    long, (June) /Ellipsoid capsules, 2" long
Full sun/Water occasionally
Sunset Zone 8, 9, 12-24
Suitable as a street tree

Silk, or silky, oak, despite its common name, is not an oak but belongs to the protea family. A large evergreen tree of eastern Australia, it is common in the rain forests of New South Wales and along adjacent watercourses. It occurs northward into Queensland, where it grows in moist hardwood forests. It is cultivated in both of these Australian states and elsewhere.

*Grevillea* is a large genus of about 250 species in the Southern Hemisphere, with most species found in Australia. It was named for Charles Greville, a prominent English botanist, known in his day "for the introduction and cultivation of many rare and interesting plants." Silk oak was introduced to the Kew Gardens, London, about 1835 by Allan Cunningham, an English botanical explorer. He wrote, in his observations of the tree, that it occurred in "thick moist woods on the banks of the Brisbane River [Queensland]...with other large forest trees....From its deeply dissected foliage and the silkiness of the underside it has obtained the name silk oak...by local people of Moreton Bay," near Brisbane. The oak part of the common name comes from the oaklike grain of the wood.

In Australia, the wood of silk oak has been used for furniture, cabinet work, and wall paneling. Young plants, with their appealing foliage, make attractive house plants.

*Grevillea robusta* was an early introduction to California according to Butterfield (1964). William C Walker offered seed at his Golden Gate

Nursery in San Francisco, and in 1871 plants were available at Belle View Nursery, Oakland. Silk oak has been much used as an ornamental tree in gardens, parks, and along streets in California, as well as in Florida and Hawaii. In Golden Gate Park, a single specimen can be seen as part of a mixed planting of shrubs and trees on the west side of Bowling Green Drive, just north of the bowling greens. A young, vigorous tree is inside, and just east of, Strybing Arboretum's Friend Gate, on the edge of the Eastern Australia collection.

Summer heat is a requirement for reliable flowering; trees in San Francisco rarely flower, while those in warmer areas like Walnut Creek, Davis, and throughout Southern California blossom beautifully. One of the most outstanding plantings is a miles-long double row along Euclid Avenue

## The Griselinias
# *Griselinia*
## Cornaceae

Named for Francesco Griselini, an Italian naturalist, the small genus *Griselinia* has about six species and occurs in New Zealand, Chile, and Brazil. The two grown in California are native to New Zealand. Griselinias are large, evergreen shrubs or small trees, with **leaves** that are alternate, leathery, glossy, bright or yellow green, and generally oval. Their foliage is the most attractive feature of these plants, making them particularly useful for screens and hedges. From a distance, plants of both species look alike. Only by close inspection of leaves and especially leaf bases, can the two be distinguished. Both male and female **flowers** are small, clustered on catkins, and inconspicuous, with no ornamental value. Only in gardens, where individuals of both sexes have been planted, do berry-like **fruits** sometimes occur. Riedel (1957) praises both species as "some of the best [plants] that have been introduced here and it is strange that they are used so little, the fresh green [of their leaves] more than compensates for their inconspicuous flowers. They are easily propagated from cuttings and quickly produce their thick white roots. They withstand pruning, are consistently green and well foliaged."

Griselinias are cultivated primarily in milder coastal areas in California. According to Butterfield (1964), the two species were exhibited at the Panama-Pacific International Exposition in San Francisco in 1915 and may have been moved to Golden Gate Park afterwards. *Griselinia lucida* was offered by the California Nursery Company in 1926. Both species were recommended for southern California by Chandler (1993), Hoyt (1938), and Riedel (1957). Both species are tolerant of shade and are usually used as screening plants.

# 74

## Kapuka
## *Griselinia littoralis*
### Cornaceae

This is the larger of the two species in Golden Gate Park, reaching almost 30 feet tall, and the most commonly planted in California. Kapuka has smaller, apple-green **leaves,** only 2 to 5 inches long and nearly equal at their bases; they are attached by a short petiole to dark gold or brownish yellow stems. The inconspicuous pale yellow or greenish **flowers,** appearing in late spring, are of no ornamental value. Some selections have been made of plants with variegated foliage.

      Fine, treelike specimens can be seen in Strybing's New Zealand collection and along the outer fence of the Demonstration Gardens. Others can be seen throughout Golden Gate Park, usually as one component of a mixed screen planting; a fine specimen is on the knoll east of the Academy of Sciences. Kapuka can be sheared into a hedge, an example of which is at the south edge of the park's Rose Garden.

Knoll E of Academy of Sciences (III-P2); Rose
   Garden (III-N2); Strybing (VI-N3 & VII-N3)
Evergreen/Fast growth/30′
Inconspicuous flowers (late spring) /Small dark
   purple berries
Full sun to part shade/Water occasionally
Sunset Zone 9, 14-17, 20-24
Color plate

# 75

## Puka
## *Griselinia lucida*
### Cornaceae

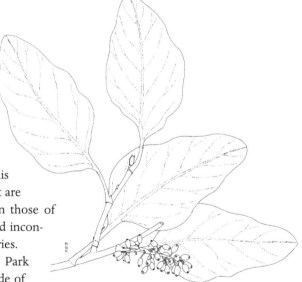

Though of smaller stature (usually no more than 12 feet tall), this species has larger **leaves,** about 4 to 7 inches long with bases that are noticeably unequal; the branches are brown black, darker than those of kapuka. The late spring **flowers** are pale yellow or greenish and inconspicuous. A selection with variegated leaves is available in nurseries.

      Puka is much less commonly planted in Golden Gate Park than kapuka. Shrubs of this species can be seen on the north side of Middle Drive East, just east of the south entrance to the Academy of Sciences. Here, both species of *Griselinia* have been treated as shrubs and sheared regularly into mounds no more than 4 or 5 feet tall; nevertheless, the distinctions between the leaves of each species can be readily seen.

Near SE corner of Academy of Sciences (III-P3)
Evergreen/Moderate growth/12′
Inconspicuous flowers (late spring) /Small, dark
   purple fruits
Full sun to part shade/Water occasionally
Sunset Zone 8, 14-17, 20-24

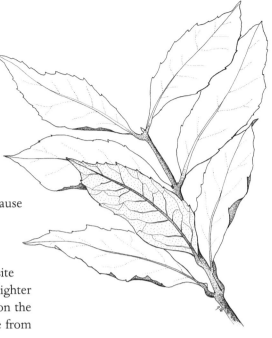

## 76

### Pigeonwood
# *Hedycarya arborea*
Monimiaceae

*Hedycarya arborea* is known as pigeonwood in New Zealand because pigeons eat its sweet, juicy fruits. The tree belongs to a family of tropical and warm regions, especially of the Southern Hemisphere. The generic name is derived from the Greek words for sweet and nut. The tree may be recognized by its smooth brown **bark** and its opposite **leaves,** 4 to 5½ inches long, dark green, shining above, dull and lighter green beneath, with scattered, coarse teeth. Venation is noticeable on the lower leaf surface, with the secondary veins joining a short distance from the margin, then branching again before reaching the margin. **Flowers** are small, with male and female flowers on separate trees in short, branched clusters. The **fruits** are fleshy, berrylike, about ½ inch long, and reddish orange. Birds eating the fruit in New Zealand are said to appear sleepy and sluggish but not otherwise harmed. The berries, leaves, and wood contain alkaloids, and the tree has been suspected of poisoning cows.

*Hedycarya* was first collected by Joseph Banks and Daniel Solander on Captain James Cook's first voyage in 1769 on the eastern coast of New Zealand's North Island. It was found again on Captain Cook's second voyage by botanists Johann and Georg Forster, who later named it. It is abundant in lowland and montane forests on both North and South islands.

Strybing Arboretum has two trees of this species in the New Zealand collection. The largest is 40 feet tall, and both have several trunks from the base. Although the trees in Strybing have not been known to flower, Eric Walther did observe flowers on a tree in the park in 1936.

Strybing (VI-N3)
Slow growth/40' - 50'
Inconspicuous flower clusters /Reddish orange,
    1/2", berrylike fruits
Full sun to part shade/Water occasionally
Sunset Zone 16,17

## 77

### Toyon
# *Heteromeles arbutifolia*
Rosaceae

Toyon is a small tree to 15 feet or more or sometimes a small shrub. Its **leaves** are stiff and leathery, 2 to 4 inches long, with toothed margins. Large terminal clusters of small white **flowers** appear in summer, followed by showy, bright red fruits in fall and winter. It is native to California in the Coast Ranges and the Sierra Nevada and southward into northern Baja California. Throughout this region, it is often a prominent member of the

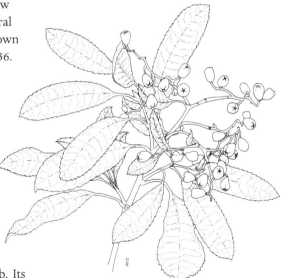

Strybing (VI-M4)
N side of Buena Vista Park
Evergreen/Moderate growth/15' or more
Terminal clusters of small white flowers (June-
    July) /Showy bright red berries
Full sun to part shade/Needs no watering
Sunset Zone 5-24

chaparral plant community. When its red, berrylike fruits are at their showiest, it is one of California's most handsome shrubs or small trees. The red berries have given the plant other common names, including Christmas berry and California holly. According to Charles Francis Saunders (1933), Hollywood was given its name because the hilly area now occupied by this city once "abounded in California holly."

Toyon is scattered throughout Golden Gate Park in areas where the native coast live oak (*Quercus agrifolia*) occurs, as in the woodland at the northeastern corner of the park, from Stanyan Street to Sixth Avenue. It is also seen in a few other places where it has been planted, including Strybing Arboretum, where it can be seen on the hill southwest of the Redwood Trail.

The relationship of toyon to the genus *Photinia* is so close that toyon was once named *Photinia arbutifolia,* a name still sometimes used. Archibald Menzies, with the Vancouver expedition, discovered the plant at Monterey in 1796 and introduced it into England.

# 78

## Chilean wine palm
## *Jubaea chilensis*
### Palmae

A handsome specimen of Chilean wine palm may be seen on the south side of Kennedy Drive opposite Conservatory Drive East. Standing by itself in the lawn, it displays its full elegance. The smooth, ashy gray trunk, among the thickest of all palm trunks, is usually 3 to 4 feet in diameter. Old trees growing in the wild in central Chile may reach 50 or 60 feet in height.

Numerous featherlike, pinnate **leaves,** as much as 15 feet long, form a dense, rounded head of foliage that crowns the massive trunk. Scattered among the bases of the leaves are the **flower** clusters and their persistent bud sheaths. Flowers produce small, rounded **fruits** just over 1 inch long, which look like miniature coconuts and have been given such common names as monkey's coconuts, coquitos, and little cokernuts.

The generic name, *Jubaea,* commemorates King Juba of Numidia, an ancient North African kingdom. In 46 BC, when his kingdom was taken by the Romans, King Juba committed suicide. The connection between King Juba and the palm, *Jubaea,* although vague, may allude to the king's reputed interest in plants. Jubaea is a genus with a single species that occurs in central Chile, the southernmost geographical limit for palms in South America. Today, perhaps the only remaining natural groves of the palm are in La Campana National Park in the Coastal Range north of Valparaiso and Santiago. At one time, it was much more widespread and abundant. Charles Darwin, in the early nineteenth century, wrote that the palm grew

S side of Kennedy Dr opposite Conservatory Dr East (IV-R2)
460 Yerba Buena Ave; Monterey Blvd between Baden and Congo
Evergreen/Slow growth/35'-60'
Dull purple, 3'-5' flower clusters (summer) /Small, yellow, coconut-like fruits
Full sun/Needs no watering
Sunset Zone 12-24

in the thousands, even hundreds of thousands, on one estate near Valparaiso. But, since Darwin's day, the palm has become greatly prized because it yields a sweet syrup; thousands of trees have been cut down to obtain it. The honeylike substance is used much like maple syrup, but unlike maple syrup, the entire tree must be sacrificed for it. A single cut trunk of the palm, allowed to drain over a period of six to eight weeks, yields seventy-five to a hundred gallons of sap. Like maple syrup, the palm sap must be concentrated by boiling. So popular a delicacy is *miel de palma de Ocoa,* or palm honey of Ocoa, that Chile has allowed its only indigenous palm to be seriously depleted.

Even though the original source of *miel de palma* is all but gone, the sap is still a popular delicacy. Clarence Elliott, an English plantsman, reported in *The Gardeners' Chronicle,* following a visit to Chile in 1929, that the substance is manufactured synthetically and sold in tins with a picture of the palm to create the illusion of the real *miel de palma.* What a pity this was not thought of years earlier! The common name, Chilean wine palm, refers to a wine made from fermented *miel de palma.*

Chilean wine palm was first listed as growing in Golden Gate Park in the 1924 *Annual Report of the Park Commissioners,* and was probably brought to the park after the park commissioners' report of 1912. The palm had been in California earlier, however. Victoria Padilla (1961) suggested that it "was introduced in the mission period, as some fine old specimens growing in San Gabriel must date back to that time." Perhaps the earliest known record for the state is that of Francesco Franceschi, who mentioned it in 1895. Franceschi reported that there were two beautiful specimens in Montecito, which he believed to be the largest in southern California. Although he does not mention their age, they must have been many years old at that time, since this palm is a slow grower. Today, specimens 30 to 40 feet tall are seen in several cities in central and southern California.

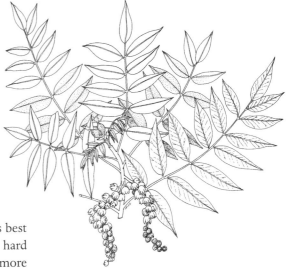

# 79

Black walnut

# *Juglans nigra*

Juglandaceae

A native of the eastern and central United States, the black walnut is best known for its timber. Its **fruits,** though edible and flavorful, have a hard shell tougher than that of English walnuts (*Juglans regia*), which are more commonly eaten. Because black walnut is one of the world's most valuable timber trees, it has become uncommon in the wild. A handsome tree reaching 100 feet or more, it has long been planted as an ornamental in the United States and Europe, although the toxic substances released by the roots prohibit the growth of some garden plants. It may be recognized by its compound **leaves,** which are made up of a number of leaflets arranged

Music Concourse (III-O2); corner of Stanyan and
   Fulton Sts (IV-S1); W side of Conservatory Dr
   East (IV-R2)
Deciduous/Moderate growth/100'-150'
Inconspicuous flowers (Apr-May) /Hard-shelled,
   1" edible nuts
Full sun/Water infrequently
Sunset Zone 1-9, 14-21

along a central rachis. Male **flowers** are held in pendant catkins in the leaf axils as the leaves are unfolding; female flowers are in short terminal spikes. One pollarded black walnut remains among the elms and planes in the Music Concourse; it is easily distinguished from the elms by its leaves. Other black walnut trees, unpollarded, are at the corner of Stanyan and Fulton streets and along Conservatory Drive East, south of the Fuchsia Garden. Black walnut is occasionally seen in cities throughout the central and northern parts of California and in the Pacific Northwest. Walnut orchards found in California and elsewhere are usually planted with English walnuts *(Juglans regia),* which are often grafted on rootstocks of the native walnut *(J. hindsii)* in California.

# 80

## Rewa-rewa
## *Knightia excelsa*
### Proteaceae

*Knightia excelsa* is an evergreen tree from New Zealand, where it is called rewa-rewa or native honeysuckle. Trees of rewa-rewa are stiffly erect, tall, attractive, and distinctive in appearance. Their habit has sometimes been compared with that of the Lombardy poplar. **Leaves** are lanceolate, up to 10 inches long and 1½ inches wide, stiff and leathery, dark green and somewhat shiny above, with a dark brown and hairy covering below, especially when young; leaf margins are distinctly toothed. **Flowers** are dark red, in short, bottlebrush-like spikes in clusters that occur along the stems; because they are more or less hidden by the leaves, they are noticed only at close range. The elongated **fruits** are narrowed at both ends, about 1½ inches long, and, when mature, split along one side and look somewhat like miniature canoes. **Seeds** are winged.

Rewa-rewa occurs from North Cape at the tip of North Island south to Marlborough Sound on the northeastern side of South Island, from sea level to 3,000 feet elevation. It is sometimes found in mixed kauri *(Agathis australis)* forests, along with *Podocarpus totara* and *Dacrydium cupressinum.* Its discovery by Europeans was in 1769 at Tolaga Bay on the eastern coast, north of Poverty Bay, during Captain James Cook's first voyage, when he was accompanied by Joseph Banks and Daniel Solander. In 1810, the plant from their collection was named for Thomas Andrew Knight, a pomologist, a friend of Banks, and an early president of the Horticultural Society of London. A member of the protea family, the genus *Knightia* has three species, one in New Zealand and two in New Caledonia.

The timber of this tree is attractive and has been used for furniture and other types of woodwork. It is not durable enough, however, for exteri-

S side of Kennedy Dr between Tree Fern Dell and
    Rhododendron Dell (IV-P2); Strybing (VI-N3)
Evergreen/Slow growth/40'
Bottlebrushlike spikes of dark red, tubular
    flowers (June-July) /Narrow pods with
    winged seeds
Full sun to part shade/Water regularly
Sunset Zone 16,17

or use. During the past century, so many trees were cut for timber that, in 1889, Thomas Kirk wrote that where trees had been plentiful in the Marlborough area of South Island, they had now become rare and localized.

Often cultivated in New Zealand, rewa-rewa has been suggested as an ideal tree for small gardens, background plantings, and along walls. Slow growing, the oldest of several trees in Strybing's New Zealand collection, about 40 feet tall, is more than sixty years old. According to Eric Walther, it was obtained before 1940 from the New Zealand nursery firm of Duncan and Davies. It is rarely planted elsewhere in California.

# 81

## Cow-itch tree
# *Lagunaria patersonii*
## Malvaceae

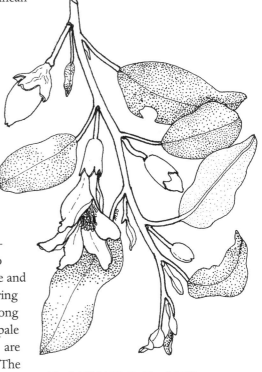

*Lagunaria patersonii* is an attractive evergreen tree, more or less pyramidal in shape, and up to 50 feet tall. The **leaves** are entire, ovate to oblong, 2 to 4 inches long and less than half as wide, dark green above and gray below. Flowering occurs in summer, the solitary **flowers** appearing in the axils of the upper leaves. The cup-shaped calyx is about ½ inch long with five shallow lobes; the five separate petals, 1 to 2 inches long, are pale pink to mauve. Like those of others in the family, the stamens are arranged along a central column that is nearly as long as the petals. The 1-inch-long **fruit** is a capsule that splits into five parts, revealing smooth, reddish brown **seeds.** Small, rough scales cover stems, leaves, and fruits and may cause an irritation of the skin.

*Lagunaria* belongs to the mallow family and is the only species in its genus. It occurs along the eastern coast of Australia and on Lord Howe and Norfolk islands. The primary difference between *Lagunaria* and the closely related genus *Hibiscus* lies in the style branches of the similarly shaped flowers: in *Lagunaria,* they are short and broad, forming a capitate, five-lobed stigma with slightly spreading stigma branches, while in *Hibiscus,* the branches are slender and, at maturity, spread widely. *Lagunaria,* however, is a distinctive enough tree to be easily recognized in spite of any similarities the flowers have to *Hibiscus.*

*Lagunaria* was named for Andreas de Laguna of Segovia, Spain, who lived at the court of Charles V, served as physician to Pope Julius III, and wrote about the botanical works of Dioscorides. The species name commemorates Colonel William Paterson, English gardener, botanist, plant explorer, and collector, who arrived in Australia in 1791; his tour of duty for the British government included service on Norfolk Island, from which he sent seeds of *Lagunaria* and other plants to England. Numerous common names have been given this tree including: primrose tree and sugar plum

Hippie Hill (IV-R2); Strybing (VI-N3)
NE corner of Washington Square Park;
    Connecticut at 17th St
Evergreen/Moderate growth/50'
Hibiscus-like flowers, 1"-2" wide, with 5 pale pink
    to mauve petals (July-Aug) /Brown capsules
    split into 5 parts
Full sun/Water infrequently
Sunset Zone 13, 15-24
Suitable as a street tree
Color plate

tree, presumably referring to the flowers and their fat buds; Queensland pyramid tree and Norfolk Island hibiscus, referring to the shape, family, and natural origins of the tree; and cow-itch tree, alluding to the skin irritation resulting from contact with stems, leaves, or fruits.

According to Riedel (1957), cow-itch tree was exhibited in San Francisco in 1870. The *Annual Report of the Park Commissioners* listed it for Golden Gate Park in the years 1897 to 1924. The cow-itch tree on Hippie Hill is a large, old specimen about 30 feet tall, somewhat pyramidal in shape, with smooth bark, and several trunks from the base. A younger tree is in Strybing's Eastern Australia collection.

Dr Francesco Franceschi of Santa Barbara records the tree there in 1895. Riedel considered it to be "an excellent streetside tree because of its narrow, compact pyramidal crown and the…pale rose hibiscus-like flowers." Muller (1974) lists cow-itch tree at several sites in Santa Barbara. Chandler (1993) includes it for Southern California in several of his habitat sites. It is occasionally seen in gardens on the San Francisco Peninsula. Although more or less coastal in its native range, a fine specimen, planted in the 1970s, thrives in The Ruth Bancroft Garden in Walnut Creek, California.

# 82

Sweet bay

# *Laurus nobilis*
Lauraceae

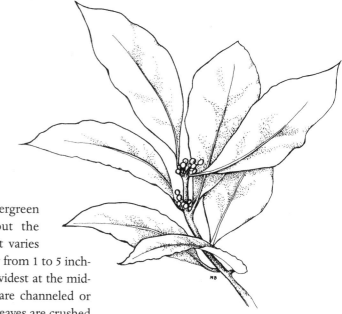

*Laurus* is a small genus consisting of two species of evergreen trees or large shrubs. Sweet bay occurs throughout the Mediterranean region, mostly along the coast, where it varies from 10 to 50 feet in height. The **leaves** of sweet bay vary from 1 to 5 inches long and from 1 to 3 inches wide; they are generally widest at the middle and tend to be lanceolate or oblong. The petioles are channeled or deeply grooved. The pungent aroma given off when the leaves are crushed is distinctive. **Flowers** of sweet bay are small, creamy yellow, and unisexual, with male and female flowers on different trees. The **fruit** is a black, fleshy berry under 1 inch in diameter

Sweet bay is the classic laurel of the ancients. Among the Greeks, it was sacred to the god Apollo; its leafy branches were symbols of triumph and were used to crown heroes. The fruiting branches were made into wreaths for distinguished poets (hence the term "poet laureate"). The crown of laurel leaves is the origin of the phrase "resting on one's laurels." The term "bachelor," referring to the degree, was derived through the French *bachelier,* which came from the Latin *bacca laureus* (laurel berry). "Baccalaureate" is also derived from the Latin term. To the Romans, the laurel was a sign of victory and of truce, like the olive branch. They

SE of McLaren Lodge (IV-S2); Strybing (VII-O3)
56-58 Parnassus; Children's Playground in
    Dolores Park
Evergreen/Slow growth/40′
Insignificant yellow flowers (early spring) /Black
    or dark purple berries to 1″ long
Full sun to part shade/Water infrequently
Sunset Zone 5-9, 12-24
Suitable as a street tree

believed that lightning would not strike the laurel, and the Emperor Tiberius is said to have worn a laurel wreath in thunderstorms. Today the only use of the leaves is commercial; sweet bay leaves are sold as a seasoning to flavor stews, soups, and sauces.

Common in European gardens for centuries, sweet bay was introduced into California in 1858 by William Walker at his San Francisco nursery. It can be seen in many places in the eastern end of Golden Gate Park: southeast of McLaren Lodge, near the Fuchsia Garden, in Peacock Meadow, and in Strybing Arboretum on the north side of the Biblical Garden (and elsewhere). It is also grown in many parks and gardens in other Pacific Coast cities, including Santa Barbara, Santa Monica, Portland, and Seattle.

# A Confusion of Names

The common names, laurel and bay, are used interchangeably for two closely related trees of the laurel family: sweet bay *(Laurus nobilis)* and California bay *(Umbellularia californica)*. Both have other common names. Sweet bay is also called Mediterranean laurel and bay laurel. California bay is often called California laurel, California olive, pepperwood, Pacific laurel, bay tree, or Oregon myrtle.

Despite the widely separated habitats of these trees, the two resemble each other so closely that, when seen in cultivation, they are not easily distinguished. Both have similar, aromatic leaves and inconspicuous yellow flowers in small clusters that might be overlooked. Differences in the flowers are technical, and close examination is needed to see them. The close resemblance of these two trees is not surprising, considering the similarity in the climates of their native regions. Each comes from one the five regions of the world having a mediterranean climate of mild, rainy winters and hot, dry summers. The two trees have evolved through natural selection under similar environmental conditions.

Sweet bay has also been confused with two other plants with laurel in their common names: English or cherry laurel *(Prunus laurocerasus)* and Portugal laurel *(P. lusitanica)*. These are members of the rose family and are not related to either sweet bay or California bay. They both contain hydrocyanic glycosides that break down to release hydrocyanic acid (prussic acid), a toxic substance. English laurel has been implicated on occasion in plant poisonings. Such poisonings may have occurred because the leaves were used for cooking in place of sweet bay's.

The common name laurel is also used for a number of other plants. Sheep laurel is a common name for *Kalmia angustifolia,* mountain laurel for *K. latifolia,* Alexandrian laurel for *Danaë racemosa,* spurge laurel for *Daphne laureola,* and great laurel for *Rhododendron maximum.* These shrubs are unrelated to sweet bay or California bay. They belong to different plant families, and none have leaves with the characteristically spicy fragrance. Their leaves, however, are evergreen and do have a laurel-like aspect.

*A story is told of a small boy who, lost in the woods, was found by searchers who heard him talking to a tree.*

UNKNOWN ORIGIN

Tea trees
# Leptospermum
## Myrtaceae

The tea trees are evergreen trees and shrubs native to Southeast Asia and Australasia (which includes Australia, New Zealand, and Melanesia). **Trunks** are short and sometimes twisted or contorted, due in part to the seaside habitat of a number of species; **bark** on mature trees exfoliates in slender strips. They generally have small, ovate to lanceolate **leaves** that are sometimes aromatic. **Flowers** typically have five sepals and five roundish petals with numerous stamens; white is the most common color, but pink is seen in some species. **Fruits** are woody capsules with small slits on the top surface opening to release tiny seeds. A member of the myrtle family, tea trees are closely related to bottlebrushes (*Callistemon*) and paperbarks (*Melaleuca*), both also native to Australia.

The aromatic leaves of several species of tea tree have been used for brewing a tea high in vitamin C and therefore useful for sailors on long voyages to prevent scurvy. New Zealand tea tree (*Leptospermum scoparium*) furnished the leaves for the tea used by Captain James Cook's crew, which led to it being called tea tree. The tea tree was discovered in 1769 by Joseph Banks and Daniel Solander, who accompanied Cook as naturalists on the first voyage of the Endeavor. During the second voyage (1773), tea tree leaves collected again and

Captain Cook mentioned their agreeable flavor in his account of this voyage. In addition to drinking the tea, Cook's crew also added it to a beer made from spruce leaves (presumably *Dacrydium cupressinum*). To quote from Cook's account, the beer was mixed "with an equal quantity of the tea plant (a name it obtained in my former voyage from our using it as a tea then, as we also did now) which partly destroyed the astringency of the other, [and] made the beer exceedingly palatable and esteemed by every one on board."

Because they occurred on the coasts of Australia and New Zealand, tea trees were noticed by the early explorers of both countries. It is not recorded who first discovered the Australian tea tree (*Leptospermum laevigatum*). Captain Cook claimed southeastern Australia for England in 1770, and, with the establishment of a permanent settlement at Sydney in 1788, English ships occasionally called at the newly settled port and seeds of nearby plants were taken back to England. In 1810, illustrations of both tea trees were published; according to the accompanying text, the Australian tea tree had already been in England for about twenty years, while the New Zealand tea tree had been introduced to King George's royal gardens at Kew as early as 1772.

# 83

White tea tree
# Leptospermum ericoides
**(syn. *Kunzea ericoides*)**
## Myrtaceae

White tea tree forms an elegant evergreen tree with branches tending to droop on mature specimens. It has small white flowers, often so abundant that the leaves are almost hidden during the flowering season. The trunk and older branches are covered with a loose, thin ragged **bark** that peels in narrow, irregular, ribbonlike strips. The maximum height of the trees varies

Strybing (VI-N3)
Evergreen/Fast growth/40'-60'
Masses of small white flowers (spring-summer)
/Cup-shaped seed capsules
Full sun/Water regularly
Sunset Zone 14-24

from 40 to 60 feet, with a trunk 1 to 3 feet in diameter; when growing at high elevations, however, some trees will grow to only 1 or 2 feet tall and may even be prostrate. **Leaves,** crowded towards the ends of branchlets, are linear, usually ¼ to ½ inch long and about ⅛ inch wide, and are dotted with oil glands. Young leaves are covered in sparse silky hairs. Small **flowers,** about ⅛ inch across, are held on short, slender stalks. Usually two to five flowers occur together in short terminal clusters; an occasional flower may be solitary. The five white petals are spreading and the stamens are numerous. **Fruits** are cup-shaped capsules, about ⅛ inch in diameter, with numerous tiny seeds.

White tea tree grows only in New Zealand, on both North and South islands, from sea level to about 3,000 feet, in montane shrubland and in forest margins. Young plants with their feathery branches and multitudes of small, white flowers are particularly graceful and attractive. Because of its small size, the tree's dense, heavy, and durable timber had only limited use in New Zealand in the past for wheel spokes and other smaller objects, but it was highly valued for firewood. Its leaves were apparently not used in New Zealand for brewing tea.

The exact date of introduction of white tea tree to California is not known, but it may have been in the early 1900s or before. Hall (1910) mentioned that it was uncommon, and suggested that it "would probably grow without care on our lower hills." It was being grown in and around San Francisco in the 1920s and 1930s. The 1924 *Annual Report of the Park Commissioners* lists it in Golden Gate Park. Victor Reiter believed the park's trees came from Robert Menzies who had obtained plants from Charles Abraham's Western Nursery in San Francisco.

White tea tree is rare in Golden Gate Park today. One specimen is in Strybing's Eastern Australia collection. It flowers abundantly during June and early July. Another large, old specimen is in Lower Orpet Park in Santa Barbara.

# 84

## Australian tea tree
# *Leptospermum laevigatum*
## Myrtaceae

The Australian tea tree occurs on the southeastern coast of Australia from southern Queensland on the north, through New South Wales, Victoria, South Australia, and Tasmania. Always in coastal areas, and usually on sand dunes not far from the sea, it often forms dense thickets. Thus, it was well suited to its early use in Golden Gate Park. A picturesque tree usually about 25 feet in height, it has gnarled trunks spreading horizontally with **bark** peeling in ribbonlike strips. Branches are dense and leafy, and spread to

N of Kennedy Dr near Stow Lake Dr (III-M2); along 6th Avenue entrance near Kennedy Dr (III-P1); surrounding Polo Field (II-G3); Strybing (VI-N3)
Great Highway at Pacheco St
Evergreen/Fast growth/25′
White, 5-petaled flowers (spring) /Woody seed capsules
Full sun/Water infrequently
Sunset Zone 14-24
Suitable as a street tree

form a broad crown. **Leaves** of the Australian tea tree are ½ to 1 inch in length, obtuse and broader at their tips, with three veins from their bases. The white **flowers,** with five separate petals spreading almost 1 inch across, do not stand out from the leaves and are not as prominent a feature of this tree as in other species.

This tea tree was among the first trees from Australia to be introduced into California. According to Butterfield (1964), it was listed by William Walker in his Golden Gate Nursery catalogue of 1858, which included a large selection of acacias, eucalypts, and other plants from seeds imported directly from Australia. Its first use in Golden Gate Park is not recorded, but sometime in the park's earliest history it was planted by the hundreds of thousands to stabilize the shifting sands. The many large, old Australian tea trees still scattered throughout the park and along Park Presidio Boulevard suggest that it has been both widely and successfully used. Particularly notable is the hedge of Australian tea tree that surrounds the Polo Grounds. Established trees can be seen at the Sixth Avenue entrance near Kennedy Drive, on the north side of Kennedy Drive opposite Stow Lake Drive, and in Stanyan Meadows near the Haight Street entrance.

As a tree for parks and gardens, the Australian tea tree is outstanding for its irregularly twisted trunks and broad crown, and in California it looks much like its wild-growing counterparts in Australia. Because it stands exposure close to the ocean it is useful for creating shelter in sandy soil and, when planted in groups, makes a good seaside hedge.

# 85

New Zealand tea tree

# *Leptospermum scoparium*

## Myrtaceae

In contrast to the Australian tea tree, the closely related New Zealand tea tree is grown for its showy, white, pink or crimson, single or double **flowers,** usually no more than ½ inch in diameter. This species forms a shrub or small tree with erect, upwardly spreading branches. It has narrow lanceolate **leaves** up to ½ inch long, sharply pointed, and with only one vein, the midvein, from the bases.

On Captain Cook's early visits to New Zealand in 1769 and 1773, this tea tree was used by the crew for making tea from its leaves. Since then, it has been found to be one of the country's most widely distributed plants. The Maoris knew it well and called it *manuka*. It occurs throughout both North and South islands and on some of the smaller islands from coast to coast and into the mountains to 5,000 feet elevation. Throughout this range, it shows great variation in growth habit, from low shrubs shaped by salty winds at the coast to still lower, creeping shrubs at high elevations. In between these extremes, it grows as a shrub, often a shapely one, and as a

Entrance to parking area
above McLaren Lodge (IV-S2); Strybing (VI-N3)
Treat St
Evergreen/Fast growth/30'
Showy white, pink or crimson flowers, 1/2" wide (Feb-June) /Small woody seed capsules
Full sun/Water infrequently
Sunset Zone 14-24
Suitable as a street tree

small tree to as much as 30 feet tall. In some areas, it forms thickets called *manuka* thickets. Along with these variations in form are differences in flower color and size. Although most wild plants have white flowers, a few have pink or crimson flowers. Many cultivars of New Zealand tea tree have been selected and grown in New Zealand, but an equally large number have been produced in California. During the 1940s, Walter Lammerts carried out a breeding program in Southern California that resulted in many new and excellent cultivars of the New Zealand tea tree.

The New Zealand tea tree also occurs in Australia, on the southeastern coast from Victoria to New South Wales and on Tasmania. Joseph Banks and Daniel Solander found it at Botany Bay, near present-day Sydney, later in 1769 during Captain Cook's third expedition; it may have been used again as a tea by those aboard the *Endeavor*.

According to Butterfield (1964), the earliest listing in California for the New Zealand tea tree was in Stephen Nolan's 1871 Belle View Nursery catalogue, in which he offered a selection of plants from Australia. This tea tree probably was not as early an introduction into Golden Gate Park as the Australian tea tree, but it was already growing in the park in 1893, according to the *Annual Report of the Park Commissioners*. Trees of this species can be seen flanking the Stanyan entrance to the parking lot north of McLaren Lodge. Many cultivars have been included in Strybing's New Zealand collection. It is now a common garden plant throughout coastal California.

# 86

## Sweet gum
# *Liquidambar styraciflua*
## Hamamelidaceae

Sweet gum, or American storax, occurs in the eastern United States along the Atlantic coast, west to the Mississippi and Ohio river valleys, and in several areas in southern Mexico and Central America. It is a large tree in the wild, 80 to 140 feet tall, but generally only about 40 to 60 feet tall in cultivation. Fully mature trees have furrowed **bark** and slightly angled branchlets. **Leaves** are deeply five to seven lobed, generally 5 to 7 inches wide, scarcely as long, heart shaped to truncate at the base, with finely toothed margins. The **fruits** are tiny capsules fused into spherical balls, about 1 to 1½ inches in diameter, that hang on slender stalks. Leaves turn color in autumn, both in the tree's native habitats and in cultivation. The wood, hard and close-grained but not very strong, takes a good polish and has been used in cabinetmaking and for small objects. The resin, or storax, obtained from the tree is seldom used in the United States, but in Mexico and Central America it is much used medicinally and for its fragrance. It was exported to Europe, where it had the same uses as in Mexico.

On slope W of McLaren Lodge (IV-S2); NW corner, Kennedy Dr and 8th Ave (III-O1); entrance to AIDS Memorial Grove (IV-Q2); Strybing (VII-N4)
Stanyan between 17th St and Belgrave
Deciduous/Moderate growth/40'-60'
Inconspicuous flowers (late spring) /Round, spiny, 1" fruits on slender stalks
Full sun/Water occasionally
Sunset Zone 1-12, 14-24
Suitable as a street tree
Color plate

In an early reference to sweet gum in Mexico, Bernal Diaz del Castillo, who accompanied Hernando Cortés in 1519 during his conquest of the Aztec empire and overthrow of the emperor Montezuma II, describes the emperor, after dining, inhaling smoke from tobacco mixed with the resin. It apparently reminded Diaz of the fragrant resin used in Europe, called Levant storax, obtained from the related *Liquidambar orientalis*. King Philip II of Spain sent his physician Francisco Hernandez to New Spain (Mexico) in 1570 to investigate the natural history and political conditions. Hernandez wrote of the resin and of the tree from which it came, "with leaves almost like those of a maple" divided into five lobes. He also described the uses of the resin by the people of the area.

American sweet gum was introduced from Virginia to England before 1683 by John Banister. It was grown in the well-known garden of Henry Compton, bishop of London and pioneer dendrologist. Philip Miller also grew it in the mid-1700s in the Chelsea Physic Garden.

According to Butterfield (1964), sweet gum was offered in 1854 by Commercial Nurseries in San Francisco. It was first listed for Golden Gate Park in the late 1890s. At present, the largest tree in the park, over 40 feet tall, is at the main entrance to the AIDS Memorial Grove at the eastern end of de Laveaga Dell. Others in the park are in the lawn area west of McLaren Lodge and near the intersection of Kennedy Drive and Eighth Avenue. In Strybing Arboretum, several trees grown from seed collected in southern Mexico have been planted in the New World Cloud Forest.

Sweet gums are planted throughout California's urban and suburban areas, along streets, in parks and campuses, and in gardens. In spite of their origin in areas with plenty of moisture, sweet gums adapt easily to the West Coast's annual summer dry period. Hodel (1988) described the tree as one of the most dependable for good autumn foliage color in the Los Angeles area. In the Pacific Northwest, sweet gums are also planted extensively. Two problems are associated with sweet gums, particularly when they are planted as street trees: their shallow roots tend to lift sidewalks and the fallen fruits can be a nuisance for pedestrians.

During the 1950s and 1960s, the Saratoga Horticultural Research Foundation introduced three cultivars of American sweet gum that are now widely used in this country and in Europe. Selected for their dependable habit and autumn leaf color, these are 'Palo Alto' (orange red to bright red fall foliage), 'Burgundy' (deep purple fall foliage lasting through winter), and 'Festival' (narrow habit).

# Liquidambars

*Liquidambar* is a small genus of about four species, of which three are used as landscape trees. Sweet gum *(L. styraciflua)* occurs in eastern North America and Central America, Oriental sweet gum *(L. orientalis)* in Asia Minor, and Formosan gum *(L. formosana)* in Taiwan and China. The scientific name of the genus comes from Latin words for liquid and amber and refers to the fragrant resin, sometimes called storax or liquid storax, which is obtained from the inner bark of Oriental and American sweet gums. The Greek word storax is derived from the Hebrew *tzori*, which appears in the Bible and refers to Levant storax, thought to be the "balm of Gilead;" this species may have occurred in Gilead, northwest of Israel, in biblical times, but it is not found there today.

# 87

Tulip tree
## *Liriodendron tulipifera*
Magnoliaceae

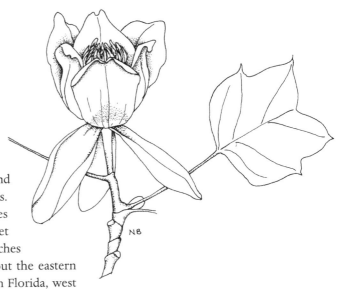

Tulip tree is one of the tallest, handsomest, most useful, and best-known trees of the eastern North American forests. Possibly the tallest deciduous tree in the world, mature trees in the wild may reach 190 to 200 feet with trunks 8 to 10 feet in diameter; the crown is narrowly pyramidal with branches only in the upper half of the trunk. It is found throughout the eastern third of the United States from Massachusetts to northern Florida, west to Lake Michigan, and south to northern Louisiana. In the southern Appalachian Mountains, it occurs at elevations of nearly 4,000 feet. Throughout this extensive region, it is known by several common names, including poplar, yellow poplar, tulip poplar, canoe wood, white wood, and popple, in addition to tulip tree.

On lawn W of McLaren Lodge (IV-S2); Strybing (VII-N3)
Duboce Park; 2242 Polk St
Deciduous/Moderate growth/30'-50'
2″ long, tuliplike, pale green and orange flowers (May-June) /Cone-shaped cluster of winged seeds
Full sun/Water regularly
Sunset Zone 1-12, 14-23
Suitable as a street tree

Tulip trees in cultivation, at least in California, do not reach the heights of those in the forests of the eastern United States; most are 30 to 50 feet tall. **Bark** of young trees is thin, somewhat scaly, and gray; on mature trees, it becomes brown, thick, and deeply furrowed. **Leaves** have a distinctive shape: the blade is about 2½ to 5 inches long, generally broader than long, with two to four lateral lobes. The top edge of the leaf, between the two upper lobes, is nearly straight across, with a shallow notch in the middle. The leaf stalk is 2 to 4 inches long, and at its base are two appendages (stipules) up to about 1 inch long; these soon fall, leaving a circular scar on the stem. From below, the **flowers** more or less resemble the garden tulip. They have three reflexed green sepals and six erect petals, 1½ to 2 inches long, pale green with an orange band near the base. Flowers are at the stem tips, but because their colors are pale, they are not showy and do not stand out from the leaves. The cone-shaped **fruit,** about 2½ inches long, is made up of a series of 1-inch-long, winged **seeds** that detach at maturity and are wind-blown. The leaves turn yellow in fall; the trees are more colorful at that time than when in flower.

Although a hardwood, the tulip tree's wood is softer than that of some pines and firs and is light enough to be used for river-going rafts. Indians and early American settlers made canoes from it. Daniel Boone carved a 60-foot canoe from a single tree and transported his family and their belongings in it from Kentucky down the Ohio River to a new home. Tulip tree wood has had many other uses. American pioneers used it for building houses, and later generations have made plywood, furniture, and paper from it.

Tulip tree was one of the earliest introductions into Europe from North America. John Tradescant, the younger, visited eastern North America several times during the mid-1600s and sent or took plants back to his father's well-known garden in London. Among these were the tulip tree, red maple *(Acer rubrum),* swamp cypress *(Taxodium distichum),* and American sycamore *(Platanus occidentalis).* Following that introduction, tulip tree was grown in English gardens. It was also taken to Holland, where a tree in the botanical garden in Leiden was described in 1687 by the garden's director, Paul Hermann, and given the name *Tulipifera arbor Virginiana.* Later, Linnaeus used *tulipifera* for the species name when he described and named the tulip tree. *Liriodendron* is taken from the Greek words for lily and tree.

Tulip tree was an early introduction into California. Butterfield (1964) lists it at Commercial Nurseries in San Francisco in 1854. It is grown in many other California cities, including Sacramento, Berkeley, Santa Barbara, Santa Monica, San Diego, and Whittier, where an avenue planting is exceptional for the size and number of trees. According to *Annual Reports of the Park Commissioners,* tulip tree has been in Golden Gate Park since the 1890s. A handsome specimen is in the lawn west of McLaren Lodge; another is in Strybing Arboretum near the fence north of Heidelberg Hill.

The genus *Liriodendron,* of the magnolia family, has only two species: *L. tulipifera* from eastern North America, and *L. chinensis* from western China and northern Vietnam. Only small differences in size and shape of the flowers and leaves separate the two species. On the other hand, flowers, fruits, and leaves of the genus are so characteristic that, once recognized, the two liriodendrons would never be confused with other members of the magnolia family. *L. chinensis* has been introduced into cultivation in the United States and Europe on several occasions but has never become as popular a landscape tree as *L. tulipifera.* Hybrids between the two species have been made at the National Arboretum in Washington, DC.

# 88

## Litsea

# *Litsea calicaris*

## Lauraceae

*Litsea calicaris* belongs to the laurel family, to which sweet bay *(Laurus nobilis)* also belongs. In its New Zealand collection, Strybing Arboretum has one tree, about 40 feet tall, with a single trunk and smooth, brown **bark.** It has alternate, ovate leaves, 2 to 5 inches long, dark green and shiny above, glaucous beneath, with inconspicuous veins. **Flowers** are small, four or five together in umbel-like clusters. Male and female flowers occur on separate trees. The **fruit** is fleshy, about ½ to ¾ inch long, with a single seed, and resembles a miniature avocado. The wood is tough, strong, elastic, and durable. At one time, it was used in New Zealand for making barrels, wheels, and wheeled vehicles.

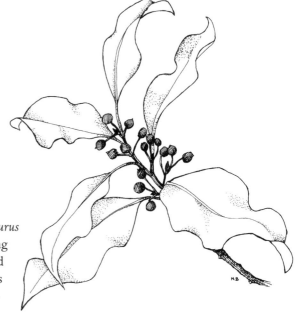

Strybing (VI-N3)
Slow growth/50′
Clusters of insignificant flowers (spring) /Fruit
    resemble a miniature avocado
Full sun to part shade/Water occasionally
Sunset Zone 16, 17

Litsea was first discovered and collected by Joseph Banks and Daniel Solander on Captain James Cook's first voyage in 1769 on the eastern coast of New Zealand's North Island. It occurs in lowland and hilly forests throughout North Island, always below 2,000 feet elevation. Though cultivated in New Zealand, it is seldom grown elsewhere.

Litsea was first mentioned in the 1924 *Annual Report of the Park Commissioners.* It may have been brought to San Francisco to landscape New Zealand's pavilion at the Panama–Pacific International Exposition in 1915, and then taken to the park after the exposition through arrangements made by park superintendent John McLaren.

# 89

## Chilean myrtle
# *Luma apiculata*
## Myrtaceae

Chilean myrtle has several synonyms, including *Myrceugenella apiculata, Eugenia apiculata,* and *Myrtus luma;* in its native Chile, it is known locally as temu or arroyan. Chilean myrtle is a large shrub or small tree, generally to about 20 feet, though in its native area it may become much taller. The attractive **bark** is orange-brown, smooth, and peels in flakes, leaving patches of white. Its evergreen **leaves** are opposite, oval, about 1 inch long, dark green above, paler beneath, abruptly pointed at their tips, and with short petioles. Fragrant white **flowers,** each less than 1 inch across, are arranged in showy clusters; they have four sepals and four cup-shaped petals. The stamens are numerous and grouped into a conspicuous ring around the style; the inferior ovary develops into a fleshy, globose, dark purple, berrylike **fruit,** about ½ inch long. The berries are sweet and edible and often used in preserves.

Chilean myrtle resembles common myrtle, but the two may be distinguished by several characters. Leaves of Chilean myrtle are not as variable in shape and size, but have rusty hairs that are lacking in common myrtle. The white flowers of Chilean myrtle have four petals, while those of common myrtle have five.

Chilean myrtle is one of the most common and widespread species of the myrtle family in western temperate South America. It occurs in cool temperate forests of south-central Chile from Concepción to the island of Chiloe and adjacent western Argentina. It was introduced to England in 1844 by William Lobb, who collected it in Chile for the Veitch and Son Nursery. Its first introduction into California was probably in the 1890s; by the 1920s, it was reported to be "sometimes grown in California." It was listed for Golden Gate Park in the 1897 *Annual Report of the Park Commissioners.* Today, it is seen scattered through the park, particularly along

W side of Kezar Dr, N of Alvord Tunnel (IV-S3); S of Kennedy Dr between Rhododendron Dell and Tree Fern Dell (III-P2); King Dr, E of Sunset Ave (II-F4); Strybing (VI-N3 & VII-O3)
Stern Grove parking lot
Evergreen/Moderate growth/20′
Fragrant clusters of white, 4-petaled flowers, to 1″ wide, with conspicuous stamens (June–July) /Dark purple berrylike fruit
Full sun/Water occasionally
Sunset Zone 14-24

Kennedy Drive where it forms a high screen with hopbush *(Dodonaea viscosa)*. Two short rows of Chilean myrtle, small trees about 12 feet tall, are on King Drive just east of the Sunset Avenue entrance to the park. Several trees can be seen in Strybing Arboretum in the South American collection, in addition to two in the Garden of Fragrance.

# 90

## Fernleaf Catalina ironwood
## *Lyonothamnus floribundus*
## *ssp. aspleniifolius*
### Rosaceae

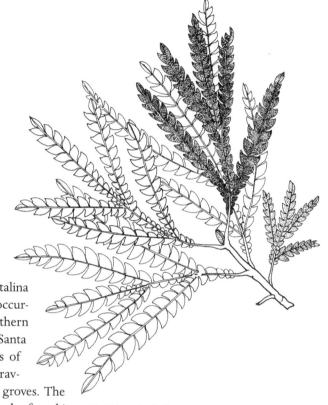

The only members of the rose family in North America to attain the size and habit of a tree are the two subspecies of Catalina ironwood. These California natives have the distinction of occurring only on the several Channel Islands off the coast of Southern California: Santa Catalina, Santa Rosa, San Clemente, and Santa Cruz. On the islands, these trees are found on steep slopes of canyons at elevations from 500 to 2,000 feet, on dry, rocky or gravelly soils; they are often seen in pure stands that form small groves. The generic name commemorates its discoverer, William S Lyon, who found it first on Santa Catalina in 1884; the second part of the generic name is from the Greek *thamnos*, or shrub. The wood is heavy, hard, and strong, giving these trees their common name.

W of Kezar Dr, S of Kennedy Dr (IV-S3); Fulton St, E of 43rd Ave (I-D1); Strybing (VII-N4)
1471 - 45th Ave
Evergreen/Moderate growth/50′
Small, white flowers in large flat clusters (June-July) /Brown seed capsules
Full sun/Water infrequently
Sunset Zone 15-17, 19-24
Color plate

Fernleaf Catalina ironwood (*Lyonothamnus floribundus* ssp. *aspleniifolius*) is a tall evergreen shrub or slender tree reaching 20 to 50 feet in height, with gray to red brown **bark** that peels in long strips. Its sessile **leaves** are opposite and palmately or pinnately compound, composed of three to nine linear leaflets, each up to 4 inches long and divided into sessile, hatchet-shaped segments. **Flowers** are numerous, held in terminal, much-branched clusters 3 to 6 inches across; individual flowers have five rounded white petals about ¼ to ½ inch across with about fifteen stamens as long as the petals. **Fruit** consists of two woody follicles, each with two seeds.

The faded flower heads are usually retained on the trees for several years, a characteristic that often results in an untidy appearance and may explain the infrequency with which fernleaf Catalina ironwood appears in cultivation. It is available from California nurseries that specialize in native plants and is recommended as a useful ornamental by landscape architect Bob Perry (1992).

In Golden Gate Park several fine trees, in flower during the summer, may be seen on the west side of Kezar Drive south of Kennedy Drive and along Fulton Street at 43rd Avenue. A fine small grove is in the Arthur Menzies Garden of California Native Plants at Strybing Arboretum, planted in the early 1970s. Outstanding groves can also be seen at the Native Plants Botanic Garden in Berkeley's Tilden Regional Park, at Rancho Santa Ana Botanic Garden in Claremont, and at the Santa Barbara Botanic Garden, where it serves as the logo for the garden. It is also the official tree of Santa Barbara County.

Santa Catalina Island ironwood *(Lyonothamnos floribundus* ssp. *floribundus)* differs in having simple leaves that may be entire or have rounded teeth. This subspecies occurs only on Santa Catalina Island and is rarely seen in cultivation. Both subspecies have been severely impacted in their island habitats by the grazing of feral animals.

## The Magnolias
# *Magnolia*
## Magnoliaceae

Magnolias are among the oldest of flowering plants, having evolved more than sixty-five million years ago when earth was dominated by ferns and conifers. The large, showy **flowers** are produced at the terminus of each shoot and have a simple arrangement of an indefinite number of thick sepals and petals, so closely resembling each other that they are called "tepals." Within the cup, or bowl, of each flower is a mass of pollen-bearing stamens spiraling around a column of pistils. Beetles, ancient forms of insect life, are thought to be the original pollinators of magnolias, feeding on both the plentiful pollen and the sweet tissue of the petals.

Most magnolias are trees, either evergreen or deciduous, with a broad rounded habit and a fairly coarse branching pattern. The usually furry **buds,** both vegetative and floral, are produced during the late summer and fall and are displayed prominently through the winter, before opening in spring. In the San Francisco area, deciduous magnolias reach their floral peak in late February or March. A few species flower in late spring or summer. Magnolias generally grow for many years before they begin flowering; in nurseries, they are often available as grafted trees, a technique for propagation that encourages earlier flowering.

Magnolia **leaves** are simple, oblong or obovate in shape, and often large, with the leaves of some temperate species reaching 2 feet in length. Deciduous species are likely to have hairy leaves, while the leaves of evergreen species will be tough and leathery, sometimes with furry undersides.

The aggregate **fruits** of magnolias are conelike in shape, made up of a series of carpels (compartments), each splitting to release one or two colorful seeds connected by a silklike thread.

Magnolias are found in Asia, particularly in the Himalayas and Japan, and from eastern North America to Central America. They have long been popular park and garden trees, the deciduous species being particularly showy when in flower in spring. The evergreen species are grown as much for their foliage as for their flowers, which are often produced sporadically and sparsely. The fragrance of many is a distinctive feature. A particularly fine collection of mostly Asiatic magnolias can be seen at Strybing Arboretum.

# 91

## Campbell's magnolia
## *Magnolia campbellii*
### Magnoliaceae

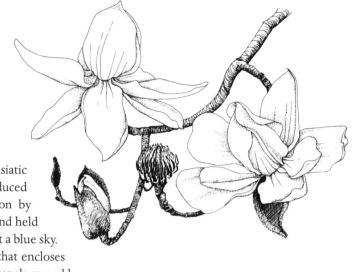

Campbell's magnolia belongs to a group of deciduous Asiatic magnolias with large, attractive **flowers** that are produced before the leaves appear; this species begins the season by flowering in January and February. Either pink or white and held upright on bare branches, they are spectacular seen against a blue sky. Their innermost tepals form an erect, conelike covering that encloses the central column of stamens and pistils; the remaining tepals spread horizontally. It is this characteristic "cup-and-saucer" flower shape that distinguishes Campbell's magnolia from other deciduous Asiatic magnolias. **Fruits** are conelike in shape and reddish.

    Trees of Campbell's magnolia may reach 80 to 100 feet in height in their native habitat in the Himalayas, often rising above other forest trees. Some trees are more stocky and broadly spreading, a form typical of many of the trees at Strybing. The light gray **bark** is striking in winter after the leaves have fallen. The **leaves** are medium green, broadly elliptical to oblong, and up to 9 inches long.

    Many trees of Campbell's magnolia have been planted at Strybing near the library, on Heidelberg Hill, and in the Asian sections. It is also seen elsewhere in Golden Gate Park: a fine specimen is west of Stanyan Street near the intersection with Page Street.

    The flowers of one of the white-flowered Campbell's magnolias in the arboretum depart from the typical shape. Its outermost tepals hang down, rather than spreading horizontally, and thus the flowers do not have the typical cup-and-saucer shape. Because this tree is unlike other trees of the species, it was given the cultivar designation 'Strybing White'. It was grown from seed received in Golden Gate Park in 1934 from G Ghose and Company in Darjeeling.

Stanyan Meadows near Page St (IV-S2); Strybing
  (VI-M3, VI-N3, & VII-N3)
Deciduous/Slow growth/60'-80'
Large pink or white upright flowers resemble a
  cup and saucer (Jan-Feb) /Reddish, conelike
  fruits
Full sun/Water regularly
Sunset Zone 6-9, 14-21
Color plates

# A Strybing First

The best known of Strybing's original trees is Campbell's magnolia, introduced into Golden Gate Park before the arboretum was established. The species had been named only in the 1860s after plants arrived in England from India; it was named for Dr Archibald Campbell, the British Political Resident in Darjeeling. In 1924, the park received a shipment of plants from the English nursery of Stuart Low and Company, and John McLaren delegated their care to Eric Walther. Among them was a two-year-old plant, first set out elsewhere in the park, then moved in 1939 to its present site in the arboretum. Its flowering at Strybing in 1940 was a historic event: it was the first tree of this species to flower in the United States. After sixteen years of waiting, the patience of Eric Walther was finally rewarded.

Other introductions of Campbell's magnolia into this country came later; trees in Seattle were not received until after World War II. Due to the efforts of Eric Walther, about twenty additional trees of Campbell's magnolia were placed in the arboretum in the 1950s; more have been added in recent years. Their flowering every year during January and February is a popular event. So prominent a feature has this magno-

# 92

## Delavay's magnolia
# *Magnolia delavayi*
## Magnoliaceae

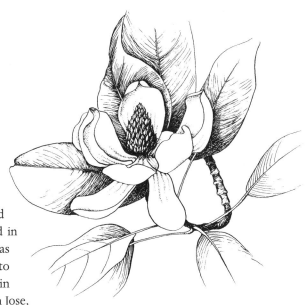

Delavay's magnolia is rarely grown and little known. An evergreen tree with creamy white flowers, it is found in Yunnan and Sichuan provinces in western China. The plant was discovered in 1886 by Pierre Delavay, a French missionary, for whom it was named. Ernest H Wilson found it again while on his first trip to western China in 1899 and introduced it into England. The tree in the arboretum may have come from WB Clarke's nursery in San Jose, where it was being offered in 1948.

Strybing's tree is mature and well established, about 30 feet tall with a broad crown. Its ovate **leaves** are up to 10 inches long (the largest of all evergreen, temperate magnolias), leathery, more or less silvery and hairy on the lower surface, with petioles to about 3 inches. The **flowers** are creamy white, bowl-shaped, 7 to 8 inches across, and fragrant. They occur sporadically, are not long lasting, and are somewhat disappointing when compared with those of southern magnolia *(Magnolia grandiflora)*. **Fruits** are conelike and dull brown. The tree in Strybing's Moon-viewing Garden is the only one in Golden Gate Park and one of the few on the West Coast. As a result of unusually heavy rains in 1998, the soil supporting this heavy and broadspreading tree gave way, allowing it to fall over slightly; it now leans on one of its major limbs but is otherwise healthy and stable.

Strybing (VI-M3)
Evergreen/Slow growth/20'-30'
Bowl-shaped, fragrant, creamy white flowers,7"-8" across (summer) /Conelike fruits
Full sun/Water regularly
Sunset Zone 7-9, 14-24

# Strybing Arboretum and Botanical Gardens

The idea for an arboretum in Golden Gate Park goes back to the park's early days and to William Hammond Hall, the original surveyor and planner of the park. However, it was not until after John McLaren became superintendent in 1887 that plans for an arboretum began to take shape. The *Annual Report of the Board of Park Commissioners* for 1889 recorded that plans were underway, in cooperation with the State Board of Forestry Commissioners, to establish an arboretum similar to that at Harvard University. The site selected for the proposed arboretum was adjacent to the waterworks along South Drive, which is the location of today's Strybing Arboretum and Botanical Gardens. Plantings of various conifers were made during the mid-1890s in this section, henceforth designated on all maps as the "Arboretum."

A proposition for raising funds for the development of the arboretum through a bond issue was placed on the San Francisco ballot sometime before 1900. The measure, unfortunately, did not receive the necessary two-thirds majority. Interest in an arboretum for the park continued, but no further development was carried out until funds became available from the bequest of Helene Strybing.

Helene Strybing, a well-to-do widow, died at the end of 1926, leaving a bequest to the City of San Francisco for an arboretum. Little is known about Mrs Strybing except that she was apparently born in Germany. Her husband, Christian M Strybing, was a successful businessman who died in the 1890s.

Most of Mrs Strybing's estate was placed in a trust fund to provide income for her brother and sisters in Germany during their lifetimes. Following their deaths (the last died in 1939), her remaining estate of about $200,000 came to the park. Mrs Strybing's instructions regarding the use of her bequest were clear and precise. The funds were to be used for "the laying out, arrangement, establishment, and completion of an Arboretum and Botanical Gardens to be situated in Golden Gate Park...preferably in the vicinity of the California Academy of Sciences...to contain especially a collection of trees, shrubs, and plants indigenous to, or characteristic of, California."

During the mid-1930s the first funds from Mrs Strybing's bequest became available and plans were begun for the development of the arboretum. Park superintendent John McLaren placed in charge his most capable gardener, Eric Walther, who set about to learn all he could about arboreta and botanical gardens in the United States and Europe. He and McLaren drew up a master plan for the layout, construction, and planting. From a central axis radiated a series of paths leading to the various planting sections. The arrangement of the sections was to be primarily geographical, with areas identified for plants from Australia, New Zealand, South Africa, the Mediterranean Basin, China, the Himalayas, Japan, Mexico, Central and South America (particularly Chile), and California. Secondary areas were to include special collections such as escallonias, magnolias, medicinal plants, and rock garden plants.

Actual construction began in November 1937 with assistance from the federally supported Works Progress Administration. A small section of four and one-half acres in the central part of the arboretum was the earliest to be developed. In this section the first tree to be formally planted was a specimen of winter's bark *(Drimys winteri)*.

Sources of plants for the new arboretum were varied. Golden Gate Park, with its large and interesting collection of ornamental trees and shrubs, was itself a kind of botanical garden; with the establishment of an arboretum in the park, it was possible to bring together in one place many of the plants scattered throughout the park's one thousand acres. Some of the earliest plants to be set out in the arboretum had come to the park from the 1915 Panama–Pacific Exposition, from the late Charles Abraham's Western Nursery, and from the Bureau of Plant Introduction of the United States Department of Agriculture. Numerous shipments of living plants were imported between 1924 and 1940 from nurseries abroad, such as Duncan and Davies in New Plymouth, New Zealand, Hillier and Sons, Winchester, England, and Stuart Low in London.

Plants were also obtained from nurseries in California, including Armstrong's in Ontario, Evans and Reeves in Los Angeles, Victor Reiter, Hallawell's, Toichi Domoto, and Leonard Coates (all in the San Francisco area), and Doty and Doerner in Oregon. Among the botanical gardens contributing plants were

The main lawn at Strybing Arboretum and Botanical Gardens, with Leyland cypress (x *Cupressocyparis leylandii)* on the right and Monterey cypress *(Cupressus macrocarpa)* emerging from the fog to the left of the fountain. Photograph by RG Turner Jr

the Washington Park Arboretum in Seattle, Huntington Botanical Gardens in San Marino, and the New York Botanical Garden. After 1940, because of increasing difficulties in the importation of living plants, seeds were imported from abroad; Henry Steedman, collector and seedsman of West Australia, and Professor RH Compton, Director of the National Botanic Gardens of South Africa at Kirstenbosch, were among the many contacts who supplied seeds from their areas.

From 1937 to 1957, under Eric Walther's supervision about twenty-five sections were laid out in forty acres and about five thousand plants had been set out at one time or another. During these years Strybing's function had been an educational one. It displayed many of the useful ornamental plants that could be grown successfully in the San Francisco area. The plants were labeled and information regarding them was made available by Walther through his guided tours, displays of cut specimens sent to school and college classes, and meetings of garden clubs and other groups, such as the California Horticultural Society.

In 1957, Eric Walther retired as the arboretum's first director, closing a career of nearly forty years in Golden Gate Park. His had been primarily a one-man operation in establishing the arboretum; the successes (and failures) of these years were due to Walther's energies and activities. The accomplishments of these years may be judged by the recognition that Strybing received from other arboreta, both at home and abroad.

In 1954, a number of Walther's friends, along with others interested in the continued development of the arboretum, organized the Strybing Arboretum Society. The early members of this society realized that Strybing had progressed beyond a one-man operation,

and they wished to broaden and develop its horticultural, educational, and scientific value and to bring its assets and potential to the people of the San Francisco Bay Area.

Percy H (Jock) Brydon was hired as Strybing's second director. One of his first tasks was to carry out a master plan drawn by Robert Tetlow, of the University of California's Department of Landscape Architecture, for the further development of the arboretum. The plan, carried out in two phases, was completed in 1966, and created the pathways and roads, the fountain, and many of the attractive vistas seen today. Remarkably, only a few trees had to be removed to accommodate the new plan.

Successive directors of the arboretum—Roy Hudson (1969–1971), John Bryan (1971–1979), Walden Valen (1979–1999), and Scot Medbury (1999–)—have continued to develop the grounds to present an exceptional array of plants from around the world. A majority of the more than 7000 kinds of plants in the collection are still arranged according to their geographic origins, in gardens such as the South African, Eastern Australian, New Zealand, Asian, and Californian sections. Other areas of the arboretum display particular groups of plants such as dwarf conifers, rhododendrons, primitive plants, succulents, and fragrant plants. The Strybing Arboretum Society continues to offer an extensive program to interpret the collections and to educate the public about plants and gardens for the San Francisco Bay Area. With the recent development of the cloud forest collections representing both the New and Old worlds, the arboretum has become a active participant in the conservation of the world's biological diversity.

# 93

Southern magnolia
## *Magnolia grandiflora*
Magnoliaceae

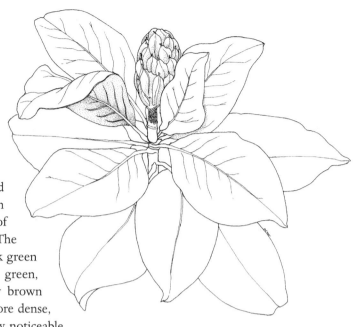

Southern magnolia, also known as evergreen magnolia and bull bay, has been called the elegant aristocrat of American trees. It usually has a pyramidal habit, attaining a height of 60 to 75 feet, or as much as 90 feet in its native habitat. The stiff, leathery **leaves** have short stalks; leaf blades are dark green and glossy above, but below the color varies from gray green, with appressed greenish hairs, to brownish, with rusty brown hairs. In some trees, the rusty brown hairy covering is more dense, giving the leaves a decidedly two-toned effect, particularly noticeable when branches and leaves are moved by a breeze. Leaf length varies from 3 to 8 inches and width from 2 to 4 inches. The large, showy, white **flowers,** 6 to 10 inches across and more or less bowl-shaped, have nine to twelve, and sometimes more, petal-like tepals that surround the central cylindrical column, on which are arranged the numerous stamens and the separate pistils. At maturity, this column enlarges to form a brown, conelike, aggregate **fruit,** 3 to 4 inches long, from which many red, fleshy **seeds,** nearly ½ inch long, are suspended by slender threads.

This handsome evergreen tree is native to the southeastern United States from the coast of North Carolina south to central Florida, westward across the coastal areas of the Gulf States to eastern Texas and along the lower Mississippi Valley to southern Arkansas. Nowhere does it occur very far inland, either from the Atlantic Ocean or from the Gulf of Mexico. Through cultivation as an ornamental tree, however, southern magnolia has been distributed around the world. It is probably more widely cultivated than any other broad-leafed evergreen tree; certainly, it is the only one with large, showy flowers that can be grown in many different climates. On the East Coast, it is grown as far north as Washington, DC; farther north, in Philadelphia and New York, it needs protection. On the West Coast it is planted from San Diego to Seattle.

Southern magnolia was introduced into California before 1860, when it was offered by two central California nurserymen. It was also an early introduction into Golden Gate Park. The 1889 *Annual Report of the Park Commissioners* listed it among the park's trees. Of the several trees in the park at present, one may be seen at the southeastern corner of McLaren Lodge, on the north side of the Lodge's parking lot, and north of Alvord Lake. Younger trees can be seen on Strybing's Main Lawn and throughout the eastern end of Golden Gate Park. It is a common tree along San Francisco streets such as Castro (between 14th and Market streets) and on the streets surrounding Dolores Park.

N side of McLaren Annex parking area (IV-S1); N of Alvord Lake (IV-S3); Strybing (VII-O3)
Dolores Park; Castro St between 14th and Market
Evergreen/Slow growth/60'-75'
White, fragrant, bowl-shaped flowers, 6"-10" across (spring, summer, fall) /Conelike fruit with exposed, red, fleshy seeds
Full sun/Water occasionally
Sunset Zone 4-12, 14-24
Suitable as a street tree

During the later decades of the twentieth century, southern magnolia became one of the popular ornamental trees in California cities from north to south. Today, we find it in the lists of those cities that have published accounts of their trees, such as Sacramento, Palo Alto, Lafayette, Santa Barbara, and Santa Monica.

The natural variation in southern magnolia—in habit, size, leaf shape, amount of rusty brown hairy covering of lower leaf surfaces, and flower size—can be observed in cultivated specimens grown from seeds. Variation is seen in young plants, sometimes even in seedlings, and variants have been selected since its introduction into Europe over 200 years ago. More recently, selections have been made in the United States. Several of these were produced at the Saratoga Horticultural Research Foundation in California; three of the most successful and best known of these are the 'Samuel Sommer', 'Russett', and 'San Marino'. Such vegetatively propagated selections have continued to increase the popularity and reliability of southern magnolia as a street tree and as an ornamental for parks, campuses, and large gardens.

# 94

## Mayten
# *Maytenus boaria*
## Celastraceae

The mayten, or maiten, is a handsome evergreen tree from the western side of southern South America. It is best known as a broad-crowned tree with drooping branches and branchlets much like those of a weeping willow. However, the branches and branchlets on some trees tend to be more or less erect. Trees of both kinds are known in the wild in South America. **Leaves** of the mayten are lanceolate, tapering at both ends, and 1 to 2 inches long. These slender leaves, on trees with a pendant habit, add to its weeping-willow appearance. In summer, the greenish white **flowers,** small and inconspicuous, occur in groups of two to five in the leaf axils. They are either male or female, with both kinds on the same plant. The **fruits,** which tend to be more conspicuous than the flowers, are rounded, nearly 1/4 inch across, and split to expose one or two seeds enclosed in a red covering. Some trees have more fruits than others and, on such trees, the branchlets are often heavily laden. Volunteer seedlings appear under old trees, and root suckers are formed by some trees.

In Argentina, mayten's range extends along the eastern side of the Andes from Chubut Province in the north, southward to Nequen Province and, in adjacent Chile, from Llanguihue Province in the south (which is approximately the same latitude as in southern Argentina) to Coquimbo Province in the north. It also is found in Brazil, Peru, and Bolivia. Its generic name is taken from *maiten,* the Chilean name for the tree. The species name *boaria* means "of or for cattle" and was chosen because cattle browse

N side of Kennedy Dr opposite entrance to Music
  Concourse area (II-O1); W of S entrance to
  Academy of Sciences (III-O3)); Strybing (VI-N3)
Evergreen/Slow growth/50'
Inconspicuous flowers (spring) /Small, round
  fruits, 1/4", which split to expose 1-2 seeds in
  a red covering
Full sun/Water occasionally
Sunset Zone 8, 9, 14-21
Suitable as a street tree
Color plate

on the leaves, preferring it to other forage. The tree forms an attractive feature of the pasturelands of the lower Andes of central Chile.

Mayten has been known in botanical literature since 1782, when it was named and described by the Chilean-born naturalist-botanist, Juan Ignacio Molina, in his account of the natural history of Chile. In the 1820s and 1830s, several British collectors took specimens of mayten to their homeland. One of these collectors was the Scottish physician-botanist John Gillies, who lived in Argentina from 1820 to 1828 and went home with a sizeable collection of plants and seeds. In 1829, he sent some of his material to London to Aylmer B Lambert; the mayten was presumably included.

Mayten is seen in California from the San Francisco and Sacramento areas south to Fresno, Santa Barbara, and the Los Angeles area, as specimen trees and sometimes as street trees. The earliest date for its introduction into California is 1878, according to Butterfield (1964). It was planted in Golden Gate Park before 1893, when the *Annual Report of the Park Commissioners* listed it. One of the largest trees in the park is in Strybing's South American section. With a single trunk and weeping habit, it is 35 feet tall and has a broad crown 50 to 60 feet across. Another old specimen is near the south entrance to the Academy of Sciences. Several maytens are part of a mixed planting on the north side of Kennedy Drive, across from the entrance to the Music Concourse.

Paperbarks, bottlebrushes, and honey myrtles
# *Melaleuca*
## Myrtaceae

*Melaleuca* is a genus with about a hundred species, mostly in Australia; a single species, *M. leucadendron,* extends northward into Southeast Asia. Melaleucas are evergreen trees and shrubs, with lanceolate, pinnately veined **leaves,** usually opposite but occasionally alternate. The name *Melaleuca* is taken from two Greek words, *melas,* black, and *leucos,* white, and alludes to the black trunk and white branches of some species. The genus is related to another Australian shrub, *Callistemon,* also called bottlebrush. Both genera have long, cylindrical clusters of **flowers** with numerous showy, colorful stamens. *Melaleuca* has stamens grouped in bundles opposite to, and longer than, the tiny petals; this characteristic separates *Melaleuca* from *Callistemon* and other closely related genera in the myrtle family.

The **bark** on many species is loose and papery, peeling off in strips; for this characteristic, some melaleucas are known as paperbarks. Some species are known for their generous production of tiny, myrtle-like flowers filled with nectar, giving rise to still another common name, honey myrtle. **Fruits** are small, woody capsules tightly clustered along the floral spike.

In their natural range, melaleucas are most commonly found in moist areas along streams, around lakes, or in swampy areas. In spite of their natural habitats, most species adapt readily to drier sites such as those found in most gardens in California. One species (*Melaleuca leucadendron*) has become a serious pest in Florida, where it was introduced as a windbreak and to drain swamps; it has naturalized in damp areas so extensively that native plant communities have been obliterated. The several species introduced into cultivation on the West Coast have behaved well in gardens and have not become naturalized. They are used in

## 95

### Bracelet bottlebrush
# *Melaleuca armillaris*
#### Myrtaceae

Bracelet bottlebrush was introduced to England from Australia in 1820. In 1854, it was offered by at least one California nursery, and by 1871, many bottlebrushes were available in California. Since these early introductions, several cultivars have been established in the United States. Harvey M Hall, of UC Berkeley, wrote in 1910 that he considered this species to be the best of the white-flowered bottlebrushes. With a little judicious pruning, it assumes a rounded, treelike habit with many drooping branchlets, each clothed in soft, 1-inch-long, needlelike **leaves** with recurved tips. He noted that it was much used in West Lake Park, Los Angeles, as well as in San Mateo and San Francisco. It was often labeled as *Melaleuca alba* in California nurseries.

An aged specimen of bracelet bottlebrush can be seen in the bed southwest of the Friend Gate, a part of Strybing's Eastern Australian collection. This tree was part of the earliest Australian plantings to be set out by Eric Walther in the 1940s. Its trunk rests on the ground for much of its length but eventually turns upward to create a gracefully rounded canopy tree about 15 feet in height. Its tiny, white **flowers** may be present in any month but are most prominent in winter and spring. Other plantings can be found in parks throughout San Francisco.

Strybing (VI-N3)
Evergreen/Moderate growth/30'
White, bottlebrush flowers on 3" spikes (winter and spring) /Woody capsules
Full sun/Water infrequently
Sunset Zone 8, 9, 12-24

## 96

### Swamp paperbark
# *Melaleuca ericifolia*
#### Myrtaceae

Swamp paperbark is a tall shrub or small tree native to Australia. It may reach 25 feet in height with a picturesque branching habit, attractive peeling **bark,** and dark green foliage. The small, whitish **flowers** that usually appear in March are arranged in short bottlebrush spikes. During some years, the spikes are abundant enough to give a snowy cast to the trees, but they are generally not conspicuous and are probably noticed only by the most observant tree watchers. The trees produce basal suckers of upright, rodlike branches that will, in time, give a coppicelike effect. In certain situations, for example where a windbreak is needed, this habit may be beneficial. However, in lawn areas the suckers

E side of Conservatory Valley (IV-Q2)
Evergreen/Fast growth/25'
Unshowy, short, bottlebrush spikes of white flowers (March) /Woody capsules
Full sun/Water infrequently
Sunset Zone 9, 12-24

need to be removed from time to time. This is done to the clump of trees in Conservatory Valley, but in the wooded area at the eastern edge of the valley, where there are additional trees, the suckers are allowed to remain.

The common name alludes to the attractive, pale brown bark, which peels in strips and to the occurrence of this tree in Australia in wet ground near swamps or streams, in the southeastern states of Victoria, New South Wales, and Tasmania. The specific epithet, *ericifolia,* which means heath-like, refers to the tree's short, slender leaves.

Swamp paperbark has been in California since 1859 when William C Walker received seeds of it from Australia at his Golden Gate Nursery in San Francisco. It was probably an early introduction into Golden Gate Park, although it was not listed in the annual reports of the park commissioners until 1924. However, the group of large, picturesque specimens in the lawn of Conservatory Valley was noted in 1910 by Harvey M Hall of UC Berkeley.

Swamp paperbark is rarely grown elsewhere in California. There are several trees on the UC Berkeley campus; one group at a corner of the Campanile Esplanade, which was planted about 1895 and cut to the ground in 1906, has grown to its present size from suckers. In Southern California, swamp paperbark has been planted in Santa Barbara, Los Angeles, and Santa Monica.

# 97

### Flaxleaf paperbark
# *Melaleuca linariifolia*
## Myrtaceae

Flaxleaf paperbark, or honey myrtle, is a shrub or small tree to about 30 feet tall, with peeling **bark,** a broad, dense habit, and branches that are more or less erect. **Leaves** are linear to narrowly lanceolate, about 1 inch long and ⅛ inch wide, nearly sessile or with short petioles. White **flowers** appear in fluffy, bottlebrushlike spikes, 2 inches or more long, with young leafy shoots growing beyond the inflorescence. Sepals and petals are small and inconspicuous, but the stamens are numerous. The white flowers are sometimes so numerous that from a distance they appear as a white cloud enveloping the tree; the plant is occasionally referred to as snow-in-summer.

This species occurs in wet places in eastern Australia from Queensland to New South Wales and northeastern South Australia. On our West Coast, it is cultivated only in coastal California, commonly as a small dense street tree. In the park, flaxleaf paperbark can be seen on the west side of Kezar Drive, just north of Alvord Tunnel. Other fine specimens can be seen at the Huntington Botanical Gardens.

W side of Kezar Dr, N of Alvord Tunnel (IV-S3)
476 27th St
Evergreen/Moderate growth/30'
Short spikes of white flowers (May-July) /Small, woody, fused capsules
Full sun/Water infrequently
Sunset Zone 9, 13-23
Suitable as a street tree

# 98

Dawn redwood
## *Metasequoia glyptostroboides*
Taxodiaceae

Dawn redwood, an unusual deciduous conifer, has become a popular ornamental tree since its discovery in China in the 1940s. Considered a living fossil, it exists even today in naturally occurring wild populations. In contrast, ginkgo or maidenhair tree *(Ginkgo biloba),* also known as a living fossil, differs from metasequoia in that it exists only in cultivation.

Metasequoia is a deciduous tree with **leaves** arranged in pairs on short branchlets; the linear, needlelike leaves are soft and bright green, especially in early spring. The leafy branchlets of metasequoia are opposite on the larger branches; at the approach of winter, these branchlets drop with their leaves attached but now golden, even in mild-winter regions like California. The **bark** is thin and flaky; the trunk on older trees is often deeply fluted. The dark brown **cones** are small, nearly globose, and attached by 1-inch stalks.

As a member of the redwood family, metasequoia is related to the sequoias of California *(Sequoia sempervirens* and *Sequoiadendron giganteum),* which are both evergreen conifers, and to the several species of bald cypress *(Taxodium).* The bald cypresses are either deciduous or evergreen, and differ from metasequoia in having leaves either linear or awl shaped and, like those of sequoia, alternate on the branchlets.

Golden Gate Park has a number of dawn redwoods. One is at the northern edge of the Fuchsia Garden, along Conservatory Drive East. Other trees, all 40 to 45 feet tall, are in Strybing Arboretum east of the Arthur Menzies Garden of California Native Plants; these were grown from seed collected in 1946 and distributed by the Arnold Arboretum. These trees are smaller than others of the same age, due undoubtedly to the cool summer temperatures in the park.

Metasequoias have been planted elsewhere on the Pacific Coast. The tree is now common in Seattle, where the tallest, at more than 90 feet, is in the Washington Park Arboretum. In Oregon, metasequoias are in the Portland's Hoyt Arboretum and in Corvallis on the Oregon State University campus and in Peavy Arboretum. In California they are found at the UC Botanical Gardens in Berkeley, at the Lakeside Park Garden Center in Oakland, in The Arboretum of LA County, at Filoli Center near Woodside, and in parks and private gardens throughout the state.

N side of Fuchsia Garden (IV-R1); Strybing (VII-N4)
Deciduous/Moderate growth/100'
(Conifer) Small, dark brown cones, 1″ long
Full sun/Water regularly
Sunset Zone 3-10, 14-24
Color plates

# The Discovery of Metasequoia

In 1941, Japanese paleobotanist Shigeru Miki, while examining fossil specimens identified as *Sequoia*, noted that cones and leaves of some, although resembling living plants and fossils of *Sequoia*, differed in certain characters. These appeared sufficiently distinct for Miki to consider them a new fossil genus that he believed had been extinct for twenty million years. He named the genus *Metasequoia*, using the Greek *meta*, meaning with or after, added to *sequoia*.

Also in 1941, a Chinese forester, T Kan, discovered an unusual conifer in the small, remote village of Modaoqi (Mo-tao-chi) in eastern Sichuan province, near the border of Hubei province. Unfortunately, he did not collect specimens for later examination. The tree grew near water and was called shui-sha, or water fir, by local villagers. A second Chinese forester, C Wang, visited Modaoqi in 1943 and made the first collections of the conifer. These eventually were seen by WC Cheng of Central University, Nanjing, who believed they represented a new genus of conifers. He sent a specimen to HH Hu, then director of the Fan Memorial Institute of Biology, Beijing, who recognized the conifer as not only new but also the same as the fossil genus described in 1941 by Miki. In 1943, Hu and Cheng named and described the conifer as a new species, *Metasequoia glyptostroboides*.

In 1946, Cheng sent specimens to ED Merrill, then director of the Arnold Arboretum of Harvard University. Realizing the significance of the newly discovered tree, Merrill made funds available for Hu and Cheng to obtain seeds. A collector was sent to Modaoqi and then south to an even more remote area, the valley of Shuishaba (Shui-sa-pa), where he found the largest known concentration of metasequoias and made a substantial collection of seed. Cheng sent a portion of the seed to Merrill, and a second lot to botanists in Copenhagen and Amsterdam. Merrill distributed his seeds to botanical gardens, parks, and individuals. Some of the old trees now growing in the United States (including those in Strybing Arboretum) are from these seeds.

After receiving seeds from Merrill, Ralph W Chaney, a paleobotanist at the UC Berkeley, made plans to visit China. In March 1948, sponsored by the Save-the-Redwoods League, Chaney and Milton Silverman, a science writer for the *San Francisco Chronicle*, flew to Chongqing, then went by steamship 175 miles on the Chang Jiang (Yangtze) River to Wan-Hsien. Accompanied by Chinese armed guards and porters, Chaney and Silverman reached Modaoqi after traveling for three days over rocky trails. At Modaoqi, they found three metasequoias growing in rice paddies in an area denuded of all natural vegetation. The largest, a fine old tree nearly 100 feet tall with a trunk over 6 feet in diameter, towered over the landscape. According to Silverman, this tree was revered by the people of the village, who considered it the home of a god. Sixteen years earlier, several village elders had raised funds to build a small mud and tile shrine at the base of the tree.

Chaney and Silverman next went to Shuishaba, from which had come the seeds sent to the Arnold Arboretum and to Europe. They spent five days in the valley, where they found metasequoias mostly in small groves in ravines, associated with native deciduous hardwoods. They collected additional seeds that were distributed later, and Chaney also brought back a few seedlings.

## Return to China

Several American botanists participated in the 1980 Sino-American Botanical Expedition to western Hubei in the People's Republic of China. Part of their field work was in the metasequoia area where Chaney and Silverman and Chinese collectors had gone in the 1940s. The expedition reported a number of changes that had occurred since that time.

Of the three metasequoias in the rice paddies at Modaoqi in 1948, only the tallest one was found, but young metasequoias, as well as Japanese cedars (*Cryptomeria japonica*), had been planted along the road that passes through the village. The small shrine, too, was gone, but the tree it honored, estimated to be about 450 years old at that time, was in good health and had seed-filled cones.

The expedition also visited Shuishaba, where the greatest concentration of metasequoias is found. Several employees of the local Bureau of Forestry had been in the valley since 1974 and had counted and measured over 5,000 trees with trunk diameters of more than

Dawn redwoods *(Metasequoia glyptostroboides)* lining a street in Madaoqi, China. Photograph by Bill McNamara

8 inches. In 1980 metasequoias were protected and not even small trees could be cut. But the government protects only the trees and not their associated vegetation. The population of the valley is dense, and as the demand for cropland increases, native vegetation is threatened, including seedlings of metasequoia. Thus, while the larger trees are protected by the government, the long term survival of metasequoia is less certain without protection of their habitat.

A British-American expedition to China in 1996 visited Madaoqi and found that the grand old dawn redwood seen on earlier expeditions was still alive, though seemingly not in excellent health, perhaps due to the tremendous compaction of the soil in its root zone. They also found that many more young trees had been planted along city streets through much of China.

## Trees in the United States

It has been over fifty years since metasequoia was introduced to the western world. Since then it has flourished in summer-rainfall areas of the eastern United States and Western Europe and also has been grown along the Pacific Coast in areas where it receives enough moisture. In 1982, the Arnold Arboretum published a list of the fifty largest trees planted in the United States between 1948 and 1967, some, but not all, grown from seed distributed by Merrill. The tallest, in Virginia, was 104 feet; others were 70, 80, and 90 feet tall. The most favorable sites for planted trees were near streams or at the edge of water, in regions that enjoyed a warm summer.

For the first thirty years after its introduction to this country, metasequoia was propagated almost entirely by cuttings. Both green softwood and dormant hardwood cuttings have rooted easily. According to John Kuser of Rutgers University, it has become more difficult to root cuttings from some older trees, but trees grown from seed obtained in the late 1940s and 1950s are now producing their own seed. Germination rates, low at first, have risen to as much as forty-five percent for seed from trees in groves where cross-pollination occurs. Seeds require no pretreatment and generally germinate within ten days. Natural reproduction by seed has occurred in some areas; seedlings are small and slow growing but appear able to start on bare soil where they have little or no competition from other plants.

# New Zealand Christmas tree and rata
# *Metrosideros*
## Myrtaceae

The name *Metrosideros* combines two Greek words: *metra,* meaning heartwood or core, and *sideros,* meaning iron. It alludes to the hardness of the heartwood of these generally red-flowered trees and climbers. New Zealand Christmas tree, rata, ironwood, and iron tree are some of the common names for the trees in this genus. Except for *M. kermadecensis,* the scientific names for the species of *Metrosideros* should end in *"-a"* instead of *"-us"* as is sometimes written.

*Metrosideros* is related to the well-known bottlebrushes, *Melaleuca* and *Callistemon.* The most obvious feature of the **flowers** of these genera is the numerous, long, colorful stamens. Their petals are small, not colorful and showy, while the stamens protrude conspicuously, giving a brushlike appearance to the flower clusters. The flowers of melaleucas and callistemons are in elongated, spikelike clusters that have given the two their common name. The flowers of Christmas trees or ratas, on the other hand, are in terminal, branched, showy, headlike clusters. The trees usually have opposite, simple **leaves,** and the **fruits** are small, dry, dehiscent capsules. Plants of the tree species from New Zealand discussed here do not always produce fruiting capsules. However, when present, they differ as follows: capsules of *Metrosideros umbellata* are enclosed within the flat-topped calyx tube; those of *M. excelsa, M. robusta,* and *M. kermadecensis* are exerted beyond the top of the calyx tube. The numerous **seeds** are wind-borne.

*Metrosideros* has about fifty species: two in northern Australia, one in South Africa, five in Hawaii, several in the South Pacific, and eleven in New Zealand. Those in Golden Gate Park and elsewhere in California are from New Zealand. Of these, four are broad-leafed evergreen trees and one is a red-flowered climber *(M. carminea).* In addition, a small white- to cream-flowered tree *(M. angustifolia)* from South Africa was introduced to Strybing Arboretum in 1988; Strybing may have the only plants of this species in cultivation in North America.

In California, the red flower clusters of metrosideros normally appear from late May to July. In New Zealand, where the seasons are the reverse of those in the Northern Hemisphere, they flower in December and became obvious Christmas decorations to early European settlers there.

A few, but not all, plants of some species of *Metrosideros* start life as epiphytes high on the branches of other trees. A wind-borne seed germinates on a branch or in a crotch of the host tree, and aerial roots are produced. Some roots eventually reach the ground, while others intertwine around the host tree's trunk, finally enclosing and often killing the tree. The epiphyte becomes a tall, free standing tree with large, spreading branches. That the epiphyte kills the host tree has been questioned by some who have suggested that the seed of the epiphyte germinates and grows only on old trees already in decline, and indeed this is often the case.

In New Zealand, trees of metrosideros had several uses. Of particular value was their hard, tough, durable wood, which was used at one time by the Maoris and early European settlers in boatbuilding. Wood of *Metrosideros excelsa* was often used to hold together boat hulls made of kauri *(Agathis australis).* The wood was also used in general carpentry. *Metrosideros excelsa* also had medicinal uses: the nectar from flowers was used for sore throats, and an infusion of the inner bark was a treatment for diarrhea.

A drive in Golden Gate Park, 1910, from a post card.

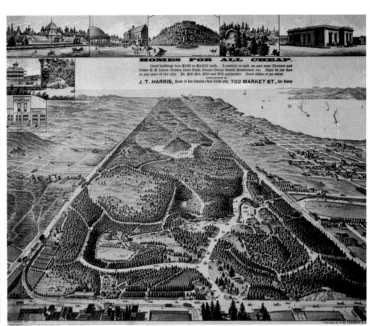

"Bird's Eye View of Golden Gate Park," 1892, prepared as part of a real estate promotion.

"A Trysting Place" in Golden Gate Park, from a post card, c. 1910.

The Dutch Windmill near the northwestern corner of Golden Gate Park, constructed to pump fresh water from beneath the park to irrigate the new plantings, c. 1900.

"A Midwinter Day at Children's Playground," from a post card, c. 1900.

A view into Golden Gate Park from the Haight Street entrance at Stanyan Street. Alvord Lake is in the lower right corner, with the historic Alvord Tunnel behind it, c. 1910.

Conservatory of Flowers in Golden Gate Park, the dome framed by Canary Island date palms *(Phoenix canariensis)*. In the foreground are elaborate beds of flowers reminiscent of the Victorian period.

The Music Concourse in winter with the stark silhouettes of pollarded London plane trees *(Platanus x acerifolia)*.

Japanese Tea Garden, 2000. Photograph by RG Turner Jr

A meadow with American elm *(Ulmus americana)* near 25th Street and Lincoln Way. Photograph by RG Turner Jr

Arthur Menzies Garden of California Native Plants, in Strybing Arboretum, near the peak of spring bloom; in the center is a California buckeye *(Aesculus californica)*. Photograph by RG Turner Jr

The Redwood Trail in Strybing Arboretum. Redwoods *(Sequoia sempervirens)* were planted about 1906, understory plantings added in the 1960s. Photograph by Saxon Holt

Ginkgo *(Ginkgo biloba)*. Photograph by RG Turner Jr

Monterey cypress *(Cupressus macrocarpa)* on the Main Lawn at Strybing Arboretum. Photograph by Saxon Holt

Rimu *(Dacrydium cupressinum)* flanks the view to the Strybing Bench and the fountain at Strybing Arboretum. Photograph by RG Turner Jr

The largest Torrey pine *(Pinus torreyana)* in the park, in Strybing Arboretum. Photograph by RG Turner Jr

*Magnolia campbellii* 'Strybing White' in Strybing Arboretum.

Mayten *(Maytenus boaria)*, a major stem covered in bromeliads, in the South American section, Strybing Arboretum. Photograph by Saxon Holt

Campbell's magnolia *(Magnolia campbellii)*.

New Zealand Christmas tree *(Metrosideros excelsa)*. Photograph by RG Turner Jr

Michelia *(Michelia doltsopa)*.

Cow-itch tree *(Lagunaria patersonii)*. Photograph by Saxon Holt

Hand-flower tree *(Chiranthodendron pentadactylon)*.

Cape chestnut *(Calodendrum capense)*. Photograph by RG Turner Jr

Talauma *(Talauma hodgsonii)*.

Purple hopseed bush *(Dodonaea viscosa* 'Purpurea').

Karo *(Pittosporum crassifolium).* Photograph by George Waters

Deodar *(Cedrus deodora).*

*Photinia davidsoniae.* Photograph by RG Turner Jr

Monterey cypress *(Cupressus macrocarpa).*

Lilly pilly *(Acmena smithii).* Photograph by RG Turner Jr

Coachwood *(Ceratopetalum apetalum)*. Photograph by
RG Turner Jr

Catalina ironwood *(Lyonothamnus floribundus)*.

*Photinia davidsoniae.*

Australian tree fern *(Sphaeropteris cooperi)*. Photograph by RG Turner Jr

Guadalupe cypress *(Cupressus guadalupensis)*.

Dawn redwood *(Metasequoia glyptostroboides)*. Photograph by Saxon Holt

Kapuka *(Griselinia littoralis).* Photograph by George Waters

Ginkgo *(Ginkgo biloba).* Photograph by Saxon Holt

Dove tree *(Davidia involucrata).*

European beech *(Fagus sylvatica).* Photograph by RG Turner Jr

Sweet gum *(Liquidambar styraciflua).* Photograph by RG Turner Jr

Victorian box *(Pittosporum undulatum).* Photograph by George Waters

Paraná pine *(Araucaria angustifolia).* Photograph by RG Turner Jr

Black tree fern *(Sphaeropteris medullaris).*

Horse chestnut *(Aesculus hippocastanum).* Photograph by RG Turner Jr

Japanese umbrella pine *(Sciadopitys verticillata).*

'Dawn redwood *(Metasequoia glyptostroboides).*

*Chamaecyparis obtusa* 'Verdonii'. Photograph by RG Turner Jr

## 99

New Zealand Christmas tree

# *Metrosideros excelsa*

(syn. *M. tomentosa*)

Myrtaceae

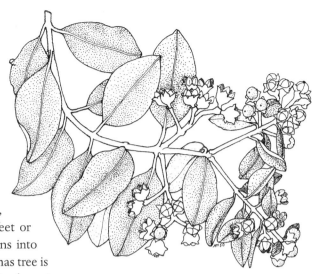

Several trees of *Metrosideros excelsa* are in Golden Gate Park, including Strybing Arboretum. This large tree (reaching 60 feet or more in height and spread) was among the early introductions into California. **Bark** on mature specimens of New Zealand Christmas tree is thick and stringy and peels in long, irregular strips. **Leaves** are leathery, 2 to 4 inches long and about half as wide, their lower surfaces densely coated with gray, woolly hairs. The leaves, as well as the gray, hairy branches, give these trees a gray-green aspect. **Flowers** are in clusters, bright crimson, with stamens generally 1 to 1¼ inches long. Old specimens of New Zealand Christmas tree (particularly those in California's coastal fog belt) often have bunches of red brown fibrous "roots" of varying lengths hanging from their trunks and main branches. Just how these function is not known. Two large, old trees, displaying such hanging roots, in Strybing's New Zealand section are among the oldest trees in the collection; they were damaged during the severe windstorm of December 1995, but are recovering nicely.

This species of *Metrosideros* was first discovered in New Zealand in 1769 by the English explorer-naturalists, Joseph Banks and Daniel Solander, on Captain James Cook's first voyage around the world. It was found on a rocky seacoast of the North Island, where it occurred abundantly. In this area, the Maoris called it *pohutu-kawa,* meaning salt sprinkled. The Maoris revered the tree, and several of their legends about it have come down to us. Allan Cunningham later collected seed of this tree in New Zealand and introduced it to the Royal Botanic Gardens at Kew.

According to Butterfield (1964), New Zealand Christmas tree was listed by William Walker at his Golden Gate Nursery in 1859. In 1900, it was included in Bailey's *Cyclopedia of American Horticulture,* and in 1905, a 40-foot flowering tree was growing in a Santa Barbara garden. In 1907, a tree was listed for Golden Gate Park. Today, a fine specimen with multiple trunks is on the south side of Kennedy Drive west of its intersection with Conservatory Drive West. It is commonly seen as a street tree in San Francisco and other California cities, including Santa Barbara, Los Angeles, and San Diego.

*Metrosideros excelsa* 'Aurea', a cultivar with pale yellow flowers, has been cultivated in New Zealand since its discovery in 1940. It was introduced into San Francisco about 1960. A single tree is in Strybing Arboretum at the north end of the Helen Crocker Russell Library.

S side of Kennedy Dr W of Conservatory Dr West
(IV-P2); Strybing (VI-N3)
4710 17th St
Evergreen/Slow growth/30'
Terminal flower clusters of brilliant red stamens
(May-July) /Dry seed capsules
Full sun/Water infrequently
Sunset Zone 17, 23, 24
Suitable as a street tree
Color plate

# 100

### Kermadec Christmas tree
# *Metrosideros kermadecensis*

Myrtaceae

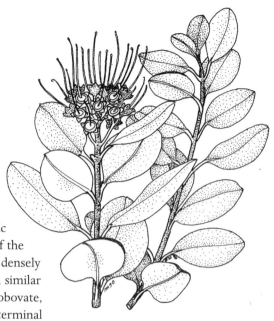

Kermadec Christmas tree grows wild only on the Kermadec Islands north of New Zealand. It was introduced into California from the New Zealand nursery firm of Duncan and Davies by Eric Walther of Strybing Arboretum in about 1950. Among the largest of the metrosideros, this species can reach 100 feet in height. **Leaves** are densely covered on the lower surface with a matting of gray, woolly hairs, similar to those of *Metrosideros excelsa,* but are only 1 to 2 inches long and obovate, differing from *M. excelsa* in size and shape. The **flowers** are held in terminal clusters and are crimson. Of the severa Kermadec Christmas trees in Strybing's New Zealand collection, two are among its oldest plants. Unfortunately, they were heavily damaged in the devastating 1995 windstorm. Other Kermadec Christmas trees are in Golden Gate Park outside the arboretum and elsewhere in California; in Los Angeles it has been sold under the name *M. villosa.*

Strybing (VI-N3)
Evergreen/Slow growth/70'
Terminal tufted clusters of crimson stamens
    (June-July) /Dry seed capsules
Full sun/Water infrequently
Sunset Zone 17, 23, 24

# 101

### Northern rata
# *Metrosideros robusta*

Myrtaceae

This species is known in New Zealand by the Maori name of rata or, because of its occurrence mostly on the North Island, as northern rata. Like New Zealand Christmas tree, northern rata usually begins life as an epiphyte; a mature tree in the wild may reach 75 feet in height. Unlike *Metrosideros excelsa* and *M. kermadecensis,* however, its leaves are green on their lower surfaces, lacking the dense covering of gray hairs seen on the leaves of the others.

The gray brown **bark** on trunks of mature trees of northern rata is thin, more or less longitudinally furrowed, and detaches in small, irregular flakes. **Leaves** are 1 to 2 inches long and nearly half as wide, and are ovate to oblong. Their upper surfaces are dark green and somewhat shiny; their lower surfaces are paler green. **Flowers** have numerous stamens that are ½ to ¾ inch long. The several northern ratas in Strybing Arboretum are the only ones in Golden Gate Park; they are mature and among the arboretum's oldest trees. These, too, suffered in the December 1995 storm. Northern ratas are also found in Santa Barbara.

Strybing (VI-N3)
893 Clayton St
Evergreen/Slow growth/75'
Terminal clusters of red stamens (May-July) /Dry
    seed capsules
Full sun/Water infrequently
Sunset Zone 17, 23, 24
Suitable as a street tree

# 102

## Southern rata
### *Metrosideros umbellata*
Myrtaceae

Abundant on New Zealand's South Island, this species is called southern rata. It is occasionally confused with northern rata, but small differences distinguish the two. Southern rata does not begin life as an epiphyte. It is also a smaller tree, up to about 45 feet tall. The gray brown **bark** of southern rata is somewhat papery and peels in thick flakes. The **leaves,** which have many oil glands, are up to 2 inches long and less than half that wide; the upper surface is dull green and the lower surface is paler. There are fewer **flowers** per cluster on southern rata than in those on northern rata, and the stamens are shorter. The somewhat smaller flowers are bright red and more brilliant than those of northern rata and New Zealand Christmas tree. Young trees, not yet old enough to flower, can be seen in Strybing's New Zealand collection.

Strybing (VI-N4)
Evergreen/Slow growth/45'
Terminal clusters of bright red stamens
  (May-June) /Dry seed casules
Full sun/Water infrequently
Sunset Zone 17, 23, 24

# 103

## Michelia
### *Michelia doltsopa*
Magnoliaceae

Another broad-leafed evergreen tree, *Michelia doltsopa* is native to the Himalayas and a magnolia relative. Trees of michelia in cultivation are generally 20 to 40 feet tall, but in their native habitat, they are reported to reach 50 to 80 feet. **Leaves** are ovate to oblong, 3 to 7 inches long, and firm in texture. The showy, white, lightly fragrant **flowers** have twelve to sixteen, somewhat floppy, petal-like tepals (like magnolias); the flowers are about 6 inches across and are scattered along the stems in the leaf axils. This position of the flowers shows one of the differences between *Michelia* and *Magnolia,* in which flowers are only at the tips of the stems. Other less obvious differences in the flowers and fruits also separate the two genera.

*Michelia doltsopa* has a wide geographical distribution in the Himalaya, extending from Nepal eastward through Assam and Myanmar (formerly Burma) to southeastern Tibet and western Yunnan Province in China. It is found in forests and thickets, or sometimes in open situations, at elevations between 4,500 and 9,000 feet. In these areas it is reported to be a valuable timber tree with wood that, although light and soft, is durable and easily worked.

Strybing (VI-M3 & VII-N4)
326 Kirkham St
Evergreen/Moderate growth/20'-40'
White, fragrant, floppy, 6" wide, saucerlike flowers
  (Feb-April) /Conelike, fleshy fruit
Full sun to part shade/Water regularly
Sunset Zone 14-24
Suitable as a street tree
Color plate

Before its observation in Sikkim (now part of India) in 1848 by Joseph Dalton Hooker, it had been discovered in Nepal by two British botanists who were among the earliest Europeans to botanize in the Himalayas. Francis Buchanan-Hamilton discovered the tree in 1803 and later suggested its name. The tree was collected for a second time by Nathaniel Wallich. In 1824, not knowing of the earlier name, he described it in his flora of Nepal as *Magnolia excelsa,* later transferred to *Michelia.* The tree was known, therefore, as *Michelia excelsa* until 1927, when James Dandy, a British specialist in the magnolia family, realized that the earlier name, *Michelia doltsopa,* had been overlooked.

It was not until the twentieth century, following Hamilton, Wallich, and Hooker that *Michelia doltsopa* was introduced into cultivation in England. George Forrest collected seed in western Yunnan, perhaps in 1918; in 1919, Reginald Farrer collected additional seed in upper Burma. From these collections, michelia was grown in the milder parts of England. The original source of *M. doltsopa* in Strybing was seed received in 1953 by the Golden Gate Park nursery from G Ghose & Company, Darjeeling, a dealer in Himalayan seeds. A seedling flowered for the first time in 1959.

A number of large specimens of this michelia can be seen in Strybing, particularly west of the Dwarf Conifer Garden and in the Asian section west of the Moon-viewing Garden. It appears elsewhere in Golden Gate Park and at the UC Botanical Gardens in Berkeley.

# Native michelia habitat

Information regarding native habitats of plants is of much interest and value to horticulturists, but is not always available. Frank Kingdon-Ward wrote of seeing many trees of *Michelia doltsopa* in what is now Myanmar during a trip he made in 1930–31 to the headwaters of the Irrawaddy River, one of the areas where this tree occurs. Trees were in the temperate rain forest above the subtropical foothill forests, at about 6,000 to 8,000 feet elevation, close to snow peaks where it is cold in winter and fairly hot in summer. Snow does not remain on the ground long at 6,000 feet but stays longer at 8,000 feet. About a third to a quarter of the forest trees are deciduous, with a few conifers, including *Pinus wallichiana,* but the area is remarkable for its twenty to thirty species of *Rhododendron.* The mountains are steep and the valleys narrow, so that the sun shines in the gorges only a few hours each day. This michelia is the earliest tree to flower in these forests.

# 104

Tree daisy
## *Montanoa grandiflora*
Asteraceae

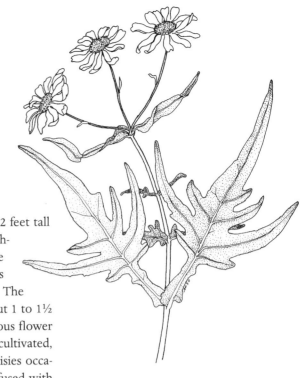

Tree daisy is a small evergreen tree or large shrub as much as 12 feet tall and irregularly branched. The lobed **leaves** are large, up to 9 inches long and often nearly as wide. In general, the irregular pinnate lobes extend no more than halfway to the midrib; their petioles are conspicuously winged, sometimes with basal, earlike lobes. The **flower** heads are arranged in open, branched clusters, each about 1 to 1½ inches wide, with ten to thirteen white ray flowers. The numerous flower heads make this tree daisy showy and attractive. It is not often cultivated, however, and not often seen in the nursery trade. Other tree daisies occasionally cultivated, mostly in southern California, might be confused with *Montanoa grandiflora*. These are *M. arborescens, M. bipinnatifida, M. hibiscifolia,* and *M. guatemalensis.*

The montanoas are all woody shrubs or trees. They all have large daisylike flower heads with white ray flowers surrounding an inner cluster of yellow disk flowers. The genus was first described in 1825 by Vicente Cervantes of the Royal Botanic Gardens, Mexico City, and named by him for Luis Montana, a physician and naturalist from Puebla, Mexico. *Montanoa* includes twenty-five species, which are distributed from Sonora, Mexico, to Peru and are often locally abundant along dry roadsides and in cloud forests, from a few hundred to over 9,000 feet elevation.

*Montanoa grandiflora* has been in Strybing Arboretum since the 1950s, but apparently has not been grown elsewhere in Golden Gate Park. Noted plantsman Victor Reiter had this species in his San Francisco garden in 1940. His plant may have been the source of the arboretum's plant, as were many other plants in his garden. Tree daisy can be seen in Strybing, on the western edge of the Redwood Trail.

Strybing (VI-M4)
Evergreen/Fast growth/12'
White daisylike flowers, 1 1/2" across, with yellow centers (fall and winter) /Clusters of papery seeds
Full sun/Water occasionally
Sunset Zone 16, 17, 20-24

*I wonder about the trees.*
*Why do we wish to bear*
*Forever the noise of these*
*More than another noise*
*So close to our dwelling place?*

ROBERT FROST, *"The Sound of the Trees"*

# 105

Ngaio
## *Myoporum laetum*
Myoporaceae

A broad-leafed evergreen tree, Ngaio's most characteristic feature, and one not found in any other ornamental tree in the state, is the numerous translucent oil glands (or pores) of the leaves, which are clearly seen when a leaf is held against the light. *Myoporum* comes from two Greek words, *myein,* meaning to close, and *poros,* meaning pore, and alludes to these oil glands. In California, it is seen as a broad-crowned tree that becomes gnarled with age. Branch tips are viscid and brownish; **leaves** are 2 to 4 inches long and somewhat fleshy. Ngaio has white **flowers,** slightly less than ½ inch across, and noticed only at close range. The purplish berrylike **fruits** are about the size of garden peas. Seedlings are likely to appear in disturbed ground.

The native home of ngaio is New Zealand, where it is found on both North and South islands. Although not restricted to the coast, it is seldom found far inland. In some places, it occurs almost within the high-water line. Its wood, dark brown in color, is dense, heavy, hard, and durable. It has been used in New Zealand for fence posts, rails, and similar purposes, as well as for cabinetwork and ornamental turnery. The Maoris made an infusion of the leaves to spread over their faces and other exposed parts of the body to prevent bites of mosquitoes and sand flies.

Ngaio is poisonous to livestock, particularly cattle. The toxin, ngaione, is a terpinoid found in its essential oil. The leaves are the most toxic part of the plant; other parts are of lesser toxicity. As a cultivated ornamental in urban areas, ngaio is not likely to be a problem to livestock. Its potential hazard will mostly be to small children.

Ngaio was an early introduction into California; according to Butterfield (1964), it was seen here "soon after 1863." It was also an early introduction into Golden Gate Park and is included in the 1902 *Annual Report of the Park Commissioners.* It is mostly seen as a windbreak in the park, particularly in the western end, as around the Beach Chalet. Fine individual specimens of ngaio can be seen around the meadow west of the conservatory and in Strybing's New Zealand collection. Ngaio is a frequent street tree in San Francisco and other coastal communities. Its use in California is limited to frost-free zones. Damage to trees only a few miles from the coast was seen in the Berkeley hills after the freeze of December 1972.

The Maoris believed that there is a ngaio tree on the moon.

> *In the moon is Rona sitting,*
> *Never to be free;*
> *With the gourd she held in flitting*
> *And the ngaio tree.*
> JESSIE MACKAY

Beach Chalet (I-B2); Meadow W of conservatory (IV-Q1)
1006 Dolores; Judah St at 48th Ave
Evergreen/Fast growth/30'
Small clusters of white, unshowy flowers, up to 1/2" wide (summer) /Purplish, pea-sized berries
Full sun/Water occasionally
Sunset Zone 8, 9, 14-17, 19-24
Suitable as a street tree

# New Zealand Trees in Golden Gate Park

Shortly after California's statehood was achieved in 1850, plants from New Zealand were being imported along with ornamental plants from other areas of the world. New Zealand plants offered for sale by nurserymen in the 1860s and 1870s included: New Zealand laurel *(Corynocarpus laevigatus)*, parrot's beak *(Clianthus puniceus)*, several species of *Hebe*, New Zealand tea tree *(Leptospermum scoparium)*, New Zealand Christmas tree *(Metrosideros excelsa)*, ngaio *(Myoporum laetum)*, karo *(Pittosporum crassifolium)*, tarata *(P. eugenioides)*, and totara *(Podocarpus totara)*.

Probably the largest number of New Zealand plants imported into California at one time were those used in the New Zealand exhibit at the Panama–Pacific International Exposition in San Francisco in 1915. The plants to be exhibited were shipped to San Francisco as living specimens. John McLaren's involvement with these plants had begun in the early planning stages of the exposition, since he served as the chief landscape supervisor for the event.

On arrival, the plants were cared for in the exposition nursery and also at the McRorie and McLaren Nursery in San Mateo, in which McLaren's son was a partner. Katherine D Jones wrote in *National Horticultural Magazine* in 1935 that, even before the exposition opened, the New Zealand plants being groomed for the exhibit were attracting attention. They were of special interest because they were unusual and different from the many Australian plants already known to Californians.

McLaren made arrangements for the acquisition of plants shown at the New Zealand exhibit after the close of the exposition. Unfortunately, we have no list of the plants that came to the park following the exposition. However, it may be assumed that many, if not all, of the New Zealand plants listed in the 1924 *Annual Report of the Park Commissioners*, and not listed in earlier reports, were acquired in this way.

Eric Walther, first director of Strybing Arboretum, had attended the 1915 exposition before he came to work in the park. He noted one specific tree brought to the park: the specimen of rimu *(Dacrydium cupressinum)* now in Strybing's New Zealand collection. This plant continues to flourish and is still producing juvenile leaves. Its growth habit does not suggest that it could ever become a large tree, yet rimu trees in New Zealand may reach 150 feet in height. Other trees that might be assumed to have been introduced to the park from the exposition include: *Olearia paniculata, Myrsine australis,* and *M. salicina,* and New Zealand chaste tree *(Vitex lucens)*. Many of these trees were initially planted around the Academy of Sciences. When that complex was enlarged many years later, some of the New Zealand trees were moved to other areas of the park; many ended up on the knoll just east of the academy where they can be seen today, while others perhaps were transplanted to Strybing.

The New Zealand botanist and horticulturist, Leonard Cockayne, published a booklet in 1914 entitled *New Zealand Plants Suitable for North American Gardens,* in which he described trees, shrubs, climbers, and ferns and made recommendations for their cultivation. The booklet was presumably distributed at the exposition. In it, Cockayne pointed out that

> *...the whole of the Pacific Coast is suitable for the open-air culture of many New Zealand plants, as also any other area where the temperature does not fall below 15°F, and where the rainfall is sufficient for everyday gardening operations. Also in those States where the winter cold is severe many species may be grown in pots which, kept in a frost-proof greenhouse during the winter, can in the summer be used for ornamental purposes in the open borders or the rock-garden.*

Many of the plants listed in Cockayne's booklet are well known today in Golden Gate Park, as well as in other places in California, and we can assume that at least some originated with the 1915 exposition. Among well-known trees included in his booklet are: New Zealand kauri *(Agathis australis)*, New Zealand cabbage tree *(Cordyline australis)*, *Fuchsia excorticata*, New Zealand lacebark *(Hoheria populnea)*, ribbonwood *(H. sexstylosa)*, *Meryta sinclairii*, *Sophora tetraptera*, and *S. microphylla*.

# 106

## Myrrhinium
# *Myrrhinium atropurpureum*
## Myrtaceae

*Myrrhinium atropurpureum* is a large evergreen shrub or small tree to 20 or, rarely, 25 feet tall. In habit, myrrhinium has a tendency to sucker and to produce multiple trunks from the base. **Leaves** are opposite, somewhat thick, narrowly elliptical, and 2 to 3 inches long, with a short petiole. The **flowers** appear on the old wood, are grouped in clusters, and have four sepals and petals. Petals are fleshy, round to oval, about ⅛ to ³⁄₁₆ inch long, mauve or lavender, and have a sweet taste; the six to eight red purple stamens have filaments nearly ½ inch long. The flowers have been likened to well-fed wood ticks caught in the tangle of stamens.

Myrrhinium, native to central Ecuador, Peru, northern Argentina, and southern Brazil, varies from area to area, particularly in leaf size and number of stamens. Throughout this wide range, several species were named and described, but the differences between them were not significant, and the genus is now considered to consist of only a single species. Synonyms still sometimes listed are *Myrrhinium rubriflorum, M. salicinum, M. lanceolatum,* and *M. peruvianum.*

Myrrhinium was introduced into California sometime before 1924, in which year *Blepharocalyx saligna,* an incorrect name for *Myrrhinium atropurpureum,* was listed for Golden Gate Park in the *Annual Report of the Park Commissioners.* Three trees are listed for Orpet Park in Muller's *Trees of Santa Barbara* (1974); one of these may be the tree reported to have been growing in Orpet Park in 1930 by Riedel (1957). Golden Gate Park has several specimens of this tree today. One is part of the dense planting edging the lawn on the north side of Kennedy Drive, west of Conservatory Drive West; another is on the knoll east of the Academy of Sciences; and a third is in Strybing's South American section. Other specimens in California are in the UCB's Blake Garden, in the Mildred Mathias Botanical Garden at UCLA, and in The Arboretum of LA County. *Myrrhinium atropurpureum* is not generally available commercially.

N of Kennedy Dr, opposite Rhododendron Dell (IV-P2); Knoll E of Academy of Sciences (III-P2); Strybing (VI-N3)
Evergreen/Slow growth/20'-25'
Clusters of flowers with fleshy, mauve or lavender petals and purplish red stamens (summer) /Small berries
Full sun to part shade/Water regularly
Sunset Zone 15-17, 19-24

*There is…a certain respect, and a general duty of humanity, that ties us, not only to beasts that have life and sense, but even to trees and plants.*

MONTAIGNE, *"Of Cruelty," Essays*

140

# Myrsine

## *Myrsine*

### Myrsinaceae

Myrsines belong to a fairly large and widespread family, but with few members in North America. *Myrsine africana,* African boxwood, is an evergreen shrub occasionally used in California for hedging; *Ardisia japonica* and *A. crenata,* evergreen shrubs from Asia, are sometimes seen indoors or in protected garden sites.

The particular feature of myrsines is their distinctive smooth, leathery evergreen **leaves,** although variations in size and shape distinguish the several species. The **flowers** are small, whitish, and clustered among the leaves. The small **fruits** are fleshy and berrylike, each containing a single seed. Both myrsines may be used as specimen trees, as sheared or unsheared hedges, and in background plantings.

# 107

## Mapau

## *Myrsine australis*

### Myrsinaceae

*Myrsine australis* is a much-branched small tree to 18 feet tall. The trunk **bark** is slightly rough and gray, while the smooth bark of the young branches and branchlets is reddish brown. The **leaves** are leathery, more or less oblong, glabrous except for a few hairs on the midrib, 1 to 2½ inches long and ½ to 1 inch wide. The petioles are red, about ¼ inch long, and the leaf margins are usually strongly wavy or undulate. **Fruits** are about ⅛ inch long and brown or black.

This species is native to New Zealand, on both main islands, from the lowlands to an elevation of 3,000 feet; the Maoris gave it the name *mapau.* It is planted in Strybing Arboretum among other plants in the New Zealand collection. It is seldom available commercially.

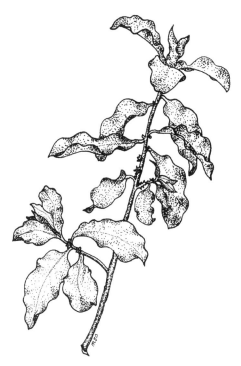

Strybing (VI-N3)
Evergreen/Slow growth/18'
Small, unshowy, white flower clusters (spring-
    summer) /Brown or black berries
Full sun to part shade/Water infrequently
Sunset Zone 16,17

## 108

### Toro
### *Myrsine salicina*

Myrsinaceae

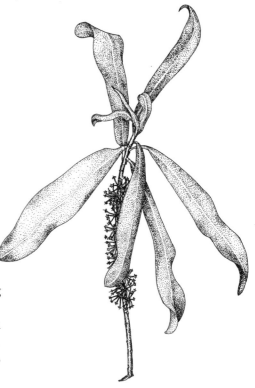

*Myrsine salicina*, a tree to 25 feet, has narrow, oblong **leaves,** 3 to 7 inches long, 1 to 1½ inches wide. The new leaves are bronzy on their lower surfaces, contrasting with the older leaves, which are entirely green. The leaves are leathery and have flat margins; the young branches lack the reddish brown color seen in *M. australis.* **Fruits** are about ⅜ inch long and red to orange.

    This myrsine, known as *toro* by the Maoris, is found naturally on both islands of New Zealand, from the lowlands to an elevation of 4,000 feet. Strybing Arboretum has a specimen in bed #43, in the section devoted to New Zealand plants. *Myrsine salicina* is seldom seen elsewhere.

Strybing (VI-N3)
Evergreen/Slow growth/25'
Small, unshowy, white flower clusters (spring-
    summer) /Red or orange berries
Full sun to part shade/Water infrequently
Sunset Zone 16,17

## 109

### Common myrtle
### *Myrtus communis*

Myrtaceae

Common myrtle is a large shrub or small tree to 15 feet or, rarely, as much as 20 to 25 feet tall. With age, it becomes a small, bushy tree with several trunks. Its **leaves** are opposite, generally 1 to 2 inches long and ½ to ¾ inch wide, green with transparent dots, and fragrant when crushed. **Flowers** are white, ¾ to 1 inch wide, with five rounded petals, and usually solitary on slender stalks. The **fruit** is a fleshy berry, purplish black, round to oblong, generally ½ inch long. In addition to the tree's use as an ornamental, its leaves, flowers, and bark are a source of scented myrtle oil used in perfumes. The wood is hard and close-grained and has been used for furniture, walking sticks, and tool handles.

    Common myrtle is variable in leaf shape and size and also in characteristics of flower and fruit. The smallest leaves may be ¼ by ⅛ inch and

S edge of Mallard Lake (II-I4); Strybing (VII-O3)
119 Collingwood
Evergreen/Slow growth/15'-25'
Fragrant, solitary, 5-petaled white flowers, 1" wide
    (July-Sept) /Small, edible, purplish black berries
Full sun to part shade/Water infrequently
Sunset Zone 8-24

the largest 2 inches by ¾ inch. The space between each leaf pair is also variable, with pairs close together or spread apart. A number of cultivars have been described and named, including 'Albocarpa' (with whitish fruits), 'Buxifolia' (boxleaf myrtle), 'Compacta' (compact myrtle), 'Flore Plena' (with double flowers), 'Microphylla' (rosemary myrtle, small-leaf myrtle), and 'Variegata' (with variegated leaves).

Common myrtle is native to the Mediterranean region and western Asia. The Greeks and Romans in ancient times considered it sacred to Venus and Aphrodite and used it as an emblem of love. In modern times, a spray of myrtle may still be used in wedding bouquets. Common myrtle is mentioned in the Bible, and it was known to biblical and post-biblical peoples of the Holy Land.

Common myrtle is also well known in northern Europe, where it is frequently cultivated outdoors in warm areas or as a container plant. It may have been one of the first plants introduced from western Asia to England, probably from the Levant prior to the sixteenth century. In the eastern United States, as in northern Europe, myrtle can be grown only in the warmest regions or in a greenhouse. In California, and in other mild-climate areas of the West, it has become a perfectly hardy, useful ornamental. However, because it is usually trimmed as a hedge, fully grown trees are seldom seen. Myrtle was introduced into California in 1853 by William Walker of Golden Gate Nursery in San Francisco, and it has been in Golden Gate Park since the late 1890s. Two treelike specimens, not well pruned over the years, are on the south edge of Mallard Lake. Common myrtle can also be seen as a hedge along Lincoln Way west of Ninth Avenue, and in Strybing's Garden of Fragrance.

# Other myrtles

Myrtle is the common name for plants in the genus *Myrtus*. It is also a common name for a number of unrelated plants in different families, including crape myrtle (*Lagerstroemia indica* and *L. hirsuta*), California wax myrtle (*Myrica californica*), Oregon myrtle (*Umbellularia californica*), creeping or running myrtle (*Vinca minor* and *V. major*), and willow myrtle (*Agonis flexuosa*).

*For humankind, the trees—their roots in the ground, their heads reaching into the sky—have seemed always to bind together the universe....Throughout the ages, humankind has looked to the trees to feed not only the flesh, but the spirit.*

GEORGE NAKASHIMA, *forward, The Soul of a Tree*

# 110

## Olive
## *Olea europaea*
### Oleaceae

The olive family includes many well-known trees and shrubs, among which are the ashes, forsythias, lilacs, and privets. Olive is a small tree, usually not more than 25 to 30 feet tall, with spreading branches that form a broad crown. Both trunk and branches have smooth, gray **bark. Leaves** are opposite, more or less lanceolate, up to 3 inches long, leathery, dark green above and silvery beneath. From a distance, the foliage appears gray green because of the silvery covering of the lower leaf surfaces. The small, white **flowers,** not a conspicuous feature of the tree, are arranged on stalks 1 to 2 inches long. Flowers are followed by black oval **fruits**—the olive of commerce—up to 1 inch long and containing a single hard seed.

Olive fruits are bitter when fresh, but are edible when treated to remove the bitterness and preserved in vinegar or a salty liquid. Almost all of the olives cultivated in the United States are grown in California. Until recently, these were used mostly in the production of table olives, but a resurgence of interest in the production of olive oil has resulted in the planting of many new olive groves, particularly in the wine country of Northern California. Olives are an important crop in the state's warmer regions, such as the Sacramento and San Joaquin valleys and the interior valleys of Southern California. Olives are also occasionally planted in southern Arizona.

Olive trees may live to a great age, their trunks becoming gnarled, knotty, often bent, and picturesque. There are said to be commercially valuable trees 400 to 500 years old still bearing fruit in Greece, Italy, and Spain. In the Holy Land in times past, old trees were venerated, and only when they were exceedingly ancient and had stopped bearing, or were much decayed, were they allowed to be cut down. Then they were cut at ground level so that regeneration through suckers would take place. It is said that in the Garden of Gethsemane there are still stumps of ancient olive trees believed to have sprouted from trees that grew during Christ's lifetime. Olive wood is hard and heavy and has been used for making tools and in cabinetwork. The use of an olive branch as a symbol of peace and goodwill predates Christianity; the origin of the practice is obscure.

Native to the eastern Mediterranean, olive is perhaps best known in the Holy Land, where it has been used for thousands of years by people living in the area. Eventually, the tree was taken to Italy, Spain, Portugal, and North Africa, where today most of the world's supply of olive oil is produced.

It is not surprising that olive, when brought to the mediterranean climate of California, should have become one of the state's best-known and most useful cultivated trees. Among the earliest trees to be introduced into California, olive was first planted in 1769 at Mission San Diego from seeds

W of Conservatory Dr East, N of Kennedy Dr (IV-R2)
101 Ocean Avenue; 2255 Lyon Street; NE side of
     Holly Park
Evergreen/Slow growth/25'-30'
Inconspicuous white flowers (early summer)/
     Oval black fruits
Full sun/Needs no watering, once established
Sunset Zone 8, 9, 11-24
Suitable as a street tree

brought from San Blas, Mexico, by Father Junípero Serra, the mission's founder. From there, the tree was taken to other missions, and subsequently planted throughout California for shade, ornament, and fruit.

Olive trees were planted in Golden Gate Park during the late 1800s. According to tree and shrub lists issued by the park's commissioners between 1902 and 1924, they may have been planted in the park a number of times. Probably none of the trees planted before 1900 have survived; those in the park today are relatively young. Several are located along Middle Drive East; a single tree is found on the west side of Conservatory Drive East, a short distance north of Kennedy Drive. These trees seldom produce fruit, perhaps because of the cool climate of San Francisco. Their foliage is likely to be greener than that of trees grown in a hotter, drier climate.

# 111

## Akiraho
## *Olearia paniculata*

### Asteraceae

*Olearia* belongs to the daisy family and occurs mainly in New Zealand and Australia. *Olearia paniculata* is a small, much-branched evergreen tree to 20 feet tall, with alternate, short petiolate **leaves** that are ovate-oblong, 2 to 3 inches long, with strongly wavy margins, and a conspicuous, silvery, feltlike covering of densely appressed hairs on the lower surface. Each **flower** head consists of only a single floret, in contrast to other composite flower heads that have several or many florets. These small flower heads, which are grouped into clusters 2 to 3 inches long, are not conspicuous but are delightfully fragrant.

*Olearia paniculata*, known to the Maoris as *akiraho*, was collected on Captain James Cook's second voyage at Queen Charlotte Sound at the southeastern corner of New Zealand's North Island, where Cook made several landings. The tree occurs on both North and South islands in coastal lowlands, from sea level to nearly 5,000 feet elevation. In New Zealand, it is reported to be easily cultivated; its main uses are as a hedge and in background plantings, especially in dry soil and windy places. It is rarely seen in California outside of Golden Gate Park, where it has been used in Strybing Arboretum as a windbreak along the southwestern edge of the Demonstration Gardens. It can be a valuable part of a shelterbelt or windbreak planting in coastal communities in California.

Strybing (VII-O3)
Evergreen/Moderate growth/20'
Fragrant, unshowy clusters, 2"-3" long, of tiny,
    white flowers (fall) /Clusters of papery seeds
Full sun/Water infrequently
Sunset Zone 16,17

# 112

## Guatemalan holly
# *Olmediella betschleriana*
### Flacourtiaceae

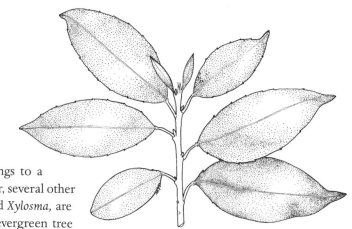

Guatemalan holly, the only species in this genus, belongs to a mostly tropical family little known in California. However, several other genera in the family, including *Azara, Dovyalis, Idesia,* and *Xylosma,* are more familiar in West Coast gardens. *Olmediella* is an evergreen tree best known for attractive **leaves** that are more or less sharply toothed and may be bronzy to dark green, depending on age and exposure. The pattern of teeth on the margins of the leaves is variable; some leaves are hollylike, while others are almost entire. Generally only 20 to 35 feet tall with a medium spread, the tree is grown as an individual specimen or in background screen plantings. The **flowers** are small, with male and female flowers on separate trees. The original tree in Strybing Arboretum is male. Female trees produce apple-shaped **fruits** about 2 inches in diameter. The Guatemalan common name, *manzanote,* alludes to the fruits. Apparently, the fruits are not edible.

Guatemalan holly is native to southern Mexico, Guatemala, El Salvador, and Honduras, where it occurs in moist mountain forests from 4,500 to nearly 9,000 feet. As a forest tree, there is little to call attention to it, except perhaps its more or less spiny leaves; nevertheless, it was introduced in central Guatemala, where, particularly in Guatemala City, it has been cultivated for many years. Fine specimens are to be seen along the Paseo de la Reforma, the city's principal boulevard, and also in the Parque Central of Antigua. Other English common names are Costa Rican holly and Puerto Rican holly, suggesting that the tree is cultivated in those countries as well. Olmediella has been cultivated in Italy for over a hundred years, but it is not listed for other European countries.

Guatemalan holly has been in Strybing Arboretum since the 1950s or perhaps earlier. According to Eric Walther, the Strybing tree was received from Paul J Howard, a well-known Los Angeles nurseryman. It was introduced into California in 1936 or 1937 by one of the Westcott brothers, associates of Paul Howard, who brought seeds of it from Guatemala. The tree is apparently not grown elsewhere in the San Francisco Bay Area. Rare in the nursery trade, it is occasionally cultivated in Santa Barbara, Santa Monica, Los Angeles, and San Diego.

The Guatemalan holly in Strybing's South American section, about 40 to 45 feet tall, has smooth bark and two trunks from near the base. Younger trees can be seen in the New World Cloud Forest collection, planted in the 1980s. It is rather slow growing, requiring little maintenance, and is resistant to frost and wind. It would be a useful tree for reforestation in Golden Gate Park and as a street or specimen tree in other coastal cities.

Strybing (VI-N3)
Slow growth/20'-45'
Inconspicuous male and female flowers on separate trees (spring) /Apple-shaped fruits, 2" wide
Full sun to part shade/Water regularly
Sunset Zone 17, 20-24

# 113

## Madeira bay
## *Persea indica*

Lauraceae

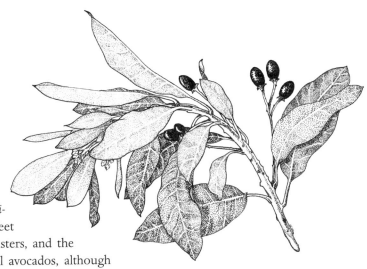

Madeira bay, like its relative the avocado *(Persea ameri-cana)*, is an evergreen tree of medium height (20 to 30 feet or more). Its small inconspicuous **flowers** are in clusters, and the black, olive-shaped, one-seeded **fruits** resemble small avocados, although only a thin layer of flesh surrounds the seed. **Bark** of the tree is slightly rough but not furrowed. **Leaves** are broadly lanceolate, 3 to 6 inches or more long; lacking the glands of the leaves of sweet bay *(Laurus nobilis)*, they are not fragrant when crushed. Throughout most of the year, a number of the oldest leaves turn red and remain on the tree for a period before falling.

W of Conservatory Dr East, S of Fuchsia Garden
   (IV-R2); Stanyan Meadows between Page and
   Haight Sts (IV-S3)
Dolores Park
Evergreen/Moderate growth/20'-30'
Inconspicuous flower clusters (spring) /Black,
   olive-sized fruits resembling avocados
Full sun/Water regularly
Sunset Zone 16, 17, 19-24

Madeira bay is found in the laurel forest, which develops in the cloud belt at middle elevations on the mountains of the two largest Canary Islands, Gran Canaria and Tenerife. In the laurel forest of Gran Canaria, several plants known in California as ornamentals are associated with Madeira bay: *Arbutus canariensis, Hedera canariensis, Semele androgyna,* Portugal laurel *(Prunus lusitanica),* and *Laurus azorica,* a close relative of the well-known sweet bay *(L. nobilis).* Unfortunately, the forest zones in these islands have long been exploited for timber. The excellent lumber from *L. azorica* and *Persea indica,* commonly called Canarian mahogany, has been used for furniture and many other items.

Madeira bay has been in Golden Gate Park since at least 1924 when it was listed in the *Annual Report of the Park Commissioners.* Francesco Franceschi introduced it to California in 1909 through his nursery in Santa Barbara. There are today a number of Madeira bays in Santa Barbara. This tree is seen elsewhere in southern California, in Santa Monica and Pasadena, and in northern California in Palo Alto, on the campus of Mills College in Oakland, and on the grounds of the State Capitol in Sacramento. An attractive broad-leafed evergreen, it deserves greater use in California as a specimen tree and for street planting.

Golden Gate Park has several trees of Maderia bay. Two are easily located on the western side of Conservatory Drive East, between Kennedy Drive and the entrance to the Fuchsia Garden; others are in Stanyan Meadows. It is also found in other parks in San Francisco, including Dolores Park, where a beautiful, small grove of multi-trunked trees is near the corner of 20th and Church streets.

# A Few Trees From the Islands

The Canary Islands, the Azores, and Madeira—all islands of Macaronesia in the eastern Atlantic off the coast of Spain and Morocco—have contributed many ornamentals to California including Canary Island date palm *(Phoenix canariensis)*, Canary Island pine *(Pinus canariensis)*, pride of Tenerife *(Echium pininana)*, pride of Madeira *(E. candicans)*, *Ilex perado*, *Clethra arborea*, and dragon tree *(Dracaena draco)*. Madeira bay *(Persea indica)* is also found on these islands, although its scientific name, given by Linnaeus, suggests that it may have come from India or the East Indies. In Linnaeus's day, world geography was not well understood and geographical terms, such as *indica*, were often used inaccurately.

## 114

Boldo

# *Peumus boldus*

Monimiaceae

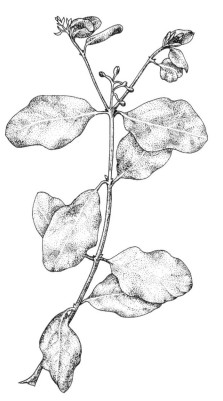

Boldo is an evergreen tree, 20 to 25 feet tall, that from a distance looks much like a California live oak, but it is little known in North America, belonging to a family found mostly in the Southern Hemisphere. Its broadly ovate **leaves** are opposite or nearly so, somewhat leathery, roughly hairy, inconspicuously glandular, slightly aromatic, and up to 2 inches long. The **flowers** are small, whitish, and unisexual, with male and female flowers on separate trees. The **fruit** is a fleshy berry about ¼ inch long.

Boldo is found in Chile from Coquimbo south to Osorno and from near sea level to about 3,000 feet elevation. Although growing under diverse conditions in this region, it is well adapted to places with little moisture and gravelly or rocky soil. In other places, however, it grows in somewhat more moist ravines along with Chilean myrtle *(Luma apiculata)* and *Citronella mucronata*, both of which are also in Golden Gate Park. Boldo trees have been valued in Chile for their bark, which is used in tanning, for their wood, which makes superior charcoal, and for their edible fleshy fruits. An alkaloid, boldina, obtained from the leaves, has had medicinal uses. The scientific names for the plant are latinized from Chilean common names.

According to Butterfield (1964), boldo was introduced into California about 1880. The tree has been in Golden Gate Park since the 1890s, when it was listed in the annual reports of the park commissioners. At present, the park has several trees: two of which are in Strybing Arboretum, one on the north edge of the Redwood Trail and another in the South American section. One tree is on the edge of Liberty Meadow, west of Conservatory Drive West. The largest specimen is at the eastern end of the park on the north side of Waller Street between Stanyan Street and Kezar Drive, adjacent to two California live oaks *(Quercus agrifolia)*. This last boldo, a broadly spreading tree, can be distinguished from the almost equally spreading oaks by the five trunks arising from its somewhat enlarged base. Leaves of

N side of Waller St between Stanyan St. and
    Kezar Dr (IV-S3); N edge of Liberty Meadow
    (IV-Q2); Strybing (VI-M4 & VI-N3)
Evergreen/Slow growth/20'-25'
Small, whitish flowers (spring) /Edible, fleshy
    berries, 1/4" long
Full sun/Water infrequently
Sunset Zone 8, 9, 14-24

the boldo and the oaks are similar except that the oak leaves have stiff, prickly margins and, on most of their lower surfaces, they have small tufts of hairs at the points where the secondary veins join the midrib.

Boldo is rare in California. There is another specimen in San Francisco's Stern Grove. The only other boldo in northern California is on the campus of UC Berkeley. In southern California, boldos are in Orpet Park in Santa Barbara and in The Arboretum of LA County.

# 115

## Canary Island date palm
# *Phoenix canariensis*
## Palmae

Canary Island date palm is easily recognized and distinguished from the few other palms in Golden Gate Park by its stout trunk, rough with persistent leaf bases, and by its large crown, with many stiffly spreading, dark green **leaves** up to 15 feet long. Its pinnate leaves group it with the feather-leafed palms. This palm has an unusually large number of leaves, some trees having as many as a hundred or more. It eventually prunes itself, leaving conspicuous leaf bases; however old leaves are often pruned off every year or two to obtain a cleaner appearance. Well-maintained trees, in which the leaf bases are cut back close to the trunk, resulting in a diamond pattern, are attractive but are seen less often than those pruned to leave about 6 inches of the leaf bases. The branched inflorescences are tucked between the leaves; the small individual **flowers** are pale yellow or orange. Like its close relative, date palm (*Phoenix dactylifera),* these palms are either male or female. **Fruits** produced by the female plants are small, yellowish dates that are edible but hardly comparable in quality to those of date palm.

The word phoenix has several meanings: it is the name of a miraculous, immortal bird in Egyptian mythology, the embodiment of the sun god; it also sometimes means red or purple; and in ancient Greece, it referred to a person from Phoenicia. Because the Phoenicians had both the dye, Tyrian purple, and date palms (with brown to purplish fruits), eventually the Greeks also applied the word phoenix to the date palms.

Canary Island date palm was introduced into California in the late 1800s and into Golden Gate Park early in the 1900s. Two of these trees can be seen in front of McLaren Lodge, a single tree is next to the Chinese Pavilion on Stow Lake, and a number of them flank the entrance to the conservatory. It is the most commonly planted palm in the boulevard of Dolores Street; in the 1990s, it was planted in large sizes along Market Street, from Laguna to Castro streets, and along the Embarcadero. This tough, hardy native of the Canary Islands is widely planted in California and grows in areas where winter temperatures sometimes drop well below freezing.

In front of McLaren Lodge (IV-S2); in front of
   conservatory (IV-Q1); near Chinese Pavilion
   on Stow Lake (III-M3)
The center medians of Dolores St, Market St, and
   the Embarcadero
Evergreen/Slow growth/60'
Hanging clusters of light yellow flowers (summer) /Small, yellowish, edible fruits
Full sun/Water infrequently
Sunset Zone 9, 12-24
Suitable as a street tree
Color plate

The Photinias
# *Photinia*
Rosaceae

Among the many members of the rose family are a number of evergreen trees and shrubs, including those in the Asian genus *Photinia,* common in gardens throughout the West Coast and in the southern states. Of the sixty or so species of *Photinia,* those in cultivation are noted for their glossy, deep green leaves, their broad clusters of tiny, five-petalled white **flowers,** and their colorful **fruits,** called pomes, that resemble tiny apples and are often popular with birds. In some species, the new leaves are bright red, adding a particularly showy note in spring, or when new leaves appear after shearing. They are tough garden plants, serving well as hedging, in backgrounds, and as shade trees.

# 116
# *Photinia davidsoniae*
Rosaceae

The largest of the three photinias in Golden Gate Park, *Photinia davidsoniae* is a broadly spreading evergreen tree that may reach 50 feet or more in height. Its dark green, glossy **leaves** are 3 to 6 inches long, narrowly elliptical, and shallowly toothed; the undersides are lighter green. The shoots are downy, reddish, and sometimes spiny when young. The tiny, creamy white **flowers** are held in terminal, hairy clusters, 3 to 4 inches in diameter and are followed by clusters of small, red orange **fruits** late in the year.

Photinia davidsoniae is known in Golden Gate Park only from several large trees in Strybing's Asian section and on the edge of its South American section, where it was among the arboretum's early plantings. It is native to western China, discovered in 1900 in western Hupeh (now Hubei) Province by EH Wilson, on his first expedition for the Veitch nursery. Wilson wrote that this photinia, one of the handsomest evergreen trees in central China, was commonly planted around shrines and tombs. He introduced it into England and in 1913 described and named it for Mrs Henry Davidson of the Friends' Foreign Mission in Sichuan, as an expression of gratitude for her assistance following an accident there in 1910, in which he was seriously injured.

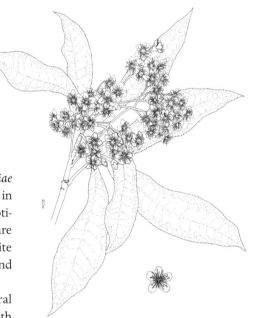

Strybing (VI-M3)
Evergreen/Moderate growth/40'
Clusters, 3-4" wide, of small, white flowers (late spring) /Red orange berrylike fruit
Full sun to part shade/Water regularly
Sunset Zone 15-24
Color plates

## 117

Hybrid photinia

# Photinia × fraseri
Rosaceae

One of the most common of evergreen shrubs in California, this photinia is a hybrid between Japanese photinia *(Photinia glabra)* and Chinese photinia *(P. serratifolia)*. Often kept as a sheared or heavily pruned large shrub, it can become a tree of 10 to 15 feet in height, with a broad, rounded canopy. The glossy **leaves** are elliptical to ovate, small-toothed, and 2 to 5 inches long. Plants of hybrid photinia are particularly conspicuous when the vivid bronze red leaves of the young growth appear in spring, in striking contrast to the dark green of the older leaves. The 4-inch terminal clusters of small, pink-tinged, white **flowers** appear only on plants that have not been sheared. Because this is a hybrid, fruit is seldom produced.

This hybrid, which has been known only since the late 1950s, originated in the Fraser Nurseries in Birmingham, Alabama. The original plant came from seed gathered from a plant of Chinese photinia growing adjacent to its Japanese cousin. The hybrid was propagated and eventually distributed, but was not named and described until 1961. Plants are easy to propagate and to grow and are most frequently seen as hedges, often clipped.

Today, hybrid photinia is seen in Golden Gate Park in several places, most commonly as a sheared hedge; a small group of unpruned trees can be seen along the north side of King Drive, east of its intersection with Sunset Boulevard. It is widely planted throughout California, particularly as large, shrubby hedges along the state's highways, where it survives with little care, other than an occasional shearing to control its size.

N side King Dr between Sunset and turnoff to
  Polo Field (II-G4)
Evergreen/Fast growth/10'-15"
Pink-tinged white flower clusters, 2"-5" wide
  (Apr-May) /Seldom-fruiting hybrid
Full sun to part shade/Water occasionally
Sunset Zone 4-24
Suitable as a street tree

## 118

Chinese photinia

# Photinia serratifolia

(syn. *P. serrulata*)

Rosaceae

Chinese photinia is a small evergreen tree or large shrub, usually 10 to 20 feet tall but occasionally taller. Its **bark** is smooth, and its glossy, dark green, oblong **leaves** tend to be slightly broader above the middle, firm and leathery, mostly 4 to 8 inches long, with margins shallowly to conspicuously toothed. Young shoots, often those on the lower trunks, show the most deeply toothed leaves. Both leaf surfaces are glabrous, with the lower pale

E side of conservatory (IV-Q1)
SE corner, 19th St at Castro St
Evergreen/Slow growth/10'-20'
Flat terminal clusters, 4"-7" across, of small, white
  flowers (Mar-May) /Soft, red berries
Full sun to part shade/Water infrequently
Sunset Zone 4-16, 18-22
Suitable as a street tree

green. Petioles are ½ to 1½ inches long, grooved on their upper surfaces at the end closest to the leaf blade and, at least when young, covered with whitish hairs along the groove; older leaves may not have any hairs. The numerous white **flowers,** about ¼ inch in diameter, are arranged in terminal, more or less flattened, branched clusters that are glabrous and 4 to 7 inches across. Flowers are followed by clusters of soft, hawthornlike red fruits about ⅜ inch in diameter. Plants are most attractive in spring when the white flowers are seen with scattered reddish new leaves. Later, the leaves are mostly green, but in the autumn, some of the oldest leaves turn red before falling.

A native of the temperate parts of China and Taiwan, Chinese photinia was said by EH Wilson to be common throughout its area. Wilson collected it twice in western China in the early 1900s, but he did not introduce it into cultivation. It had been introduced into England from China in 1804 by a ship captain of the English East India Company, and by the 1820s it was being cultivated in both England and France.

Chinese photinia has been grown in California at least since 1874, when James Hutchinson sold it at his nursery in Oakland. It has been in Golden Gate Park since the 1880s and is listed in reports of the park commissioners from 1889 to 1924. Several trees with multiple trunks from their bases are to be seen in front of the conservatory on its eastern side. Since its arrival in California, Chinese photinia has occasionally been planted in cities throughout the state from north to south. It is better adapted to regions away from California's coastal fog, where its leaves are likely to be disfigured by powdery mildew, often noticeable on trees within Golden Gate Park.

## The Pines
# *Pinus*
## Pinaceae

Pines are among the trees most often seen in Golden Gate Park. One of the earliest trees planted, and one that makes up the backbone of the park, is Monterey pine (*Pinus radiata*), but many others are also found here.

There are several hundred species of pines in the world, distributed in habitats ranging from coastal bluffs and sand dunes to windswept mountaintops. Some species are early pioneer trees, quickly populating areas laid bare by fire or other disturbance of the land. Some mingle with other conifers and broadleafed trees in mixed forests. Others dominate forests of a few species covering millions of acres.

Pines are distinguished from other conifers by their **leaves,** which are long, slender needles always clustered into bundles called fascicles; a sheath of thin, papery tissue wraps the base of the needles, holding them together. Needles are typically bundled in twos, threes, and fives; occasional species have single needles, and a few have bundles of four needles. The number of needles in each bundle is usually consistent within a species, and allows division of the species into the black pines (two or three needles) and the white pines (five needles).

The fruits of pines are **cones,** usually large and woody, conical in outline, with segments called scales protecting the developing seeds. Scales are distinguished by their size, shape, and the presence or absence of prickles or bumps on their outer surface. The **seed** usually possesses a papery wing, similar to that of a maple seed, which aids in its distribution. Seeds of many species are edible, constituting an important part of the diet of some native peoples, valued as a delicacy in that of others. Some species ripen their cones in the first year, while others take two to three years to do so. A number of species, such as the Monterey pine, require fire or intense heat to open their cones and release their seeds; they are known as closed-cone pines.

Pines provide wood for construction, cabinetry, furniture, utensils, and ornaments. Paper is produced from the pulpwood of some species. Turpentine and other substances are extracted from the wood of pines and have important commercial uses. However, the massive quantities of pollen produced by pines provide a significant allergen for many people.

# 119

### Japanese red pine
# *Pinus densiflora*

## Pinaceae

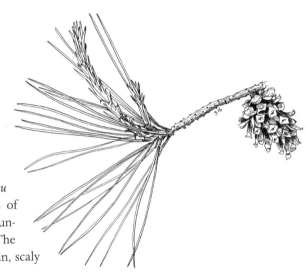

Japanese red pine, known in Japan as *aka-matsu* and *me-matsu* (female pine), is widely distributed on the three main islands of Japan and also in Korea. Japanese red pine has two **needles** per bundle, slender with a rounded point; they persist for three years. The **cones** are ovoid, less than 3 inches long. The reddish brown, thin, scaly **bark** peels or flakes irregularly.

According to EH Wilson (1916), red pine has been abundantly planted in Japan for reforestation from ancient times, but it was not planted in parks, temple grounds, and gardens, where the similar black pine (*Pinus thunbergii*) was favored. The Japanese also planted a number of dwarf, variegated, and other variants of red pine, which were great favorites and were propagated by grafting them onto black pine.

Japanese red pine was discovered by Carl P Thunberg, introduced to Holland by Philipp Franz von Siebold, and introduced to England by John Gould Veitch. It was brought to this country in 1862 by George R Hall. Several specimens may be seen in the Japanese Tea Garden: one southwest of the Pagoda is 25 feet tall and treelike; others are carefully shaped dwarf trees. In Strybing's Moon-viewing Garden is the slow-growing cultivar 'Umbraculifera', commonly called Tanyosho pine.

Japanese Tea Garden (V-N2); Strybing (VI-N3)
Evergreen/Slow growth/100'
(Conifer) Light brown, oval cones, less than 3"
Full sun to part shade/Water occasionally
Sunset Zone 2-9, 14-24

*Pines are the largest and most diverse genus of conifers; they are the most important genus economically and are found throughout the Northern Hemisphere and in Indonesia, just across the equator.*

KEITH RUSHFORTH, *Conifers*

# 120

Montezuma pine

# *Pinus montezumae*

Pinaceae

Montezuma pine is widespread in the mountains of central Mexico and extends into western Guatemala. Its name commemorates the last emperor of the Aztecs, Montezuma II, who lost his life at the time of the Spanish conquest (1520) under Hernando Cortés.

Montezuma pine is reported to reach 60 to 100 feet when mature. **Bark** on young trees is rough and scaly; on mature trees, it has deep, irregular fissures that form rough, scaly plates. The drooping **leaves** are mostly five in a cluster, less often four or six, and range from 6 to 10 inches long. The sheath at the base of the leaf cluster is about ½ to 1 inch long. The **cones** are also variable. In shape, they are an elongated oval, usually slightly curved, sometimes more or less straight. Cones are 4 to 6 inches long, occasionally longer, and generally 3 or 4 inches wide. Cone **scales** are thick, hard, and stiff, and their tips have a small prickle that usually drops off.

Over their wide geographic range in Mexico, Montezuma pines grow in cold to warm temperate regions at elevations ranging from 6,000 to 10,000 feet. They are reported to grow best in well-drained soil on high mesas and mountain slopes, but they also are found on arid sites, where growth is slower and trees are not as tall as those in wetter areas.

Montezuma pine was first observed in Mexico by Alexander von Humboldt and Aimé Bonpland during their early explorations of South America and Mexico from 1799 to 1804. They observed trees of it near Mexico City in 1803. The pine was later seen by other European plant explorers in Mexico, including German-born Karl Theodore Hartweg, who introduced it to England in 1836.

In Golden Gate Park, there are three Montezuma pines at the edge of a well-established planting behind McLaren Lodge. These are over 40 feet tall and produce cones. Their age is not known, but Montezuma pine has been in the park since at least 1893. Another tree can be seen above Strybing's Succulent Garden. Other trees are in the UC Botanical Garden in Berkeley.

W side of the lawn, N of McLaren Lodge (IV-S2);
    Strybing (VI-M4)
Evergreen/Fast growth/60'-100'
(Conifer) Tan, ovoid cones (3"-4" x 6" or more)
Full sun/Water infrequently
Sunset Zone 14-24

# 121

### Italian stone pine
# *Pinus pinea*
Pinaceae

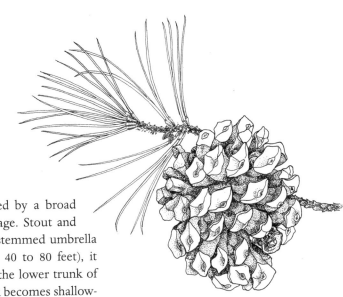

The Italian stone pine, although typically characterized by a broad umbrella-shaped crown, varies in habit depending on age. Stout and shrubby when young, it takes on the shape of a thick-stemmed umbrella after a few years. With greater age and height (from 40 to 80 feet), it becomes high headed and almost flat on top. **Bark** on the lower trunk of young trees is rough and flaky. As trees mature, the bark becomes shallowly furrowed. In older trees, it is deeply and longitudinally furrowed with irregular ridges; only on upper branches is it still scaly. **Leaves** are in twos (rarely threes), 3 to 6 inches long, with basal sheaths about ¼ inch long. **Cones,** which need three years to mature, are sessile, one or sometimes two together, broadly ovoid to globose, rounded at the tip, 4 to 6 inches long, nearly as broad, and symmetrical. **Scales** are irregularly four sided, and a horizontal ridge bisects the well-defined central portion, which has a stout, slightly pointed tip. Seeds are oblong, ½ to ¾ of an inch long, with a short wing that detaches before the seed falls. **Seed** coats are hard, but the seeds are wonderfully edible.

In addition to its easily recognized spreading crown, Italian stone pine has other unusual features. As a species, it is remarkably stable. The only described variant, var. *fragilis,* characterized by a soft, thin seed coat, is possibly the result of selection for this character in cultivated plantings rather than a naturally occurring variant. Some thirty different turpentine components occur in pines. *Pinus pinea,* among the few pines with only one kind of turpentine, has almost pure limonene turpentine.

The natural area of distribution of the Italian stone pine in the Mediterranean region extends from Spain eastward to Turkey. Like the olive, also found widely in the region, it has been extensively planted for centuries, making it difficult to determine whether it occurred naturally in the areas where it is found today or originated from plantings. Away from the Mediterranean region, it is cultivated only where the climate is mild; in these areas, it is grown as a distinctive and attractive landscape tree. According to Butterfield (1964), Stephen Nolan offered it in 1871 at his Belle View Nursery in Oakland. Its exact date of introduction into Golden Gate Park is not known, but it is listed in annual reports of the park commissioners from 1893 to 1924.

Today, many Italian stone pines may be seen in the park. One is in Stanyan Meadows near Page Street. Additional trees include two groups of three flanking the main entrance to the California Academy of Sciences, a grove in the traffic island on Kennedy Drive between Spreckels Lake and the Buffalo Paddock, and a single tree in Strybing Arboretum, just inside the main entrance, opposite the imposing Monterey cypress *(Cupressus*

Near Stanyan St between Oak and Page Sts
 (IV-S2); entrance to the Academy of Sciences
 ( III-O2); Strybing (VII-O4)
Washington Square; Westwood Park; 140
 Turquoise Way
Evergreen/Slow growth/40'-60'
(Conifer) Sessile, shiny, brown, roundish cones,
 4"-6" long
Full sun/Needs no watering once established
Sunset Zone 6-9, 13-24
Suitable as a street tree

*macrocarpa*). Although stone pines have been in the park for about a century, none that were originally planted have survived. Those in the park today were planted in the 1950s and 1960s. Larger and older ones are seen in other cities in California such as Berkeley, Palo Alto, San Mateo, Salinas, Whittier, Santa Monica, and the Los Angeles and San Diego areas. In Santa Barbara, where stone pines are frequently seen, trees 40 to 60 feet tall can be seen along several streets. Of several on the capitol grounds in Sacramento, one, perhaps among the oldest in the state, is over 90 feet tall, with a trunk 11 feet in diameter.

# Pines in Literature

Along with other pines of southern Europe, the Italian stone pine has had a long association with people. Theophrastus (372–287 BC), a Greek philosopher and student of Aristotle, made an early and significant reference to it in his *Enquiry into Plants*. He recognized pines as different from other trees and wrote of their usefulness; the stone pine was among the five he described. In Roman times, Pliny the Elder, who lived during the first century of our era, discussed two of the pines described by Theophrastus, of which one was apparently the Italian stone pine.

An early record of cultivation of this pine in the Mediterranean region was its introduction by fourth- and fifth-century monks into the vicinity of Ravenna in Italy, probably for its edible seeds. These trees flourished and spread from their planted areas, gradually forming groves *(pineta)* for several miles north and south along the Adriatic coast. Eventually, the groves became known as the pines of Ravenna *(la pineta di Ravenna)* made famous by the writings of Dante, Boccaccio, and Byron. Dante finished the *Divine Comedy* in Ravenna and died there in 1321; Boccaccio used the Ravenna forest as the setting for his *Decameron;* and Byron wrote *Don Juan* while living in Ravenna, where he spent time in the "evergreen pine forest."

Unfortunately, this human-made forest, which has existed for about 1,500 years, has declined in recent decades. Its trees have suffered from neglect and cutting, and measures have not been taken to protect the remaining trees or to reforest the decimated groves.

## 122

Monterey pine
## *Pinus radiata*

Pinaceae

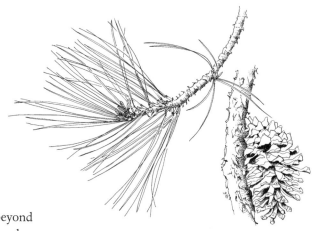

One of the major canopy trees planted throughout the park (I-E2); Japanese Tea Garden (V-N2); Strybing (VII-O4)
1450 Divisadero Street; Buena Vista Park.
Evergreen/Fast growth/30'-100'
(Conifer) Unevenly conical, light brown, cones, 3"-5" long, with prickly upper scales
Full sun/Water occasionally
Sunset Zone 15-17

Monterey pine is the most widely planted of all pines, cultivated far beyond its limited natural range on California's central coast. It has an irregular, somewhat rounded crown and varies from 30 to 100 feet tall, with a trunk 2 to 6 feet in diameter, covered with a thick, deeply furrowed, dark brown **bark. Needles** are in bundles of three, are 2 to 5 inches long on mature trees, and are flexible, dark green, and very dense on the branches, remaining for three to four years; persistent leaf sheaths are ¼ to ½ inch long. **Cones** have little or no stalk, point more or less downward, and are unevenly conical, 3 to 5 inches long and 2 to 3 inches wide. The inner side of the cone next to the branch is imperfectly developed; the lowermost cone **scales** on the side away from the branch form thickened, rounded knobs, while the upper scales are somewhat diamond-shaped with a small prickle in the center.

Monterey pine belongs to the closed-cone pine group, with cones remaining on the trees and closed for several years. Heat causes the cones to open, releasing the seeds. In rare instances, Monterey pines in Golden Gate Park have been known to open their cones in early fall after several unusually warm days. Cones open with a slight crackling sound and release their seeds, which drift to the ground like heavy snowflakes.

Monterey pine is restricted in nature to three coastal areas of central California. The northernmost is in the vicinity of Año Nuevo Point (southern San Mateo County) and the adjacent area around Waddell Creek (northern Santa Cruz County). About 130 miles to the south, in northern San Luis Obispo County, is a fairly extensive forest around Cambria, and immediately north is a small, isolated stand near Pico Creek. The best known locality, however, is on the Monterey Peninsula, where extensive pine woodlands occur on the picturesque low coastal hills and ocean bluffs from Monterey to Pacific Grove and Point Lobos, extending inland for several miles and south to Malpaso Creek. A variant, *Pinus radiata* var. *binata,* occurs on Guadalupe Island off the coast of Baja California, Mexico. Because of its limited distribution, Monterey pine is considered rare, but it is not an endangered species.

David Douglas, the first professional plant collector to visit California, introduced Monterey pine into England in 1833. During the years since, it has been grown in England and Europe, but its most extensive plantings have been in the Southern Hemisphere. There, it is the most common pine for reforestation and afforestation in South Africa, South America, Australia, and New Zealand; it is harvested in those regions for both lumber and paper.

Monterey pine can be seen throughout the park, with many trees now in a serious state of decline due to old age. A fine, small grove of vigorous trees can be seen at the Main Entrance to Strybing Arboretum; other good specimens are along Kennedy Drive, just west of the Buffalo Paddock. Many young groves are visible, particularly in the western end of the park, the result of a reforestation program begun in the late 1970s. In the Japanese Tea Garden, most of the tallest pines, carefully shaped according to Japanese custom, are, in fact, Monterey pines.

*He that plants trees loves others besides himself.*

THOMAS FULLER, 1732

# 123

## Japanese black pine
# *Pinus thunbergii*

### Pinaceae

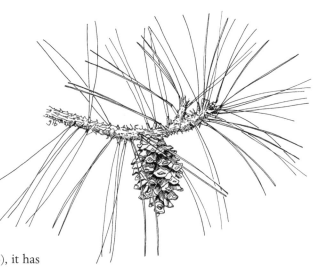

Japanese black pine, known in Japan as *kuro-matsu* and o-matsu (male pine), occurs on Japan's main islands, Honshu, Shikoku, and Kyushu, where it is common along the coast and in the lowlands. According to EH Wilson (1916), it has been so widely planted from time immemorial that it is not possible to determine precisely the tree's original distribution. It was planted along important highways and on palace and temple grounds. At some sites, trees were tall and erect to nearly 100 feet, with trunks 5 to 6 feet in circumference. However, Wilson says that this pine usually has a crooked trunk, heavy sprawling branches, dark green leaves, and an irregular crown, a picturesque habit that accounts for its wide use in Japan. This pine has two **needles** in each bundle; they persist for three years and are stout and sharply pointed. The ovoid **cones** are less than 3 inches long. The **bark** is dark gray, thick, and furrowed or fissured, forming irregular plates or sections. Black pine is often represented in Japanese paintings and crafts.

Carl Thunberg collected Japanese black pine while living in Japan in the late 1700s. Philipp von Siebold introduced it into Holland in 1855, and John Gould Veitch introduced it into England in 1861. In Wilson's day, the Arnold Arboretum had large specimens of black pine grown from seed sent from Sapporo, Hokkaido, in 1880, and from seed collected in Japan in 1892 by CS Sargent.

A Japanese black pine is the oldest tree in Golden Gate Park's Japanese Tea Garden, planted near the main entrance and conspicuous as a waist-high layered tree stretched along the tops of a number of wooden supports. According to the late George Hagiwara, it was planted by his grandfather, Makoto Hagiwara, who estimated its age at 300 years. A relatively young black pine is on the western edge of Strybing's Primitive Plants Garden. A group of black pines has been planted at Doughboy Meadow.

Japanese Tea Garden (V-N2); Doughboy Meadow (III-M1); Strybing (VII-N3)
Washington Square Park
Evergreen/Slow growth/100'
(Conifer) Green brown, oval cones, up to 3" long
Full sun/Water occasionally
Sunset Zone 2-12, 14-24

# Japanese Tea Garden

Golden Gate Park's Japanese Tea Garden originated in the California Mid-Winter Exposition held in the park from January to December 1894. The exposition, which covered about sixty acres, was a huge success, and one of its most popular exhibits was the Japanese Village. At the close of the exposition the San Francisco Board of Park Commissioners bought the village from George Turner Marsh, who had designed and built it, and the Park Department took over its maintenance. Today's Japanese Tea Garden, although changed from the original Japanese Village, retains a few reminders of the 1894 exposition. These include the splendid two-storied Main Gate, the Moon (or Drum) Bridge, the Tea House, and the pond with its small island in front of the Tea House.

George Marsh was born in Australia in 1857. He went to Japan with his family when he was twelve and, during the next six years, studied the history, art, and language of the country. In 1875, he came to San Francisco and a year later opened an Oriental art goods store. When plans were underway for the Mid-Winter Exposition, he became one of the exposition's backers. He proposed a Japanese exhibit and, through his efforts, the Japanese Village was built.

Shortly after the close of the exposition, John McLaren asked Makoto Hagiwara to take charge of the maintenance of the Japanese garden. Born in Japan in 1854, Hagiwara came to San Francisco in 1885 and worked as landscape gardener in the area. Beginning in 1895, he maintained the Japanese Tea Garden but left for a period in 1900. After his return in 1908, he moved his family into a house he built within the Tea Garden and was responsible for many of the changes made in the garden during the following years. After Hagiwara's death in 1925, his daughter and her husband continued to care for the garden until early 1942. After the United States entered World War II, the Hagiwara family, like thousands of other Japanese-Americans, were forced to leave San Francisco for life in an internment camp until the end of the war. Sadly, the family never returned to live in, and maintain, the garden. A bronze plaque, placed inside the Main Gate in 1974 by the John McLaren Society, commemorates the contributions of the Hagiwara family to the Japanese Tea Garden during the nearly forty years of their association with it.

The design for the Japanese Village followed the pattern of a traditional Japanese stroll garden. Two tea houses were part of the original design, but only one remains today. Though many of the garden's features today follow the basic pattern of the original design, parts of the garden have seen additions or changes, among which were those that came from the Japanese exhibit at the Panama–Pacific Exposition of 1915. These included the Pagoda, the Temple Gate and the South Gate. In 1966, a collection of dwarf trees amassed by the Hagiwara family was planted below the Temple Gate.

Most of the plants in the Japanese Tea Garden are from Japan. Many of the dwarf trees are old; some were among the earliest to be planted in the garden. The oldest plant in the garden is a Japanese black pine (*Pinus thunbergii*) espaliered on a bamboo frame in front of the Tea House. It came from Japan as a potted plant and was planted by Makoto Hagiwara. The tall Japanese umbrella pine (*Sciadopitys verticillata*) behind the Tea House was also planted by Hagiwara.

The tall Monterey pines (*Pinus radiata*) were planted in the late 1800s. They have been pruned through the years to allow light to filter through their branches. The pruning has shaped them in a manner so completely in keeping with the rest of the plants in the garden that they are not readily recognized as being native California pines. The smaller, twisted pine just inside the Main Gate is also a Monterey pine. Makoto Hagiwara brought it from the park's western end as a young tree and planted it in its present location around 1900.

Adapted from *The Japanese Tea Garden*
by Elizabeth McClintock, 1977

# 124

## Torrey pine
# *Pinus torreyana*

### Pinaceae

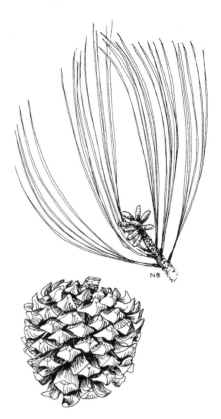

Torrey pines in their native habitats vary from low or nearly prostrate to about 30 feet tall in exposed sites; in sheltered sites, they are taller, up to 60 feet, and more erect. Torrey pine is characterized by its five stout **needles,** 6 to 12 inches long, sharply serrate on the margins, and generally blue green or grayish yellow green. Needles remain on the tree for several years. The cylindrical male pollen-bearing cones are 1 to 2 inches long and occur in terminal clusters of five to fifteen. The bulky seed **cones** grow slowly, taking about three years to mature. At maturity, they are broadly ovoid, 4 to 6 inches long, and almost as broad. The prominent cone **scales** are four-sided, pyramidally thickened at the apex, and end in a stout spine. **Seeds** are about ½ inch long with a hard shell. At the apex, they have a wing ¼ to ½ inch long. The seeds are edible, either roasted or raw.

Torrey pine, the rarest of California's pines, has one of the most limited distributions in the genus. It occurs only in two small areas in Southern California. One population is on the coastal mainland, within the city of Del Mar and to the immediate south in Torrey Pines State Reserve. Scattered over a few square miles to the north and south of Soledad Valley, this population was estimated by the California Department of Parks and Recreation in 1975 to include about 3,400 mature trees. The second population, to the northwest on Santa Rosa Island offshore from Santa Barbara County, covers less than one square mile. It includes about 1,000 mature trees, but has a higher proportion of young trees than the mainland population. These two populations, which show small morphological differences, are recognized within *Pinus torreyana* as ssp. *torreyana* and ssp. *insularis*.

According to Butterfield (1964), Torrey pine was first offered commercially in California by Stephen Nolan in 1871 at his Belle View Nursery in Oakland. The giant of cultivated Torrey pines is in the city of Carpinteria in Southern California. When measured recently, it was 126 feet tall, with a trunk circumference of 20 feet and a branch spread of 130 feet. Another magnificent Torrey pine in Beverly Hills was reported in 1988 as being 110 feet tall, with a trunk diameter of 20 feet and a spread of 75 feet. Other Torrey pines in cultivation are in San Diego, Santa Monica, Santa Barbara, and Sacramento. One planted in The Ruth Bancroft Garden in Walnut Creek in the mid-1970s is now 50 feet tall and nearly as broad.

Torrey pine was one of the earliest trees planted in Golden Gate Park; it was listed in annual reports of the park commissioners from 1893 through 1924. It is scattered throughout the park, with particularly notable specimens along Kennedy Drive just west of Chain of Lakes Drive, on Fulton Street near the 30th Avenue entrance to the park, and along Lincoln Way near 21st Avenue. There are also a number of Torrey pines in Strybing Arboretum, with a particularly large one just north of the arboretum's nursery.

Fulton near 30th Ave (II-H1); Lincoln at 21st Ave (II-K4); Kennedy Dr W of Chain of Lakes Dr (I-D3); Strybing (VI-N4)
Castro St at Henry St
Evergreen/Fast growth/60'-100'
(Conifer) Broadly oval, dark brown cones, 4"-6" long, with scales ending in tiny pyramids
Full sun/Water infrequently
Sunset Zone 17, 20-24
Color plate

# 125

### Himalayan pine
## *Pinus wallichiana*

Pinaceae

Himalayan pine, also called Himalayan white pine, blue pine, and Bhutan pine, has smooth **bark** when young; on mature trees, it is thicker and breaks into irregular, shallow plates. Trees have five **needles,** 5 to 7 inches long, with sharply toothed margins, and remain on the tree for two to three years. Needles often bend abruptly near the base so that they hang down. Color of the needles varies from gray green to bluish. The **cones** are cylindrical, generally 6 to 10 inches long and 1½ to 2 inches wide. They are solitary or two to three together, on stalks 1 to 2 inches long, erect when young but pendant later. Cone **scales** are about 1½ inches long and an inch wide with an acute, thickened lip. **Seeds** are about ¼ inch long with a thin, nearly inch-long wing.

Himalayan pine is widely distributed in the Himalayas from Afghanistan to Assam and Nepal. It was discovered by Francis Buchanan-Hamilton, a Scottish physician and botanist, who mentioned the pine in 1802 in an account of travels in Nepal. It was later found in Nepal by Nathaniel Wallich, who described and named it as a new species, *Pinus excelsa*. In later years, it was learned that this name had been used earlier for another conifer, and *P. excelsa* was renamed *P. wallichiana*. Other names, published later and sometimes still used, are the synonyms *P. nepalensis* and *P. griffithii*.

In their native area, trees of Himalayan pine, presumably of considerable age, have been described as up to 150 feet in height. In cultivation, they are not as tall, but perhaps also not as old. However, there are records in England and Ireland of Himalayan pines from 75 to 120 feet.

Himalayan pines have been planted in several cities on the Pacific Coast. In Vancouver, British Columbia, they are found in Queen Elizabeth Park and Stanley Park, in VanDusen Botanical Garden, and on the campus of the University of British Columbia. In Seattle, Washington, they can be seen in Washington Park Arboretum, on the campus of the University of Washington, in the gardens at Chittenden Locks, in Woodland Park Zoological Garden, and in residential gardens. In Portland, Oregon, they are planted in Hoyt Arboretum, and in Berkeley, California, they can be seen on the UC campus. A single specimen, planted in the mid-1970s, can be seen at The Ruth Bancroft Garden in Walnut Creek. According to Butterfield (1964), this pine was first listed in 1897 by Francesco Franceschi for his Santa Barbara nursery. It has been in Golden Gate Park at least since 1893. Today, trees in the park include two in Strybing Arboretum, east of the Succulent Garden.

Strybing (VI-M4)
Evergreen/Moderate growth/75'-120'
(Conifer) Light brown, cylindrical cones, 2" x 6"-10"
Full sun/Water occasionally
Sunset Zone 4-7, 14-17

# Pines for Food

Throughout the Mediterranean region, the Italian stone pine *(Pinus pinea)* has been planted more for its edible seeds, often called pine nuts, than for its attractive habit and picturesque appearance in the landscape. Pine seeds, with varying amounts of fats and proteins, are a useful human food, but only about eighteen species of pines have seeds large enough and of sufficiently good flavor to be considered edible. Some have too pronounced a turpentine flavor to be palatable.

An excellent American edible seed comes from the southwestern pinyon pine *(Pinus edulis)*. In Europe, the best known and most important of edible pine seeds are those of the Italian stone pine. Their use as food goes back many centuries. Pine nuts preserved in honey have been found among the ruins of Pompeii. Pine nut shells found in refuse dumps of Roman camps in England indicate that they may have been included in food rations of Roman legions. Traditionally in Italy, the seeds were used in soups and ragouts, but they have also been used in desserts and candies, and have been eaten raw, roasted, and salted, much as Americans eat peanuts.

In Italy, Spain, and southern France, the seeds have been an important item of commerce. Efficient methods have been developed for collecting cones and seeds, extracting the seeds, and sorting them to obtain the best ones for export. In addition to their use as human food, they are fed to animals and are the source of an oil used for pharmaceutical purposes. Pine nuts are so well known in these countries that each has its common names for them: *pinocchio* and *pinoli* in Italy, *pinones* in Spain, *pomme de pin* in France. Imported into England, they are called *pignolias* or *pignoli*. The English common name for the tree, stone pine, refers to its hard seed coats.

# The Pittosporums
# *Pittosporum*

## Pittosporaceae

The genus *Pittosporum* has about 150 to 200 species and is widely distributed in warm temperate, subtropical, and tropical regions of the Old World. Australia and New Zealand have over thirty species, and most pittosporums grown in California come from these two countries. Pittosporums are evergreen trees or shrubs. Several are attractive in habit, foliage, and flowers, and are planted frequently as ornamentals in gardens and parks, as street trees, and in hedges.

Pittosporum **leaves** are alternate and evergreen. **Flowers** generally are white to yellow or pink to purple. The petals cohere in their lower portion to form a tube below the reflexed or spreading tips. Although the flowers are small, they form showy, generally umbel-like clusters. **Fruits** are capsules that split into two or three divisions to reveal several to many **seeds** embedded in a resinous fluid. When the capsules open, the seeds become somewhat dry but remain sticky, and are dispersed by birds. The name *Pittosporum* is taken from two Greek words for pitch and spore, in reference to the sticky seeds. In California and a few other places, seeds of several cultivated pittosporums (*P. crassifolium, P. tenuifolium, P. tobira,* and *P. undulatum*) germinate in disturbed areas.

Several pittosporums were collected by early European explorers. The earliest collection was made by Engelbert Kaempfer, a German-born naturalist serving as medical officer of the Dutch East India Company in the late 1600s. He collected a number of plants, including one that he illustrated and described in 1712 using its Japanese name, *tobera*. Nearly a century later, at Kew, England, it was given the name that we know it by today, *Pittosporum tobira*.

During 1769 and 1770, five species of *Pittosporum* were collected by Joseph Banks and Daniel Solander, naturalists on Captain James Cook's first voyage to New Zealand and Australia. Among these was tawhiwhi *(Pittosporum tenuifolium)*, now widely cultivated in California.

# 126

## Karo
## *Pittosporum crassifolium*
### Pittosporaceae

Known by the Maori common name karo, this much-branched large shrub or small tree, generally 15 to 25 feet tall, is a native of New Zealand. It is found around forest margins and along streams on North Island and on the Kermadec Islands, about 600 miles northeast. In its native habitat, it is always found close to the coast and is most abundant on the tiny islands off the northeast coast of North Island.

The thick, leathery **leaves,** about 4 inches long and 2 inches wide, with margins rolled under, have a dull green upper surface and a white to buff, densely hairy lower surface. The fragrant **flowers,** several in a terminal umbel-like cluster, are dark red to purple, their petal tips folded back against the tube. The ½-inch long woody **fruits** split in threes, revealing many shiny, black, sticky seeds.

Karo was discovered in late 1833 by the Kew-trained English botanical explorer Richard Cunningham. It was taken to England sometime before 1872, the year in which it was illustrated in *Curtis's Botanical Magazine* from a plant grown at Tresco Abbey on the Isles of Scilly. It was probably introduced there by Joseph Banks. It has been in California since before 1871, when it was sold by Stephen Nolan at his Belle View Nursery in Oakland. As one of the hardiest pittosporums, it is widely planted. It was first listed as being in Golden Gate Park in the 1899 *Annual Report of the Park Commissioners.*

Several karo plants may be seen along Kennedy Drive from Sixth to Tenth avenues; others are in Strybing Arboretum, near the main entrance, around the perimeter of the gardens, and on the north side of the Dwarf Conifer Garden. Elsewhere in the San Francisco Bay Area, karo is on the campuses of the UC Berkeley, Stanford University in Palo Alto, and Mills College in Oakland. It can also be seen at UC Davis, and, in Southern California, in Santa Barbara, the Los Angeles area, and San Diego. Karo is among the most coast tolerant of shrubs and is commonly planted in coastal parks and gardens. It is one of only a few trees (or large shrubs) that can survive along San Francisco's windswept Great Highway, where it can be seen along with Monterey cypress *(Cupressus macrocarpa),* Australian tea tree *(Leptospermum laevigatum),* and ngaio *(Myoporum laetum).*

N side Kennedy Dr between 8th and 10th Avenues (III-N1); S side of Kennedy Dr opposite 8th Ave (III-O2); Strybing (VII-O4)
Great Highway near Quintara St
Evergreen/Moderate growth/15'-25'
Fragrant dark red to purple flowers in small clusters (spring) /Marble-sized woody fruits containing shiny, black, sticky seeds
Full sun to part shade/Water occasionally
Sunset Zone 9, 14-17, 19-24
Suitable as a street tree
Color plate

# 127

## *Pittosporum daphniphylloides*

Pittosporaceae

Native to Taiwan and lacking a common name, *Pittosporum daphniphylloides* is a small tree with fragrant yellow flowers. It has leathery **leaves** to 6 inches long and 2 inches wide with leaf stalks ½ to ¾ inch long. Pale yellow **flowers,** about ¼ inch long, occur in elongated flower clusters consisting of two or three umbel-like groups one above the other. This arrangement of flowers is not seen in other pittosporums discussed here. The small, round **fruits,** about ⅜ inch in diameter, split into two parts and contain ten to fifteen seeds.

The only location in Golden Gate Park for *Pittosporum daphniphylloides* is in Strybing's Asian section, where it is found in the Moon-viewing Garden; this small tree has been in the arboretum since before 1958. This pittosporum is rare in California, since there are no records of plants other than the one at Strybing. In the 1930s, it was in EO Orpet's garden in Santa Barbara and in Elysian Park in Los Angeles.

Strybing VI-M3)
Evergreen/Slow growth/15'
Fragrant pale yellow flowers, 1/4" long, in tiered
 clusters (Apr-May) /Round leathery capsules
Full sun to part shade/Water occasionally
Sunset Zone 14-24

# 128

## *Pittosporum erioloma*

Pittosporaceae

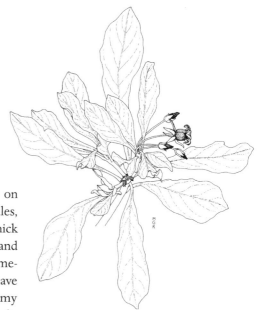

*Pittosporum erioloma,* a shrub or small tree to 15 feet tall, occurs only on Lord Howe Island, about 400 miles off the coast of New South Wales, Australia, and in the Solomon Islands in the South Pacific. **Leaves** are thick and leathery, glabrous, 2 inches long, with margins slightly thickened and rolled under. Because the leaves are vaguely laurel-like, the species is sometimes called Lord Howe's laurel, joining the many other plants said to have laurel-like leaves. The **flowers** are few, in a loose, umbel-like cluster, creamy white with a pink basal tinge. Rounded **fruits,** ¼ to ¾ inch in diameter, split in threes to reveal fifteen to twenty black, sticky seeds.

There are no records of the date of introduction of *Pittosporum erioloma,* but presumably it has been in the state since the 1920s. It has been in Golden Gate Park since 1924, when it was listed in the *Annual Report of the Park Commissioners.* At present, several plants may be seen on Kennedy Drive between Eighth and Tenth avenues. Of Strybing's several trees, two have been there since 1958. Most these are in the New Zealand collection; another is at the edge of the Demonstration Gardens.

N side Kennedy Dr between 8th and 10th
 Avenues (III-O1); Strybing (VI-N4)
Evergreen/Moderate growth/15'
Few, creamy white flowers with a basal pink
 tinge, in loose clusters (spring) /Round cap-
 sules, 3/4" wide, containing black, sticky seeds
Full sun to part shade/Water infrequently
Sunset Zone 14-17, 19-22

# 129

## Tarata

### *Pittosporum eugenioides*

Pittosporaceae

Said to be the largest of the pittosporums in New Zealand, tarata (its Maori name) may reach 40 feet in height with a trunk 2 feet in diameter. A second common name, lemonwood, refers to the strong lemony scent of the crushed leaves. Generally 3 to 6 inches long and 1 to 2 inches wide, **leaves** are somewhat leathery and yellow green with a yellowish midvein prominent on the upper surface. The undulate margins are wavier than those of Victorian box *(Pittosporum undulatum)*. The fragrant yellow **flowers** have a sweet, honeylike scent that can be overpowering. The flowers occur in terminal, umbell-like, showy clusters; the narrow petal tips spread outward. The **fruits,** smaller than those of other pittosporums in cultivation, are about 3/8 inch wide and generally split into two, revealing sticky, black seeds.

Tarata occurs on both islands of New Zealand. The Maori mixed the flowers with fat for anointing their bodies and extracted the sap for its scent. It is commonly cultivated as both an ornamental tree and as a hedge in New Zealand and Europe. It was introduced into California before 1871, when it was offered by Stephen Nolan at his Belle View Nursery in Oakland. It is commonly cultivated in California, and has been in Golden Gate Park since the late 1890s, when it was first listed in the annual reports of the park commissioners. Today, many plants are in the park, particularly along Kennedy Drive between Eighth and Tenth avenues. A large tree is near the western entrance to the AIDS Memorial Grove in de Laveaga Dell. Several are in Strybing Arboretum including some, such as the one on the south side of the Main Lawn, that were planted before 1958.

N side Kennedy Dr between 8th and 10th
  Avenues (III-O1); W entry to AIDS Memorial
  Grove (III-P2); Strybing (VII-O4)
Evergreen/Fast growth/40'
Fragrant yellow flowers in showy terminal clus-
  ters (spring) /Woody capsules, 3/8" long, con-
  taining sticky black seeds
Full sun to part shade/Water occasionally
Sunset Zone 9, 14-17, 19-22
Suitable as a street tree

# 130

## Tawhiwhi

### *Pittosporum tenuifolium*

Pittosporaceae

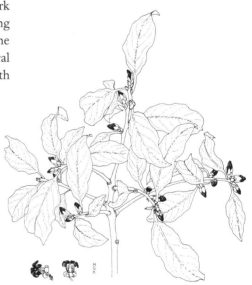

Another species from New Zealand, this pittosporum has two Maori names, *tawhiwhi* and *kohuhu;* only tawhiwhi has been adapted for it outside of New Zealand. It is a shrub or tree sometimes reaching a height of 30 feet or more. The young shoots are dark red to blackish and make a pleasing contrast with the bright green leaves. The **leaves,** thin to somewhat thickish in texture, have slightly wavy margins and are glossy. **Flowers,** one to three in the leaf

S side Kennedy Dr at entrance to Music
  Concourse (III-O2); Strybing (VI-N3)
Evergreen/Fast growth/30'
Purple flowers with spreading petals in leaf axils
  (late spring) /1/2' round, woody capsules
  with sticky, black seeds
Full sun to part shade/Water occasionally
Sunset Zone 9, 14-17, 19-24

axils, are purple or rarely white to yellow, with petals spreading outward. The rounded, somewhat woody **fruits** are generally about ½ inch in diameter and open into three parts, revealing sticky, black seeds.

Tawhiwhi, cultivated in England and elsewhere in Europe, is variable, and several selections are occasionally listed. It has been in California since 1865, when a Mr Walsh brought it by boat, perhaps to San Francisco. It has been in Golden Gate Park since 1924, when it was included in the *Annual Report of the Park Commissioners*. A number of trees can be seen along Kennedy Drive from Sixth to Eighth avenues, and at the southeast corner of Kennedy and Tea Garden drives, surrounding the Thomas Starr-King Monument. Several others are in Strybing Arboretum. It is widely planted in California for hedging and screening.

# 131

## Tobira
# *Pittosporum tobira*

## Pittosporaceae

Commonly called tobira or Japanese pittosporum, this is a large shrub or small tree to 15 feet, densely branched to the base. **Leaves,** 2 to 4 inches long, are generally broadest in the upper half, thick and leathery, with margins turned under. **Flowers,** carried in terminal umbel-like clusters of about ten, are yellowish white and so powerfully fragrant that sometimes the plant is called mock orange. The petals are about ½ inch long with spreading tips. **Fruits** are nearly round, three parted, ½ inch in diameter, and densely hairy. The numerous seeds are reddish.

Tobira comes from Japan, the Ryukyu Islands, and China. It has been in California since 1871. The 1899 *Annual Report of the Park Commissioners* listed it for Golden Gate Park. It is widely planted in California parks and gardens, popular for its low care and delightful fragrance when in flower. However, the only tobiras found in the park today are the dwarf, shrubby selection called 'Wheeler's Dwarf'; this cultivar never reaches the stature of a tree.

E side 7th Ave, N of Lawton St; 450 27th St
Evergreen/Moderate growth/15'
Fragrant, yellowish white flowers, about 1"
    across, in terminal clusters (early spring)/
    Roundish, hairy capsules with sticky red
    seeds
Full sun to part shade/Water occasionally
Sunset Zone 8-24

# 132

## Victorian box
### *Pittosporum undulatum*
Pittosporaceae

Native to eastern Australia, Victorian box is a tree to about 35 feet tall, much branched with a spreading habit. Its glabrous **leaves** are 6 inches long, 2 inches wide, dark green and shining above, with irregularly wavy margins, although less so than those of tarata *(Pittosporum eugenioides)*. The pale yellowish **flowers,** as many as fifteen in each terminal, umbel-like cluster, are pleasantly fragrant and, like those of tobira *(P. tobira),* are sometimes likened to mock orange. Its leathery, yellow orange **fruits,** about ⅜ inch long, divide into two, or rarely, three parts, exposing reddish black, sticky **seeds.**

Joseph Banks brought Victorian box into cultivation in England from New South Wales, Australia, in 1789. It is widely cultivated in warm parts of Europe, as well as in Madeira, the Azore and Canary islands, and California. It has been in California since 1858, when William C Walker sold it at his Golden Gate Nursery in San Francisco. The park commissioners listed it in their annual reports from 1879 through 1924. At present, it may be seen along the north side of Kennedy Drive between Sixth and Tenth avenues; a fine small grove is just inside the Tenth Avenue gate to Strybing's tiny parking lot. It is a common street tree throughout the San Francisco Bay Area.

N side of Kennedy Dr between
    6th and 8th Avenues (III-P1); Strybing VII-O4)
3367 22nd St
Evergreen/Moderate growth/35'
Fragrant, yellowish flowers in terminal clusters (early
    spring, sporadic year-round) /Leathery, yellow
    orange capsules with reddish black, sticky seeds
Full sun to part shade/Water occasionally
Sunset Zone 16, 17, 21-24
Suitable as a street tree
Color plate

*In me be the windswept truth of shore pine,*
    *fragrance of balsam and spruce,*
        *the grace of hemlock.*
*In me the truth of Douglas fir, straight, tall,*
    *strong-trunked land hero of fireproof bark.*
*Sheltering tree of life, cedar's truth be mine,*
    *cypress truth, juniper aroma, strength of yew.*

                    *"Chinook Psalter," Earth Prayers*

# 133

London plane
## *Platanus × acerifolia*

Platanaceae

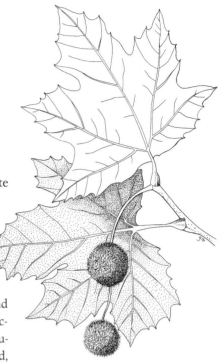

London plane, one of the most frequently planted urban trees in temperate regions around the world, is so called because of its wide use in parks and along streets in London. A hybrid between Oriental plane *(Platanus orientalis)* from Asia Minor and American sycamore *(P. occidentalis)* from the eastern United States, it has been grown in London for nearly 300 years. Early in the seventeenth century, the two parent trees were introduced into England. About 1670 and thereafter, seedling-grown plane trees, different from the two species in and around London, were noticed for their vigor, hardiness, and intermediate characters. The vigorous, new plane trees flourished in London and were eventually taken to other cities in Europe and America, where they also thrived, showing remarkable tolerance of various soils, smoke, dust and, eventually, smog, and of heat reflected from pavement and buildings.

**Leaves** of London planes are usually 5 to 7 inches long, 6 to 8 inches wide, and have three to seven lobes. Their texture is unusually thick and leathery, and they do not disintegrate readily after falling. They have a leaf stalk with a swollen base that encloses the young bud—a useful means of identification. The small **flowers** of London plane, as well as those of other planes, are grouped together into spherical clusters about 1 inch wide. Two to four clusters hang on long pendant stalks, another unusual feature. The **fruits** are globose, about 1 inch in diameter, and bristly. The patchy, exfoliating **bark** is light in color and distinctive.

London plane is among the most amenable of trees to the pruning practices known as pollarding and pleaching. Pollarded trees can be seen in the Music Concourse in Golden Gate Park and in the plaza on the east side of San Francisco's City Hall. On the campus of the UC Berkeley, the pollarded trees at the Campanile Esplanade came from the 1915 Panama–Pacific International Exposition in San Francisco. Elsewhere on the campus, an arbor of pleached trees can be seen on the south side of Mulford Hall. Unpruned London planes are common street trees throughout California, including San Francisco where they were planted along Market Street in the 1970s, following subway construction. There are also a number of unpruned London planes in Golden Gate Park; one is at Mallard Lake, another near Lincoln Way and 25th Avenue, and a third in front of the County Fair Building.

Music Concourse (III-O2); Meadow E of 25th Ave, between King Dr and Lincoln Way (II-J4); N side Mallard Lake (II-I3); Strybing (VI-M3)
Civic Center Plaza; 163 and 147 Tenth Ave
Deciduous/Fast growth/80'
Rounded clusters, 1" wide, of insignificant flowers on long stalks (spring) /2-4 hanging green brown seed balls
Full sun/Water infrequently and deeply
Sunset Zone 2-24
Suitable as a street tree
Color plate

# The Music Concourse

Golden Gate Park's first Music Concourse, dedicated July 4, 1888, was near the present-day tennis courts. After the close of the Midwinter Fair, it was decided to move the Music Concourse to the "Concert Valley" of the fair site, opposite today's DeYoung Museum. Construction of the new bandstand was begun in 1899. At the time of its dedication on September 9, 1900, it was called the Spreckels Temple of Music in honor of the generosity of Claus Spreckels, whose contribution of $75,000 made its construction possible. Designed by the brothers James and Merrit Reid in Italian Renaissance style and built of Colusa sandstone, it is still impressive. Its central arch is 55 feet wide and 70 feet high and is flanked on both sides by Corinthian columns. The bandstand faces an open area called, at the time of its dedication, the Great Court. According to an account of the dedication in the 1902 *Annual Report of the Park Commissioners,* "The Great Court in front has been carefully turned, and a profusion of shrubbery and trees add picturesqueness to the scene." Seating was provided for 20,000 people among the trees. On the day of the dedication, there were 75,000 people "bending their heads to listen," and "this great crowd not only overtaxed this immense seating capacity, but the terraced grounds along the outer boundaries of the court were [alive] with humanity."

Nothing more is said of the trees planted in the Great Court in the account of the dedication, but a contemporary photograph that features the bandstand gives an impression of a fairly uniform planting of trees facing it. The trees were uniform because they were planted with geometric regularity, were all the same age, and were pruned in a formal manner called "pollarding" that would allow them to be maintained at a uniform size and shape.

Several different trees in the Music Concourse can be picked out by their trunk and bark characteristics, but they are more easily distinguished and identified by their leaves. London planes *(Platanus x acerifolia)* and Scotch elms *(Ulmus glabra)* are the most common trees in the Music Concourse. A number of other trees have been grown there, but only a single tree of hedge maple *(Acer campestre)* and one of black walnut *(Juglans nigra)* can be seen today among the planes and elms.

The trees in Golden Gate Park's Music Concourse are relatively uniform in appearance, suggesting that they were planted about the same time. They are deciduous, and their appearance changes with the seasons, but a close look at the trees shows that their uniformity in height and shape is the result of pruning used to maintain them. During most of their years, they have been severely pruned once a year by a method called pollarding. Although drastic, this kind of pruning does the trees no harm as long as it is properly done. In particular landscape situations, such as in the Music Concourse, where it is desired to keep the trees uniform in appearance, it serves a useful purpose. By this method of pruning, the secondary branches are cut back annually, almost to the main trunk. This results in a dense head of long, slender new shoots that grow from the upper ends of the secondary branches, giving the tree a broad, dome-shaped crown of a consistent height.

Pollarding does no harm to trees so pruned, but it drastically changes their appearance. Long, slender branches, produced each spring, leaf out during the summer. The following winter, when these branches are removed, the cuts must heal by callusing over; when pollarding is done year after year, the callused ends of these short secondary branches become enlarged and knobby. The resulting knobby enlargements are more prominent during the winter after the trees have lost their leaves; the shortened secondary branches give these trees an appearance very different from those allowed to grow naturally.

Certain trees can stand more severe pruning than others; among those that can be successfully pollarded are London planes, elms, maples, willows and black locusts. Pollarding has not been commonly practiced in America; it is more often seen in Europe, where it is also carried out for such utilitarian purposes as, on certain willows, to obtain long, slender twigs for basket and furniture making.

Pollarding should not be confused with pleaching, another severe method of pruning. Pleaching, done on closely planted trees or shrubs, involves shearing the upper branches as a means of encouraging horizontal branches that will intertwine and form a high wall of foliage, a hedge, or an overhead arbor.

# 134

## Totara
## *Podocarpus totara*
### Podocarpaceae

Totara, an evergreen tree of New Zealand, is one of a small number of trees and shrubs brought directly from Australia and New Zealand to California in the middle of the last century. Totara is a densely leafy tree having a broadly pyramidal habit, with dark, somewhat gray green, stiff, pointed **leaves,** about 1 inch long and ⅛ inch wide. In Golden Gate Park, trees are over 30 feet tall. However, in its native habitat of New Zealand, totaras may be 50 to 100 feet tall with massive trunks. The dark brown to silver gray, fibrous **bark** peels off in strips. The curious **fruits** are actually swollen, fleshy receptacles, red or orange, with a single seed attached.

Maoris used totara in a number of ways. The straight trunks were made into outrigger canoes, timber was used for building, and the fibrous bark, peeled into long strips, was used in roofing and for storage baskets. The wood is extremely durable and long lasting. Ancient Maori carvings made of totara and buried for centuries were in an excellent state of preservation when unearthed. The Europeans who came to New Zealand also found many uses for its durable wood in construction and boat-building.

According to Butterfield (1964), totara was brought to San Francisco about 1865 on a cargo ship. The ship, in the charge of James Welsh, had come from New South Wales and carried Australian and New Zealand plants, as well as a few which "may have been picked up in Japan." In spite of its early introduction, totara is rarely planted in California today. In the park, a tree can be seen near the south entrance to the Academy of Sciences, while another is between Stow Lake and the Japanese Tea Garden. Several trees are in Strybing's New Zealand collection, planted by Eric Walther in the early years of the arboretum; these trees were brought from New Zealand to landscape that country's pavilion at the Panama–Pacific International Exposition in San Francisco in 1915. A single tree, planted in the 1970s, is in The Ruth Bancroft Garden in Walnut Creek, and several trees have been noted in the Santa Barbara area.

Near staircase between Japanese Tea Garden and Stow Lake (III-N2); near S entrance to Academy of Sciences (III-O3); Strybing (VI-N3)
Evergreen/Slow growth/25'-30'
(Conifer) Round red fruits, 1/2" across
Full sun to part shade/Water regularly
Sunset Zone 8, 9, 14-24

The cherries and laurels
# Prunus
Rosaceae

The rose family is among the most important in the fields of horticulture and agriculture. Few plants can surpass the rose in popularity worldwide. Our fruit and vegetable gardens are filled with apples, pears, cherries, plums, peaches, apricots, raspberries, and strawberries—all members of the rose family. Many other trees, shrubs, and perennials from the family brighten our gardens: spiraea, potentilla, cotoneaster, geum, alchemilla, and pyracantha, to name just a few.

An important genus within the rose family is *Prunus,* whose members serve us in diverse ways, some as ornament, others providing food for the table or a green framework for the garden. All are trees or shrubs, easily organized into two groups: a small group of evergreen species and a large group of deciduous species. Evergreen cherries and laurels offer the gardener good foliage and solid screening, with the added benefit of flowers (mostly white) and fruit that is popular with birds and other wildlife. Deciduous species are grown for their flowers and, more importantly, for their fruits. All of the stone fruits (cherries, plums, peaches, nectarines, apricots, and almonds) belong to the genus *Prunus,* as do their ornamental counterparts, which color our landscapes so delicately in spring.

Over 400 species in the genus *Prunus* occur throughout the Northern Hemisphere, with a few appearing in South America. Whether they evergreen or deciduous, members of the genus are easy to identify. The **bark** is often dotted with tiny slits or pores, known as lenticels, which allow the passage of gases through the bark. **Leaves** are usually alternate and toothed, with tiny stipules attached to the petioles. **Flowers,** often clustered in spikes or racemes, have five petals and a ring of ten stamens within a five-lobed calyx; white is the most common color, but pink and red occur in some species. **Fruits** are fleshy, often colorful, and contain a single, hard **seed.**

Both evergreen and deciduous species can be seen in Golden Gate Park. The evergreen laurels are usually small trees or large shrubs serving as screening and background plants. The deciduous flowering cherries light up the park in springtime with their flowers, and again in fall as their leaves turn color before dropping. Both deciduous and evergreen species are common throughout California in parks and gardens, as well as along city and suburban streets.

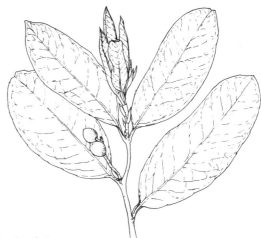

# 135

English laurel
# Prunus laurocerasus
Rosaceae

English laurel (sometimes called cherry laurel, particularly in England) is a small evergreen tree, usually with multiple stems from the base. It is native to mountainous, forested areas of southwestern Asia and Eastern Europe. It attains a height of 20 feet or more and sometimes has a spread twice as great. Its thick, leathery **leaves** are usually oblong, 4 to 7 inches or, rarely 10 to 12 inches, long and 2 to 5 inches wide. Small, white **flowers,** ⅓ inch across and reminiscent of miniature, single roses, occur on flowering spikes 3 to 5 inches long. The purple black cherrylike **fruit** is oval in shape, about

S edge of meadow W of conservatory (IV-Q1); around Goethe-Schiller statue near Academy of Sciences (III-O2); Strybing (VII-N3)
Evergreen/Fast growth/25'
White, 5-petaled flowers, 1/3" wide, on 3"-5" long spikes, Mar-Apr) /Purple black, 1/2" long, cherrylike fruit
Full sun to part shade/Water occasionally
Sunset Zone 4-6, 15-17

½ inch long, with a small amount of flesh covering a large stone. The flowers appear in March and April in the Bay Area and, because the flowers are small and their stems shorter than the leaves, they do not stand out from the foliage. In its natural distribution and also in cultivation, there is variation in leaf shape and size and in plant height. Some of these variants have been named as cultivars, and, in California, we are likely to find 'Otto Luyken', 'Schipkaensis', and 'Zabeliana'.

English laurel was taken to Western Europe for cultivation in gardens as early as the middle of the sixteenth century, when it was grown in the garden of Prince Oria at Genoa. In 1576, the Flemish-born botanist Jules Charles de l'Ecluse (better known as Clusius), then in the service of Emperor Maximilian II in Vienna, received English laurel in a shipment of rare trees and shrubs sent by the Emperor's ambassador at Constantinople. English laurel was known at that time as the date or plum of Trebizond (a seaport city now known as Trabzon, south of the Black Sea in northeastern Turkey). The plant received in Vienna by Clusius was propagated and distributed. Material from it reached England early in the seventeenth century and, in 1629, John Parkinson included English laurel in his account of English garden plants. Later in the century in England, cherry laurel (as it is known there) was commonly used for hedges. In 1754, Philip Miller said that the cherry laurel "is so well known, as to need no description, it being very common in every garden."

English laurel also became known for another reason; it was soon learned that the leaves contained a substance that produced hydrocyanic acid. By 1662, the leaves were used in cooking to give an almondlike flavor, and water distilled from them became popular as a flavoring. However, when used in larger quantities than for flavoring, English laurel water was found to be toxic. As early as 1731, a Dublin physician reported the accidental deaths of two women who used it as a cordial.

English laurel has been in the state since 1871, when Stephen Nolan listed it in the catalogue for his Belle View Nursery in Oakland. Today it is frequently seen in California parks and gardens. It was introduced to Golden Gate Park before 1893, when it was listed in the *Annual Report of the Park Commissioners*. It is used as a background planting in various areas, such as around the Goethe-Schiller statue near the Academy of Sciences. It is also seen as part of a shrub mass on the south side of the meadow west of the conservatory. It forms part of the background planting for Strybing's Fragrance Garden.

# 136

## Portugal laurel
### *Prunus lusitanica*

Rosaceae

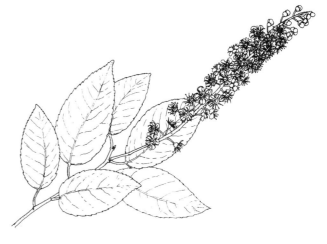

Portugal laurel, a native of Spain, Portugal, the Azores, and the Canary Islands, is a large evergreen shrub or small tree, 10 to 20 feet tall; its **leaves** are thick but not as thick and leathery as those of English laurel. The ½-inch diameter **flowers** are white, with five petals, similar in appearance to those of English laurel, but their flowering spikes are longer so that the flowers stand conspicuously above the foliage. Flowers are produced in profusion in May and June and are a great feature of the park's Portugal laurels. Later, the dark purple, cherrylike **fruits** appear. Like those of English laurel, they have a large stone covered by a small amount of flesh, but they are smaller—only about 1/3 inch long.

In England, Portugal laurel has been cultivated since the seventeenth century. It was probably introduced into California about the same time as English laurel, since it was also listed in 1871 by Stephen Nolan. The earliest listing of Portugal laurel for Golden Gate Park is in the 1897 *Annual Report of the Park Commissioners.*

Portugal laurels are common in Golden Gate Park today. A grove of the trees can be seen northwest of the western end of Alvord Tunnel, and a tall, unsheared hedge of them is east of the Academy of Sciences and north of Middle Drive East. A fine specimen can be seen at the western entrance to the Demonstration Gardens at Strybing Arboretum.

Grove NW of W end of Alvord Tunnel (IV-S3); between Goethe-Schiller statue and Middle Dr (III-P3); Strybing (VII-O3)
Evergreen/Moderate growth/10'-20'
White, 5-petaled flowers, 1/3" wide, on long spikes above the leaves (May-June) /Dark purple cherrylike fruits, 1/3" long
Full sun/Water infrequently
Sunset Zone 4-9, 14-24

# 137

## Yoshino cherry
### *Prunus × yedoensis*

Rosaceae

Among the many Asian flowering cherries, Yoshino or Tokyo cherry is the most frequently cultivated in Japan and perhaps elsewhere. Its origin in cultivation is not known, nor is its origin known in the wild. EH Wilson (1916) suggested that it might be of hybrid origin, the result of a cross between *Prunus serrulata* and *P. subhirtella,* both native to Japan; experimental crossings have since proven Wilson's theory. He further wrote that this cherry was distinct from other Japanese or Chinese cherries and one of the most floriferous and beautiful of them all. He noted that it was generally

Stanyan Meadow near Page St (IV-S3); King Dr S of Japanese Tea Garden (III-N3); Strybing (VI-N3)
Deciduous/Fast growth/25'
Clusters of single, white to pink, fragrant flowers (April) /1/4" wide cherrylike fruit with large pit
Full sun/Water regularly
Sunset Zone 2-7, 14-20
Suitable a a street tree

planted in the parks, temple grounds, cemeteries, and streets of Tokyo; in fact, its flowers herald an annual national holiday decreed by the emperor. In all, over 50,000 trees of this species are growing in the city of Tokyo.

Yoshino cherry is a deciduous tree, 30 to 50 feet tall, with a rounded or spreading habit; its **bark** is smooth, and young shoots have a light covering of soft hairs. The serrate **leaves** are 2 to 5 inches long and about half as wide, elliptical to ovate or obovate, and have thirteen to fifteen veins on each side of the midvein. Clusters of two to six white or light pink **flowers** are held on ½ to 1 inch stems at the tip of 1-inch-long stalks; flowers appear before the leaves, usually around the first of April in San Francisco. Typical of the rose family, the sepals and petals number five, the petals being about ½ inch long with rounded tips. The bitter, inedible **fruit** is round, about ¼ inch wide, and contains a single stone or pit, like most cherries.

In the early years of this century, Yoshino cherry was introduced into Europe and America. In 1902, the Arnold Arboretum in Boston received a tree from Tokyo and, in 1909, a tree was recorded in Germany. In about 1910, the Royal Botanic Gardens at Kew, England, received trees from the Hillier and Sons' Nursery in Winchester. The well-known avenue of 800 cherry trees around the Tidal Basin in Potomac Park, Washington, DC, exist as a gift from the mayor of Tokyo.

No date is known for the first planting of this cherry in California, but the smaller-growing cultivar, 'Akebono', was introduced by the WB Clarke Nursery of San Jose in 1925. This selection of Yoshino cherry, chosen for its pinker flowers, has been widely planted in Golden Gate Park, particularly along Martin Luther King Drive opposite Strybing's main entrance and near the Japanese Tea Garden. It can also be seen in Stanyan Meadows near Page Street and in Strybing's Moon-viewing Garden. It has been in the collection at the Washington Park Arboretum in Seattle since World War II. In Japan, this cultivar is known as 'Amerika'.

# 138

Evergreen pear

# *Pyrus kawakamii* (syn. *P. taiwanensis*)

Rosaceae

Strybing (VII-O4)
NE corner Green and Fillmore Sts
Evergreen/Slow growth/25'
Clusters of white flowers (mid to late winter)/
    Tiny, hard fruit
Full sun/Water occasionally
Sunset Zone 8, 9, 12-24
Suitable as a street tree

The genus *Pyrus* gets its name from the classical word for pear. Plants in this genus are mostly deciduous shrubs or small trees with alternate, simple leaves. The typical flowers of the genus are white, sometimes tinged yellow, green, or rose. They are arranged in terminal clusters, with five sepals and petals and, usually, numerous stamens. The pear-shaped fruits contain numerous hard-walled cells, giving the characteristically gritty texture to the flesh. Black brown seeds are enclosed in parchment-like cell walls.

Evergreen pear differs from most species of *Pyrus* in being mostly evergreen. Generally 12 to 30 feet tall with handsome, rough-textured, dark brown **bark,** the much-branched, often drooping stems, sometimes graced with sharp thorns, make a broad, rounded shrub or small tree. The lustrous, bright green, ovate or obovate **leaves,** 2 to 4 inches long, have thickish margins with short, fine, rounded teeth and 1-inch-long petioles. Clusters of white flowers are produced in mid to late winter; the **flowers** are more abundant and more visible in areas away from the mild coast, where warmer summers encourage bud set and leaves are more likely to be shed in the colder winters. The smooth, rounded **fruits** are about ½ inch across—hard, inedible, and of little consequence.

Evergreen pear is native to China and Taiwan. In Golden Gate Park, a tree of this species can be seen on the east side of the County Fair Building, near the gates to the gallery. It is common in parks, gardens, and along streets throughout Central and Southern California.

# A Brief History of Pears

Common pear *(Pyrus communis),* the best-known species of the genus, is often mentioned in classical Greek and Roman literature. Pears have a long history of cultivation in Great Britain, probably having been introduced there during the Roman occupation. Their cultivation in England and Wales is now widespread both in gardens and orchards. They are reported to be the most long-lived of fruit trees.

Pears played an important role in West Coast agriculture during the late 1800s and early 1900s. The fine alluvial soils of California's interior valleys were ideal for pears, and pears were a major crop in orchards inland from San Francisco Bay. Today, few of those orchards remain. The land in places like Walnut Creek—once known for its pear production—is now covered with vast suburbs, its streets lined with ornamental trees such as, ironically, evergreen pears.

The Oaks
# *Quercus*
Fagaceae

Approximately 400 species of oaks—mostly trees with a few shrubs—are included in the genus *Quercus,* which is widely distributed throughout North America (including Mexico) and in Central America, the Columbian Andes, Europe, North Africa, and Asia. Oaks may be evergreen or deciduous, with **leaves** being generally lobed or toothed. Their small, wind-pollinated **flowers** are usually overlooked; numerous male flowers occur in hanging catkins, while the few female flowers generally occur singly. Their constant and recognizable feature is the characteristic **fruit,** a nut called an acorn that is partially enclosed in a cuplike cap made of tightly held scales.

Oaks have had widely varying uses. Traditionally, the sturdy wood was used in construction and boatbuilding. The bark of many species was a source of tannin, and one species with unusually spongy bark provided the cork used in bottling wine. Acorns have been a valued source of food for humans and wildlife. Oaks are now most often cultivated as ornamentals.

*Quercus* is the ancient Latin name for oak tree. Several plants that are neither oaks nor members of the family are also called oaks. Poison oak *(Toxicodendron diversilobum)* is found naturally throughout much the West; silk oak *(Grevillea robusta)* and swamp oaks *(Casuarina* spp.) are both native to Australia and cultivated in California and elsewhere in North America. Tan oak, or tanbark oak, belongs to *Litho-carpus,* a large genus also in the beech family and there-fore related to *Quercus.* One species occurs in western North America *(L. densiflorus),* while the nearly 300 other species are found in Asia.

# 139

## Coast live oak
# *Quercus agrifolia*
### Fagaceae

Coast live oak, one of California's most picturesque oaks, is found in the Coast Ranges from northern Sonoma County southward to northern Baja California. It grows in a variety of habitats—rich valley lands, rocky and dry hillsides, and even windswept sites. These broad-crowned, evergreen trees vary in height, usually reaching 25 to 40 feet, but sometimes being much taller. The oaks in Golden Gate Park have not attained the heights of live oaks in other areas, but they do have broad, spreading crowns.

The characteristically shaped, brittle **leaves** are roundish to ovate or oblong, generally with several spine-tipped teeth, rarely entire, mostly 1 to 2 inches long, and usually convex when seen from above. On the lower, somewhat cupped surface, small tufts of hairs may usually be seen at points where the few secondary veins join the midrib; the tufts of hairs may not be present on every leaf of a tree, but they will be seen when a number of leaves are examined. **Fruits** mature during their first autumn; thin-scaled, shallow cups enclose the lower third of the slender, pointed acorns, each 1 to 1½ inches long.

Early Spanish explorers in California found and wrote about the coast live oaks, which they called *encina*. These oaks were noted by Gaspar de Portola, who discovered San Francisco Bay in 1769, and by Father Juan Crespi, who accompanied Portola. In 1770, the Franciscan Father Junípero Serra landed at Monterey Bay; the story is told that, shortly thereafter, he placed his cross beneath a large, old live oak, and there said his first mass. Jepson (1909) pointed out that the location of the chain of Franciscan mis-sions "corresponded closely" with the distribution of coast live oak.

An expedition sent out by the Spanish government, under the com-mand of Italian-born Alessandro Malaspina, spent several days during September 1791 at Monterey. Here, two of the ship's officers collected spec-imens of coast live oak and valley oak *(Quercus lobata)*. They were given to Luis Nee, one of the botanists attached to the expedition. In 1801, Nee pub-lished the botanical names and descriptions of the two oaks.

Before Europeans came to California, the Native Americans prepared acorns of several native oaks for food; in fact, acorn meal was a staple of life

On either side of Hayes St entrance (IV-S1); AIDS Memorial Grove (III-P3); Strybing (VII-N4)
CMPC (Davies Campus) across from 43 Noe St
Evergreen/Moderate growth/20'-40'
Insignificant flowers (early spring) /Slender acorns, 1"-1-1/2" long, shallow caps
Full sun/Needs no watering once established
Sunset Zone 5, 7-24
Suitable as a street tree

for these first Californians. Acorns of coast live oak were among those used. The wood of this live oak is hard, heavy, and very strong. In times past, it was used for wagon repairs and similar purposes. It also makes excellent firewood; no doubt Golden Gate Park oaks were used for this purpose in 1906, when many earthquake victims lived in the park. Significant groves of oaks can be seen in the northeastern corner of Golden Gate Park from the Hayes Street entrance to Fulton Street, and at the western end of the AIDS Memorial Grove in de Laveaga Dell. Beautiful, free-standing specimens of coast live oak can also be seen in Strybing's Arthur Menzies Garden of California Native Plants.

# The Park's Original Trees

Among the many trees to be seen in Golden Gate Park, only the coast live oak *(Quercus agrifolia)* is native there; the others have been planted. Before the park was developed, there were likely seepages in which native willows grew, but the willows in the park today, such as those around Stow Lake, were all planted; like most of the bodies of water in the park, Stow Lake is human-made. Prior to its development in the 1870s, the park was almost entirely shifting sand dunes, which were not conducive to the natural growth of trees.

Trees, in fact, were never a prominent feature on the northern tip of the narrow, windswept San Francisco Peninsula. Archibald Menzies, the British surgeon-naturalist with the Vancouver expedition who visited the peninsula in 1792, wrote of its "scrubby oaks" *(Quercus agrifolia)* and "dwarf" horse chestnuts *(Aesculus californica)*. Those trees had been naturally pruned low by the persistent winds off the ocean. In the years since Vancouver's visit, the trees have given way to the development of San Francisco. Fortunately, the area set aside in 1870 for Golden Gate Park contained several small stands of coast live oaks. (The San Francisco Presidio, established in 1776, also has stands

of these oaks.) Perhaps the best of the groves in the park is in its northeastern corner along Fulton Street, extending from Stanyan Street to Sixth Avenue, behind McLaren Lodge and the conservatory.

In the northeastern section of the park, together with the coast live oaks, are toyons *(Heteromeles arbutifolia)*, another well known and widely distributed California native. Toyon is a small tree to about 15 feet tall but sometimes only a large spreading shrub.

Those who frequent Golden Gate Park have doubtless observed that nearly all of the park's trees are evergreen. Other than the two conifers, Monterey cypress *(Cupressus macrocarpa)* and Monterey pine *(Pinus radiata)*, that make up most of the forest canopy, the majority of trees in the park are broad-leafed evergreens, including the coast live oak and toyon. John McLaren and others who chose trees for the park realized that climatic conditions in San Francisco were particularly favorable to evergreen trees. Even before John McLaren came to the park in the late 1880s, early California nurserymen were importing broad-leafed evergreens for the San Francisco Bay Area.

*...the trees
That whisper round a temple become soon
Dear as the temple's self...*

JOHN KEATS, *"A Thing of Beauty"*

# 140
## Holly oak
## *Quercus ilex*
### Fagaceae

The holly oak, or holm oak, occurs in the Mediterranean region of southern Europe and northern Africa. The specific epithet *ilex* was the ancient Latin name for this species; the word is also used as the genus name *Ilex* for the hollies. Holly oak is an attractive evergreen tree. It has been cultivated in northwestern Europe since the 1500s and in California since 1858. Trees vary in height from 40 to 70 feet, with a crown of equal spread. The **bark** is smooth, gray, and shallowly split. Its leathery **leaves** vary in size and shape, but are usually 1 to 3 or 4 inches long and ½ to 1 inch wide; leaf margins are variable, often entire, but may be irregularly toothed (hollylike), especially on young leaves. The relatively glossy upper surface of the leaf contrasts with the white or gray, densely woolly underside. The **fruits** are generally 1 inch long, with the thin-scaled caps covering as much as half their length.

A single, large, old holly oak stands above the four-foot retaining wall facing Stanyan Street between Fulton and Hayes streets, opposite St Mary's Hospital. Here, this specimen is seen among several native coast live oaks. Fine plantings of holly oak can also be seen in Oakland's Lakeside Park and on the UC Berkeley campus. Holly oak is often used as a street tree or plaza tree in cities along the West Coast from southwestern British Columbia to Southern California.

Stanyan St, N of Hayes St entrance (IV-S1)
25th St at Castro St
Evergreen/Moderate growth/40'-70'
Insignificant flower (spring) /Acorns, 1" long,
  caps cover almost 1/2 of length
Full sun/Needs no watering once established
Sunset Zone 4-24
Suitable as a street tree

# 141
## English oak
## *Quercus robur*
### Fagaceae

The deciduous English oak, or pedunculate oak, is the common oak of the British Isles, occurring almost throughout the islands and in Europe, northern Africa, and the Caucasus of western Asia. In English history, it is said to be the oak of the druids, of Robin Hood's cudgel, and of King Arthur's round table; the ornately carved interiors of castles and cathedrals were often of English oak. It is one of the longest-lived and most valuable timber trees in the world. Its timber is in less demand now for ship building than it was before iron and steel came into use, but it is still used in some areas for

E side of McLaren Lodge (IV-S2); meadow E of
  Pioneer Log Cabin (III-M2); Children's
  Playground on King Dr, E of Crossover Dr (III-
  L3); Strybing (VI-N3)
Deciduous/Moderate growth/60'-80'
Insignificant flowers (spring) /Acorns, 1-1/2"
  long, cap covering 1/3 of length
Full sun/Water infrequently
Sunset Zone 2-12, 14-21
Suitable as a street tree

building construction. The species name *robur* is an ancient Latin word for oak wood and refers to its strength or hardness.

English oaks are large, spreading trees; when given time and space, they may reach 60 to 80 feet in height and spread. The **bark** is thick and densely furrowed. Its **leaves** are 2 to 4 inches long and about ¾ to 2½ inches wide, stalkless or with a very short stalk, and with five to seven rounded lobes. The leaves are not particularly colorful in late autumn before they drop. The **fruits** are about 1½ inches long with the cap covering a third of the acorn; they occur on slender, 1- to 4-inch-long peduncles or stalks, hence the tree's other common name, pedunculate oak.

In Golden Gate Park, an English oak can be seen on the east side of McLaren Lodge, shading the small parking lot. A single large, spreading English oak stands by itself at the edge of the large meadow east of the Pioneer Log Cabin. Another fine specimen is adjacent to the playground on King Drive, just east of Crossover Drive. Large specimens can also be seen on the UC Berkeley campus and in many other parks and arboreta along the West Coast. The columnar selection 'Fastigiata' can be seen near the Zellerbach Garden in Strybing Arboretum and in The Ruth Bancroft Garden in Walnut Creek.

# 142

## Soapbark tree
## *Quillaja saponaria*

### Rosaceae

Soapbark tree is native to central Chile, from the coast to the mountains, in areas of open woodland to about 5.000 feet elevation. It is evergreen, 30 to 40 feet tall, and oaklike in appearance. Its **leaves** are alternate, simple, oval, shallowly and remotely toothed, 1 to 2 inches long, and with short petioles. When open, the greenish yellow, autumn **flowers** are somewhat less than 1 inch across, not typically roselike, with five spreading sepals and petals, and ten stamens arching upward. The **fruit** splits at maturity into five spreading separate seed pods, each to about ½ inch long, opening along one side to release numerous, winged seeds. The fruits, which also appear in autumn, are not conspicuous on the tree but, seen at close range, are distinctive.

When crushed and mixed with water, the inner bark foams like soap. In Chile, this mixture has been used as an emulsifying agent for laundry purposes and as a shampoo. During the eighteenth century, the bark was imported into Europe for use as an emulsifier. A less laudable use was to produce a head on stale beer. Soapbark tree was named botanically in 1782 by a Chilean Jesuit, Juan Ignacio Molina. *Quillaja* was adapted from the local names *qillai* or *cullay*; the specific name *saponaria* alludes to the soaplike quality of the bark.

Slope above lawn W of McLaren Lodge (IV-R2); Knoll east of Academy of Sciences and N of meadow (III-P2); Strybing (VI-N3)
Evergreen/Slow growth/30'-40'
Greenish yellow flowers, up to 1" wide, with 5 fused sepals and 5 petals (Sept) /Brown, 5-parted capsules with winged seeds
Full sun/Water infrequently
Sunset Zone 8, 9, 14-24

Seeds of soapbark tree were first brought to San Francisco in 1878 from Chile. The date of its introduction into Golden Gate Park is not known, but it is listed in the 1912 and 1924 annual reports of the park commissioners. Today, the park has a fine specimen about 30 feet tall, located near the lower edge of the planting above the lawn west of McLaren Lodge and another on the knoll east of the Academy of Sciences. Other trees in California, some used as street trees, are in Palo Alto, Santa Barbara, San Diego, The Arboretum of LA County, and on the campus of UC Berkeley.

# A Chilean Botanist

Juan Ignacio Molina was born in Chile in 1737 and lived there until 1768, when the Spanish monarch, Carlos III, expelled him and other Jesuits from his possessions. Molina then went to Italy, where he lived in Bologna until his death in 1829. In 1782, he published a classic work on the geography and natural and civil history of Chile. In this work, written in Italian and translated later into other European languages, Molina named and described for the first time Chilean plants well known today in California, including soapbark tree *(Quillaja saponaria),* a puya *(Puya chilensis),* mayten *(Maytenus boaria),* and Chilean wine palm *(Jubaea chilensis).*

# 143

## Italian buckthorn
# *Rhamnus alaternus*
## Rhamnaceae

Buckthorn is the name frequently given to members of the genus *Rhamnus,* because of the stubby thorns that often characterize the branchlets or stem tips. The genus contains over a hundred species of shrubs or small trees; it takes its scientific name from the classical Greek name for a species found in Greece. Many species have medicinal uses, including the West Coast's native *R. purshianus,* which is the source of the laxative cascara sagrada. In the same family is *Ceanothus,* a group of native shrubs familiar to most gardeners on the West Coast.

Italian buckthorn is an attractive, evergreen, mostly glabrous shrub or small tree, up to 25 feet tall. Unlike many members of the family, it lacks thorns on its stems and gray branchlets. Its alternate **leaves** are 1 to 2½ inches long and nearly as wide, ovate to oblong, with few serrations on the margins, and may have three veins originating at the base; petioles may be short or nonexistent. The tiny cream yellow **flowers** are crowded in small clusters along the stems in early spring; they are followed by black, globose **fruits,** about ¼ inch in diameter, each containing three seeds.

SE corner of conservatory (IV-Q1); Strybing (VI-N3 & VII-N4)
W side of Funston, S of Balboa
Evergreen/Fast growth/25'
Inconspicuous,cream yellow flowers (Apr-May)/ Small, black, berrylike fruit
Full sun to part shade/Water infrequently
Sunset Zone 4-24
Suitable as a street tree

Italian buckthorn is a native of southern Europe, particularly the Mediterranean region from Portugal and Morocco east to the Crimea. It was introduced into cultivation in northern Europe about 1700 or perhaps earlier.

Although Italian buckthorn, with its small flowers and black fruits, lacks the beauty and appeal to be widely popular, it is an attractive shrub that can be useful in a well-tended garden. To quote from Bean (1974), this "useful, cheerful evergreen…makes a dense mass of pleasant greenery." It is often used for background or screening and is useful as part of a windbreak. It serves the latter purpose in Strybing Arboretum, where it can be seen along the eastern edge of the lawn just west of the New Zealand collection, buffering the persistent west wind for portions of the collection in its lee. It can also be seen at the southeast corner of the conservatory and in other locations within Strybing and Golden Gate Park. A hedge of the attractive variegated selection 'Argenteovariegatus' partially encloses one of the smaller gardens within Strybing's Demonstration Gardens.

# 144

## Japanese umbrella pine
# *Sciadopitys verticillata*
## Taxodiaceae

As a forest tree in Japan, umbrella pine may be 100 to 120 feet tall, though usually less in cultivation. The **bark** is thin, gray to brown, and peeling in long, thin strips. Its **leaves** are of two kinds: the larger and more showy leaves are linear, grooved on both surfaces, 2 to 5 inches long, about ⅛ inch wide, and are arranged in whorls of ten to twenty-five; the smaller ones are scale-like, triangular, ⅛ to ¼ inch long, and are arranged in a ring at the base of the larger leaves. The round male **cones,** in clusters, are ¼ to ½ inch long. The solitary female cones are ovoid, 2 to 4 inches long, with woody fan- or wedge-shaped bracts, their upper margins round and recurved; there are five to nine seeds on each scale. Cones take two years to mature. Propagation is by seed, although seeds can be difficult to germinate. Nursery seedlings may not be ready to plant out for five or six years; trees are generally slow growing.

Japanese umbrella pine was observed on the island of Deshima by three Dutch East India Company officers, who also recorded sightings of cryptomeria. Engelbert Kaempfer described the tree in his 1712 monograph on Japanese plants. Carl Thunberg included it in his flora of Japan, calling it *Taxus verticillata;* apparently he had not seen a cone. Philipp Franz von Siebold also observed the tree and sent seed to the botanical garden at Buitenzorg (now Bogor) on the island of Java. In 1830, he published a description of it under the name *Pinus verticillata*. In 1842, realizing that it was not a pine, he described it as a new genus with a single species,

Japanese Tea Garden (V-N2); Strybing (VII-O4)
Evergreen/Slow growth/40'
(Conifer) Ovoid, woody cones, 2"-4" long, with
   curving bracts protruding from the scales
Full sun/Water regularly
Sunset Zone 4-9, 14-24
Color plate

*Sciadopitys verticillata.* The generic name is taken from two Greek words that translate literally as umbrella pine. The name refers to the spreading whorl of narrowly linear leaves that resemble the ribs of an umbrella. The specific name also refers to the whorled leaves.

The first introduction of umbrella pine to Europe was sent by Thomas Lobb in 1853 from Buitenzorg to the Veitch nursery in England. In 1861, John Gould Veitch sent cones and seeds to England from Japan, and from these many specimens were grown. Umbrella pine reached the United States in 1861, when it was included in an early collection of living plants sent from Japan. The collection had been brought together and established in Wardian cases (portable glass terrariums) for shipment to Boston by Dr George Rogers Hall, an American living at the time in Yokohama. Hall's collection came into the hands of Francis Parkman, horticulturist, rosarian, and historian, who cared for it for several years. Umbrella pine proved hardy in the Boston area, and today a grove of trees is established at the Arnold Arboretum.

Umbrella pine is native to the mountains of the large Japanese islands of Honshu, Kyushu, and Shikoku. EH Wilson observed it in 1914 in two areas of central Honshu. One of these was Koya-san, the mountain from which the Japanese name for the tree, *koya-maki,* was taken. Wilson found it there between 2,400 and 3,000 feet elevation, in both pure stands and in groves with other conifers, including Hinoki cypress *(Chamaecyparis obtusa),* often the dominant tree. His observations showed that the umbrella pine does best in steep, rocky situations, where it is cool and moist but sheltered from strong winds.

The wood of umbrella pine is durable and resistant to water, making it useful for boatbuilding. It is also resistant to decay; timbers used in the Sensu Bridge in Tokyo lasted for 300 years without painting. The most important use of the Japanese umbrella pine today, however, is as an attractive landscape tree.

In California, umbrella pine was first offered by RD Fox in 1884 at his Santa Clara Valley Nursery in San Jose. It has been in Golden Gate Park since the 1890s, although the earliest plantings have not survived. Several trees can be seen in the Japanese Tea Garden; the largest one is above the Tea House. A small tree is in Strybing's Asian Discovery Garden. Umbrella pines are on the capitol grounds in Sacramento and in Santa Barbara. They are also seen in parks and gardens from Portland, Oregon to Victoria, British Columbia.

*Of all man's works of art, a cathedral is greatest. A vast and majestic tree is greater than that.*

HENRY WARD BEECHER, 1870

# The Redwoods
# *Sequoia and Sequoiadendron*
## Taxodiaceae

The sequoias—coast redwood *(Sequoia sempervirens)* and giant sequoia *(Sequoiadendron giganteum)*—are two of California's remarkable conifers. Their great size, age, and beauty have given them a place among the world's best-known trees.

The two sequoias occupy widely separated forested areas in California. Giant sequoias occur on the western slopes of the southern Sierra Nevada, where they form a narrow, broken belt about 250 miles long at elevations from 4,500 to 8,500 feet. They occur in more or less continuous groves in Tulare and southern Fresno counties and in more widely scattered groves northward to southern Placer County. Coast redwood occurs along the Pacific Coast from the southwestern corner of Oregon south to the Santa Lucia Mountains in Monterey County. Along this strip, the trees form an interrupted forest belt about 450 miles long and from one to forty miles wide along the region of coastal fog, mostly below 2,000 feet. Fossil records indicate, however, that the coast redwood had a much greater distribution in past geological times, when the climate was wetter than California's today. They have been able to continue in their current range because of the extra moisture provided by coastal fogs during otherwise dry summers.

Coast redwood was first named *Taxodium* in 1832 by the British botanist David Don, from a specimen collected at Santa Cruz by Archibald Menzies in 1792 while on the Vancouver Expedition. Don recognized the similarity of the Menzies plant to the already known genus, *Taxodium,* the deciduous bald cypress of the southeastern United States. Because of its ever-green leaves, Don named the newly discovered plant *Taxodium sempervirens.* In 1847, the Austrian botanist Stephan Endlicher considered that the differences between coast redwood and bald cypress were greater than their similarities and placed coast redwood in a new genus, to which he gave the name *Sequoia.* This name honored Sequoyah (1760-1843), born in Cherokee country in the state of Georgia, son of a British trader and a Cherokee mother. In 1820, Sequoyah published a syllabic Cherokee alphabet that enabled tribe members to become literate, but Endlicher gave no reason for having honored Sequoyah in this manner.

In 1853, in San Francisco, William Lobb, a plant collector for the Veitch Nursery in England, learned of the discovery of a remarkable "big tree." In late summer, he left for the Calaveras region, where he obtained seeds, specimens, and living plants and left immediately for England, arriving in early December. He turned his material over to botanist John Lindley, who apparently lost no time in naming Lobb's big tree. His description appeared in Richardson's *Gardener's Chronicle,* December 24, 1853, under the name *Wellingtonia gigantea.* The generic name honored the Duke of Wellington, the "greatest of modern heroes," who had died a year earlier. However, unknown to Lindley, the name *Wellingtonia* had been used several years earlier for another plant and therefore could not be used for Lobb's tree. A year later, Lobb's big tree was renamed *Sequoia gigantea.*

After some time, it was realized that giant sequoia differed in several ways from coast redwood, but it was not until 1939 that these differences were pointed out in a publication by the American botanist John T Buchholz. Giant sequoia was then renamed *Sequoiadendron giganteum.* This was necessary because, in addition to differing in their geographic distribution, size, and age, the two sequoias differed in several key botanical characters, including leaves, cones, and bark.

Coast redwood, the first to be cultivated in Europe, was taken to the botanical garden in St Petersburg, Russia, in 1840, and from there in 1843 to Great Britain. Giant sequoia was introduced twice in 1853 to Great Britain. Early in the year, a Scottish plant collector, John D Mathew, sent seed from the Calaveras region of the southern Sierra Nevada to Scotland. Later in the same year, Lobb arrived in England with his collections. Following these original introductions, the two sequoias were grown in other European countries.

Both sequoias were early introductions in Golden Gate Park. Beginning in the late 1880s, they were listed in the annual reports of the park commissioners. Their potential for use in other of the city's parks is shown by the several hundred of each tree that were being grown in the park's nursery during the late 1890s and early 1900s.

Both sequoias were logged for lumber, though only coast redwood proved profitable. Their bark has proven more problematic. The bark of both is thick, cinnamon red, fibrous, spongy, up to 18 inches thick on giant sequoia, and 12 inches or less on coast redwood. In the early days of lumbering, redwood bark was discarded; however, after methods were devised for separating the bark into its constituent fibers, attempts were made in the 1960s to use the fibers commercially for fabrics, felts, and insulation. These uses apparently proved unprofitable and are not continued today. The bark of coast redwood is used primarily as an organic mulch and soil conditioner.

# 145

## Coast redwood
## *Sequoia sempervirens*

### Taxodiaceae

Coast redwoods are the taller of the two redwoods, reaching up to 367 feet in their natural range. Their trunks, however, are less wide, up to only 20 feet, and their maximum age is lower, about 2,000 years. The trees have a slender, graceful, conical form, which they retain until great age. **Leaves** of coast redwood are of two kinds: one is linear, about 1 inch long and spreading along both sides of short branchlets on the tree's main branches; the other is short, lance-shaped, and overlapping on vigorous terminal branches, often high in the tree and generally not seen until they fall to the ground. Seed **cones** of coast redwood mature the first year, are about 1 inch long, and have ten to twenty scales; tips of the scales are easily broken off.

Redwood Memorial Grove (III-M1); Heroes Grove (III-N1); AIDS Memorial Grove (IV-Q2); Strybing (VI-M4)
Park next to Transamerica building; Castro St at Duboce St
Evergreen/Fast growth/100' or more
(Conifer) Round cones, to 1" long, at the tips of branches
Full sun/Water regularly
Sunset Zone 4-9, 14-24
Color plate

Coast redwood is one of the few conifers that is able to reproduce vegetatively from the stump or root crown. Scattered around the basal trunks of living redwoods, around stumps left from felled trees, and around trees gutted by fire are burls, or buds, that sprout into young shoots. From these are formed the circle of young trees—the "fairy ring"—often seen around the trunks of old parent trees. Young trees of this generation, however, are clones of the parent trees and are not comparable to seed-produced offspring.

Wood of coast redwood is of excellent quality, durable, knot free, straight grained, insect resistant, and easily worked, which has made it a desirable commercial tree. The great success of redwood lumbering operations, however, resulted in the cutting of vast redwood forests, and eventually prompted the founding of the Save-the-Redwoods League in 1918. The organization's ongoing efforts have preserved many coast redwood groves.

The park has several well-established groves of coast redwoods. One, planted in the first decade of the 1900s in Strybing Arboretum, defines the section called the Redwood Trail; in it are plants that grow with redwood trees in their natural habitat. This grove is an excellent example of a redwood plant community.

Two groves are on the north side of the park. Heroes Grove is between Tenth Avenue and Park Presidio Drive on the north side of Kennedy Drive. It was dedicated by the Gold Star Mothers of America in memory of those San Franciscans who lost their lives in World War I. Their names are inscribed on a large granite monument, erected in 1932 not far from the Tenth Avenue entrance to the park. Redwood Memorial Grove is to the west of Park Presidio Drive, also on the north side of Kennedy Drive. This grove is dedicated to the memory of members of the Native Sons of the Golden West who lost their lives in World Wars I and II. Their names are inscribed on a tablet below a statue of the doughboy that is close to the grove's entrance and can be seen from Kennedy Drive. A small grove makes up the heart of the National AIDS Memorial Grove in de Laveaga Dell. There are many other coast redwoods scattered throughout the eastern half of the park. Coast redwoods also occur in other parks in San Francisco, including a grove planted in the 1970s in the financial district on the eastern side of the Transamerica Building.

# 146

## Giant sequoia
# *Sequoiadendron giganteum*
### Taxodiaceae

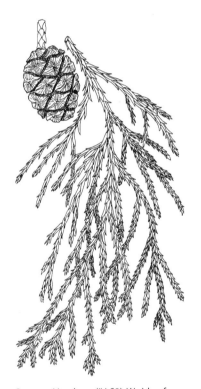

Giant sequoias are remarkable for their height, to about 325 feet; for the width of their trunks, to 30 feet or more (at 6 feet above ground); and for their great age, estimated at 2,500 to 3,500 years. Though not as tall as coast redwoods, they are considered to be the world's largest trees based upon their mass. They maintain a broad, dense, conical shape until reaching great age. **Leaves** of giant sequoia are all alike: small, short, lance shaped, overlapping, and somewhat similar to the shorter, overlapping leaves of coast redwood. **Cones** of giant sequoia mature in the second year, are about 2 inches long with twenty-five to forty scales, and are stout; the tips are not easily broken off. Giant sequoia is not able to reproduce vegetatively.

Wood of giant sequoia, light in weight, soft, and coarse-grained, was used locally for minor purposes, but harvesting and commercial use of these giant trees was given up as uneconomical. Because of their large size, trees generally shattered as they were felled. In addition, the rugged terrain in which they grew made it difficult to remove cut trees, and they were often left to decay on steep hillsides. Eventually preservation of the groves was ensured by the US Congress, which, in 1890, created Yosemite, Sequoia, and King's Canyon national parks. This prevented further commercial exploitation of these magnificent trees.

Today, a giant sequoia of historical interest may be seen at the western end of Conservatory Valley near Kennedy Drive. This tree, a gift of the

Stanyan Meadows (IV-S2); W side of
    Conservatory Valley (IV-Q2); Hippie Hill (IV-
    R2); Strybing (VI-N4)
26 Graystone Terrace; 664 Carolina St
Evergreen/Fast growth/100' or more
(Conifer) Roundish cones to 2" long, with stout
    scales
Full sun/Water infrequently and deeply
Sunset Zone 1-24

Sequoia Chapter of the Daughters of the American Revolution, was planted on April 19, 1894, the 119th anniversary of the Battle of Lexington. Soils from the battlefields of the Revolutionary War were placed at the base of the young tree. Other giant sequoias are in Stanyan Meadows, on the top of Hippie Hill, and in the Panhandle of Golden Gate Park, on a path at the northeast corner near the junction of Baker and Fell streets. Several trees are in Strybing Arboretum, including one north of the reservoir. Though less commonly planted than coast redwoods in California, a number can be seen in parks and campuses throughout the state; several can be seen on the capitol grounds in Sacramento. Being hardier to cold temperatures, they are also common park and campus trees in the Pacific Northwest.

# 147

### African linden
# *Sparmannia africana*
## Tiliaceae

African linden may be described either as a large shrub or a small tree. It has numerous basal stems that form clumps and are mostly about 12 feet tall. The many stems are covered with heart-shaped, irregularly toothed **leaves** several inches long, which look like leaves of some of the lindens to which it is related. The white, five-petaled **flowers,** with numerous yellow stamens and staminodes, superficially resemble roses in appearance more than they do lindens, in whose family they are placed. **Fruits** are five-segmented, globose capsules.

S side of Kennedy Dr opposite 8th Ave entrance
    (III-O1); E side of Stow Lake Dr (III-M2);
    between King Dr and Metson Rd (II-G4)
Evergreen/Fast growth/12'
Single, 5-petaled, 1 1/2" wide flowers with white
    petals, numerous yellow stamens (midwinter-
    early spring) /Globose capsule
Full sun/Water regularly
Sunset Zone 15-24

Known locally in South Africa as *stokroos,* or stock rose, African linden is remarkable for the behavior of its stamens and staminodes. When an insect visits a flower, the stamens bend and deposit pollen on the insect. The stamens need not be touched for this movement to take place since the stimulus comes from the staminodes, which the insect has touched.

The generic name *Sparmannia,* commemorates the Swedish botanist, Anders Sparmann, who collected plants in South Africa in and around Cape Town in the 1770s. In 1775, he was on the coast east of Cape Town where he found this large shrub with its showy white flowers, later named for him by Linnaeus.

According to Butterfield (1964), Francesco Franceschi first introduced African linden into California in 1908, but there was likely an earlier introduction since it was reported growing in Southern California in the early 1900s. The 1924 *Annual Report of the Park Commissioners* lists *Sparmannia* growing in the park. Today, large clumps are seen around Stow Lake Drive, between King Drive and Matson Road, on the south side of Kennedy Drive opposite Eighth Avenue, as well as many other places in Golden Gate Park and Strybing Arboretum.

## Tree ferns
# *Sphaeropteris*
## Cyatheaceae

These large, broad-spreading tree ferns are natives of the tropics and subtropics around the world. The distinguishing characters are finely divided **fronds** (leaf blades), triangular in shape, bi- or tripinnate, with petioles covered in dark papery **scales,** which are sometimes tipped with a spine that can be irritating to the skin. The trunks are relatively slender, particularly compared to the genus *Dicksonia*, which also occurs in the park, and there are fewer fronds than on *Dicksonia*. When old fronds fall, they leave behind large oval scars where they were previously attached to the trunk.

These ferns are more tender to cold temperatures than are the species of *Dicksonia* grown in Golden Gate Park, but they are faster growing, sometimes increasing in height by several feet a year when grown with plenty of moisture. Plants of two species of *Sphaeropteris, (S. cooperi* and *S. medullaris)* were once found in the Tree Fern Dell and can still be seen in Strybing Arboretum and elsewhere in the park.

# 148
## Australian tree fern
# *Sphaeropteris cooperi*
## Cyatheaceae

Australian tree fern is sometimes still listed by two botanical synonyms, *Alsophila cooperi* and *Cyathea cooperi,* as well as a third incorrect name, *A. australis*. At one time, there were numerous specimens of this large, graceful fern in the Tree Fern Dell, but none remain; a small, scattered grove is on the south side of King Drive west of 25th Avenue, and others can be seen in Strybing's Primitive Plants Garden.

This is probably the most frequently and most successfully cultivated of all tree ferns. Planted in both California and Florida, it reaches 10 to 12 feet in height, although in its native habitat in eastern Australia, plants reach three times that height. The broad, triangular **fronds** may be 20 feet long and half as wide; the fine-textured fronds are tripinnately divided, with dark brown, papery **scales** on the petioles. The **trunks** are usually no more than 6 inches in diameter, marked by oval leaf scars, and covered in brown, hairy scales.

S side of King Dr between Mallard Lake and 25th
    Ave (II-J4 ); Strybing (VII-N3)
Evergreen/Moderate growth/12' or more
(Fern) Spores under fertile fronds
Part shade to full sun on coast/Water regularly
Sunset Zone 15-24
Color plate

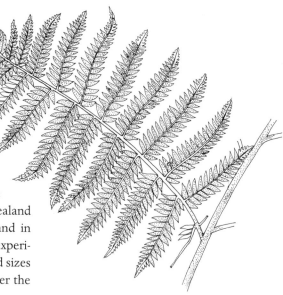

# 149

## Black tree fern
# *Sphaeropteris medullaris*
Cyatheaceae

Black tree fern is the largest and most impressive of the cultivated tree ferns. In Golden Gate Park, large, splendid specimens of this New Zealand native once existed in the Tree Fern Dell, around Quarry Lake, and in Strybing Arboretum; these succumbed to the cold temperatures experienced in the early 1990s. Today, several specimens of varying ages and sizes can be seen in Strybing's Primitive Plants Garden, mostly planted after the freeze of 1990.

Sometimes listed as *Cyathea medullaris,* this species can be as much as 50 feet tall in the wild, with tripinnate **fronds** 8 to 10 feet long, making a striking silhouette against the sky. The pith of the stem and the lower petiole bases of this fern was used as food by the Maoris of New Zealand, and the outer part of the stems has been used for making decorative containers and bowls called ponga ware. In mature specimens, the persistent, broken petiole bases remain on the upper portion of the **trunk,** but on lower stems, the bases break off cleanly, like those of *Sphaeropteris cooperi,* leaving only oval scars. The distinguishing feature of this fern is its shiny, black petioles, which give it the common name of black tree fern. In some young plants, the petioles are greenish, but in others, even some that have not yet developed a trunk, they are black, and young specimens can be recognized by this character. The dark brown **scales** on the petioles are minutely spine-tipped.

Strybing (VI-M4)
Evergreen/Slow growth/25'
(Fern) Spores under fertile fronds
Shade/Water regularly
Sunset Zone 17, 22-24
Color plate

## Beefwood and firewheel trees
# *Stenocarpus*
Proteaceae

The protea family is found primarily in the Southern Hemisphere, particularly in South Africa and Australia. The family has been used in support of the theory of continental drift, since closely related genera within the family can be found on all the continents that were originally connected in the supercontinent Gondwana. The two species of *Stenocarpus* grown in Golden Gate Park are both native to eastern Australia, as is silk oak *(Grevillea robusta),* another member of this family included among the trees of Golden Gate Park.

*Stenocarpus* is a genus of woody trees and shrubs, found in Australia, Malaysia, and New Caledonia. **Leaves** may be entire or pinnately lobed; in some species, juvenile leaves are lobed, while adult leaves are entire. Small tubular **flowers,** clustered in umbels, appear in the leaf axils. The **fruits** are small, narrow, leathery capsules.

# 150

Beefwood
## *Stenocarpus salignus*
Proteaceae

*Stenocarpus salignus* is generally called beefwood in Australia because its wood, particularly when freshly cut, is dull red, suggesting raw beef. The second part of its name, *salignus,* Latin for willowlike, alludes to the shape of the leaves. **Leaves** of beefwood on old trees are entire, lanceolate, 2 to 4 inches long, with three indistinct veins from the base; on young trees, leaves may be longer and shallowly, pinnately lobed. The **flowers,** appearing in spring, are white, about ½ inch long, and arranged somewhat like the spokes of a wheel, but being small and white, they are not showy as are those of fire-wheel trees. The wood of beefwood was at one time used in Australia for furniture, veneers, and, to a limited extent, as shingles.

One tree of beefwood can be seen in Strybing's Eastern Australian collection. It is not particularly showy, but the flowers are fascinating on close inspection and the layered branching on this 15-foot tree is appealing. This tree is among the oldest in the arboretum, planted there by Eric Walther before the arboretum was officially dedicated in 1940. Francesco Franceschi had a tree of beefwood in his Santa Barbara garden in 1897, according to Butterfield (1964), but the tree is seldom seen in gardens or nurseries today.

Strybing (VI-N3)
Evergreen/Slow growth/40'
White tubular flowers, 1/2" long with protruding
    stigmas, in spokelike clusters (early summer)/
    Small woody capsules
Full sun/Water occasionally
Sunset Zone 16, 17, 20-24

# 151

Firewheel tree
## *Stenocarpus sinuatus*
Proteaceae

In New South Wales, Australia, where they are native, firewheel trees sometimes reach 60 to 100 feet in height. The **leaves** are large, glossy, leathery, generally pinnately lobed, and up to 12 inches long, with two to four irregular large lobes on each side. Sometimes, however, they are entire, broadly lanceolate, and 6 to 8 inches long. The lobed leaves are so distinctive that a tree is easily recognized even when not in flower. The clusters of twelve to eighteen bright red **flowers** are showy and attractive. The individual flowers, about 1 inch long, radiate more or less symmetrically from a central point, like the spokes of a wheel, giving rise to the common name. The flowers, which occur occasionally during summer and autumn, are pro-

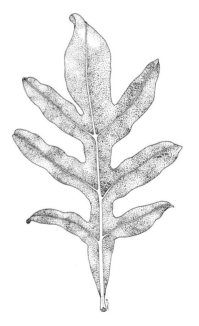

Strybing (VI-N3)
Evergreen/Slow growth/30'
Showy, spokelike clusters of bright red, 1" long,
    tubular flowers (summer-fall) /Woody fruit to
    4" long
Full sun/Water occasionally
Sunset Zone 16, 17, 20-24

189

duced on the old wood and are more or less hidden by the leaves, but trees with a profusion of flowers can be spectacular. Firewheel trees, however, need summer heat to flower, and trees in Golden Gate Park seldom flower.

Firewheel tree was discovered in 1828 by the early British botanical explorer Allan Cunningham near Moreton Bay in Queensland. Another tree from the same locality, now seen in Golden Gate Park and elsewhere in California, is Moreton Bay fig *(Ficus macrophylla)*. Because of its attractive flowers, firewheel tree has a long history in Australia as an ornamental. In addition, its wood, which is close-grained, moderately hard, and durable, has been used there for cabinetwork, veneers, and in some areas where abundant enough, for general building purposes. Today, it is seen in botanical gardens in Southern California and, occasionally, as a park or street tree there. Firewheel tree has been in California since 1871, when it was listed by Stephen Nolan at his Belle View Nursery in Oakland. It has been in Golden Gate Park since 1910. The larger of two firewheel trees in the Strybing's Eastern Australia collection is about 30 feet tall; it was planted in the 1930s by Eric Walther.

# 152

## Turpentine tree
## *Syncarpia glomulifera*
## Myrtaceae

*Syncarpia* is a genus with only two species, both native to Australia, only one of which is an ornamental tree. The generic name comes from two Greek words for together and fruit, referring to the several fruits united into a rounded cluster. Turpentine tree is erect, generally reaching 50 to 100 feet tall in Australia, but it is usually shorter in cultivation. The **bark** is thick, fibrous, and furrowed. The **leaves** are opposite, up to 5 inches long, ovate with a somewhat wavy margin, the upper dark green surface contrasting with the gray, hairy underside. White **flowers,** generally six to ten, are joined in a somewhat woody cluster. The conspicuous part of each flower is the dense, showy ring of white stamens; the petals are small and inconspicuous. Superficially, the flower clusters resemble those of some eucalypts, to which the tree is related. The flowers are followed by clusters of rounded, woody **fruits** about ¾ inch in diameter. The common name derives from the resinous sap exuded when the trunk is cut. The resin, which originates between the bark and the wood, has scarcely any odor and is not flammable, despite the tree's common name.

In Australia, turpentine tree occurs in mixed forests, often in the transition between rainforest and eucalypt forest. The durable wood is resistant to fire damage and to certain local insects. One of its important uses has been for saltwater pilings, but it has also been used for poles, heavy con-

SE corner 6th Ave and Fulton St (III-P1); main
    footpath E of conservatory (IV-R1)
McCoppin Square; 24th Ave between Taraval and
    Santiago Sts
Evergreen/Moderate growth/40'-50'
Roundish cluster of 6-10 flowers with showy,
    creamy white stamens (spring-summer)/
    Round, woody, fused fruits,1/2" wide
Full sun to part shade/Water infrequently
Sunset Zone 16, 17, 20-24

struction, and other building purposes. It is an attractive shade, shelter, and windbreak tree and is used for ornamental planting. Turpentine tree, probably because of its reputation as a timber tree in Australia, has been planted experimentally in other countries, but its growth there has been poor.

Turpentine tree was introduced to California before 1871, when it was first listed in the state by Stephen Nolan at his Belle View Nursery in Oakland. In Golden Gate Park, turpentine tree was first mentioned in the 1893 *Annual Report of the Park Commissioners.* Today, it can be seen in several locations within the park. The largest trees are along a path just east of the conservatory, where several are planted close together; a cluster of three trees is at the Sixth Avenue entrance from Fulton Street. The height and obvious age of these trees suggest that they may go back to the earliest record of this tree in the park. They may be recognized, when not in flower, by their large size and thick, longitudinally furrowed, fibrous bark. Though the tree can be seen in Santa Barbara, it is not commonly planted elsewhere in California.

# Hippie Hill

Many points within Golden Gate Park have acquired names that do not appear on official maps, but that are known to park gardeners and users alike and give character and a sense of history to the park. One such location near the eastern end of the park is Hippie Hill, a pleasant tree-topped knoll whose gentle southern slope, overlooking Sharon Meadow, became a popular sunning spot for the flower children of the late sixties. On its western side are the tennis courts and to the north is Kennedy Drive. Many old and attractive trees are on the hill, including such familiar ones as coast live oaks, Monterey pines and cypresses, and blue gums, and several uncommon trees: coast banksia (*Banksia integrifolia*), titoki (*Alectryon excelsus*), turpentine tree (*Syncarpia glomulifera*), and cow-itch tree (*Lagunaria patersonii*).

# 153

## Talauma
# *Talauma hodgsonii*

## Magnoliaceae

*Talauma hodgsonii* is an evergreen tree that, in its natural area, becomes 50 to 60 feet tall and has a trunk girth of 3 to 6 feet; trees are smaller in cultivation. **Leaves** are exceptionally large and leathery, 8 to 20 inches long, and up to 6 inches wide. The showy **flowers,** 6 inches across, have six inner petal-like tepals that are creamy white and faintly rose tinged, plus three outer tepals that are white on the inner side and purplish outside.

Talauma, with flowers like those of a magnolia, differs from *Magnolia* only in the manner in which its fruits open and release their seeds. Even the

Strybing (VII-N4)
Evergreen/Slow growth/50'-60'
Showy, magnolia-like, white flowers tinged with
    rose and purple, 6" wide (early summer)/
    Cone-like fruit
Full sun to part shade/Water regularly
Sunset Zone 17, 20-24
Color plate

**seeds,** like those of magnolia, dangle from silky threads. The two genera have long been considered separate, although some botanists have now transferred *Talauma* to *Magnolia*. *Magnolia hodgsonii* may thus be considered a synonym of *Talauma hodgsonii*.

*Talauma hodgsonii* is native to forests of the eastern Himalaya. In part of its geographic range, it occurs with *Magnolia campbellii* and *Michelia doltsopa,* both also in Strybing Arboretum. Talauma was discovered in 1848 by Joseph Dalton Hooker in a forested valley in Sikkim, between 5,000 and 6,000 feet elevation. *Magnolia globosa, Michelia champaca,* and *Manglieta insignis* occur in the same area. According to Hooker, "of these the prince is, no doubt, *Magnolia campbellii* and next to it is *Talauma hodgsonii*"—this in an area remarkable for its handsome magnolia-related trees.

Of Strybing's two trees of *Talauma hodgsonii,* the one on the eastern edge of the New World Cloud Forest is the finest. Planted about 1953, the first flowers opened in 1967. Flowering in Strybing does not occur every year but is sporadic. This and a smaller tree west of the Moon-viewing Garden are the only talaumas in Golden Gate Park. Others in California are in the Blake Garden, Kensington; Lotusland in Montecito near Santa Barbara; and Huntington Botanical Gardens, San Marino. Talauma is otherwise rare in the California landscape. The source for the Huntington tree is the old Evans and Reeves Nursery, Los Angeles, which introduced talauma in the 1930s. This also may have been the source of the other talaumas in California, including the ones in Strybing.

# 154

Bald cypress
# *Taxodium distichum*

Taxodiaceae

One of the trees seen by everyone who enters Golden Gate Park from the Panhandle is a bald cypress, or swamp cypress, at the edge of the lawn west of McLaren Lodge. It stands close to, and somewhat overshadows, a dome-shaped Camperdown elm. About 50 feet tall, it is densely branched. Its lowest branches root when they touch the ground, giving it a spread of nearly 30 feet.

The outermost leafy branchlets are slender, flexible, drooping, and feathery in appearance. The soft **leaves** are about ½ inch long and scarcely ⅛ inch wide. **Cones** appear on new spring branchlets but are not always seen on cultivated trees. The smaller, pollen-bearing male cones are scattered on leafless branchlets 4 to 6 inches long. Female seed-bearing cones usually occur singly or in pairs on leafy branchlets. They are rounded to oval, about 1 inch in diameter, green at first, later turning brown.

This deciduous tree goes through several seasonal stages during the year. From late spring through summer and fall, its foliage is a pleasant bright green. This changes to an attractive golden or cinnamon brown dur-

Edge of lawn W of Mclaren Lodge (IV-R2); North
    Lake (I-D2); Strybing (VII-N3)
SE corner Dolores Park
Deciduous/Moderate growth/40'-100'
(Conifer) Round or oval, 1" green cones, brown
    when mature
Full sun/Water regularly
Sunset Zone 2-9, 14-24

ing the winter before the leaves drop, leaving the tree "bald." New, fresh, light green leaves appear early the following spring. Some park visitors, seeing the tree after the leaves have fallen and assuming that all conifers are evergreen, inquire at the lodge about the health of the tree. They are assured that, while most conifers are evergreen, bald cypress is deciduous and loses its leaves during part of each winter.

Cypress as a common name is used for a number of different trees. The association of the name cypress with *Taxodium distichum* goes back to accounts of the tree from late sixteenth and early seventeenth century English visitors to eastern North America.

The English first noted the tree when they came to Virginia in early colonial times. Upon seeing it in 1586, Thomas Hariot called it "cypres" and took it back to England, along with other plants. William Strachy visited the English colony on the James River in 1610 and, in the account of his visit, mentioned a tall "cypres." In 1637, John Tradescant, the younger, again introduced the tree into England, planting it in his father's garden in London. No trees are known to have survived in England from these two early introductions, but three trees planted about 1750 are still standing. Bald cypress is said to be one of the most beautiful and interesting trees that can be grown in both wet and dry places in England.

The geographical range of bald cypress extends along the coastal plain of the eastern United States from Delaware south to Florida and west to eastern Texas, and through the Mississippi Valley north to southern Illinois and Indiana. Bald cypress grows in low, wet places, usually along streams, rivers, and often in swamps, sometimes in almost pure stands. In some situations, trees produce flaring or buttressed trunks and "knees," which are roots that stand above the water. The knees may also appear on trees in cultivation when they are growing in or near water.

The wood of bald cypress is hard, heavy, straight grained, durable, resistant to decay, and easy to work. It has been highly prized since colonial times and has had commercial value as barrels, shingles, railroad ties, and bridge beams. Trees are slow growing in their native stands, and their natural reproduction has not kept up with the demands of industry for their lumber. Now, with thousands of acres of swamps drained, the number of mature bald cypress trees has declined significantly throughout their range.

The date of the introduction of bald cypress into Golden Gate Park is not known, but the tree was listed among the park's plantings in 1893. It is possible that the tree seen today west of McLaren Lodge was planted at this site before 1893; it may also have been part of the plantings set out around the Lodge upon its completion in 1897. Several bald cypresses on one of the islands in North Lake were planted after the lakes were constructed. Work began on the lakes in 1899, and plans for each of their small islands called for them to be planted differently. One was to be planted with "Louisiana swamp cypress." Bald cypresses can also be found at the eastern end of Strybing's Duck Pond.

Bald cypress trees are to be seen in other California cities, including Palo Alto, Berkeley, Oakland, Sacramento, Arcadia, Santa Monica, and Pasadena. *Taxodium distichum* is closely related to Mexico's Montezuma cypress *(T. mucronatum)*. So similar are the two that it is difficult to distinguish them, and trees in cultivation are likely to be confused.

## The Yews
# *Taxus*
### Taxaceae

*Taxus* is the best known of the six genera in its family. It occurs in the Northern Hemisphere in North America, Europe, eastern Asia, and Asia Minor, extending into Mexico and central Malaysia. It is thought to include three to ten species, which are closely related and so similar that it is difficult to distinguish between them. Because some species are limited in distribution, they may more easily be separated by range, when known, rather than by morphological characters.

The yews are evergreen conifers, with linear, needlelike **leaves** arranged spirally or appearing to be in two ranks along the branchlets; leaves are usually dark green and glossy, sometimes with their undersides a slightly different shade of green. The solitary **fruit** is an ovoid seed, covered, at least in part, by a brightly colored, fleshy aril that is attractive to birds and aids in the seed's dispersal.

Several species of *Taxus* are important garden plants; selected forms of each and hybrids between some of the species have created a wide range of yews available for the gardener looking for dependable and adaptable evergreen shrubs or small trees.

# 155

### English yew
# *Taxus baccata*
### Taxaceae

English yew is widely distributed in Europe and Asia Minor. Slow growing and extraordinarily long-lived, it is second only, perhaps, to western bristlecone pine *(Pinus longaeva)* for longevity records. English dendrologist Alan Mitchell estimated an English yew in Perthshire, Scotland, to be over 4,000 years old and another in Kent, England, to be over 3,000 years. But old and very large yews are hollow, so their ages cannot be accurately dated by ring counts.

English yew is a broad tree, heavily branched in its typical form, with mature specimens reaching over 50 feet in height. Its **leaves** are dark, glossy green and may be up to 1½ inches long, gradually tapering to a point. The **fruit,** a red, fleshy aril, may be ⅓ inch long, extending beyond the seed but not enclosing it completely. English yew is well known for its highly toxic taxine alkaloids. The entire plant is poisonous, especially the **seeds,** and ingesting them can be fatal. The bright red aril covering the seed, however, is not toxic, making it suitable food for birds that, in turn, distribute the undigested seeds. Wood of English yew, which is tough, hard, and elastic, was used for the long bows of medieval archers. Popular today as garden plants, a great many named cultivars have been selected from seedling-grown and wild-collected plants of English yew; they vary in height, form, and branching characters, and in the color and size of the leaves.

W side of McLaren Lodge lawn (IV-S2); S of
    Kennedy Dr opposite conservatory (IV-Q2);
    Japanese Tea Garden (V-N2); Strybing (VI-N4)
2766 California St
Evergreen/Slow growth/25'-40'
(Conifer) Bright red, juicy fruit to 1/2" wide, with
    a single seed
Full sun to part shade/Water infrequently
Sunset Zone 3-9, 14-24

In pre-Christian Great Britain, English yews were sacred trees. The druids built their temples near them; later, early Christians used the druid sites for their churches. This association of yews with religious sites has continued to the present.

Of the several species of *Taxus,* English yew is the most commonly cultivated. According to Butterfield (1964), English yew has been in California since the 1870s and 1880s. Stephen Nolan offered it at his Belle View Nursery, Oakland, in 1871, and RD Fox followed at his Santa Clara Valley Nursery, San Jose, in 1884. Many English yews are in Golden Gate Park: one is west of the McLaren Lodge lawn; another is in front of the conservatory; several broad, sheared columns are along Kennedy Drive opposite the conservatory; and others are in the Japanese Tea Garden and north of the reservoir in Strybing Arboretum. It is cultivated in many West Coast cities from Vancouver, British Columbia, to Santa Barbara and elsewhere in Southern California.

# 156

## Japanese yew
# *Taxus cuspidata*

Taxaceae

Strybing (VII-N4)
Evergreen/Moderate growth/50'
(Conifer) Juicy, scarlet fruit to 1/2" wide, with a
  single seed
Full sun to part shade/Water occasionally
Sunset Zone 1-6, 14-17

Japanese yew is occasionally cultivated on the Pacific Coast, although not as commonly as English yew. Because it is more cold hardy than English yew, it is frequently planted in the northern United States, where it was introduced in 1862. Japanese yew can usually be distinguished from English yew by its **leaves,** which are generally shorter, to 1 inch long, and somewhat erect, producing a v-shaped groove between the two rows; the leaf tips taper abruptly to a point. Also, the lower surface of the leaf is tawny or yellow-green. The **fruit** is a scarlet, fleshy aril that does not completely cover the seed; like English yew, all parts of the plant are poisonous except for the aril. The buds are generally several in a small cluster. Also like English yew, Japanese yew is a variable species with many cultivars differentiated by their size and growth habits.

Japanese yew is native to all the islands of Japan. It has been in Golden Gate Park since 1902, with fine specimens once seen in the Panhandle, along with dwarf or slow-growing selections in Strybing's Dwarf Conifer Garden and in the Japanese Tea Garden. Today, one fine, mature specimen of Japanese yew is on the knoll between the Main Lawn and the New World Cloud Forest at Strybing. Most of the other yews found in the park appear to be English yews *(Taxus baccata).* Japanese yew is less commonly available in nurseries in California than is its English cousin.

# Yews in Medicine

The recent discovery of the usefulness of the bark of Pacific yew *(Taxus brevifolia)* as a source of the cancer-fighting drug called taxol has brought attention to this tree. A forest tree of Northern California, Oregon, and Washington, Pacific yew had previously been considered of no economic value, and trees in the path of lumbering operations were often destroyed. Efforts are now being made to preserve these trees in their native habitats, as well as to look to other species of *Taxus* as possible sources of taxol. In 1992, Thomas Elias, director of the National Arboretum in Washington, DC, and a Russian collaborator, Vladislav V Korzhenevshy, reported the discovery of taxane, a taxol compound, in trees of *T. baccata* native to the Ukraine, Georgia, and southern Russia.

# 157

## Western red cedar
# *Thuja plicata*
## Cupressaceae

Western red cedar is widely distributed in the mountains of western North America. It is found from southeastern Alaska south to northwestern California and east to the Rocky Mountains. Because it is so well known, it has many additional common names including red cedar, Pacific red cedar, canoe cedar, giant cedar, shingle-wood, arborvitae, and giant arborvitae.

West side of Conservatory Valley (IV-Q2); Strybing (VII-O4)
Evergreen/Fast growth/120' or more
(Conifer) Oblong cones, 1/2"-3/4" long, that point backwards, with 9 spreading scales
Full sun/Water regularly
Sunset Zone 1-9, 14-24

A tall tree, generally pyramidal in outline, Western red cedar can reach 120 feet or more in height and have a trunk diameter of 12 feet or more. Its leafy branches are fragrant when crushed. The **bark** is reddish brown, thin, irregularly ridged, and somewhat flaking. The branchlets making up the flattened branches are shiny green on their upper surfaces, and ⅛ to ³⁄₁₆ inch wide. The scalelike **leaf** pairs are closely appressed, ¹⁄₁₆ to ³⁄₁₆ inch long. The lower surfaces of leaves may be marked with small, white streaks, but the markings vary from tree to tree and between branches on the same tree. The oblong **cones** are ½ to ¾ inch long; they bend backwards on the branch, and their nine scales spread apart upon ripening.

Western red cedar is an important Pacific Coast timber tree. Its wood is soft, reddish brown, coarse-grained, and durable; it has been used for posts, shingles, doors, and interior finishes. Native Americans of the Pacific Northwest used the trunks for totem poles, buildings, and canoes, hence one of the common names, canoe cedar. The inner bark, also used by Native Americans, was cut into strips and woven into mats, baskets, and bags. The trees are excellent for windbreaks and background plantings. Because their foliage remains green through winter, they are better suited for northern climates than white cedar *(Thuja occidentalis)* of eastern North America, whose foliage turns brownish in winter.

According to Butterfield (1964), western red cedar was first offered in California in 1871 by Stephan Nolan at his Belle View Nursery. It has been in Golden Gate Park since the early 1890s, when it was listed in the annual reports of the park commissioners. A group of western red cedars may be seen at the western end of Conservatory Valley. A number of trees are in Strybing Arboretum, south of the Dwarf Conifer Garden and in the Arthur Menzies Garden of California Native Plants. Western red cedar is a common feature of the landscape in the Pacific Northwest.

# 158

### Hiba cedar
# *Thujopsis dolabrata*
## Cupressaceae

Japanese Tea Garden (V-N2); Strybing (VI-N3)
Evergreen/Slow growth/50'-90'
(Conifer) Round cones, 1/2" wide, with blue grey
    scales that turn brown
Full sun/Water regularly
Sunset Zone 3-7, 14-17

Hiba cedar occurs widely in the mountains of Japan. Trees are pyramidal or irregular in shape and may reach 90 feet, but in cultivation they are smaller. Hiba cedar is distinguished from western red cedar and incense cedar by its wider flattened branches, which are ³⁄₁₆ to ³⁄₈ inch wide, dark green and shiny above, and with a characteristic pattern of white streaks on the lower surface. The scalelike **leaf** pairs spread outward and are ⅛ to ¼ inch long, the lateral pair being sometimes longer and wider than the inner pair. The white streaks on the lower surfaces of the leaves bear a slight resemblance to the blade of a hatchet, a *dolabra* (Latin for hatchet), from which comes *dolabrat* in the name of the species. The somewhat succulent, ovoid **cones,** each with eight to ten scales, are solitary, ⅓ to ½ inch in diameter, and glaucous, becoming woody when ripe.

In Japan, where it is also called *asunaro,* this cedar grows in moist, dense forests and is shaded by taller adjacent trees. But in one area of northern Honshu, EH Wilson (1916) noted that Hiba was common and formed "a magnificent and almost pure forest."

Hiba was first offered by RD Fox at his Santa Clara Valley Nursery, San Jose, in 1884. It has been in Golden Gate Park since the early 1890s, when it was mentioned in the annual reports of the park commissioners. It can be seen today as a hedge in the Japanese Tea Garden, between the *torii* and the Temple Gate; and as erect, multi-stemmed trees at the edge of the main pond and near the South Gate. Another tree is among the conifers on the lawn south of Strybing's Moon-viewing Garden. As an ornamental and at its best, Hiba is an attractive conifer, but its use is limited in California, perhaps because it requires cool, moist summers. Several cultivars have been selected in Europe and in Japan, where it is widely grown.

## The Lindens
# *Tilia*
### Tiliaceae

With common names like linden, basswood, whitewood, and lime, *Tilia* is a genus of about thirty to forty-five species having a wide geographical distribution in the Northern Hemisphere, including North America, Europe, and parts of Asia. *Tilia* is a classical Latin name, perhaps derived from the Greek *ptilon*, meaning feather, an apparent reference to the narrow, winglike bract to which flower clusters and fruits are attached.

Lindens are deciduous trees with alternate, generally heart-shaped **leaves,** often slightly unequal at their bases. The **flowers** are small, frequently fragrant, and occur in loose clusters; they are so uniform in appearance that they are of little value in defining individual species. The **fruits** are round, dry, about the size of peas, and generally covered with hairs. The characteristic and readily identifiable feature of all lindens is the long, narrow, leafy bract to which the lower half of the inflorescence is fused. The bract serves as an aid in the distribution of seeds in much the way a samara propels the seeds of maples and ashes through the air.

Based on leaf characters, the species can be divided into two groups: those in which the leaves have a showy covering of white hairs on their lower surfaces (the silver lindens); and those in which the lower surfaces have few or no hairs.

# 159

### Little-leaf linden
# *Tilia cordata*
### Tiliaceae

The little-leaf linden is the common linden of England and northern Europe, though another tree is known as the European linden *(Tilia x europaea)*. Its **leaves** are heart shaped, about 2 to 3 inches long, and the margins are saw-toothed. They are glossy and dark green above and somewhat glaucous on their undersides, with tiny tufts of hairs in the axils of the veins. The pale yellow, fragrant **flowers** are clustered in the typical fashion with five to seven flowers attached to a slender, bracted stalk; they appear in late spring.

Little-leaf linden was one of the trees pollarded in the Music Concourse in Golden Gate Park to establish a uniform size and shape, though none exist there now. Today, a little-leaf linden can be seen at the entrance to the Rose Garden from Kennedy Drive. This species is widely planted throughout North America, as a street and plaza tree. It is usually seen as one of its named cultivars, selected for the uniformity of the branching pattern. One such cultivar, 'Rancho', can be seen at the northern edge of Strybing's Main Lawn.

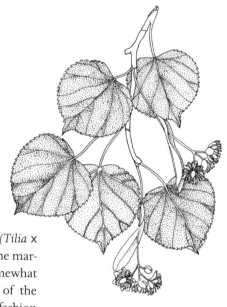

Rose Garden (III-N2); Strybing (VII-O3)
Deciduous/Slow growth/30'-50'
Clusters of slightly fragrant, small, pale yellow
    flowers fused below a long narrow bract
    (May-June) /Hard, oval seeds
Full sun/Water regularly
Sunset Zone 1-17
Suitable as a street tree

## 160

European linden
# *Tilia* x *europaea*
Tiliaceae

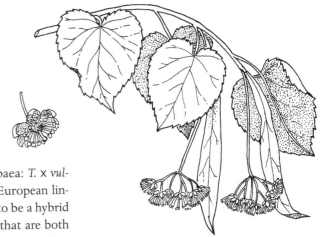

A variety of scientific names have been used for *Tilia* x europaea: *T.* x *vulgaris, T. intermedia,* and *T. hybrida.* It is commonly known as European linden, European basswood, whitewood, and lime. It is believed to be a hybrid between two European species *(T. platyphylos* and *T. cordata)* that are both native to England. The hybrid, which occurs along with the parent species, is widely cultivated in the British Isles and continental Europe; it has naturalized in areas where lindens are not native. A fairly large tree, it has **leaves** that are broadly ovate, generally 4 inches long by 3 inches wide, and abruptly pointed at their tips. The leaves are dark green above and glabrous on the lower surfaces, except for a small tuft of hairs in the axils of the secondary veins and the midrib. **Flower** clusters have up to ten small, fragrant, pale yellow flowers fused below the narrow bract. This hybrid species produces an abundance of suckers that are a disadvantage in cultivation.

Although European linden was first introduced to the United States in Williamsburg, Virginia, in 1724, it apparently is rarely cultivated in North America. Butterfield (1964) listed it in California in 1854, when it was offered by Commercial Nurseries of San Francisco. In Golden Gate Park, a tree of this species may be seen in the mass of shrubbery along a path southwest of the Ghirardelli Rustic Shelter; another is at the edge of the small lawn northeast of Lincoln Way at 25th Avenue.

Meadow W of conservatory (IV-Q1)
Deciduous/Moderate growth/100'
Loose clusters of small, white, fragrant flowers
    fused below a long, narrow bract (May-June)/
    Dry, pea-sized, hairy fruits
Full sun/Water regularly
Sunset Zone 1-17
Suitable as a street tree

## 161

Silver linden
# *Tilia tomentosa*
Tiliaceae

Silver linden, or European white linden, is a native of southeastern Europe and adjacent Asia Minor. It takes its common names from the covering of dense, white hairs on the undersides of its **leaves;** this character distinguishes silver linden from European linden and gives the tree a distinctive and attractive appearance when its leaves twist in a breeze. The leaves are heart shaped, 3 to 6 inches long and wide, and abruptly pointed. The loose cluster of up to ten white **flowers** is fused to the prominent bract. **Fruit** is usually ovoid, up to about ⅜ inch long, and covered by white hairs and minute, wartlike projections.

W of North Lake (I-D2); Meadow W of conservatory (IV-Q1)
Deciduous/Moderate growth/40'-50'
Loose clusters of small, white, fragrant flowers
    fused below a long, narrow bract (June) /Dry,
    pea-sized, hairy fruits
Full sun/Needs no watering once established
Sunset Zone 1-21
Suitable as a street tree

Silver linden is a variable species with a number of listed cultivars. It is more drought tolerant than most lindens and is commonly cultivated in North America. In California, it was first offered for sale in 1884 by RD Fox's Santa Clara Valley Nursery in San Jose.

Silver linden may be seen in Golden Gate Park in the same area as the European linden, southwest of the Ghirardelli Rustic Shelter, and also on the western side of North Lake. A grand old specimen in Strybing Arboretum succumbed to the severe windstorm of December 1995 and no longer exists. A young specimen, planted in the 1970s, can be seen in The Ruth Bancroft Garden in Walnut Creek. Silver linden is occasionally seen in other parks and public places in California, where its drought tolerance makes it particularly suitable.

# 162

California nutmeg
## *Torreya californica*
Taxaceae

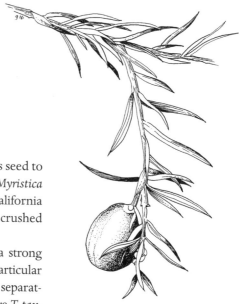

Strybing (VI-N4)
Evergreen/Slow growth/15'-50'
(Conifer) Olive-shaped, green cones, often
    streaked with purple, containing flesh-cov-
    ered seeds
Full sun to part shade/Water occasionally
Sunset Zone 7-9, 14-24

California nutmeg is so named for the superficial resemblance of its seed to nutmeg, but the commercial spice is obtained from the unrelated *Myristica fragrans,* native to the Asian tropics. Other common names for California nutmeg, stinking cedar and stinking yew, refer to the odor of its crushed leaves and green bark. It is also known as California torreya.

*Torreya* is related to the yews *(Taxus),* and its foliage bears a strong resemblance to theirs. A small genus of five species, *Torreya* is of particular interest to botanists and plant geographers for its disjunct or widely separated areas of distribution. North America has one other species, the rare *T. taxifolia* in Florida. The other species are in Asia—two in China and one in Japan.

California nutmeg has rough, more or less cross-checked **bark** and spreading or somewhat drooping branches. **Leaves** are stiff, 1 to 3 inches long and about ⅛ inch wide, ending in a sharp point. Pollen and seed cones occur on separate trees. The pollen cones are ovoid, about ⅓ inch long. The **fruits** are olive shaped, about 1 to 1½ inches long, and green, sometimes streaked with purple. A thin, fleshy layer covers the single seed. California nutmeg occurs in California in scattered locations along streams and in protected places, such as creek bottoms and moist canyons. It is found in the Coast Ranges from Mendocino to Santa Cruz counties and in the Sierra Nevada.

Seeds of California nutmeg were offered in 1859 by William Walker of Golden Gate Nursery, San Francisco, and plants were offered in 1871 by Stephen Nolan of Belle View Nursery, Oakland. California nutmegs are grown in the Santa Barbara Botanic Garden and on the campus of San Jose State University. Lenz and Dourley (1981) record the survival of twelve

California nutmegs out of seventy planted on the original site of the Rancho Santa Ana Botanic Garden in Santa Ana Canyon. The trees were forty-seven years old when located; the north-facing slope apparently had given the trees just enough protection from the heat to survive.

In Golden Gate Park, California nutmeg was listed in the annual reports of the park commissioners from 1893 to 1924. Two large trees once existed in de Laveaga Dell on the wooded slope below Middle Drive. Today, a large tree that produces fruits is in Strybing Arboretum near the nursery area; a second tree is on Strybing's Redwood Trail.

Several uses have been reported for California nutmeg. It is a handsome ornamental tree, although probably only rarely offered in the nursery trade. The nuts have an agreeable, aromatic taste somewhat like that of peanuts; they were roasted and eaten by Native Americans. The nut's oil could probably be used in cooking; an oil used for cooking has been obtained in Japan from the seeds of Japanese nutmeg.

# Torrey—the Man and the Trees

Two California conifers were named for John Torrey, one of the most distinguished and best known American botanists of the nineteenth century. Torrey named and made known hundreds of plants collected on many of the government expeditions that explored unknown areas of western North America. He collaborated with Asa Gray (the two were lifelong friends) on their two-volume *Flora of North America,* published between 1838 and 1842.

*Torreya* was named in 1838 by George Walker Arnott, a Scottish botanist whom Torrey had met on a trip to England in 1833. A specimen collected along the Apalachicola River in Florida was sent to Arnott. From it, he described *Torreya* as well as the first known species of the new genus, *T. taxifolia.*

In 1851, William Lobb collected California nutmeg in the Sierra Nevada and introduced it to English horticulture. It is not known whether Torrey received a part of Lobb's collection, but an early collection was sent to Torrey, who recognized it as belonging to the same genus as *Torreya taxifolia.* Torrey named the second species *T. californica.*

Charles Christopher Parry made the first collection of Torrey pine *(Pinus torreyana)* in 1850. Parry sent his collection to Torrey in New York. Torrey believed the collection to be a new species and sent part of it to the French botanist EA Carriere, who was preparing a monograph on conifers. Carriere's monograph, published in 1855, included the description of the new pine named for Torrey.

*In the intimate and humanized landscape, trees become the greatest single element linking us visually and emotionally with our surroundings….It's no wonder that when we first think of a garden we think of a tree.*

THOMAS D. CHURCH, *Gardens Are for People*

# 163

### Windmill palm
# *Trachycarpus fortunei*

## Palmae

Windmill palm, also known as Japanese windmill palm, Chinese windmill palm, Chusan palm, Fortune's palm, and hemp palm, is a fan palm with rounded leaves like those of a paper fan. It is the most cold tolerant of all cultivated palms, hardy in Vancouver, British Columbia, the British Isles, and Beijing. It is considered native to central and southern China, where it has long been cultivated for economic reasons, but because it naturalizes readily, it is not known whether it is native to all the areas in which it now occurs. In Japan, it is native only to the southernmost large island, Kyushu, but it has long been cultivated throughout Japan as an ornamental tree.

The windmill palm has a straight, slender trunk about 25 or sometimes 40 feet tall. The **trunk** is covered with a loose matting of coarse, dark, stiff fibers that are the remnants of old leaf bases. The fan-shaped, nearly round **leaves** are 2 to 4 feet across, divided more than halfway into stiff, somewhat erect to drooping segments. The petiole is generally 2 to 3 feet long, with small but sharp irregular teeth along the margins. The numerous small, yellow **flowers** are carried on a large, hanging, branched inflorescence at the top of the trunk, among the younger leaves in early summer. The blue black, nearly round **fruits** are about ½ inch in diameter.

The windmill palm is not only widely grown but is probably the most economically useful palm in China. The trunks are used in the construction of houses, the fresh flowers are eaten, and the seeds are used as food for domestic animals. The fibrous matting on the trunk (called Chinese coir) have been harvested in Sichuan Province and exported for the making of ropes, mats, mattresses, scrubbing brushes, hats, and raincoats. From the outer portion of the fruit, a wax has been obtained that is comparable in quality to the wax from carnauba palm (*Copernicia prunifera*) of Brazil. A drug with the Chinese name *hsuen an,* obtained from the seeds, is used to control internal bleeding. Because of these many uses, the cultivation of windmill palm is an important industry in China.

*Trachycarpus* is a small genus, generally considered to have six species, although two (*T. wagnerianus* and *T. caespitosus*) may be variants of *T. fortunei*. Rare in cultivation are *T. martianus, T. nanus,* and *T. tikal,* and their names are often used incorrectly. The most widely grown species is *T. fortunei,* which is sometimes listed incorrectly as *T. excelsus, Chamaerops fortunei,* and *C. excelsus.*

The generic name comes from two Greek words meaning rough and fruit, alluding to the rough covering on the fruits of some species. The specific name was selected in honor of Robert Fortune, who saw the palm on Zhoushan Island in eastern China and sent seeds of it to England.

Japanese Tea Garden (V-N2); Strybing (VI-N3)
990 Monterey Blvd
Evergreen/Moderate growth/25'-40'
Numerous, small, yellow flowers on hanging,
     branched inflorescence (early summer) /Blue
     black, berrylike fruits, 1/2" in diameter
Full sun/Water occasionally
Sunset Zone 4-24
Suitable as a street tree

Windmill palm was introduced to Europe by Philipp von Siebold, who sent seeds from Japan to Leyden, Holland, in 1830. Of those few seedlings, one was sent to Kew Gardens in England in 1836. It was not expected to be hardy outdoors and was placed in the palm house. In 1849, Robert Fortune sent a plant to England from Chekiang (now Zhejiang) Province, China, and perhaps on his recommendation, it was planted outside; in 1979, it was reported that the tree had survived every winter since its planting. In 1860, Fortune sent seeds from the Ningbo area of the province to Glendenning's Nursery in England, and from these the first general distribution of the palm was made when the nursery auctioned young plants.

The date of introduction of the windmill palm to the United States is not known. Today, it is cultivated in the southeastern states and on the Pacific Coast from California to Vancouver, British Columbia. It has been in Golden Gate Park at least since 1924. The Japanese Tea Garden has a small grove of well-established trees west of the main pond. A single tree can be seen in Strybing south of the Zellerbach Garden. Windmill palm is common as a street and park tree throughout much of California.

# 164

## Brisbane box
# *Tristania conferta*
## Myrtaceae

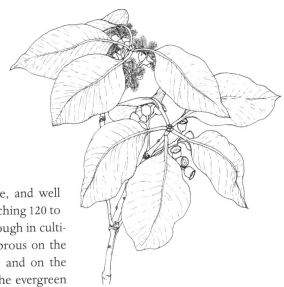

Brisbane box, a broad-leafed evergreen tree, is tall, attractive, and well shaped; old trees in their native habitat have been reported reaching 120 to 150 feet in height, with trunk diameters of 8 feet or more, though in cultivation trees are much smaller. The **bark** is persistent and fibrous on the lower trunk but smooth, reddish brown, and flaking above and on the branches. In Australia, the bark has been used for tanning. The evergreen **leaves,** usually 3 to 6 inches long, are alternate except at the tips of the branches, where they are crowded into indistinct whorls. The white **flowers** are about 1 inch across in groups of three to seven, distinctive but not particularly showy. The stamens, the most conspicuous feature of the flowers, are grouped together in feather-like bundles. The **fruits** are hard capsules, resembling those of some eucalypts, and contain numerous tiny seeds.

Because of its bark and the shape of the evergreen leaves, Brisbane box bears a superficial resemblance to California's madrone *(Arbutus menziesii)*. Old capsules or flowers will immediately identify Brisbane box, but without one or the other, the two trees can also be distinguished by their leaves. Leaves of Brisbane box are green on both surfaces and borne on petioles ¾ to 1½ inches long, whereas those of madrone are more or less glaucous on their lower surfaces and are borne on petioles ½ to 1 inch long.

Stanyan Meadows N of Alvord Lake (IV-S3)
1098 Valencia; Castro St between Duboce and
      14th Sts
Evergreen/Moderate growth/60'
White flowers with conspicuous stamens, 1"
      across, in groups of 3-7 (summer) /Woody
      fruit capsules
Full sun/Water infrequently
Sunset Zone 16-24
Suitable as a street tree

*Tristania* belongs to the myrtle family and is related to *Eucalyptus*. Its flowers and the whorled leaves at the ends of its branches, however, immediately distinguish Brisbane box from any eucalypt.

Brisbane box occurs naturally in Australia in the central part of the eastern coast near the city of Brisbane, usually in a forest mixture forming a transition between rain forest and moist eucalypt forest. In these forests, it is found with several transition-zone eucalypts and turpentine tree *(Syncarpia glomulifera)*. It is this habitat that gives Brisbane box its second common name, brush box, the name usually used in Australia for this tree. In Australia, brush designates dense and luxuriant vegetation.

*Tristania conferta* was first discovered in Australia on the coast of New South Wales by Robert Brown, a naturalist with the Flinders Expedition. After his return, he worked on his extensive collections and also those of other early collectors in Australia and, in 1810, published the first systematic account of the Australian flora. Among the many new species that he described from his own collections was *T. conferta*. He also named the genus *Tristania*, in honor of a contemporary French botanist, Jules Marie Claude, Marquis de Tristan. Some botanists have recently proposed, however, that *Tristania* be transferred to the genus *Lophostemon*.

Brisbane box was one of the earliest Australian trees to be imported into California. According to Butterfield (1964), William C Walker imported seed of Brisbane box in 1859 for his Golden Gate Nursery in San Francisco. Another early San Francisco nurseryman, F Lüdemann of the Pacific Nursery, listed the tree in his catalog of 1874. Brisbane box, an early introduction to Golden Gate Park, was growing there in 1893. Today, one can be seen north of Alvord Lake. As a street tree, it can be seen on Castro Street between Duboce and 14th streets, and on many streets in the South of Market area.

From San Francisco, Brisbane box was distributed to other California coastal cities including Berkeley, Santa Barbara, Pasadena, Los Angeles, Santa Monica and San Diego. Because it is adapted to frost-free Australian coastal areas, it cannot be used where winter frosts are severe.

*In the tree world may be found just as diverse groups, types, and characters as in the human family—the strong, the self-willed, the reliant and masterful, the weak and clinging, those who only have strength when gathered into crowds, the beautiful, the ugly, the useful, the worthless, the fighter, the slacker, and so on ad infinitum.*

ERNEST H WILSON, *Aristocrats of the Trees*

# 165

Water gum
## *Tristaniopsis laurina*

Myrtaceae

The genus *Tristaniopsis* occurs in eastern Australia and eastern Asia. Of its approximately thirty species, only water gum *(T. Iaurina)* is known in cultivation. The name *Tristaniopsis* is taken from the related genus *Tristania*, a genus in which it was once placed. It is still often known as *Tristania laurina*.

This species is remarkable for its wide distribution and for its variable habit, ranging from a shrub in dry parts of its range to a tall tree, sometimes reaches 70 feet, in moist forests. The scaly **bark** is eventually shed in irregular flakes. Young branchlets and flowers are covered in silky hairs. **Leaves** vary from 3 to 4 inches long, are lanceolate, dark green above and paler beneath, and narrow at the base to a short leaf stalk. The five-petaled, white **flowers** are about ¼ inch across in small clusters among the leaves, with calyx lobes shorter than the ⅛-inch petals. Grouped in five bundles are numerous stamens of unequal lengths, as long as or shorter than the petals. The pistil has a long style, and the **fruit** is a small capsule with winged seeds.

Water gum occurs in eastern Australia from Queensland south to Victoria. Its common name alludes to its frequent occurrence along watercourses. The second part of the scientific name, *laurina,* acknowledges a resemblance of its leaves to sweet bay *(Laurus nobilis)*.

Water gums are attractive ornamentals and are often used as street trees throughout coastal California because of their tolerance of dry conditions. The timber in Australia has been used for coaches and boats, for cabinetry, and for smaller objects such as tool handles.

Several trees of water gum in the Eastern Australian collection at Strybing are among the oldest trees in the garden, having been planted by the arboretum's first director, Eric Walther. Others in the arboretum can be found in the courtyard of the Helen Crocker Russell Library. Water gums are commonly planted as street trees in San Francisco.

Strybing (VI-N3)
E side Castro St between 16th St and Market St
Evergreen/Slow growth/30'
Small, yellow, fragrant flowers in profuse clusters (late spring-early summer) /Round fruit capsules
Full sun/Water infrequently
Sunset Zone 15-24
Suitable as a street tree

## The Elms
# *Ulmus*
Ulmaceae

Elms are among the few deciduous trees in Golden Gate Park. There are more than forty species of *Ulmus* distributed throughout the Northern Hemisphere. All are trees or shrubs, deciduous or nearly so. Their leaves are usually elliptical to ovate, with saw-toothed margins. **Leaves** of elms are always more or less lopsided, which provides an identification feature. At their bases, where the blades join the leaf stalks, their two halves are unequal, one half being somewhat longer than the other. Elms have small **flowers,** mostly in spring before or as the leaves appear, and these are followed by roundish, papery, winged **fruits** that are distributed by the wind.

Elms are subject to Dutch elm disease, so called because of its discovery in the Netherlands in 1921. It first appeared in the United States on the East Coast in 1930 and has destroyed native elms throughout the eastern half of the United States. It has been particularly destructive to the American elm. From the East Coast, Dutch elm disease has spread westward, and, although there are no native elms in the western states, introduced ornamental species have also been affected and killed by the disease.

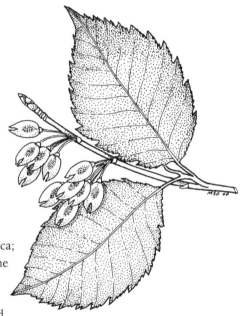

# 166
American elm
# *Ulmus americana*
Ulmaceae

American elm is the largest of the six species native to North America; many reach 65 to 100 feet, and a few have reached 120 feet. It is also the most widespread of the American elms, occurring in southeastern Canada and throughout the eastern half of the United States.

American elm is distinct among elms for its graceful vase-shaped **form.** A single trunk rises to 20 feet or more before dividing into several secondary trunks, each continuing to rise and arch outward. As the branches become thinner, they also begin to droop, so that the slender, outermost branches on a typical American elm will be pendant. The **bark** is deeply grooved, with ridges interweaving in an elongated, vertical pattern. **Leaves** are typically elmlike: strongly toothed, elliptical in outline, with unequal bases, and 3 to 6 inches long. The tiny **flowers** are clustered in the leaf axils in spring, as the leaves are appearing. They are followed quickly by masses of ¼-inch thin, disklike **fruits,** each a single seed centered in a round, flat, papery wing.

Because of Dutch elm disease, American elm is rarely planted today. A number remain in cities throughout the West, including in Berkeley and Sacramento, planted in the early part of the twentieth century. Golden Gate Park has a few American elms, best represented by several trees east

Meadow E of 25th Ave, between King Dr and
    Lincoln Way (II-J4); Historic Tree Lane, E of
    Pioneer Log Cabin (III-M2)
Around the edge of South Park
Deciduous/Fast growth/100'
Insignificant, red flowers before leaves (spring)/
    Roundish, green, papery winged seeds
Full sun/Water occasionally
Sunset Zone 1-11, 14-21
Suitable as a street tree

of the Pioneer Log Cabin at the intersection of Kennedy and Stow Lake drives; the tree nearest the stop sign is an American elm, as are two large specimens a few yards further east on a slope above the large meadow. Two other American elms can be seen on either side of the small meadow northeast of the intersection of Lincoln Way and 25th Avenue.

# 167

## Scotch elm
## *Ulmus glabra*
### Ulmaceae

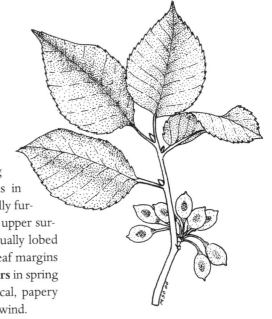

Scotch elm usually has a dome-shaped crown with spreading branches that become pendulous toward their tips. Old trees in England have attained considerable size. The **bark** is longitudinally furrowed. The oval **leaves,** somewhat rough to the touch on their upper surfaces and downy below, are usually 2 to 6 inches long and unequally lobed at their bases, the longer lobe partially hiding the short petiole. Leaf margins are irregularly and doubly toothed. Scotch elms have small **flowers** in spring before the leaves appear; these are followed by broadly elliptical, papery winged **fruits,** up to 1 inch long, which are blown about by the wind.

Music Concourse (III-O2); AIDS Memorial Grove
   (IV-P3); Alvord Lake (IV-S3)
Deciduous/Slow growth/120'
Insignificant, red flowers before leaves (spring)/
   Roundish, green, papery, winged seeds
Full sun/Water occasionally
Sunset Zone 1-11, 14-21
Suitable as a street tree

The Scotch elm, also called wych elm, is native to the British Isles where its wood, considered stronger and more easily worked than that of other elms, has been used for furniture and other purposes. In Great Britain as well as in the United States, it has often been planted because it thrives in cities despite their smoke, dust, smog, and poor soil. The word wych, as used in the British Isles, originally meant pliant or supple, but it has also been used for any elm tree.

There are many Scotch elms in Golden Gate Park, some quite large. A fine specimen can be seen on the north edge of Alvord Lake. There are several Scotch elms in the AIDS Memorial Grove in de Laveaga Dell. This species was often used for pollarding, which controls the size and shape of trees; several of the trees so treated in the Music Concourse were of this species, although the majority pollarded today are London plane trees *(Platanus* x *acerifolia).*

# 168

## Camperdown elm
# *Ulmus glabra* 'Camperdownii'
## Ulmaceae

A Camperdown elm in Golden Gate Park stands adjacent to the bald cypress *(Taxodium distichum)* at the western edge of the lawn west of McLaren Lodge; another is on the eastern edge of Alvord Lake. They are easily recognized by their extremely pendulous branches. **Leaves** are elm-like, with doubly toothed margins and unequal bases. Clusters of tiny **flowers** occur in early spring, as the leaves are appearing. **Fruits** are typical of elms: flat, disklike, papery, and about 1 inch in diameter.

In cultivation, Scotch elm *(Ulmus glabra)* has produced several variants; of these, two have a strongly weeping habit, and both originated in Scotland during the nineteenth century. The first to be found was named *Ulmus glabra* 'Horizontalis'. It was discovered in 1816 in a bed of seedlings of the Scotch elm in a nursery in Perth. A prostrate plant, it was propagated by top grafting on stock of English elm *(U. procera)* and eventually distributed in England and the rest of Europe.

A second form of Scotch elm was found about 1880 as a seedling growing near Dundee at Camperdown House, the estate of the earl of Camperdown, from which its cultivar name derives. Upon first seeing it, Richardson (1911) noted that the seedling was of "considerable age, prostrate in habit, creeping along the ground amongst other elms." This seedling was also propagated by top grafting. Both cultivars, as grafted trees, make handsome ornamentals when they are well grown and have attained considerable size and age, although 'Camperdownii' is usually considered choicer of the two. Bean (1980) describes 'Camperdownii' as "pendulously branched, a small arborlike tree, with a rounded crown, sinuously branched," and 'Horizontalis' as a "flat-topped tree with horizontal or low-arching branches and pendulous branchlets."

The date of introduction of the Camperdown elm into Golden Gate park is not known, but it was sometime prior to 1924 when it was included in the *Annual Report of the Park Commissioners.* The tree had been introduced into California sometime before 1884—the year in which RD Fox listed it in his catalog for the Santa Clara Valley Nursery in San Jose.

Other Camperdown elms in northern California can be seen on the UC Berkeley campus; on the campus of Mills College, Oakland; at Filoli Center, Woodside; and at Dunsmuir House and Gardens, Oakland. It occasionally appears in parks and estate gardens throughout the Pacific Northwest.

Lawn area W of McLaren Lodge (IV-S2); Alvord Lake (IV-S3)
Deciduous/Slow growth/10'-20'
Insignificant, red flowers before leaves (spring)/ Roundish, green, papery, winged seeds
Full sun/Water occasionally
Sunset Zone 1-11, 14-21

# 169

## California bay
## *Umbellularia californica*

### Lauraceae

California bay is also called California laurel, California olive, pepperwood, Pacific laurel, bay tree, and Oregon myrtle. The only species within its genus, it is found from southwestern Oregon through the length of coastal California to northern Baja California and in the Sierra Nevada. It varies from a low, wind-sculpted shrub on coastal bluffs to a tall, often multi-trunked tree in moist canyons, where it may associate with oaks, California buckeyes *(Aesculus californica),* and big-leaf maples *(Acer macrophyllum).*

The **leaves** of California bay vary from 1 to 5 inches long and from 1 to 3 inches wide; they tend to be widest in the lower third and are lanceolate, sometimes broadly so. The petioles are nearly flat to slightly grooved. Like its distant relative sweet bay *(Laurus nobilis),* California bay gives off an aroma when its leaves are crushed. The leaves, however, are decidedly more pungent than those of sweet bay; they can be used as seasoning, but must be used sparingly because of their greater pungency. Crushed lightly and inhaled, the effect is refreshing, but too much can cause sneezing and headaches in some people. (This has produced yet another common name: headache tree.) The leaves, wood, and fruit contain oils, the most abundant of which is umbellulone, an essential oil that may irritate the skin.

In mid to late winter, the yellow **flowers** are produced in small clusters, abundant enough to be noticeable from a distance when trees are in full bloom; unlike those of sweet bay, California bay's flowers have both stamens and pistils in the same flower. The **fruits** of the California bay, which are about the size and shape of large olives, have kernels or nuts surrounded by thin, fleshy coverings. The acrid kernels were used as food and seasoning by Native Americans, but only after thorough parching or roasting. They may have been used as either a condiment or stimulant. They contain starch, which, along with the oil, has some food value.

The wood of California bay is hard, heavy, and attractively grained. It has been used for making furniture. In southwestern Oregon, the tree is called Oregon myrtle, and its wood is used for making small objects such as bowls, trays, and decorative boxes. These are sold as souvenirs in roadside shops where visitors are told, erroneously, that Oregon myrtle grows naturally only in Oregon and in the Holy Land.

*Umbellularia californica* was first discovered by Archibald Menzies in 1792, probably at Monterey. David Douglas found it again in southwestern Oregon in 1826 and introduced it into England. It has been cultivated in Golden Gate Park since the late 1890s. California bay is in Strybing Arboretum and on the western slopes of the AIDS Memorial Grove in de Laveaga Dell. A magnificent freestanding tree is at the southern edge of the large meadow east of Pioneer Log Cabin. California bay is also grown in many other Pacific Coast cities from Santa Barbara to Seattle.

AIDS Memorial Grove (IV-P3); Meadow E of
   Pioneer Log Cabin (III-M2); Strybing (VI-N4)
McAllister St at Willard North
Evergreen/Fast growth/80'
Yellow flowers in small clusters (Feb) /Fleshy,
   green, olivelike fruits holding single nuts
Full sun to part shade/Needs no watering, once
   established
Sunset Zone 4-10, 12-24

# 170

New Zealand chaste tree
## *Vitex lucens*

Verbenaceae

New Zealand chaste tree is an attractive ornamental, usually 20 to 30 feet tall, but in its native habitat it may reach 60 feet. It has a broadly spreading crown, and large trees have massive trunks, 3 to 5 feet in diameter. The opposite **leaves** are palmately divided into three, four, or five leaflets, each 2 to 5 inches long, with one or two smaller than the others. They are dark green and glossy above, somewhat leathery, and with margins that are entire and slightly wavy. On the lower leaf surface, at the junction of the main vein with the secondary veins, are very small pits or domatia, similar in appearance to those seen on the leaves of *Citronella mucronata;* these small pits may be inhabited by tiny mites. The pink to red **flowers** are produced in clusters, as many as ten to fifteen in each cluster. Petals are united to form a swollen, two-lipped, tubular corolla about 1 inch long. The fleshy, nearly round **fruits** are almost 1 inch in diameter and tend to be clustered inconspicuously among the leaves.

Large trees of this species produce a valuable hardwood, dark brown, dense, and of great strength. The wood is difficult to work, but because of its durability and resistance to decay, it has been used in New Zealand for railroad ties, gate and fence posts, house blocks, furniture, and cabinetwork. Because of the tree's ornamental appearance and fairly rapid growth on good soils, it is planted in gardens in New Zealand, especially on North Island.

*Vitex lucens* belongs to the verbena family. It is not as well known as its deciduous shrubby relative, the chaste tree *(V. agnus-castus)* of the Mediterranean. The name of the genus, *Vitex,* was taken from the Latin name of the Mediterranean shrub.

New Zealand chaste tree is found in New Zealand only on North Island, mostly in the northern half from along the coast to the interior at elevations up to 2,500 feet. Banks and Solander in 1769 found it on the eastern coast, a short distance north of where they had found New Zealand laurel *(Corynocarpus laevigatus).*

New Zealand chaste tree was first listed for Golden Gate Park in the 1924 *Annual Report of the Park Commissioners,* and undoubtedly came to the park following the 1915 Panama–Pacific International Exposition. One tree is on the north side of Mothers Meadow; a second can be seen on King Drive at the southwest corner of the park's nursery. Other trees are in Strybing's New Zealand collection. Trees may also be seen in Santa Barbara and Santa Monica.

N side of Mothers Meadow (IV-R3); King Dr, W of
    Park Nursery gate (IV-P4); Strybing (VI-N3)
Dolores Park, on Church St at end of
    Collingwood St
Evergreen/Moderate growth/20'-30'
Large clusters, pink to red, 2-lipped, tubullar
    flowers, 1" long (late spring) /Roundish,
    bright red fruits
Full sun/Water occasionally
Sunset Zone 16, 17, 22-24

# Appendices

# Appendix A: Maps

## How to Use the Maps

The maps on the next several pages are numbered I through VII; check the Map Index below to see their relationship to one another. Numbers in bold on the maps correspond to the tree numbers given at the top of each entry in the field guide portion of this book (pages 23–210). Map coordinates (e.g. VI-N3) are shown in parentheses in the sidebar data for each tree; the Roman numeral denotes the map (I–VII) and the alphanumeric designation locates the tree on its map.

## Map Index

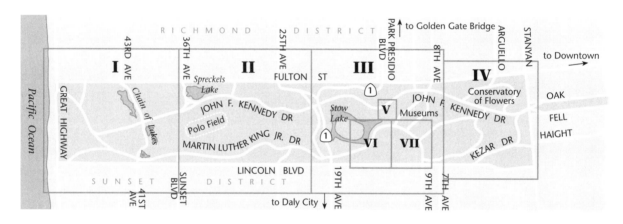

## Map Legend

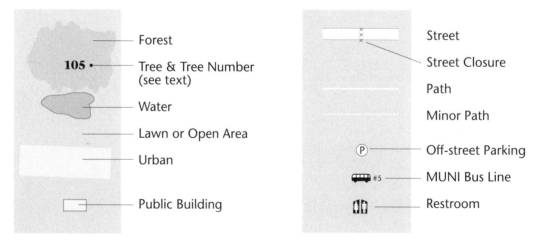

| | |
|---|---|
| Forest | Street |
| **105** • Tree & Tree Number (see text) | Street Closure |
| Water | Path |
| Lawn or Open Area | Minor Path |
| Urban | ⓟ Off-street Parking |
| | #5 MUNI Bus Line |
| Public Building | Restroom |

# Map I: From Ocean Beach to 37th Ave

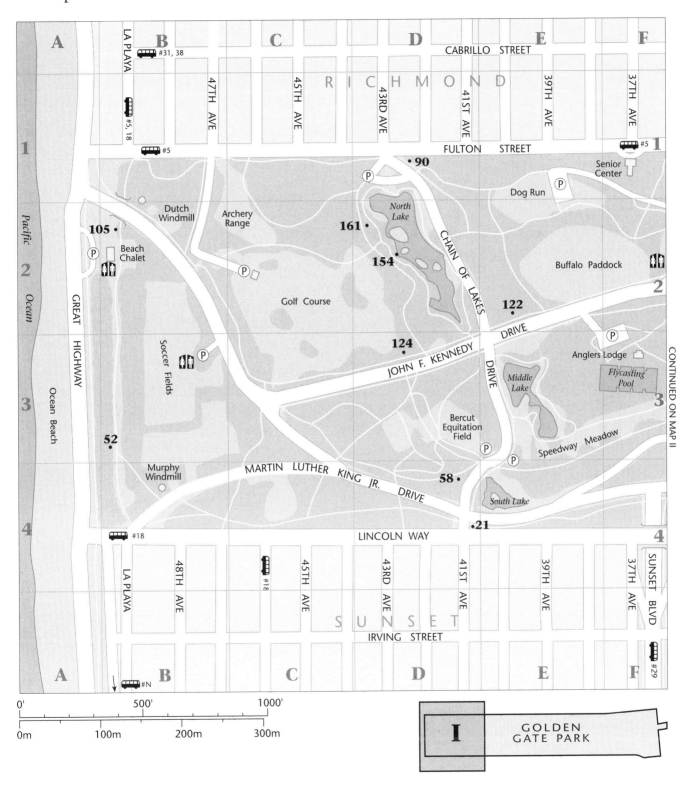

## Map II: From 36th Ave to 21st Ave

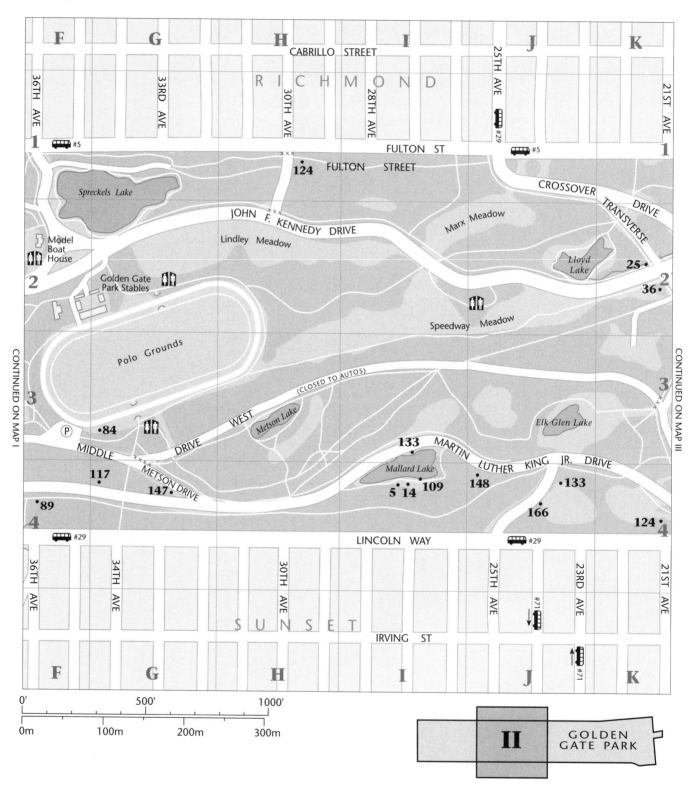

# Map III: From 20th Ave to 6th Ave

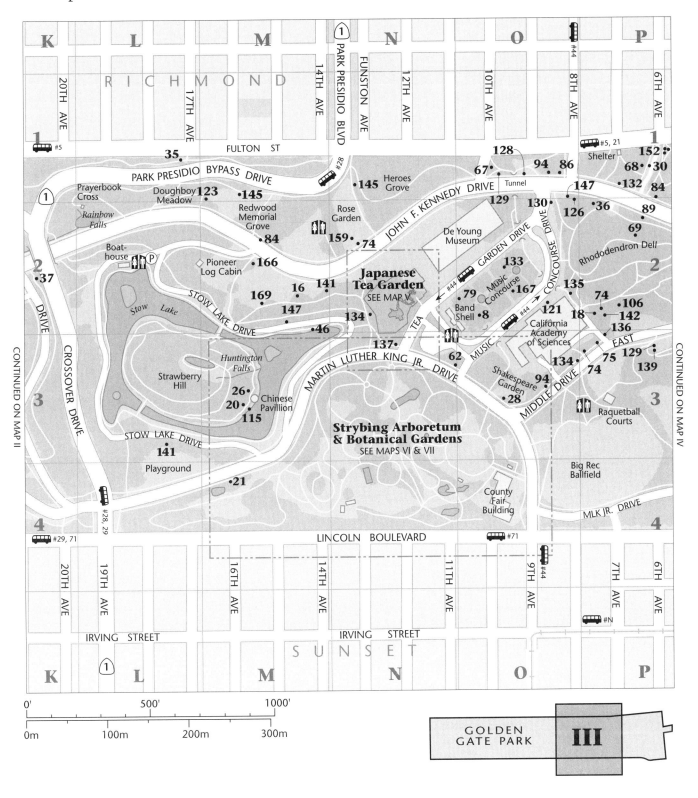

# Map IV: From 5th Ave to Stanyan St

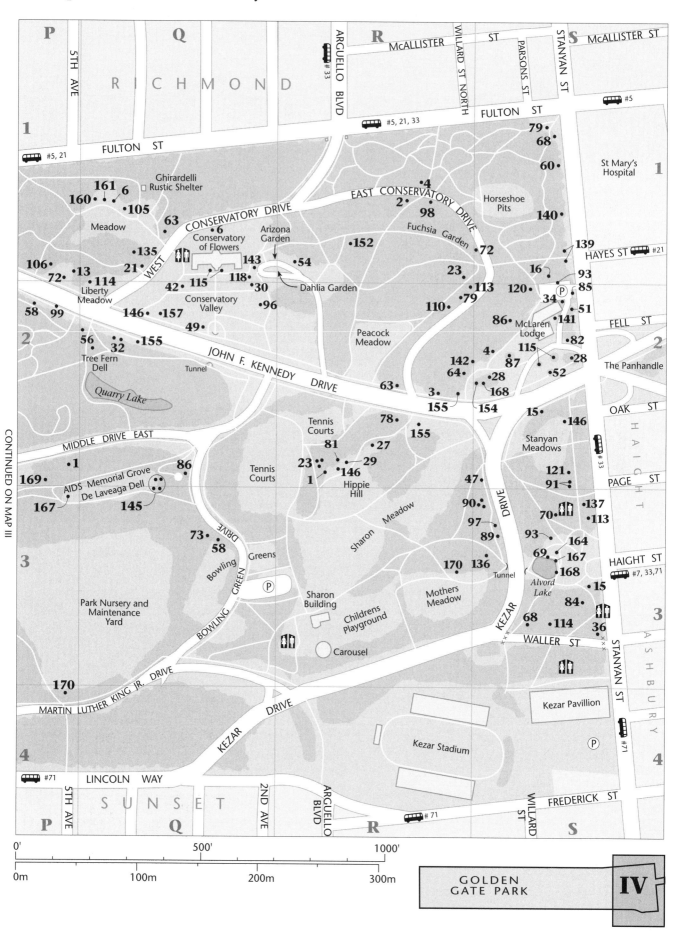

# Map V: The Japanese Tea Garden

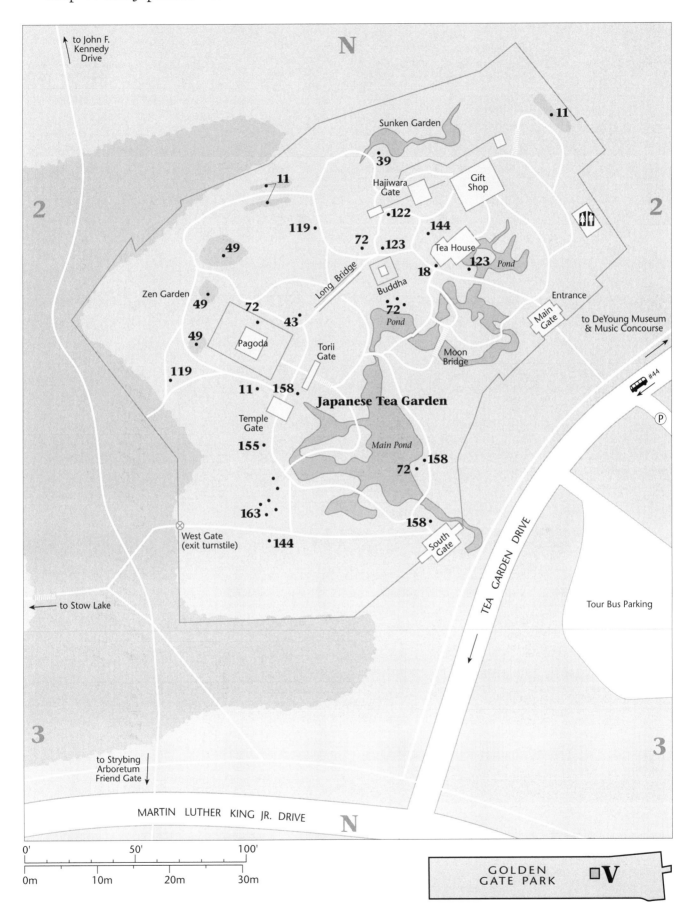

to John F. Kennedy Drive

N

Sunken Garden

• 11

• 39

Hajiwara Gate

Gift Shop

2

2

• 11

• 122

119 •

144

72

• 123

Tea House

• 123

Pond

49

18

Entrance

Zen Garden

49

Buddha

72

Main Gate

to DeYoung Museum & Music Concourse

72

43

Pond

Long Bridge

Moon Bridge

#44

Pagoda

49

Torii Gate

119

Japanese Tea Garden

P

11

158

Temple Gate

155 •

Main Pond

158

72

163

158

West Gate (exit turnstile)

144

South Gate

TEA GARDEN DRIVE

to Stow Lake

Tour Bus Parking

3

3

to Strybing Arboretum Friend Gate

MARTIN LUTHER KING JR. DRIVE

N

0'    50'    100'

0m  10m  20m  30m

GOLDEN GATE PARK   □V

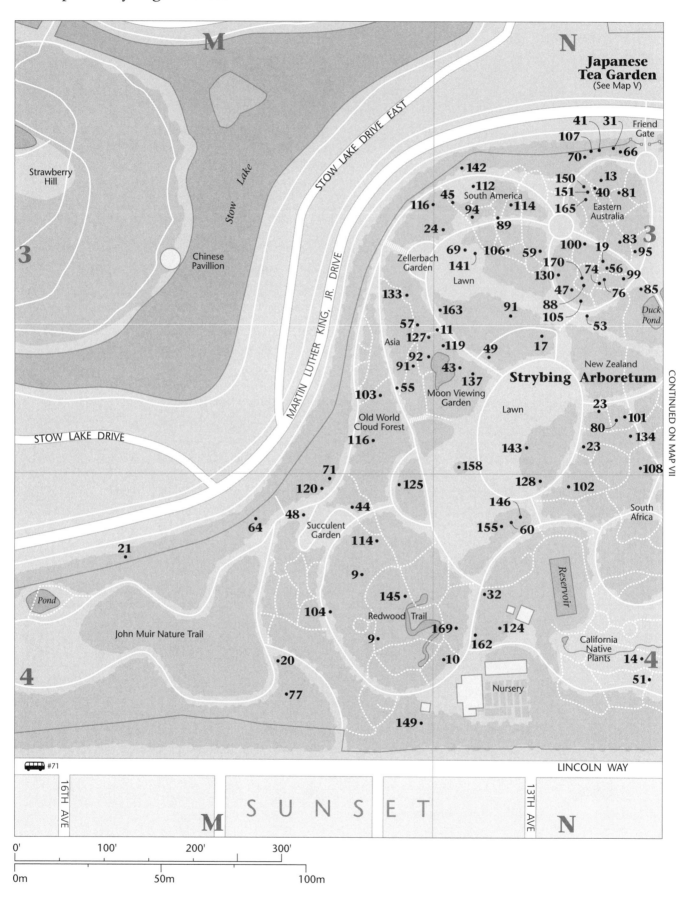

M

N

**Japanese
Tea Garden**
(See Map V)

41   31   Friend
107        Gate
70        66

•142
•112
South America
45        •13
116   94   •114   150   •40   •81
24   89   151   165   Eastern
        Australia

69   106   59   100   19   •83
Zellerbach   141   170   •95
Garden   Lawn   130   74   56   99
        47   76   85
133        88
•163   91   105   53

57   •11   Duck
Asia   127   •119   49   17   Pond
92   43   Strybing   Arboretum
91   137   New Zealand
103   •55   Lawn   23
Moon Viewing   80   •101
Old World   Garden   •23   •134
Cloud Forest   143   •108
116   •158   South
71   128   102   Africa
120   125   146
48   •44   Succulent   155   60
64   Garden
21   114   Reservoir
9   California
104   145   32   Native
9   Redwood   Trail   124   Plants   14   •4
•20   169   162   51
•77   •10
149   Nursery

Strawberry
Hill

Stow Lake

Chinese
Pavillion

3

STOW LAKE DRIVE EAST

MARTIN LUTHER KING, JR. DRIVE

STOW LAKE DRIVE

Pond

John Muir Nature Trail

4

🚌 #71

LINCOLN WAY

16TH AVE

M   S U N S E T   N

13TH AVE

CONTINUED ON MAP VII

3

4

0'      100'      200'      300'

0m      50m      100m

# Map VII: Strybing Arboretum

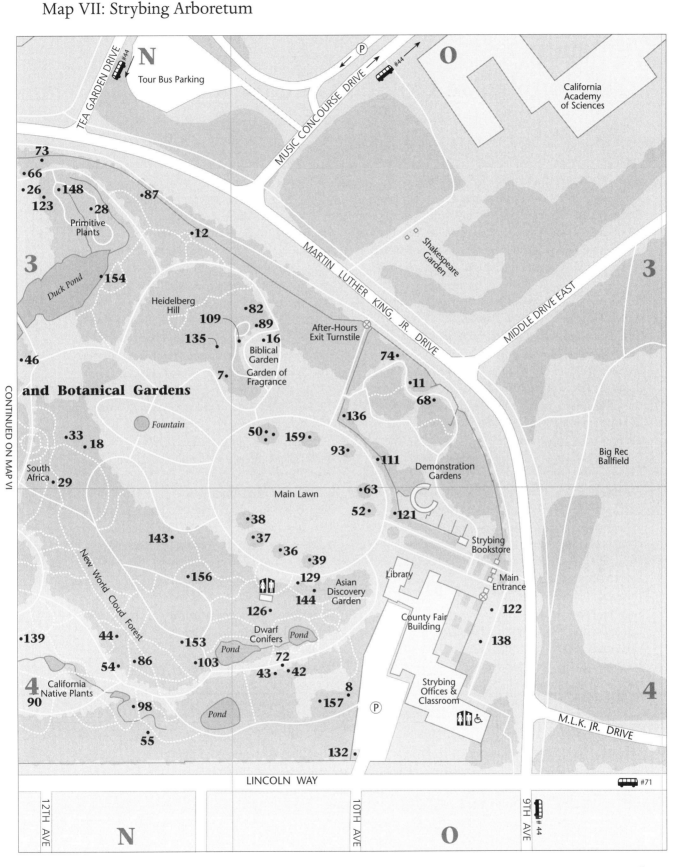

**N**

Tour Bus Parking

TEA GARDEN DRIVE

MUSIC CONCOURSE DRIVE

**O**

California Academy of Sciences

73
•66
•26 •148
123
•28
Primitive Plants
•87
•12

**3**

Duck Pond
•154

Heidelberg Hill

MARTIN LUTHER KING, JR. DRIVE

Shakespeare Garden

MIDDLE DRIVE EAST

**3**

•82
109
•89
135
•16
7•
Biblical Garden
Garden of Fragrance
After-Hours Exit Turnstile

74•
•11
68•
•136

•46

**and Botanical Gardens**

Fountain

•33 •18
South Africa •29

50•• •159
93•
•111
•63
52•
•121

Main Lawn

Demonstration Gardens

Big Rec Ballfield

Strybing Bookstore

Library

Main Entrance

•122

•38
•37
•36
•39
143•
•156
•129
144
126•
Asian Discovery Garden

County Fair Building

•138

New World Cloud Forest

•139
44•
•153
54• •86 •103
43• 72 •42
8•
•157
(P)

Dwarf Conifers
Pond
Pond
Pond

Strybing Offices & Classroom

CONTINUED ON MAP VI

**4**
California Native Plants
90
•98
55•
132•

**4**

M.L.K. JR. DRIVE

LINCOLN WAY

12TH AVE
**N**
10TH AVE
**O**
9TH AVE
#44

#71

GOLDEN GATE PARK **VI** **VII**

# Appendix B:
# Tree Families in Golden Gate Park

Trees and other plants are grouped into families that share certain characteristics. Family names usually end in –aceae. Following each of the families listed below are the tree genera (printed in *italics*) that will be found in the field guide portion of this book (pages 23–210).

Aceraceae (maple family): *Acer, Dipteronia*

Agavaceae (agave family): *Cordyline*

Araucariaceae (araucaria family): *Agathis, Araucaria*

Arecaceae: see Palmae

Asteraceae (daisy family): *Dahlia, Montanoa, Olearia*

Buxaceae (boxwood family): *Buxus*

Casuarinaceae (she-oak family): *Casuarina*

Celastraceae (bittersweet family): *Maytenus*

Compositae: see Asteraceae

Cornaceae (dogwood family): *Davidia, Griselinia*

Corynocarpaceae (corynocarpus family): *Corynocarpus*

Cunoniaceae (cunonia family): *Ceratopetalum*

Cupressaceae (cypress family): *Calocedrus, Chamaecyparis,* x *Cupressocyparis, Thuja, Thujopsis*

Cyatheaceae (a tree fern family): *Sphaeropteris*

Dicksoniaceae (a tree fern family): *Dicksonia*

Ericaceae (heather family): *Erica*

Fabaceae: see Leguminosae

Fagaceae (beech family): *Fagus, Quercus*

Flacourtiaceae (flacourtia family): *Olmediella*

Ginkgoaceae (ginkgo family): *Ginkgo*

Grossulariaceae: *Escallonia*

Hamamelidaceae (witch hazel family): *Liquidambar*

Hippocastanaceae (horse chestnut family): *Aesculus*

Icacinaceae (icacina family): *Citronella*

Juglandaceae (walnut family): *Juglans*

Lauraceae (laurel family): *Laurus, Litsea, Persea, Umbellularia*

Leguminosae (pea family): *Acacia*

Magnoliaceae (magnolia family): *Liriodendron, Magnolia, Michelia, Talauma*

Malvaceae (mallow family): *Lagunaria*

Monimiaceae (monimia family): *Hedycarya, Peumus*

Moraceae (mulberry family): *Ficus*

Myoporaceae (myoporum family): *Myoporum*

Myrsinaceae (myrsine family): *Myrsine*

Myrtaceae (myrtle family): *Acca, Acmena, Agonis, Callistemon, Eucalyptus, Leptospermum, Luma, Melaleuca, Metrosideros, Myrrhinium, Myrtus, Syncarpia, Tristania, Tristaniopsis*

Oleaceae (olive family): *Fraxinus, Olea*

Palmae (palm family): *Jubaea, Phoenix, Trachycarpus*

Pinaceae (pine family): *Cedrus, Pinus*

Pittosporaceae (pittosporum family): *Pittosporum*

Platanaceae (plane tree family): *Platanus*

Podocarpaceae (podocarp family): *Afrocarpus, Dacrydium, Podocarpus*

Proteaceae (protea family): *Banksia, Grevillea, Knightia, Stenocarpus*

Rhamnaceae (buckthorn family): *Rhamnus*

Rosaceae (rose family): *Crataegus, Heteromeles, Lyonothamnus, Photinia, Prunus, Pyrus, Quillaja*

Rutaceae (citrus family): *Calodendrum*

Sapindaceae (soapberry family): *Alectryon, Dodonaea*

Simaroubaceae (quassia family): *Ailanthus*

Sterculiaceae (sterculia family): *Chiranthodendron*

Taxaceae (yew family): *Taxus, Torreya*

Taxodiaceae (redwood family): *Cryptomeria, Metasequoia, Sciadopitys, Sequoia, Sequoiadendron, Taxodium*

Tiliaceae (linden family): *Sparmannia, Tilia*

Ulmaceae (elm family): *Ulmus*

Verbenaceae (vervain family): *Vitex*

Winteraceae (winter's bark family): *Drimys*

# Appendix C:
# List of Common Names

If you know only the common name of a tree (usually in English), use that name here to find the corresponding botanical name (in Latin and printed in *italics*). The trees in this book are organized alphabetically according to their botanical names. This List of Common Names includes only those trees discussed in this book.

acacia, Bailey, *Acacia baileyana*
acacia, black, *Acacia melanoxylon*
acacia, blackwood, *Acacia melanoxylon*
acacia, everblooming, *Acacia retinodes*
acacia, star acacia, *Acacia verticillata*
akiraho, *Olearia paniculata*
arborvitae, giant, *Thuja plicata*
ash, Shamel, *Fraxinus uhdei*
banksia, coast, *Banksia integrifolia*
banksia, tree, *Banksia integrifolia*
basswood, European, *Tilia* x *europaea*
bay tree, *Umbellularia californica*
bay, bull, *Magnolia grandiflora*
bay, California, *Umbellularia californica*
bay, Madeira, *Persea indica*
bay, sweet, *Laurus nobilis*
beech, European, *Fagus sylvatica*
beefwood, *Casuarina*
beefwood, *Stenocarpus salignus*
big tree, *Sequoiadendron giganteum*
blackwood, *Acacia melanoxylon*
boldo, *Peumus boldus*
bottlebrush, bracelet, *Melaleuca armillaris*
bottlebrush, weeping, *Callistemon viminalis*
box, *Buxus sempervirens*
box, Brisbane, *Tristania conferta*
box, brush, *Tristania conferta*
box, Victorian, *Pittosporum undulatum*
boxwood, English, *Buxus sempervirens*
buckeye, California, *Aesculus californica*
buckeye, red, *Aesculus pavia*
buckthorn, Italian, *Rhamnus alaternus*
bull bay, *Magnolia grandiflora*
bunya-bunya, *Araucaria bidwillii*
cabbage tree, New Zealand, *Cordyline australis*

California buckeye, *Aesculus californica*
California holly, *Heteromeles arbutifolia*
Cape chestnut, *Calodendrum capense*
cedar of Lebanon, *Cedrus libani* ssp. *libani*
cedar, Atlas, *Cedrus libani* ssp. *atlantica*
cedar, canoe, *Thuja plicata*
cedar, Cyprian, *Cedrus libani* ssp. *brevifolia*
cedar, deodar, *Cedrus deodara*
cedar, giant, *Thuja plicata*
cedar, Hiba, *Thujopsis dolabrata*
cedar, Himalayan, *Cedrus deodara*
cedar, incense, *Calocedrus decurrens*
cedar, North African, *Cedrus libani* ssp. *atlantica*
cedar, Pacific red, *Thuja plicata*
cedar, red, *Thuja plicata*
cedar, stinking, *Torreya californica*
cedar, western red, *Thuja plicata*
chaste tree, New Zealand, *Vitex lucens*
cherry, Akebono, *Prunus* x *yedoensis* 'Akebono'
cherry, flowering, *Prunus* x *yedoensis*
cherry, Tokyo, *Prunus* x *yedoensis*
cherry, Yoshino, *Prunus* x *yedoensis*
chestnut, Cape, *Calodendrum capense*
chestnut, horse, *Aesculus hippocastanum*
chestnut, red horse, *Aesculus* x *carnea*
Christmas berry, *Heteromeles arbutifolia*
Christmas bush, New South Wales, *Ceratopetalum gummiferum*
Christmas tree, Kermadec, *Metrosideros kermadecensis*
Christmas tree, New Zealand, *Metrosideros excelsa*
coachwood, *Ceratopetalum apetalum*
cow-itch tree, *Lagunaria patersonii*
cypress, bald, *Taxodium distichum*
cypress, false, *Chamaecyparis*
cypress, Guadalupe, *Cupressus guadalupensis*
cypress, hinoki, *Chamaecyparis obtusa*
cypress, Lawson, *Chamaecyparis lawsoniana*
cypress, Leyland, x *Cupressocyparis leylandii*
cypress. Monterey cypress, *Cupressus macrocarpa*
cypress, Port Orford, *Chamaecyparis lawsoniana*
cypress, swamp, *Taxodium distichum*
dahlia, tree, *Dahlia imperialis*
daisy, tree, *Montanoa grandiflora*
date palm, Canary Island, *Phoenix canariensis*

deodar, *Cedrus deodara*
devil's hand, *Chiranthodendron pentadactylon*
dipteronia, *Dipteronia sinensis*
dove tree, *Davidia involucrata*
elm, American, *Ulmus americana*
elm, Camperdown, *Ulmus glabra* 'Camperdownii'
elm, Scotch, *Ulmus glabra*
elm, wych, *Ulmus glabra*
escallonia, *Escallonia revoluta*
eucalypt, *Eucalyptus*
fern pine, African, *Afrocarpus gracilior*
fern, Australian tree, *Sphaeropteris cooperi*
fern, black tree, *Sphaeropteris medullaris*
fern, Tasmanian tree, *Dicksonia antarctica*
fig, Moreton Bay, *Ficus macrophylla*
firewheel tree, *Stenocarpus sinuatus*
ginkgo, *Ginkgo biloba*
guava, pineapple, *Acca sellowiana*
gum, blue, *Eucalyptus globulus*
gum, ghost, *Eucalyptus pauciflora*
gum, manna, *Eucalyptus viminalis*
gum, Murray red, *Eucalyptus camaldulensis*
gum, red, *Eucalyptus camaldulensis*
gum, red-flowering, *Eucalyptus ficifolia*
gum, river red, *Eucalyptus camaldulensis*
gum, snow, *Eucalyptus pauciflora*
gum, sweet, *Liquidambar styraciflua*
gum, water, *Tristaniopsis laurina*
hand-flower tree, *Chiranthodendron pentadactylon*
handkerchief tree, *Davidia involucrata*
hands, tree of little, *Chiranthodendron pentadactylon*
hawthorn, Mexican, *Crataegus pubescens*
headache tree, *Umbellularia californica*
heath, tree, *Erica arborea*
Hiba, *Thujopsis dolabrata*
hibiscus, Norfolk Island, *Lagunaria patersonii*
hinoki, *Chamaecyparis obtusa*
holly, California, *Heteromeles arbutifolia*
holly, Costa Rican, *Olmediella betschleriana*
holly, Guatemala, *Olmediella betschleriana*
holly, Puerto Rican, *Olmediella betschleriana*
hopseed bush, *Dodonaea viscosa*
horse chestnut, *Aesculus hippocastanum*
horse chestnut, red, *Aesculus x carnea*
horsetail tree, *Casuarina*
incense cedar, *Calocedrus decurrens*
ironwood, *Eucalyptus, Lyonothamnus, Metrosideros*
ironwood, fernleaf Catalina, *Lyonothamnus floribundus*
    ssp. *aspleniifolius*
kapuka, *Griselinia littoralis*
karo, *Pittosporum crassifolium*
kauri, New Zealand, *Agathis australis*
kauri, Queensland, *Agathis robusta*
laurel, bay, *Laurus nobilis*

laurel, California, *Umbellularia californica*
laurel, cherry, *Prunus laurocerasus*
laurel, English, *Prunus laurocerasus*
laurel, Mediterranean, *Laurus nobilis*
laurel, New Zealand, *Corynocarpus laevigatus*
laurel, Pacific, *Umbellularia californica*
laurel, Portugal, *Prunus lusitanica*
lemonwood, *Pittosporum eugenioides*
lilly pilly, *Acmena smithii*
lime, *Tilia* x *europaea*
linden, African, *Sparmannia africana*
linden, European, *Tilia* x *europaea*
linden, European white, *Tilia tomentosa*
linden, little-leaf, *Tilia cordata*
linden, silver, *Tilia tomentosa*
litsea, *Litsea calicaris*
London plane tree, *Platanus* x *acerifolia*
magnolia, Campbell's, *Magnolia campbellii*
magnolia, Delavay's, *Magnolia delavayi*
magnolia, evergreen, *Magnolia grandiflora*
magnolia, southern, *Magnolia grandiflora*
mahogany, swamp, *Eucalyptus robusta*
maidenhair tree, *Ginkgo biloba*
maiten, *Maytenus boaria*
mapau, *Myrsine australis*
maple, big-leaf, *Acer macrophyllum*
maple, English, *Acer campestre*
maple, five-leaf, *Acer pentaphyllum*
maple, hedge, *Acer campestre*
maple, Japanese, *Acer palmatum*
maple, vine, *Acer circinatum*
mayten, *Maytenus boaria*
messmate stringybark, *Eucalyptus obliqua*
messmate, swamp, *Eucalyptus robusta*
michelia, *Michelia doltsopa*
mimosa, *Acacia*
monkey puzzle tree, *Araucaria araucana*
monkey's hand, *Chiranthodendron pentadactylon*
myrrhinium, *Myrrhinium atropurpureum*
myrsine, *Myrsine australis, M. salicina*
myrtle, Chilean, *Luma apiculata*
myrtle, common, *Myrtus communis*
myrtle, Oregon, *Umbellularia californica*
myrtle, willow, *Agonis flexuosa*
naranjillo, *Citronella mucronata*
ngaio, *Myoporum laetum*
nutmeg, California, *Torreya californica*
oak, coast live, *Quercus agrifolia*
oak, English oak, *Quercus robur*
oak, holly oak, *Quercus ilex*
oak, holm oak, *Quercus ilex*
oak, pedunculate oak, *Quercus robur*
oak, silk, *Grevillea robusta*
olive, *Olea europaea*

olive, California, *Umbellularia californica*
palm, Canary Island date, *Phoenix canariensis*
palm, Chilean wine, *Jubaea chilensis*
palm, Chinese windmill, *Trachycarpus fortunei*
palm, Chusan, *Trachycarpus fortunei*
palm, Fortune's, *Trachycarpus fortunei*
palm, hemp, *Trachycarpus fortunei*
palm, Japanese windmill, *Trachycarpus fortunei*
palm, windmill, *Trachycarpus fortunei*
paperbark, flaxleaf, *Melaleuca linariifolia*
paperbark, swamp, *Melaleuca ericifolia*
parana pine, *Araucaria angustifolia*
pear, evergreen, *Pyrus kawakamii*
peppermint tree, *Agonis flexuosa*
pepperwood, *Umbellularia californica*
photinia, hybrid, *Photinia x fraseri*
pigeonwood, *Hedycarya arborea*
pine, African fern, *Afrocarpus gracilior*
pine, Australian, *Casuarina*
pine, Bhutan, *Pinus wallichiana*
pine, blue, *Pinus wallichiana*
pine, Brazilian, *Araucaria angustifolia*
pine, bunya, *Araucaria bidwillii*
pine, Chile, *Araucaria araucana*
pine, fern, *Afrocarpus gracilior*
pine, Himalayan, *Pinus wallichiana*
pine, Himalayan white, *Pinus wallichiana*
pine, hoop, *Araucaria cunninghamii*
pine, Italian stone, *Pinus pinea*
pine, Japanese black, *Pinus thunbergii*
pine, Japanese red, *Pinus densiflora*
pine, Japanese umbrella, *Sciadopitys verticillata*
pine, Monterey, *Pinus radiata*
pine, Montezuma, *Pinus montezumae*
pine, Norfolk Island, *Araucaria heterophylla*
pine, paraná, *Araucaria angustifolia*
pine, Torrey, *Pinus torreyana*
pine, umbrella, *Sciadopitys verticillata*
pineapple guava, *Acca sellowiana*
pittosporum, Japanese, *Pittosporum tobira*
plane tree, London, *Platanus x acerifolia*
poplar, yellow, *Liriodendron tulipifera*
poplar, tulip, *Liriodendron tulipifera*
prickly Moses, *Acacia verticillata*
primrose tree, *Lagunaria patersonii*
puka, *Griselinia lucida*
pyramid tree, Queensland, *Lagunaria patersonii*
rata, northern, *Metrosideros robusta*
rata, southern, *Metrosideros umbellata*
redwood, coast, *Sequoia sempervirens*
redwood, dawn, *Metasequoia glyptostroboides*
redwood, Japanese, *Cryptomeria japonica*
redwood, Sierra, *Sequoiadendron giganteum*
rewa-rewa, *Knightia excelsa*

rimu, *Dacrydium cupressinum*
sequoia, giant, *Sequoiadendron giganteum*
Shamel ash, *Fraxinus uhdei*
she-oak, drooping, *Casuarina verticillata*
she-oak, river, *Casuarina cunninghamiana*
shingle-wood, *Thuja plicata*
silk oak, *Grevillea robusta*
soapbark tree, *Quillaja saponaria*
stink tree, *Ailanthus altissima*
stink wood, *Ailanthus altissima*
storax, American, *Liquidambar styraciflua*
stringybark, messmate, *Eucalyptus obliqua*
sugar plum tree, *Lagunaria patersonii*
swamp mahogany, *Eucalyptus robusta*
sweet bay, *Laurus nobilis*
sweet gum, *Liquidambar styraciflua*
talauma, *Talauma hodgsonii*
tarata, *Pittosporum eugenioides*
tawhiwhi, *Pittosporum tenuifolium*
tea tree, Australian, *Leptospermum laevigatum*
tea tree, New Zealand, *Leptospermum scoparium*
tea tree, white, *Leptospermum ericoides*
titoki, *Alectryon excelsus*
tobira, *Pittosporum tobira*
toro, *Myrsine salicina*
torreya, California, *Torreya californica*
totara, *Podocarpus totara*
toyon, *Heteromeles arbutifolia*
tree fern, Australian, *Sphaeropteris cooperi*
tree fern, black, *Sphaeropteris medullaris*
tree fern, Tasmanian, *Dicksonia antarctica*
tree of heaven, *Ailanthus altissima*
tulip tree, *Liriodendron tulipifera*
turpentine tree, *Syncarpia glomulifera*
umbrella pine, Japanese, *Sciadopitys verticillata*
walnut, black, *Juglans nigra*
wattle, Cootamundra, *Acacia baileyana*
wattle, silver, *Acacia dealbata*
wattle, Sydney golden, *Acacia longifolia*
whitewood, *Liriodendron tulipifera*, *Tilia x europaea*
willow myrtle, *Agonis flexuosa*
winter's bark, *Drimys winteri*
yew, English, *Taxus baccata*
yew, Japanese, *Taxus cuspidata*
yew, stinking, *Torreya californica*

# Appendix D:
# People and Places

*Trees of Golden Gate Park* is as much the story of a great urban park as it is a history of plant exploration in the sixteenth through twentieth centuries. Extracted from the original articles in *Pacific Horticulture* are these short descriptions of some of the botanists, horticulturists, plant explorers, and nursery people, mentioned in the articles, who worked to bring trees from their wild homes to our parks and gardens on the West Coast of North America. Consult the trees listed after each entry for more of the story of these people and their role in the history of Golden Gate Park's trees.

**Abraham, Charles Christian** (1851–1929)—born in Germany, worked for F Lüdemann in 1878; opened Western Nursery on Greenwich Street in San Francisco in 1881 (closed in the early 1940s); helped plant the State Capitol grounds in Sacramento. *Leptospermum ericoides*

**Banks, Sir Joseph** (1743–1820)—an English naturalist and plantsman who, with Daniel Solander, collected the first banksias and other plants on Australia's east coast while accompanying Captain James Cook's first voyage around the world on the ship Endeavor (1768-1771). Banks later became president of the Royal Society and advisor to London's Kew Gardens, at the time a private garden of the royal family. Through these positions, he influenced plant-collecting expeditions worldwide, but especially in Australia. *Banksia integrifolia, Araucaria heterophylla, Cordyline australis, Corynocarpus laevigatus, Dacrydium cupressinum, Hedycarya arborea, Knightia excelsa, Leptospermum scoparium, Litsea calicaris, Metrosideros excelsa, Pittosporum crassifolium, P. tenuifolium, P. undulatum, Vitex lucens*

**Bartram, John** (1699–1777)—America's first botanist, a Quaker farmer in Pennsylvania, who collected plants in nearly all the American Colonies, sending seeds and plants to Peter Collinson, among others, in England; he was eventually appointed the King's Botanist. His personal botanical garden near Philadelphia is now an historic site. *Aesculus hippocastanum*

**Belle View Nursery**—see Stephen Nolan

**Bidwill, John Carne** (1815–1853)—an English-born botanist who visited Australia in 1838 and moved there in 1844, eventually becoming the Commissioner of Crown Lands and the first director of the Royal Botanic Gardens, Sydney. *Araucaria bidwillii*

**Bonpland, Aimé Jacque Alexandre** (1773–1858)—a French physician-botanist who traveled throughout South America with Alexander von Humboldt. He later supervised the gardens for Empress Josephine at Malmaison in France. *Chiranthodendron pentadactylon, Pinus montezumae*

**Brown, Robert** (1773–1858)—a Scottish-born botanist who spent three and one-half years in Australia as a naturalist with the Flinders Expedition. He inherited Joseph Banks's personal library and herbarium collections. *Acacia melanoxylon, Tristania conferta*

**Buchanan-Hamilton, Francis** (1762–1829)—a Scottish-born physician and botanist who spent about twenty years in eastern Asia in the Bengal Medical Service and as superintendent of the botanic garden at Calcutta, making many contributions to early botanical knowledge of the area. *Michelia doltsopa, Pinus wallichiana*

**California Nursery Company**—founded by Richard D Fox, John Rock, and Georg Christian Roeding in Niles, California in 1884. Became one of the largest nurseries in Northern California, ultimately closing in the late 1970s when land was sold and subdivided for housing. *Griselinia*

**Candolle, Augustin Pyramus de** (1778–1841)—a French botanist who developed the system of plant classification, based on morphology, that is still in use today. *Crataegus pubescens*

**Cervantes, Vicente** (1755–1827)—one of the Spanish botanists sent by Charles III to Mexico City in 1788 to help establish the ill-fated Royal Botanic Gardens (funding was later eliminated by Charles IV). Later founded a chair of botany and remained in Mexico until the early 1800s. *Montanoa grandiflora*

**Church, Thomas Dolliver** (1902–1978)—a San Francisco-based landscape architect, considered one of the most influential in post-war California garden design; author of several books, including Gardens are for People. *Acmena smithii*

**Cockayne, Dr Leonard** (1855–1934)—a schoolteacher who became one of New Zealand's best-known botanists and early ecologists. *Dacrydium cupressinum*

**Colenso, Rev William** (1811–1899)—an English-born printer, missionary, and plantsman who moved to New Zealand in 1833 in the employ of the Church Missionary Society. He helped JD Hooker with his Flora Novae-Zelandiae. *Cordyline australis*

**Collinson, Peter** (1694–1768)—and English merchant and naturalist who, through exchanges with plant collectors in the American Colonies, introduced many trees to cultivation in Europe. He was a patron to John Bartram, providing funding for his plant collecting efforts in the Colonies. *Aesculus hippocastanum*

**Commercial Nurseries**—operated by John Center (né Juan Centre) near Folsom and 16th streets in San Francisco in early 1850s; later managed by James Saul, and ultimately leased to John O'Hare, and Son. *Acer macrophyllum, Aesculus hippocastanum, A. pavia, Liquidambar styraciflua, Liriodendron tulipifera, Tilia ×europaea*

**Cunningham, Allan** (1791–1839)—a pioneering English botanist and explorer of eastern Australia, he spent most of his adult life studying and collecting the plants of that country, plus Norfolk Island and New Zealand. He succeeded his brother Richard as Colonial Botanist in Australia from 1835 until his death. *Araucaria cunninghamii, Grevillea robusta, Metrosideros excelsa, Stenocarpus sinuata*

**Cunningham, Richard** (1793–1835)—a Kew-trained, English botanical explorer who collected in New Zealand and Australia, where he served as colonial botanist and superintendent of the Royal Botanic Garden, Sydney from 1833 until his death. *Pittosporum crassifolium*

**Dallimore, William** (1871–1959)—English horticulturist and forester who worked at Kew Gardens in London with BD Jackson and supervised the development of the National Pinetum. × *Cupressocyparis leylandii*

**David, Abbé Jean Pierre Armand** (1826–1900)—a French-born, Lazarist missionary and naturalist in China, who found the giant panda and the rare Père David's deer, in addition to the dove tree and other plants now common in gardens. An exceptional scientific collector, he was sponsored by the Musée d'Histoire Naturelle in Paris and spent nearly fifteen years exploring much of Mongolia and western and southern China, before returning to Paris in 1974 because of poor health. *Davidia involucrata*

**de Laguna, Andreas** (1499–1560)—a native of Segovia, Spain, who lived at the court of Charles V, served as physician to Pope Julius III, and wrote about the botanical works of Dioscorides, the first century Greek physician and herbalist. *Lagunaria patersonii*

**del Castillo, Bernal Diaz** (1492–1580)—accompanied Hernando Cortés in 1519 during his conquest of the Aztec empire and overthrow of the emperor Montezuma II. *Liquidambar styraciflua*

**Delavay, Père Jean Marie** (1834–1895)—a French botanist who collected mostly herbarium specimens, and some seeds, on his many travels in China from 1867 to 1895. His extensive collections overwhelmed the Musée d'Histoire Naturelle in Paris, and most remained unknown until rediscovered by later collectors. *Magnolia delavayi*

**Domoto, Toichi** (b. 1902)—proprietor of the Domoto Nursery in Hayward, California until its closing in 1981; originally operated as Japanese Nursery in east Oakland, opening about 1885 and operated by brothers Tom (Toichi's father) and Henry Domoto. The nursery specialized in plants of Japanese origin, particularly camellias, tree peonies, azaleas, and Japanese maples, and plants for bonsai. *Acer pentaphyllum*

**Douglas, David** (1798–1834)—a Scottish-born naturalist and plant collector employed by the Glasgow Botanic Garden, and then sent by the Horticultural Society of London to western North America.

Stationing first in Vancouver, British Columbia, he spent three years exploring the Pacific Northwest. He was the first professional plant collector to visit California, sent to North America by the society, arriving in Monterey in 1830, and travelling the state until 1832. *Acer circinatum, Pinus radiata, Umbellularia californica*

**Duncan and Davies Nursery**—located in New Plymouth, New Zealand; provided plants for that country's pavilion at the Panama–Pacific International Exposition in San Francisco in 1915, from which trees were transplanted into Golden Gate Park; nursery still in business today. *Dacrydium cupressinum, Knightia excelsa, Metrosideros kermadecensis*

**Evans and Reeves Nursery**—located in Los Angeles, California; notable for introducing a wide array of mediterranean climate plants as well as subtropical plants to California horticulture. Co-proprietor Bill Evans was heavily involved in the landscape design and planting of Disneyland and Disney World in Florida. *Callistemon viminalis, Talauma hodgsonii*

**Farges, Père Paul** (1844–1912)—a French missionary-botanist sent to China in 1867, based in northeastern Sichuan Province. He was the first collector to send back seeds of dove tree, among others, to Maurice de Vilmorin, a nurseryman in France. *Davidia involucrata*

**Farrer, Reginald** (1880–1920)—a prolific English writer and plant collector of the early twentieth century, he scoured the European Alps and the mountains of southwestern China for good garden plants. He was best known for his life-long study of alpine plants and their cultivation in the rock garden. *Michelia doltsopa*

**Fischer, Friederich Ernest Ludwig von** (1782–1854)—a Russian botanist, director of the Imperial Botanic Garden, St Petersburg. *Cupressus macrocarpa*

**Forrest, George** (1873–1932)—a Scottish botanist and plant hunter, employed by the herbarium at the Royal Botanic Garden, Edinburgh, who collected extensively in southwestern China and the Himalayas, hiring and carefully training local collectors to assist in his work. His many expeditions were financed privately. He introduced to horticulture some of the plants origi-nally found by Delavay, as well as a great many plants he discovered himself. *Michelia doltsopa*

**Forster, Johann Georg Adam** (1754–1794) and Johann Reinhold Forster (1729–1798)—a son and father team of German naturalists and botanists on Captain James Cook's second voyage (1772–1775). Cordyline australis, *Hedycarya arborea*

**Fortune, Robert** (1812–1880)—a Scottish plant collec-tor and writer who spent many years in China and Japan on behalf of the Horticultural Society in London during the 1840s and early 1850s, and for the US government in the late 1850s. He wrote several books in which he described plants that he had intro-duced into England and elsewhere. He scoured nurs-eries for interesting garden plants, especially in Japan, in addition to collecting in the wild. *Trachycarpus fortunei*

**Fox, Richard D** (1852–1928)—born in Dublin, Ireland, arrived in San Jose 1864. He took over his uncle's Santa Clara Valley Nursery in San Jose in 1881; later joined with John Rock in founding the California Nursery Company in Niles. *Aesculus × carnea, Cryptomeria japonica, Sciadopitys verticillata, Taxus baccata, Thujopsis dolabrata, Tilia tomentosa, Ulmus glabra 'Camperdownii'*

**Franceschi, Dr Francesco** (dates unknown; also known as Dr Emanuele Orazio Fenzi)—arrived from Italy in Santa Barbara in 1893, and returned to Italy in 1913. In Santa Barbara, he founded the Southern California Acclimatizing Association, a nursery through which he introduced several hundred plants to California horticulture. His home in the hills above Santa Barbara is known today as Franceschi Park and continues to display many of the unusual plants he introduced. *Acca sellowiana, Calodendrum capense, Chiranthodendron pentadactylon, Crataegus pubescens, Cupressus guadalupensis, Jubaea chilensis, Lagunaria patersonii, Persea indica, Pinus wallichiana, Sparmannia africana, Stenocarpus salignus*

**Fraser Nurseries**—a large wholesale grower of trees and shrubs in Birmingham, Alabama. *Photinia × fraseri*

**G Ghose & Company**—a dealer of Himalayan seeds in Darjeeling, India; source of some of the magnolias in Golden Gate Park. *Michelia doltsopa*

**Golden Gate Nursery**—see William Connell Walker

**Greville, Charles Francis** (1749–1809)—a prominent English botanist, horticulturist, member of Parliament, founder and vice-president of the (Royal) Horticultural Society. Known for introducing and cultivating many rare and interesting plants. A close friend of Joseph Banks. *Grevillea robusta*

**Hagiwara, Makoto**—see Japanese Tea Garden, page 159

**Hall, Dr George Rogers** (1820–1899)—an American physician who practiced medicine in Shanghai beginning in 1846. He became active in plant collecting in China and was one of the first to bring back plants to America from Japan, where he had established a garden in Yokohama by 1860. *Pinus densiflora, Taxus cuspidata*

**Hall, Harvey Monroe** (1874–1932)—a leading taxonomist of the early twentieth century, working at both UC Berkeley and the Carnegie Institution. Co-authored a series of botanical essays ("Nature and Science on the Pacific Coast") that were published in the tour guide for the Panama–Pacific International Exposition in 1915. *Melaleuca ericifolia*

**Hall, William Hammond**—self-taught surveyor, horticulturist, and park planner who served as landscape engineer and superintendent of Golden Gate Park from 1870 until 1876. See chapter one.

**Hariot, Thomas** (1560–1621)—British mthemetician, surveyor, and historian who traveled to the Virginia Colony in 1585-1586, after which he wrote a Briefe and True Report of the New Found Land of Virginia (1588). *Taxodium distichum*

**Hartweg, Karl Theodor** (1812–1871)—a Germany plantsman sent by the Horticultural Society of London to Mexico and Guatemala in 1836, remaining there for several years before traveling to California. He is important today for many plants, such as fuchsias, that he introduced into England from Central and South America. He also explored California, Jamaica, and Madeira. *Cupressus macrocarpa, Pinus montezumae*

**Henry, Augustine** (1857–1930)—an Scottish-born physician, sent from England to China in 1880 to join the Imperial Chinese Maritime Customs Service in eastern Sichuan Province, where his duties as customs officer allowed him periods of time off to explore in the vicinity. Out of boredom, he began to collect plants and eventually became exceedingly knowledgeable about the plants of that area of Sichuan and, later, Yunnan and Taiwan. *Cryptomeria japonica, Davidia involucrata*

**Hernandez, Dr Francisco** (1515–1578)—a Spanish physician sent, in 1570 by Philip II of Spain, to investigate the natural and political history of New Spain (Mexico), where he remained for seven years. He traveled throughout Mexico, studying native plants that were used for food and medicine by the local people. A portion of his extensive portfolio was published in the mid-1600s. *Chiranthodendron pentadactylon, Crataegus pubescens, Liquidambar styraciflua*

**Hillier Nurseries Ltd** (originally Hillier and Sons' Nursery)—one of the most highly respected nurseries in England, located in Winchester. The gardens are now the Hillier Arboretum. *Prunus x yedoensis*

**Hooker, Sir Joseph Dalton** (1817–1911)—an English botanist and plant collector who began traveling in 1839, first to the Antarctic islands, New Zealand, and Tasmania, later to the Himalayas, where he collected extensively, and finally to the Atlas Mountains of Morocco. He succeeding his father, Sir William Jackson Hooker, as the second director of the Royal Botanic Gardens, Kew, from 1865 to 1885. He was a friend of Charles Darwin and a supporter of his theory on the origin of species. *Cedrus, Michelia doltsopa, Talauma hodgsonii*

**Howell, John Thomas** (1903–1994)—a California botanist who, as head of the botany department of the California Academy of Sciences in San Francisco, traveled widely around the state and neighboring regions studying plants. *Cupressus guadalupensis*

**Humboldt, Baron Friedrich Heinrich Alexander von** (1769–1859)—a German scientist who traveled with Aimé Bonpland throughout South America and Mexico from 1799 to 1804. The pair brought plants back with them to Paris, many new to horticulture, and later published approximately thirty books on their journeys. *Chiranthodendron pentadactylon, Pinus montezumae*

**Hutchison, James** (b. 1824)—born in Scotland, arrived in California 1850, and began Hutchison's Nursery Depot in 1853, involving several sites, first in Alameda, then in Oakland and Piedmont and known as Bay Nursery, which continued in existence until about 1920. *Photinia serratifolia*

**Incarville, Pierre Nicholas le Chéron d'** (1706–1757)—a French Jesuit missionary and botanist who lived in Peking from 1740 until his death. Despite government restrictions at the time on travel and collecting by foreigners, he was probably the first European botanical collector in China, sending his plant and seed collections to Paris. *Ailanthus altissima*

**Jackson, Benjamin Daydon** (1846–1927)—a Swedish-born botanical historian who worked at Kew Gardens with William Dallimore and served for many years as general secretary of the Linnean Society. x *Cupressocyparis leylandii*

**Kaempfer, Engelbert** (1651–1716)—a German physician, botanist, and naturalist who spent two years (1690–1692) on an island in Nagasaki Bay, Japan, as a medical officer of the Dutch East India Company. He studied the plants around the island and was also able to get to the mainland of Kyushu. Upon his return to Europe, he published the first book on Japanese plants. *Cryptomeria japonica, Ginkgo biloba, Pittosporum* spp., *Sciadopitys verticillata*

**Kingdon-Ward, Frank** (1885–1958)—an English plant collector, explorer, and author who traveled throughout western and southwestern China, plus Tibet and Burma, from 1909 to 1958. He sent back seeds and plants to nurseries, private patrons, and botanial gardens; many of his extensive collections have now become popular gardens plants. He writings, photographs, and maps filled twenty books, the publication of which helped finance his travels. *Michelia doltsopa*

**L'Héritier de Brutelle, Charles Louis** (1746–1800)—a French botanist in London who named and described Eucalyptus as a new genus, from specimens collected by David Nelson and William Anderson, traveling on Captain James Cook's third voyage (1777). *Eucalyptus obliqua*

**Labillardière, Jacques-Julien Houtou de** (1755–1834)—a French botanist and member of the D'Entrecasteaux expedition that left France for Australia in 1791, in search of the lost French explorer, Phillipe Picot de La Pérouse. He spent only few weeks in Australia, mostly collecting plants on the west coast. *Eucalyptus gobulus, Eucalyptus viminalis*

**Lambert, Aylmer Bourke** (1761–1842)—an Englishman well known for his botanical and horticultural activities. He received seeds from various collectors in the New World and in turn, introduced plants from those collections to horticulture. Served as vice-president of the Linnean Society for forty-six years. *Crataegus pubescens, Cupressus macrocarpa, Maytenus boaria*

**Lammerts, Dr Walter E** (dates unknown)—botanist and plant breeder who, while at UCLA, carried out a breeding program that resulted in many new and excellent cultivars of New Zealand tea tree, in addition to roses, camellias, lilacs for warm climates, and other garden plants. *Leptospermum scoparium*

**l'Ecluse, Jules Charles de** (1526–1609)—a Flemish botanist, better known as Clusius, who served the Holy Roman Emperor Maximilian II from 1573 to 1576 as prefect of the imperial gardens in Vienna. He traveled throughout Europe and western Asia, collecting bulbs and other flowering plants. He became a specialist in tulips and other bulbs, and is considered a "father" of gardens in Europe for his extensive introductions of ornamental plants now common in gardens. *Aesculus hippocastanum, Prunus laurocerasus*

**Linnaeus, Carl** (1707–1778)—a Swedish naturalist who developed the binomial (two-word) system for naming plants (and other living things). While working as a physician in the Netherlands from 1735 to 1738, he developed his ideas on an orderly system for classifying and naming plants and animals. After returning to Stockholm and becoming a professor at the University of Uppsala, he published many books and papers, including Species Plantarum in 1753, in which he detailed his new system. Though his ideas for classification have been superceded by those of Candolle, the binomial system remains in use today. *Aesculus hippocastanum, Cryptomeria japonica, Sparmannia africana*

**Lobb, Thomas** (1820–1894)—an English botanist and plant explorer sent by Veitch & Sons Nursery, Exeter, England, in the 1840s and 1850s to India and Southeast Asia. Highly respected, and occasionally aided, by Joseph Hooker, he was one of the earliest collectors of orchids. *Sciadopitys verticillata*

**Lobb, William** (1809–1863)—the first of about twenty gardeners sent out by the James Veitch & Sons Nursery, Exeter, England, to collect plants in the New World, beginning in 1840 to South America and eventually to California and the Sierra Nevada. *Aesculus californica, Cryptomeria japonica, Luma apiculata, Sciadopitys verticillata, Sequoiadendron giganteum, Torreya californica*

**Loddiges, George** (1784–1846)—second generation English florist and nurseryman in Hackney, London. *Crataegus pubescens*

**Low, Sir Hugh** (1824–1905)—British plantsman who collected plants in the East Indies for his father's nursery, especially orchids and other hothouse exotics. He was the first European to climb Mt Kinabalu in Borneo, where he worked as secretary to the Rajah for twenty-eight years. *Cupressus macrocarpa*

**Low, Stuart Henry Jr** (1863–1952)—an English nurseryman, proprietor of London Royal Nurseries in Clapton, Middlesex. *Magnolia campbellii*

**Lüdemann, Frederick** (dates unknown)—founder of Pacific Nurseries in Cow Hollow district of San Francisco in 1869; later moved nursery to Colma, and sold to Paul von Kempf in 1910; nursery exists today. x *Cupressocyparis leylandii, Tristania conferta*

**Masson, Francis** (1741–1805)—A Scottish gardener and plant collector, the first to be sent out officially from Kew Gardens (before it became the Royal Botanic Gardens) to South Africa (1772), where he often traveled with Carl T Thunberg and brought back many choice new garden and greenhouse plants. He later traveled to the Canary Islands and North America. *Calodendrum capense*

**Mattioli, Pier Andrea** (1501–1577)—an Italian physician and botanist, who studied the plants of Italy and surrounding regions and published, in Latin, a translation of the six Books of Dioscorides, with his own commentaries. Served as personal physician to both Archduke Ferdinand and Emperor Maximillian II in Austria. *Aesculus hippocastanum*

**McLaren, John** (1846–1943)—Scottish-born horticulturist who served as superintendent of San Francisco's parks from 1887 until 1943. See chapter one.

**Menzies, Archibald** (1754–1842)—a Scottish surgeon-naturalist with the Vancouver Expedition, which explored the West Coast of North America. He was among the first European explorers to study the flora of California and the Pacific Northwest, as well as parts of South America. *Acer macrophyllum, Araucaria araucana, Heteromeles arbutifolia, Sequoia sempervirens, Umbellularia californica*

**Mociño Suares Losad, José Mariano** (1757–1820)—a Mexican physician, botanist, and naturalist who explored large areas of Mexico between 1787 and 1803 with Martin de Sessé y Lacasta. Plants they collected were sent to the botanic garden in Madrid. Their books on the flora of Mexico were not published until the 1880s. *Crataegus pubescens*

**Molina, Juan Ignacio** (1737–1829)—a Chilean-born Jesuit and naturalist-botanist, one of the earliest South American botanists to study the natural history of his country; the results of his work were published in 1782. *Maytenus boaria, Quillaja saponaria*

**Née, Louis** (dates unknown)—a Spanish botanist who, while visiting Mexico and California on the Alexandro Malaspina Expedition from 1789 to 1794, was the first to describe and name two California oaks: coast live oak (*Quercus agrifolia*) and valley oak (*Q. lobata*). *Quercus agrifolia*

**Nolan, Stephen** (1834–1919)—English-born founder of the Belle View Nursery in Oakland in 1860. The nursery was one of first to offer California native plants and was notable for its selection of plants from Australia; in 1877, he gave eucalypts to UC Berkeley, still seen in the grove at the west end of campus. He closed the nursery in 1879 when he began a landscape business. *Agonis flexuosa, Eucalyptus, Grevillea robusta, Leptospermum scoparium, Pinus pinea, P. torreyana, Pittosporum crassifolium, P. eugenioides, Prunus laurocerasus, P. lusitanica, Stenocarpus sinuata, Syncarpia glomulifera, Taxus baccata, Thuja plicata, Torreya californica*

**Nuttall, Thomas** (1786–1859)—an English printer who became interested in plants on his first journey to Philadelphia in 1808. He collected seeds and plants on expeditions throughout much of North America, including the region along the West Coast. He was professor of botany at Harvard University from 1822 to 1834. *Aesculus californica*

**Olbrich, Marshall** (1920–1991)—cofounder, with Lester Hawkins, of Western Hills Nursery in Occidental, California, noted for its offerings of plants from mediterranean climate regions around the world; an occasional contributor to Pacific Horticulture. *Acer pentaphyllum*

**Pacific Nurseries**—see Frederick Lüdemann

**Parry, Charles Christopher** (1823–1890)—an English-born botanist who settled in Iowa. Served as botanist with the Mexican Boundary Survey from 1849 to 1861 and later with the Pacific Railway Survey. Became an expert on flora of Colorado. *Pinus torreyana*

**Paterson, Colonel William** (1755–1810)—an English gardener, botanist, plant explorer, and collector, who arrived in Australia in 1791 as a military commander for the British government. He sent plants collected back to Robert Brown and Joseph Banks in London. *Lagunaria patersonii*

**Pursh, Friedrich Traugott** (1774–1820)—a German botanist who, after immigrating to America in 1799, produced an early work (1914) on North American plants that was published in London and said to be "the first flora on a continental scope...that included Pacific Northwest species." *Acer circinatum, A. macrophyllum*

**Riedel, Peter** (dates unknown)—plantsman who settled in Santa Barbara in 1905, working first with Dr Franceschi until 1909, later running his own nursery, teaching, and consulting. *Crataegus pubescens, Fraxinus uhdei, Griselinia, Lagunaria patersonii, Myrrhinium atropurpureum*

**Reiter, Victor Jr** (1903–1986)—one of San Francisco's most renowned plant enthusiasts, a hybridizer of many plants including fuchsias, and proprietor of La Rochette Nursery at his home on Stanyan Street. He worked closely with Eric Walther on the development of the collections at Strybing Arboretum and Botanical Gardens. *Montanoa grandiflora*

**Roberts, Warren** (b. 1942)—a botanist-horticulturist, California historian, past president of the California

Horticultural Society, and currently superintendent of the UC Davis Arboretum. *Cupressus guadalupensis*

**Rock, Joseph Francis Charles** (1884–1962)—an Austrian-born, American botanist and explorer who was sent on numerous expeditions to China from 1922 to 1949, including one to western China sponsored by the National Geographic Society in 1929. He was also an authority on woody plants of Hawaii, where he served on the university faculty from 1907 to 1919. *Acer pentaphyllum*

**Roezl, Benedict** (1824–1885)—a Czechoslovakian gardener and botanist who traveled extensively in Mexico and western North America. He had a nursery in Mexico City, invented a machine for extracting fibers from plants for making cloth, and introduced many orchids and other tropical plants into Europe from his travels in South America. *Dahlia imperialis*

**Ruiz Lopez, Hipólito** (1754–1816) and José Antonio Pavón y Jiménez (1754–1840)—Spanish pharmacist-botanists sent by the scientifically minded Charles III of Spain to study the vegetation of the vice-kingdom of Peru (now Peru and Chile), from 1777 to 1788. Their collections went to botanic gardens in both Madrid and Paris. They were particularly interested in plants of economic value. *Citronella mucronata*

**Santa Clara Valley Nursery**—see Richard D Fox

**Saratoga Horticultural Research Foundation**—non-profit research organization founded in the early 1950s, responsible for introducing many new plants to cultivation in California. Originally located in Saratoga, it is now in San Martin, California. *Ginkgo biloba, Liquidambar styraciflua, Magnolia grandiflora*

**Sargent, Charles Sprague** (1841–1927)—an American botanist and first director of the Arnold Arboretum at Harvard University, serving there from 1873 until his death. His primary interest was in woody trees and shrubs, collecting many himself on travels to Asia and elsewhere. He eventually hired EH Wilson to collect on behalf of the arboretum. *Pinus thunbergii*

**Sellow, Friedrich** (1789–1831)—a German naturalist whose family name was spelled Sello; South American plants named for him may follow either spelling. He traveled throughout South America searching for useful plants. *Acca sellowiana*

**Sessé y Lacasta, Martin de** (d. 1809)—a Spanish physician, botanist, and naturalist sent to Mexico by Charles III to establish a botanic garden. He explored large areas of Mexico between 1788 and 1803 with José Mariano Mociño Suares Losad. Their books on the flora of Mexico were not published until the 1880s. *Chiranthodendron pentadactylon, Crataegus pubescens*

**Siebold, Philipp Franz von** (1796–1866)—a German-born physician-naturalist who worked for the Dutch East India Company on Deshima Island, Japan, in the late 1820s and on Kyushu in the early 1860s, developing a passion for the country, the people, and the plants. In between, he operated a nursery in Leiden that accepted plants from other collectors in Japan and introduced them to horticulture in Europe. *Cryptomeria japonica, Pinus densiflora, P. thunbergii, Sciadopitys verticillata, Trachycarpus fortunei*

**Smith, Sir James Edward** (1759–1828)—an important English botanist who purchased Linnaeus's scientific collections and library from his widow and joined with other naturalists in founding the Linnean Society in London in 1788, serving as its president for the first forty years. *Acmena smithii*

**Solander, Daniel Carlsson** (1733–1782)—an Swedish-born naturalist and student of Linnaeus, who traveled with Joseph Banks on Captain James Cook's voyages to Australia and New Zealand. He later settled in England, serving as Banks's librarian and herbarium curator. *Banksia integrifolia, Cordyline australis, Corynocarpus laevigatus, Dacrydium cupressinum, Hedycarya arborea, Knightia excelsa, Leptospermum scoparium, Litsea calicaris, Metrosideros excelsa, Pittosporum tenuifolium, Vitex lucens*

**Sparrmann, Anders** (1748–1820)—a Swedish naturalist-botanist on Captain James Cook's second voyage (1772–1775), collecting plants in and around Cape Town, South Africa. (There are many spellings of his name, including Andreas Sparrman.) *Cordyline australis, Sparmannia africana*

**Stuart Low and Company**—a nursery located in England; source of the first *Magnolia campbellii* planted in Golden Gate Park. *Magnolia campbellii*

**Thunberg, Carl Peter** (1743–1828)—a Swedish-born physician-naturalist and student of Linnaeus who traveled to South Africa, Java, and Japan, where he spent nearly two years (1775-1776) on Deshima Island in Nagasaki Bay on Kyushu as a surgeon with the Dutch East India Company. He later returned to Sweden, became a professor at Uppsala, and published the first flora of Japan. *Cryptomeria japonica, Pinus densiflora, P. thunbergii, Sciadopitys verticillata*

**Tradescant, John the younger** (1608–1662)—An English gardener and plant collector who collected in the American colony of Virginia on three visits and later became head gardener to the royal family in England, succeeding his father who was also a plant collector. *Aesculus hippocastanum, Liriodendron tulipifera, Taxodium distichum*

**Veitch and Sons Nursery**—one of England's oldest and most important nurseries, begun about 1800, and managed over four generations at several locations. The nursery sponsored many plant collectors and expeditions, particularly in Asia. *Aesculus californica, Chamaecyparis obtusa, Cryptomeria japonica, Davidia involucrata, Dipteronia sinensis, Photinia davidsoniae, Sequoiadendron giganteum*

**Veitch, John Gould** (1839–1870)—second generation English nurseryman with Veith & Sons Nursery in southern England. *Pinus densiflora*

**Veitch, Sir Harry James** (1840–1924)—English horticulturist and nurseryman, fourth generation proprietor of Veitch & Sons Nursery, Coombe Wood, Exeter, England, and sponsor of many plant-collecting expeditions around the world in the 1800s and early 1900s. *Davidia involucrata*

**Vilmorin Nursery**—located in Les Barres, France; sponsor of plant-collecting expeditions around the world in the 1800s, and distributor of many plants collected by French missionary-botanists in China. *Davidia involucrata*

**von Mueller, Baron Ferdinand Jacob Heinrich** (1825–1896)—a German-born botanist who went to Australia in 1847 and spent the rest of his life exploring the country, collecting plants, and eventually becoming the greatest of Australia's nineteenth-century botanists and the greatest proponent of the magnificent Australian flora. *Eucalyptus* spp.

**Walker, William Connell** (1814–1871) –Philadelphia-born proprietor of the Golden Gate Nursery (1850-1877) in San Francisco, with three acres of greenhouses and fields near South Park. During the late 1850s and early 1860s, he imported and offered many Australian plants for the first time in California; nursery operated by David Neely after 1866. *Acacia, Araucaria heterophylla, Calocedrus decurrens, Casuarina verticillata, Chamaecyparis lawsoniana, Cryptomeria japonica, Eucalyptus, Ficus macrophylla, Grevillea robusta, Laurus nobilis, Leptospermum laevigatum, Melaleuca ericifolia, Metrosideros excelsa, Myrtus communis, Pittosporum undulatum, Torreya californica, Tristania conferta*

**Wallich, Nathaniel** (1786–1854)—a Danish-born physician, botanist, and director of the Calcutta Botanic Garden where he worked for nearly thirty years, traveling frequently to the Himalayas, Burma, and Nepal to search for new plants to collect and send back to botanical gardens at Kew and Edinburgh. *Michelia doltsopa, Pinus wallichiana*

**Walther, Eric** (?–1958)—a German-born gardener and an internationally recognized plantsman who became the first director of Strybing Arboretum and Botanical Gardens (1937–1957). He communicated with nurserymen and plant collectors around the world in the interest of gathering new trees and other plants for Golden Gate Park and the developing arboretum. See chapter one. *Citronella mucronata, Dodonaea viscosa, Magnolia campbellii*

**Warren and Son's Garden and Nursery**—see Colonel James Lloyd Lafayette Warren

**Warren, Colonel James Lloyd Lafayette** (1805–1896)—born in Massachusetts, arrived in San Francisco 1849; proprietor of Warren and Son's Garden and Nursery in Sacramento in early 1850s. Their 1853 catalog was the first published for a California nursery. He sold the nurseries (several locations including one in San Francisco) in 1854 to become editor of The California Farmer, begun that year. He was also a founder of the California State Agricultural Society. Acacia, *Ailanthus altissima*

**WB Clarke & Co Nursery**—a well-known nursery in San Jose, founded along Coyote Creek by Walter B Clarke in 1856. Specializing in the selection and breeding of trees, shrubs for the mild California climate, including lilacs, quince, and peonies, the nursery was in existence until 1938 as J Clarke Nursery Co. *Prunus x yedoensis* 'Akebono'

**Western Hills Nursery**—see Marshall Olbrich

**Western Nursery**—see Charles Christian Abraham

**Wilson, Ernest Henry** (1876–1930)—an English plant collector and author who, as a gardener at Kew Gardens, was chosen to be sent to China as a collector for the Veitch & Sons Nursery in 1899 and 1903 and became the last and greatest of the Veitch collectors. He was then hired by Charles Sprague Sargent of the Arnold Arboretum at Harvard University to further explore China and Japan, on several journeys from 1909 to 1919, returning to Boston as curator and eventually director of the arboretum. *Cryptomeria japonica, Davidia involucrata, Dipteronia sinensis, Magnolia delavayi, Photinia davidsoniae, P. serratifolia, Prunus x yedoensis, Sciadopitys verticillata, Thujopsis dolabrata*

# Glossary

**alternate**  an arrangement of leaves or other plant parts placed singly on the stem or rachis, not in pairs (opposite) or in whorls

**angiosperm**  one of a group of seed-bearing, flowering plants whose seeds are enclosed within an ovary

**anther**  the terminal part of the stamen that contains the pollen

**appressed**  lying flat for its entire length, usually applied to hairs but can also be applied to other parts of a plant

**aril**  an appendage or outer covering of a seed, sometimes fleshy and colorful

**axil**  the angle or space between a petiole and the stem to which it is attached

**bipinnate**  having leaflets that are divided pinnately

**bloom**  a bluish or grayish, powdery covering of a stem, leaf, or fruit that can be rubbed off; also a flower or the season of flowering

**bract**  a modified, often reduced leaf subtending a flower or an inflorescence; sometimes the modified leaves between the calyx and the normal leaves (often showy, as in the red bracts of poinsettia)

**calyx**  a collective term for all the sepals of a flower that form the outermost whorl of flower parts

**capitate**  ending in a rounded tip, as the stigma at the end of a pistil; also referring to an inflorescence in which the flowers are arranged in a head, as in members of the daisy family (Asteraceae)

**compound**  divided into two or more parts, as a leaf

**conifer**  a cone-bearing tree or shrub, such as pine, fir, juniper, and cypress

**corolla**  a collective term for the petals of the floral whorl, whether the petals are free or fused

**crotch**  the angle formed by two branches or trunks of a tree

**crown**  the top of a tree, including the upper trunk, branches, and branchlets

**cultivar**  a cultivated variety of a plant, maintained in cultivation through propagation by cuttings, divisions, or other asexual means (not by seed); because it is propagated asexually, all plants of a cultivar are essentially identical; noted by a name enclosed in single quotation marks (eg 'Akebono')

**deciduous**  characterized by the falling of plant parts when no longer useful, usually applied to trees whose leaves are shed in autumn

**decurrent**  characterized by a leaf blade that extends down and attaches directly to the sides of a stem

**dehiscent**  characterized by the splitting open of a seed capsule along specific lines when ripe (opposite of indehiscent)

**dentate**  pointing straight out, applied to the teeth on a leaf margin

**disjunct**  separated from the main cluster, applied to a plant's natural distribution

**domatium**  (plural, domatia) tiny holes on the surface of a leaf, often occupied by mites or minute insects

**entire**  having a smooth margin, lacking indentations or serrations; usually applied to a leaf

**evergreen**  characterized by leaves that persist for two or more seasons; in some evergreen trees the leaves may be shed over a period of time; in contrast to deciduous plants that shed their leaves annually

**exerted**  projecting beyond the surrounding structure, often applied to stamens and pistils which protrude from the perianth

**fascicle**  a cluster of leaves or flowers all arising from a common point

**flower**  the reproductive part of a plant, consisting of some combination of sepals, petals, stamens, and pistil

**follicle**  a dry, dehiscent fruit that opens along a single line

**frond**  the leaf blade of a fern or palm

**fruit**  the ripened ovary that protects and aids in the dispersal of the seeds of a plant

**glabrous**  smooth, without pubescence, not hairy

**glaucous**  possessing a bluish or grayish coloration, usually applied to leaves with a powdery or waxy coating that can be rubbed off

**gymnosperm**  one of a large group of seed-bearing plants (spermatophytes) whose seeds are not enclosed in an ovary, including cycads, conifers, podocarps, and ginkgoes

**habit**  the growth pattern of a plant

**hardy** tolerant of cold or other adverse cultural conditions

**indeterminate** describing an inflorescence that lacks a terminal flower, as in a raceme or panicle

**inflorescence** a floral cluster; the arrangement of the flowers on a floral stem

**keeled** having a pronounced ridge, like the keel of a boat, on the underside of the leaves, petioles, sepals, or petals

**key** a colloquial name for the fruit of maples (Acer)

**lanceolate** lance shaped, longer than broad, wider above the base and tapered toward the apex

**leader** the main stem of a tree

**leaflet** a distinct and separate division of a compound leaf

**leaf** scar on a stem, the mark where a leaf had been attached

**legume** the flattish, beanlike pod containing the seeds of a member of the legume family (Leguminosae)

**montane** of the mountains, applied to plants or other things found in the mountains

**node** the point at which a leaf or leaves are attached to a stem

**oblique** characterized by leaf bases that are unequal in their angle and size

**obovate** in a leaf, characterized by the terminal half being broader than the basal half

**obtuse** characterized by a base or tip that gradually tapers to a blunt or rounded end

**operculum** a cover, lid, or cap, as in the flowers of eucalypts

**opposite** characterized by an arrangement of leaves, or other plant parts, in pairs on opposite sides of the stem or rachis

**ovate** egg-shaped, broader near the base that the outer tip, applied to leaves

**ovule** a body within the ovary of a flowering plant that, when fertilized by a pollen grain, will develop into a seed

**palmate** lobed or divided, as the fingers of a hand; usually applied to leaves

**panicle** an inflorescence in which the main axis is branched, with the pedicels of individual flowers arranged on the secondary branches

**pedicel** a flower stalk

**peduncle** the stalk of an inflorescence

**peltate** resembling an umbrella, referring to a leaf whose petiole is attached at the center of the leaf blade

**perianth** the calyx and petals collectively, whether or not they are distinguishable

**petal** the corolla or showy part of the floral whorl found within the calyx and often conspicuously colored

**petiole** a leaf stalk

**photosynthesis** the process by which plants combine hydrogen (from water), carbon dioxide (from air), and energy from the sun to produce their own food (carbohydrates)

**phyllode** an enlarged leaflike petiole that functions in photosynthesis, sometimes reduced to a spinelike structure; often found in acacias

**pinnate** having divisions like a feather, with leaflets arranged on opposite sides of the rachis

**pistil** the female organ of a flower composed of an ovary, style, and stigma

**pleach** to prune vertical growths from a tree, encouraging lateral growths that can be intertwined, for the purposes of shaping a trees growth into a horizontal pattern

**pod** any of several types of fruit that are dry and dehiscent

**pollard** to prune back the stems on a tree to the same point annually, for the purposes of controlling the size and shape of the tree's crown

**pollen** a grainlike structure, produced by the anther, containing the male, reproductive body of a seed-bearing plant

**pollen cone** the male cone of a gymnosperm that produces the pollen

**pubescent** having a hairy surface, usually of short, fine hairs

**raceme** an unbranched, indeterminate inflorescence with individual flowers arranged on pedicels

**rachis** the central stem of a compound leaf (or fern frond) to which the leaflets are attached

**receptacle** the end of the floral stem to which all the floral parts are attached

**reflexed** turned or curled back on itself, referring to flower petals

**revolute** rolled under, referring to a leaf margin

**samara** a dry, indehiscent, winged fruit with one or two seeds

**seed** the ripened ovules of a flowering plant, combining an embryo and food reserves for a new plant

**sepal** one of the outermost, sterile, separate parts of the calyx, normally outside of the petals and enclosing the other floral parts

**serrate** pointing to the outer tip, referring to teeth on a leaf margin

**sessile** lacking a stalk, sitting directly on its base

**simple** not divided, not compound

**sorus** (plural, sori) a cluster of sporangia in ferns

**spermatophyte** a seed producing plant

**spike** an inflorescence in which a long, unbranched stem having flowers attached directly to it, without pedicels

**sporangia** a container (of plant tissue) that contains the spores, as on the underside of a fern frond

**spore** a reproductive cell in ferns

**spur** a hollow projection of the calyx or corolla, usually containing nectar

**spur shoot** a short branchlet bearing tightly arranged leaves, flowers, and fruits

**stamen** the male, pollen-producing organ of a flower, consisting of an anther and a stalk-like filament

**staminode** a sterile stamen that does not produce pollen, sometimes petal-like and showy

**stigma** the tip of a pistil, often sticky or hairy to receive pollen grains

**stipule** a leafy appendage, often part of a pair, at the base of a petiole, sometimes falling early and leaving a distinctive scar

**style** the slender, stalk-like extension of the pistil that connects the ovary to the stigma

**subtend** to appear beneath and enclose, applied to leaves of bracts beneath a flower

**sucker** a shoot growing from a plant's root or underground stem

**syconium** a fruitlike inflorescence in which the flowers line the interior of the fleshy receptacle, as in the figs (Ficus)

**tepal** a segment of a perianth that cannot be differentiated as a sepal or petal; typical of the magnolia family

**tripinnate** having leaflets that are divided pinnately, with those divisions further divided pinnately

**umbel** a convex or flattened inflorescence in which the pedicels all arise from the apex of a common stalk

**unisexual** flowers that have either male (stamens) or female (pistils) parts but not both

**variegated** having two or more colors on a single leaf or flower

**viscid** covered in a sticky exudation

**whorled** characterized by three or more parts arising from a common node, usually referring to leaves or branches

# Further Reading

Most of these publications can be found in the Helen Crocker Russell Library of Horticulture, just inside the Main Gate to Strybing Arboretum and Botanical Gardens.

Amundsen, Ronald, and Brian Tremback. "Olmsted's Law Refuted." *Pacific Horticulture* 50, no. 4 (Winter 1989): 52–56.

Bailey, Liberty Hyde. *Standard Cyclopedia of Horticulture*. New York: Macmillan Company, 1914.

———. *Cyclopedia of Horticulture*. New York: Macmillan Company, 1900–1902.

Bailey, Liberty Hyde, Ethel Zoe Bailey, and Staff of Liberty Hyde Bailey Hortorium. *Hortus Third: A Concise Dictionary of Plants Cultivated in the United States and Canada*. New York: Macmillan Company, 1976.

Bean, William J. *Trees and Shrubs Hardy in the British Isles,* 8th edition. 4 vols. London: John Murray, 1970–1980.

Beatty, Russell A. "Metamorphosis in Sand: The first Five Years of Golden Gate Park." *California Horticultural Journal* 31, no. 2 (April 1970): 41–46, 73.

Black, Michael. "Searching for a Genius of Place: The Ambiguous Legacy of Golden Gate Park." In the symposium proceedings of *The Environmental Spirit Past, Present, & Prospects*. University of California, Berkeley, 1995.

Brenzel, Kathleen Norris. *Sunset Western Garden Book*. Menlo Park, Calif.: Sunset Publishing Corporation, 2001.

Brown, Thomas A. *Horticulturists and Plant Raisers*. Petaluma, Calif: Thomas A Brown, 1998.

———. *A List of California Nurseries and Their Catalogs, 1850–1900*. Petaluma, Calif: Thomas A Brown, 1993.

Butterfield, Harry M. "Some Pioneer Nurseries in California and their Plants." Parts 1 and 2. *Journal of the California Horticultural Society* 27, no. 3 (July 1966): 70–77; 27, no. 4 (October 1966): 102–108.

———. *Dates of Introduction of Trees and Shrubs into California*. 1964. Mimeographed.

———. "The Golden Gate Nursery of the 'Fifties."*Journal of the California Horticultural Society* 1, no. 2 (April 1940): 87–91.

———. "The Introduction of Acacias into California." *Madroño* 4 (1938): 177–187.

Caen, Herb. *Herb Caen's Guide to San Francisco*. Garden City, NJ: Doubleday & Co, Inc, 1957.

Carr, Denis John and SGM Carr. *People and Plants in Australia*. Sydney, Australia: Academic Press Australia, 1981.

Cave, Yvonne, and Valda Paddison. *The Gardener's Encyclopaedia of New Zealand Native Plants*. Aukland, New Zealand: Random House New Zealand, 1999.

Chandler, Philip E. *Reference Lists of Ornamental Plants for Southern California Gardens*. Los Angeles: Southern California Horticultural Society, 1993.

Chesnut, Victor King. *Plants Used by the Indians of Mendocino County*. Fort Bragg, Calif: Mendocino County Historical Society, 1902.

Clarke, Desmond L, ed. *Bean's Trees and Shrubs Hardy in the British Isles*. Vol 5. Supplement. London: John Murray, 1988.

Clary, Raymond H. *The Making of Golden Gate Park: The Growing Years: 1906–1950*. San Francisco: Don't Call It Frisco Press, 1987.

————. *The Making of Golden Gate Park: The Early Years: 1865–1906*. San Francisco: California Living Books, 1980.

Coats, Alice. *The Quest for Plants: A History of the Horticultural Explorers*. London: Studio Vista, 1969.

Cockayne, Dr Leonard. *New Zealand Plants Suitable for North American Gardens*. Wellington, New Zealand: J Mackay, Government Printer, 1914.

Cockrell, Robert A, and Frederick F Warnke. *Trees of the Berkeley Campus*. Berkeley: University of California, Division of Agricultural Sciences, 1976.

Dallman, Peter R. *Plant Life in the World's Mediterranean Climates*. Berkeley, Calif: University of California Press, 1998.

Dirr, Michael A. *Manual of Woody Landscape Plants*. 3rd ed. Champaign, Ill: Stipes Publishing Company, 1983.

Downing, Andrew Jackson. *Treatise on the Theory and Practice of Landscape Gardening Adapted to North America*. New York: George P Putnam, 1850.

Elias, Thomas A. *The Complete Trees of North America*. New York: Gramercy Publishing Company, 1987.

Elliot, W Rodger, and David L Jones. *Encyclopaedia of Australian Plants suitable for cultivation*. Vol. 1-5. Melbourne, Australia: Lothian Books, 1980–1990.

Elwes, Henry John, and Augustine Henry. *The Trees of Great Britain and Ireland*. Privately printed, 1906–1913.

Emmerson, George B. *A Report on the Trees and Shrubs Growing Naturally in the Forests of Massachusetts*. Vol 2. Boston: Little, Brown & Co, 1887.

Evelyn, John. *Sylva*. 3rd ed. London: J Martin, printer to the Royal Society, 1679.

Forestry, State of California Department of. *Golden Gate Park Forest Management Plan*. Sacramento: State of California, Department of Forestry, 1980.

George, Alex. *The Banksia Book*. Kenthurst, Australia: Kangaroo Pass, 1984.

Giffen, Guy, and Helen Giffen. *The Story of Golden Gate Park*. San Francisco: Phillips and Van Orden Co, 1949.

Goode, Patrick, and Michael Lancaster, eds. *The Oxford Companion to Gardens*. New York: Oxford University Press, 1986.

Gray, Asa, and John Torrey. *Flora of North America*. 2 vols. New York: Wiley & Putnam, 1838–1842.

Griffiths, Mark, ed. *Index of Garden Plants*. Portland, Ore.: Timber Press, 1994.

Hickman, James C, ed. *The Jepson Manual: Higher Plants of California*. Berkeley: University of California Press, 1993.

Hillier, Harold G. Hillier's *Manual of Trees and Shrubs*. 5th ed. Newton Abbot, England: David & Charles, 1981.

Hodel, Donald R. *Exceptional Trees of Los Angeles*. Arcadia, Calif: California Arboretum Foundation, 1988.

Holliday, Ivan, and G Watton. *A Field Guide to Banksias*. Adelaide, Australia: Rigby Ltd, 1975.

Hoyt Arboretum. *Hoyt Arboretum Tree Inventory 2000*. Portland, Ore: Hoyt Arboretum, 2000.

Hoyt, Roland Stewart. *Checklists for the Ornamental Plants of Subtropical Regions*. Los Angeles: Livingston Press, 1938.

Hudson, Roy. "Brief History of Golden Gate Park." *California Horticultural Journal* 31, no. 2 (April 1970): 38–40.

————. "John McLaren As I Knew Him." *California Horticultural Journal* 31, no. 2 (April 1970): 47–51.

Hyam, Roger, and Richard Pankhurst. *Plants and Their Names: A Concise Dictionary*. Oxford: Oxford University Press, 1995.

Jacobson, Arthur Lee. *North American Landscape Trees*. Berkeley: Ten Speed Press, 1996.

Janoff, Clifford, ed. *Trees for San Francisco.* San Francisco: Friends of the Urban
Forest, 1995.

Jepson, Willis Linn. *Flora of California.* Vol. 2. San Francisco: Cunningham, Curtiss,
and Welch, 1936.

———. *Trees of California.* San Francisco: Cunningham, Curtiss, and Welch, 1909.

Johnson, Hugh. *The International Book of Trees.* New York: Bonanza Books, 1980.

Justice, Clive L. *Mr. Menzies' Garden Legacy: Plant Collecting on the Northwest Coast.*
Delta, BC, Canada: Cavendish Books, 2000.

Keator, Glenn. *The Life of an Oak.* Berkeley, Calif: Heyday Books, 1998.

Kirk, Thomas. *Forest Flora of New Zealand.* Wellington, New Zealand: G Didsbury,
government printer, 1889.

Lenz, Lee W, and John Dourley. *California Native Trees and Shrubs.* Claremont,
Calif.: Rancho Santa Ana Botanic Garden, 1981.

Mabberley, David J. *The Plant-Book: A Portable Dictionary of the Higher Plants.* New
York: Cambridge University Press, 1987.

Marinelli, Janet, ed. *The Brooklyn Botanic Garden Gardener's Desk Reference.* New
York: Henry Holt and Company, Inc, 1998.

McClintock, Elizabeth, and Andrew T Leiser. *An Annotated Checklist of Woody
Ornamental Plants of California, Oregon and Washington.* Berkeley: University of
California Press, 1979.

McLaren, John. *Gardening in California.* San Francisco: AM Robertson, 1908; second edition 1927.

———, *Gardening in California: Landscape and Flower.* San Francisco: AM
Robertson, 1909.

Miller, Philip. *The Gardeners Dictionary.* Abridged edition. London: printed for the
author, 1754.

Morrison, Ben Y. *Street and Highway Planting.* Sacramento: State Printing Office,
1913.

Muller, Katherine K, with Richard E Broder and Will Beittel. *Trees of Santa
Barbara.* Santa Barbara: Santa Barbara Botanic Garden, 1974.

Mulligan, Brian O, comp. *Woody Plants in the University of Washington Arboretum.*
Seattle: University of Washington, 1977.

Olmsted, Vaux and Company. *Preliminary Report to a Plan of Public Pleasure Grounds
for the City of San Francisco.* New York: WC Bryant & Co, 1866.

Padilla, Victoria. *Southern California Gardens.* Berkeley: University of California
Press, 1961. (reprinted by Allen A Knoll, 1994).

Park Commissioners, San Francisco Board of. *Catalogue of Trees and Shrubs in
Golden Gate Park.* San Francisco, 1895.

———. *To His Excellency: William Irwin, Governor of the State of California, from the
Park Commissioners of San Francisco.* San Francisco: BF Sterrett, 1876.

———. *Second Biennial Report of the San Francisco Park Commissioners, 1872–1873.*
San Francisco: Francis & Valentine, 1874.

———. *Annual Reports of the Park Commissioners.* San Francisco: Board of Park
Commissioners, 1872–1924.

Parkinson, John. *Paradisi in Sole Paradisus Terrestris.* 1629. Facsimile edition.
London: Dover Publications, 1976.

Peattie, Donald Culross. *A Natural History of Trees of Eastern and Central North
America.* Boston: Houghton Mifflin Company, 1964.

———. *A Natural History of Western Trees.* Boston: Houghton Mifflin Company,
1953.

Perry, Bob. *Landscape Plants for Western Regions.* Claremont, Calif: Land Design
Publishing 1992.

Perry Jr, Jesse P. *The Pines of Mexico and Central America.* Portland, Ore: Timber
Press, 1991.

Phillips, Roger. *Trees of North America and Europe.* New York: Random House, 1978.

Popenoe, Wilson. *Manual of Tropical and Subtropical Fruits.* New York: Macmillan, 1920.

Recreation and Park Department, San Francisco. *Plan for Golden Gate Park.* San Francisco: Recreation and Park Department, 1979.

Reynolds, Phyllis C, and Elizabeth F Dimon. *Trees of Greater Portland.* Portland, Ore: Timber Press, 1993.

Richardson, Adam Dewar. *Gardeners' Chronicle* 50 (1911): 221.

Riedel, Peter. *Plants for Extra-Tropical Regions.* Arcadia, Calif: California Arboretum Foundation, 1957.

Saunders, Charles Francis. *Western Wild Flowers and Their Stories.* Garden City, NJ: Doubleday, Doran & Company, 1933.

Skinner, MW, and BM Pavlik. *Inventory of Rare and Endangered Vascular Plants of California.* Sacramento: California Native Plant Society, 1994.

Spring, John. "The Park Nursery: 1870–1970." *California Horticultural Journal* 31, no. 2 (April 1970): 69–71.

Starr, Kevin. *Material Dreams: Southern California Through the 1920s.* New York: Oxford University Press, 1990.

Stearn, William T. *Stearn's Dictionary of Plant Names for Gardeners.* New York: Sterling, 1992.

Thompson, Peter. *The Looking-Glass Garden: Plants and Gardens of the Southern Hemisphere.* Portland, Ore: Timber Press, 2001.

Walther, Eric. "Notes from the Arboretum in Golden Gate Park: First Flowering of Magnolia campbellii." *Journal of the California Horticultural Society* 1, no 2 (April 1938): 115-116.

Whittle, Tyler. *The Plant Hunters.* New York: PAJ Publications, 1988.

Wilson, Ernest H. *Aristocrats of the Trees.* Boston: The Stratford Company, 1930.

———. *Aristocrats of the Garden.* Boston: The Stratford Company, 1926.

———. *Conifers and Taxads of Japan.* Cambridge, Mass: Harvard University Press, 1916.

Wolf, Carl. *The New World Cypresses.* Anaheim, Calif: Rancho Santa Ana Botanic Garden, 1948.

Wyman, Donald. *Wyman's Gardening Encyclopedia.* Updated ed. New York: MacMillan, 1987.

Young, Terence. "Trees, the park and moral order: the significance of Golden Gate Park's first plantings." *Journal of Garden History* 14, no. 3 (1994): 158–170.

Zohary, Michael. *Plants of the Bible.* Cambridge: Cambridge University Press, 1982.

# Author Biographies

## Elizabeth McClintock, PhD

It would not be an exaggeration to say that this book, *Trees of Golden Gate Park and San Francisco,* has been in preparation for nearly fifty years. In the early 1950s, as she began her work as curator in the botany department of the California Academy of Sciences, Dr Elizabeth McClintock became intrigued with the diversity of trees she observed in the forest that is Golden Gate Park. Discovering that many of the trees there were poorly recorded and documented, she began adding significant numbers of specimens to the academy's extensive herbarium, particularly of trees and other plants she found growing in the park.

Dr McClintock is an uncommon botanist in her passion and dedication to the world of horticulture, and the many challenges presented in maintaining consistency in the nomenclature of plants of ornamental value. As botanical editor for the *Journal of the California Horticultural Society* (later the *California Horticultural Journal),* Dr McClintock reviewed each manuscript for botanical accuracy; she also provided many articles on the plants within Golden Gate Park, and particularly in the developing Strybing Arboretum and Botanical Gardens. As associate editor for the first twenty-five years of *Pacific Horticulture,* the successor to the *California Horticultural Journal,* she continued to review the nomenclature and to contribute articles on a wide array of subjects, but most notably on the trees of Golden Gate Park. What began as a couple of one-page articles to help fill the pages of the new journal in its first year grew into a series of seventy-one articles, over twenty-five years, covering in excess of 170 kinds of trees growing in Golden Gate Park.

Dr McClintock's involvement with *Pacific Horticulture* (published by the non-profit Pacific Horticultural Foundation) was just one of her many contributions to public horticulture during a long and distinguished career. A native of Southern California, she received undergraduate and graduate degrees in botany from UCLA. She obtained her PhD in botany from the University of Michigan; her specialty was taxonomy—the classification, naming, and distribution of plants. Returning to California, she settled in the Bay Area, working first at the herbarium of the University of California, then taking a position as curator in the botany department of the California Academy of Sciences, where she worked until retirement. In later years, she also worked as a research associate in the Jepson Herbarium.

Her connection with Strybing Arboretum and Botanical Gardens began in her earliest years in the Bay Area, when she became friends with Eric Walther, the first director of the gardens. Walther's extensive knowledge of Strybing's plant collection was kept in his head. Recognizing the need to make this information accessible to the visiting public, Dr McClintock worked with Walther to create the first plant records system for Strybing, strengthening the educational value of its plant collection. In the mid-1950s, support for the arboretum was waning at City Hall. To ensure that the gardens would continue, Dr McClintock joined with others in forming the Strybing Arboretum Society and served the society over the years in a variety of volunteer capacities.

She has been a founder, board member, or active participant in the other organizations collaborating on this book: Friends of Recreation and Parks, Friends of the Urban Forest, and the Tree Advisory Board. She is widely respected among the foresters working for the city in the Recreation and Parks Department and in the Department of Public Works.

Publications have always been a significant part of Dr McClintock's professional work. Her booklet entitled *Trees of the Panhandle* established the importance of Golden Gate Park's panhandle and northwest corner, and helped prevent construction of a freeway through that area in the 1960s. *A Flora of San Bruno Mountain,* co-authored with Walter Knight, was influential in creating a county park on the slopes of this mountain treasure south of San Francisco. Her *Checklist of Woody Ornamental Plants of California, Oregon, and Washington* has been of tremendous value to those in the horticulture industry since its publication in 1979. She collaborated on the preparation of *Hortus III* (1976) and *The Jepson Manual* (1993), and has published monographs on the genera *Hydrangea, Monarda,* and *Teucrium.*

Dr McClintock has worked tirelessly throughout the West to preserve natural areas and to identify and control the spread of invasive exotic plants that threaten our native plant communities. She has worked with the California Natural Areas Coordinating Council, was a charter member and fellow of the California Native Plant Society, and has served on the board of trustees of the Northern California Chapter of The Nature Conservancy and on the executive committee of the Sierra Club's San Francisco Bay Chapter. For her many efforts, Dr McClintock has received several awards over the years. In 1977, the Massachusetts Horticultural Society presented her with their Silver Medal. In 1982, she was listed in *American Men and Women of Science.* In 1986, she was awarded the Liberty Hyde Bailey Medal by the American Horticultural Society.

In 1997, Dr McClintock received two awards for her contributions to the world of horticulture. Recognizing "her community involvement, scientific achievements, and tireless work on behalf of San Francisco's trees," Friends of the Urban Forest bestowed on her the fourth annual Emily Prettyman Lowell Award. Dr McClintock had been influential in establishing the City's street tree ordinance and in forming, and serving on, the Tree Advisory Board. At the national level, she was given the Award of Merit by the American Association of Botanical Gardens and Arboreta (AABGA) at its annual meeting in New York City. This award is presented to individual members of AABGA who have performed with distinction in the area of public gardens. Dr McClintock served on the board of AABGA, as its president from 1962 to 1963, and actively participated in the programs of this professional organization over a forty-year period.

And in 2001, Dr McClintock received the Gold Veitch Memorial Award, the highest award given by the Royal Horticultural Society to a non-British horticulturist who has worked to advance the science and practice of horticulture. She was honored for her many contributions to horticulture and conservation, particularly in California.

## Russell A Beatty

Russell Beatty is retired from the University of California, Berkeley, where he taught for twenty-eight years in the Department of Landscape Architecture. Currently, he is a consulting landscape architect in Santa Cruz, California. His professional interests include the restoration of historic gardens and cultural landscapes, vegetation management, and urban forestry. Notable work includes the Garden Restoration and Maintenance Master Plan for Rancho Los Alamitos, Long Beach, and a Tree Selection and Planting Guide for the East Bay Regional Park District, Oakland. He is the author of *Trees for Lafayette* and co-author of *Gardens of Alcatraz.* He contributes frequently to *Pacific Horticulture.* His professional work has garnered numerous awards from local and national organizations.

## Peter Ehrlich

Peter Ehrlich received a bachelor's degree from the University of California in Forestry and Natural Resource Management. For ten years, he worked as a reforestation gardener in Golden Gate Park, where he did site preparation, planting, and reforestation tree maintenance in the San Francisco Recreation and Park Department's reforestation program. After serving as gardener supervisor of the reforestation crew, he was promoted to urban forester for the San Francisco Recreation and Park Department, coordinating all tree management programs on department lands. In 2000, he became the forest manager for the Presidio Trust, and has begun a Historic Forest Tree Replacement Program for the Presidio National Park in San Francisco.

# Art Credits

All photographs reproduced courtesy of the Helen Crocker Russell Library of Horticulture, unless otherwise noted in caption.

Maps provided courtesy of Ben Pease.

Botanical illustrations provided courtesy of the following artists:

Nancy Baron: pages 40, 41(top), 48(bottom), 53(top), 60, 71, 73, 87–90, 92, 108, 113–117, 120, 121, 135(bottom), 160, 179, 190–191.

G. Lee Boerger: pages 30–31, 45, 53(bottom), 70, 76, 103(top), 106, 129, 135(top), 153–154, 156–158, 161, 168, 170, 176, 181, 184, 196–197, 200.

Leslie Bohm: page 81.

Virginia Gregory: page 149.

Lee Adair Hastings: pages 42, 51, 55–56, 104, 110–112, 125, 127(bottom), 138, 171, 173(top), 186, 203.

Kristin Jakob: pages 144, 194–195.

Martha Kemp: pages 29, 35, 38, 59, 66, 97, 102, 103(bottom), 150, 151(top), 164–167, 209.

Carolyn Mullinex: page 163.

Mimi Osborne: pages 26–28, 32–34, 36–37, 39, 41(bottom), 44, 46–47, 48(top), 50, 52, 57–58, 61–63, 65, 67–68, 75, 77–78, 80, 82–85, 91, 93–95, 98, 100, 105, 107, 118, 124, 127(top), 128, 133–134, 137, 140–142, 145–148, 151(bottom), 155, 173(bottom), 174, 178, 180, 185, 187–189, 192, 198–199, 202, 205–208, 210.

# Sponsoring Organizations

Each of the following five non-profit organizations has, as a part of its mission, a commitment to the study, appreciation, or care of trees in Golden Gate Park and in the city at large. From their first meeting in December 1997, they pledged their enthusiastic support for the publication of *The Trees of Golden Gate Park and San Francisco,* offering information, volunteer assistance, funding, and promotion.

**Friends of Recreation & Parks** is a membership-based support group providing leadership, education, and funding for all city parks. It raises money for unbudgeted capital projects and programs in city parks, supplies project management for funded projects, seeds new ideas, and enables other park support groups.

> Friends of Recreation & Parks
> McLaren Lodge, Golden Gate Park
> 501 Stanyan Street, San Francisco, CA 94117-1898
> (415) 750-5105; www.sfparks.org

**Friends of the Urban Forest** is a membership-based group working to promote a larger, healthier urban forest, as part of the urban ecosystem, through community planting, maintenance, education, and advocacy.

> Friends of the Urban Forest
> Presidio of San Francisco, Bldg #1007
> PO Box 29456, San Francisco, CA 94129-0456
> (415) 561-6890 x100; www.fuf.net

**Pacific Horticultural Foundation** is a non-profit educational foundation whose mission is to stimulate and inspire gardeners in the art and science of horticulture on the West Coast. The foundation publishes the quarterly *Pacific Horticulture* magazine, organizes garden and natural history tours, and sponsors symposia and occasional lectures.

> Pacific Horticultural Foundation/
> *Pacific Horticulture*
> PO Box 680, Berkeley, CA 94701
> (510) 849-1627; www.pacifichorticulture.org

**Tree Advisory Board** is a group of nine citizen foresters committed to protecting San Francisco's urban forest through volunteer advocacy and public education. Created by the Urban Forestry Ordinance in 1986, the board advises the Department of Public Works on tree management issues.

> Tree Advisory Board
> Department of Public Works
> 875 Stevenson Street, Room 460, San Francisco, CA 94103
> (415) 554-6700

**Strybing Arboretum Society** is a membership-based organization which raises funds for the ongoing development of the city's Strybing Arboretum and Botanical Gardens in Golden Gate Park, operates the Helen Crocker Russell Library of Horticulture, and provides education in horticulture, gardening, conservation, botany, and the natural environment.

> Strybing Arboretum Society
> 9th Avenue at Lincoln Way
> Golden Gate Park, San Francisco, CA 94122
> (415) 661-1316; www.strybing.org

## Tree Tours

Contact Strybing Arboretum Society for a schedule of free tours of the arboretum.

Contact Friends of Recreation and Parks for a schedule of free tours of Golden Gate Park.

Contact Friends of the Urban Forest for a schedule of free tours of trees in the parks and along neighborhood streets in San Francisco.

# Individual Sponsors

The following individuals and groups provided financial support for the publication of *Trees of Golden Gate Park and San Francisco*. Their generous contributions not only permitted publication of the book but allowed proceeds from sales of the book to be allocated to the Elizabeth McClintock Fund for Trees, to support the ongoing management of the park's forest.

Clarellen Adams
Michael and Susan Addison Living Trust
Joseph Barbaccia, MD
Carol J Barnes
Edward Brennan
Julie Brook
F Joseph Butler, Architect
California Horticultural Society
California Native Plant Society, Yerba Buena Chapter
Columbia Foundation
Dorothy Clifford
Diana Cohen and Jerry H Robinson
Albert and Janet Collins
Laurence R Costello
Elliott Donnelley
Mary Falk
Brian Fewer
Friends of Recreation and Parks
Friends of the Urban Forest
Janice V Gendreau
Ann Gitlis
Carlyn Jean Halde
Amanda Hamilton
Anne Hicks

John C Hooper
Mary Unkovic Jensen
Chapin Koch
Roy C Leggitt II and Courtney S Clarkson
Linda Liebelt
Molley Lowry
G Karl Ludwig, Jr
Malcolm Margolin
Kathryn Kendrick McNeil
Ernest Ng
Pacific Horticultural Foundation
Julia H Parish
Barbara and Roland Pitschel
Jack Porter Living Trust
Earl and Viola Raab
Harold L Retler
Allan Ridley and Helen McKenna
Alice Russell-Shapiro
San Francisco Department of Public Works and Tree Advisory Board
Michele Schaal
Fred H Smith IV
Stanley Smith Horticultural Trust
John J Spring
Charles Starbuck
Strybing Arboretum Society
Shirley Suhrer
Michael Sullivan
Urban Resource Systems Inc
Juliana VerSteegt
Isabel Wade and Neighborhood Parks Council
Emily D Warner

244